Cloud Native Security Cookbook

Recipes for a Secure Cloud

Josh Armitage

Beijing · Boston · Farnham · Sebastopol · Tokyo

Cloud Native Security Cookbook

by Josh Armitage

Copyright © 2022 Joshua Hagen Armitage. All rights reserved.

Published by O'Reilly Media, Inc., 1005 Gravenstein Highway North, Sebastopol, CA 95472.

O'Reilly books may be purchased for educational, business, or sales promotional use. Online editions are also available for most titles (*http://oreilly.com*). For more information, contact our corporate/institutional sales department: 800-998-9938 or *corporate@oreilly.com*.

Acquisitions Editor: Jennifer Pollock	**Indexer:** Judith McConville
Development Editor: Corbin Collins	**Interior Designer:** David Futato
Production Editor: Jonathon Owen	**Cover Designer:** Karen Montgomery
Copyeditor: Sonia Saruba	**Illustrator:** Kate Dullea
Proofreader: Piper Editorial Consulting, LLC	

April 2022:   First Edition

Revision History for the First Edition

2022-04-20:   First Release

See *http://oreilly.com/catalog/errata.csp?isbn=9781098106300* for release details.

978-1-098-10630-0

[LSI]

Table of Contents

Preface

In the early 2000s, public cloud emerged as a new a paradigm that revolutionized how technology is consumed across the world. Rather than waiting weeks to months for new computers to be ordered, delivered, and racked, access to machines is mere seconds away. The company bringing you one-click shopping was now bringing you one-click computing.

In my first job out of university, I was working in the mainframe division of IBM, building a cloud-delivered virtualized mainframe environment. We were looking to bring DevOps to the world's most venerated enterprises. What became a focus of the customer conversations over time was security. How can they be assured that their data is safe when they upload it to the cloud?

When the cloud was making waves in even the most risk-averse industries, I became convinced that it was the way forward for businesses looking to excel in the digital age.

Since IBM, I have spent the majority of my time working as a consultant in Australia and the UK, focused on helping start-ups and enterprises alike use the cloud as their innovation engine, empowering their developers to deliver exceptional outcomes.

Through my experience I have seen many false steps, patterns, and anti-patterns that reappear as businesses and engineers make their first forays into a cloud-native world. This book is focused on how to use the cloud *securely*.

The recipes in this book show you how to build a secure foundation in your cloud environment and how to leverage the first-party security solutions to stay on top of your estate as it organically scales.

Who This Book Is For

This book is about getting hands-on with the cloud. Each recipe comes with a fully worked solution in Terraform, the most widely used infrastructure-as-code tool.

For each problem presented, there is a recipe for each of the three primary cloud providers, Amazon Web Services, Microsoft Azure, and Google Cloud Platform. As the modern world is becoming increasingly multi-cloud, it is ever more valuable to be cloud multilingual.

Although the three clouds have significant overlap in the services they provide, the design decisions that went into the cloud itself have massive ramifications for security. With this book you'll become empowered to translate between the three clouds and rapidly solve problems wherever they present.

How This Book Is Organized

This book has nine chapters of recipes, each focused on a particular theme. These range from how to structure your estate and manage users to how to ensure compliance at scale to the intricacies of identity and access management on each cloud provider.

What You Need to Use This Book

In order to complete the recipes in this book, you will need access to your cloud of choice. Depending on the recipe, you will need highly privileged credentials to make the required changes.

All the recipes were developed using Terraform version 1.0. If you have not used Terraform before, then going through Chapter 11 will show you how to safely authenticate against your cloud.

Conventions Used in This Book

The following typographical conventions are used in this book:

Italic

    Indicates new terms, URLs, email addresses, filenames, and file extensions.

`Constant width`

    Used for program listings, as well as within paragraphs to refer to program elements such as variable or function names, databases, data types, environment variables, statements, and keywords.

`Constant width bold`

    Shows commands or other text that should be typed literally by the user.

`Constant width italic`

    Shows text that should be replaced with user-supplied values or by values determined by context.

This element signifies a general note.

 This element indicates a warning or caution.

Using Code Examples

Supplemental material (code examples, exercises, etc.) is available for download at *https://github.com/Armitagency/cloud-native-security-cookbook-tf*.

If you have a technical question or a problem using the code examples, please send email to *bookquestions@oreilly.com*.

This book is here to help you get your job done. In general, if example code is offered with this book, you may use it in your programs and documentation. You do not need to contact us for permission unless you're reproducing a significant portion of the code. For example, writing a program that uses several chunks of code from this book does not require permission. Selling or distributing examples from O'Reilly books does require permission. Answering a question by citing this book and quoting example code does not require permission. Incorporating a significant amount of example code from this book into your product's documentation does require permission.

We appreciate, but generally do not require, attribution. An attribution usually includes the title, author, publisher, and ISBN. For example: "*Cloud Native Security Cookbook* by Josh Armitage (O'Reilly). Copyright 2022 Joshua Hagen Armitage, 978-1-098-10630-0."

If you feel your use of code examples falls outside fair use or the permission given above, feel free to contact us at *permissions@oreilly.com*.

O'Reilly Online Learning

 For more than 40 years, *O'Reilly Media* has provided technology and business training, knowledge, and insight to help companies succeed.

Our unique network of experts and innovators share their knowledge and expertise through books, articles, and our online learning platform. O'Reilly's online learning platform gives you on-demand access to live training courses, in-depth learning paths, interactive coding environments, and a vast collection of text and video from O'Reilly and 200+ other publishers. For more information, visit *http://oreilly.com*.

How to Contact Us

Please address comments and questions concerning this book to the publisher:

> O'Reilly Media, Inc.
> 1005 Gravenstein Highway North
> Sebastopol, CA 95472
> 800-998-9938 (in the United States or Canada)
> 707-829-0515 (international or local)
> 707-829-0104 (fax)

We have a webpage for this book, where we list errata, examples, and any additional information. You can access this page at *https://oreil.ly/cloudNativeCkbk*.

Email *bookquestions@oreilly.com* to comment or ask technical questions about this book.

For news and information about our books and courses, visit *http://oreilly.com*.

Find us on LinkedIn: *https://linkedin.com/company/oreilly-media*

Follow us on Twitter: *http://twitter.com/oreillymedia*

Watch us on YouTube: *http://www.youtube.com/oreillymedia*

Acknowledgments

This book stands upon the shoulders of other people's ideas and knowledge. I am indebted to the many people who have readily shared their expertise so that we can explore further and higher rather than continually relearn the same lessons.

Above the main coworking space in my home city of Perth is the Greek proverb "A society grows great when old men plant trees whose shade they know they shall never sit in," an ideal I try to hold close. I truly feel that everyone has valuable stories to share. Wherever you are on your journey, there are people behind you or next to you on their own journey who could benefit from your experience. This book is my attempt to help people develop safer systems, protect their users, and have a more fulfilling and happier working life.

Having spent a number of years consulting with the world's biggest enterprises, I have firsthand experience of both the pains and triumphs that come with digital and cloud transformation, especially in the security domain. This book is a distillation of those days in the trenches, with a bias for action that is imperative for real change to happen.

Working with computers was almost preordained for me, as it seems the occupation of choice for my family. My father and I both got jobs as mainframe developers straight out of university about 30 years apart, much to his enjoyment when he found out.

I started writing this book while in lockdown in the UK, attempting to find a project to help keep me sane. I finished it in Australia just before my daughter was due to arrive. I couldn't have finished this book without the never-ending support of my wife, Rebecca, who has had to deal with many late nights and weekends of me hammering the keyboard. In the end, the timing could not have worked out better as I move on from this herculean labor to being a father.

Thank you to my triumvirate of tech reviewers who have challenged me and kept me honest through the book, Marcus Maxwell, JK Gunnink, and Pete Yandell. Your hours spent dissecting my writing has taken the book to a higher level and I am forever grateful.

To the amazing staff at O'Reilly, especially Corbin Collins for supporting me throughout this endeavor, Jennifer Pollock for giving me the chance to write this book, and the production team, thank you for having the requisite patience and ensuring that this book became a reality.

It's hard to imagine this book existing were it not for the support of each and every one of you.

CHAPTER 1

Security in the Modern Organization

In this chapter, you will learn the following:

- Why security is becoming ever more critical in the modern age
- What is meant by cloud native security
- Where security fits in the modern organization
- What the purpose of security is
- What DevSecOps really is
- How to measure the impact of security
- The underlying principles of security

This foundation is critical for you to compellingly articulate why investment into security is and will continue to be mandatory and how the advent of the cloud has not invalidated the fundamental principles of security but has transformed how they are applied.

1.1 Why Security Is Critical

Seeing as you're reading this, you probably already believe in the criticality of security; however, it's important to understand how security continues to be ever more important day to day and year to year.

Life in the 21st century is digital first—our lives revolve around the internet and technology. Everyone's personal information is given to and stored by trusted third parties. We all believe that it will be handled safely and securely. What recent history has shown us, however, is that security breaches are the norm; they are to be expected.

This information is the gold filling the 21st-century bank vaults of technology titans. Where you have concentrations of wealth, you must scale your security to match.

Human instinct makes us believe that to go slowly is to go safely, which often manifests as lengthy security assessments, full multiweek penetration tests on every release, and security being the slowest moving part on the path to production.

This is actively harmful in two ways. First, the systems that businesses operate are inherently complex. Complexity theory and other models of complexity, such as the Cynefin framework, shown in Figure 1-1, teach us that it is impossible to think our way through a complex system. No amount of reading code and looking at architecture diagrams can allow you to fully understand all the possibilities and potential vulnerabilities within a system. Being able to react and apply fixes quickly when issues are discovered, such as the Log4j vulnerability in December 2021, results in a superior security posture when compared to lengthy, time-intensive review cycles.

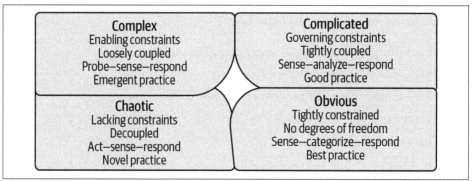

Figure 1-1. Cynefin framework

But even if it were possible with sufficient time to root out all security vulnerabilities, for a business, moving slowly in the 21st century is a recipe for disaster. The level of expectation set by the Googles, Microsofts, and Amazons of the world has laid down a gauntlet. Move fast or die. Security teams are caught between two unstoppable forces: the business imperative for agility through speed and the exponential growth in breach impacts.

When a breach happens, the business suffers in a number of ways, to name but a few:

- Reputational damage
- Legal liabilities
- Fines and other financial penalties
- Operational instability and loss of revenue
- Loss of opportunity

The vast majority of businesses are either already in the cloud or are exploring how they can migrate their estates. With the near ubiquity of cloud infrastructure, both governments and regulators are investing significantly in their understanding of how companies are using the cloud. Examples such as the General Data Protection Regulation (GDPR) and the California Consumer Privacy Act are just the tip of a wave of increased security expectations, controls, and scrutiny. Over time, the damage suffered by a business from a breach will exponentially and catastrophically increase. Our principles of security are not invalidated by this new reality, but how they are applied, embedded, and upheld needs to fundamentally transform.

1.2 What Is Meant by Cloud Native Security?

A common trope of the technology industry is that definitions become loose over time. In this book, *cloud native* is defined as *leveraging technology purpose-built to unlock the value of, and accelerate your adoption of, the cloud*. Here is a list of common properties of cloud native solutions:

- It is automation friendly and should be fully configurable through infrastructure as code (IaC).
- It does not place unnecessary, artificial constraints on your architecture. For example, per machine pricing is not considered a cloud native pricing model.
- It elastically scales. As your systems and applications grow in size, the solution scales in lockstep.
- It natively supports the higher-level compute offerings on the cloud platforms. It should support serverless and containerized workloads, as well as the plethora of managed service offerings.

In this book, where possible, the recipes use the managed services provided by the cloud platforms themselves. They have all the previous properties, are purpose-built to support customers in their cloud journey, and are easily integrated into your estate.

IT security has existed from the day there was something of value stored on a computer. As soon as things of value were stored on computers, it was necessary to defend them. As an industry, IT has proven the ability to undergo seismic shifts with frightening regularity; embracing cloud native is simply the most recent. As more value is poured into technology and systems, the potential value to be gained by attacking them increases, therefore our security must increase in kind. The cloud can bring so much good, but with it comes new challenges that will need cloud native people, processes, and tools to overcome.

The Beginnings of the Cloud

Back in 2006, Amazon first announced Amazon Web Services (AWS), offering pay-as-you-go technology to businesses. Over the intervening 15 years, a tectonic shift fundamentally altered how companies approach technology. Historically, businesses ordered and managed hardware themselves, investing huge sums of capital up front and employing large teams to perform "undifferentiated heavy lifting" to operate this infrastructure. What Amazon started, followed in 2008 by Google and 2010 by Microsoft, allowed businesses to provision new infrastructure on demand in seconds, as opposed to waiting months for the hardware to arrive and be racked, configured, and released for use.

Infrastructure became a commodity, like water or electricity. This enabled businesses to rapidly experiment, become more agile, and see technology as a business differentiator rather than a cost center. Over time, the cornucopia of services offered by the Cloud Service Providers (CSPs) has grown to encompass almost everything a business could need, with more being released every day. Nearly every company on the planet, including the most ancient of enterprises, is cloud first. The cloud is here to stay and will fundamentally define how businesses consume technology in the future.

Old Practices in the New Reality

When something as transformational as cloud computing occurs, best practices require time to emerge. In the intervening gap, old practices are applied to the new reality. The security tools and processes which served us well in the pre-cloud age were not built to contend with the new normal. The pace of change posed by the cloud presented new security challenges the industry was not equipped to face. Through effort, time, and experimentation, it is now understood how to achieve our security objectives by working with, not against, the cloud. You can now have cloud native security.

Cloud native security is built around the following fundamental advantages of cloud computing:

Pay for consumption
    In a cloud native world, expect to only pay for services as you use them, not for idle time.

Economies of scale
    As the CSP is at hyperscale, it can achieve things which cannot be done in isolation, including lower pricing, operational excellence, and superior security postures.

No capacity planning
> Cloud resources are made to be elastic; they can scale up and down based on demand rather than having to go through the effort-intensive and often inaccurate process of capacity planning.

Unlock speed and agility
> By allowing companies and teams to rapidly experiment, change their mind, and move quickly, the cloud allows for capturing business value that would be impossible otherwise.

Stop spending money on "undifferentiated heavy lifting"
> Rather than focus on activities that cannot differentiate you from your competition, allow the CSP to focus on those tasks while you focus on core competencies.

Span the globe
> The CSP allows businesses to scale geographically on demand by having locations all over the world that operate identically

When you look at the processes and tools that constitute cloud native security, you enable the consumption and promised benefits of the cloud, not constrain them.

1.3 Where Security Fits in the Modern Organization

Historically, security has operated as a gatekeeper, often as part of change advisory boards (CABs), acting as judge, jury, and executioner for system changes. This siloed approach can only take you so far. The waste incurred by long feedback loops, long lead times, and slow pace of change is incompatible with a digital-first reality.

By looking to block rather than enable change, the security and delivery teams are forced into a state of eternal conflict, creating friction that breeds animosity and prevents the business from achieving its goals. *Team Topologies*, by Matthew Skelton and Manual Pais (IT Revolution Press), examines the four team archetypes that are fundamental to exceptional technology performance: enabling teams, platform teams, complicated-subsystem teams, and stream-aligned teams, as shown in Figure 1-2.

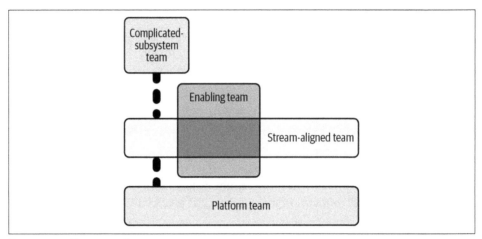

Figure 1-2. Team topologies

Stream-aligned teams are how the business directly delivers value. They build the systems and services that allow the business to function, interact with customers, and compete in the market.

Complicated-subsystem teams look after systems that require their own deep domain expertise, such as a risk calculation system in an insurance company.

Platform teams produce compelling internal products that accelerate stream-aligned teams, such as an opinionated cloud platform, which is the focus of Chapter 2.

Enablement teams are domain specialists who look to impart their understanding of other teams within the business.

Simply put, all other teams are there to enable the stream-aligned team. Security needs to operate as an enablement team; i.e., they are domain experts that actively collaborate with other teams. It is unrealistic and infeasible to expect that all engineers become security experts throughout a company, although it is not unrealistic or infeasible to expect and embed a base level of security competency in all engineers. Even in a highly automated world, developing systems is knowledge work—it is people who determine the success of your security initiatives.

It is through this enablement lens that many of the recipes in this cookbook make the most sense. Through working with enterprises around the world, I have seen that the paradigm shift from gatekeeper to enabler can be difficult to undertake; the animosity and lack of trust between security and delivery built over many years are powerful inhibitors of change. However, to take full advantage of cloud native security, this shift must happen, or misaligned incentives will scupper any and all progress.

1.4 The Purpose of Modern Security

Security operates in the domain of risk. Perfect security is not a realistic or achievable goal; at any one time, you cannot provide services and be known to be immune to all threats. This reality is even borne out in how fines are handed out following breaches: a substantial percentage of the fine is negated if reasonable attempts have been made to prevent the breach. So, if you cannot achieve complete security, then what is your north star? What is your goal?

At the macro level, your goal is to make commercially reasonable efforts to minimize the chance of security incidents. What is deemed commercially reasonable varies wildly among companies. Often, startups have a significantly higher risk tolerance for security than regulated enterprises, as common sense would lead us to predict. What is important to keep in mind is that this much lower risk tolerance does not mean that an enterprise cannot move as fast as a startup due to overbearing security concerns. Throughout this book you will see how, with the correct principles and recipes in place, you do not handicap your stream-aligned teams.

At the micro level, your goal is to ensure that a single change does not present an intolerable amount of risk. Again, what is tolerable is highly context specific, but thankfully, techniques to minimize risk are often universal. Later in this chapter, as I discuss DevSecOps, I will drill into what properties of changes allow you to minimize the risk and how embracing a DevSecOps culture is required for aligning teams around security objectives.

1.5 DevSecOps

Before I can dive into what DevSecOps is, you first need to understand its precursor, DevOps.

What Is DevOps?

At its heart, DevOps is a cultural transformation of software delivery. It is heavily influenced by lean theory and is most simply described as bringing together what historically were two disparate silos, development and operations, hence *DevOps*, or the commonly used soundbite, "You build it, you run it."

To put it into numbers, elite teams operating in a DevOps model do the following:

- deploy code 208 times more frequently
- deploy code 106 times faster
- recover from incidents 2,604 times faster
- make 1/7 the amount of changes that fail

As you can see from the numbers, DevOps was revolutionary, not evolutionary, and DevSecOps has the same potential.

Understanding these numbers is crucial for modern security as it allows for alignment around a common set of constraints—security objectives need to be achieved without preventing teams from becoming elite performers. Being elite for lead time means that changes are in production within an hour, meaning that mandatory security tests that take a day to complete are incompatible with the future direction of the company. A classic example of this in the enterprise is a mandatory penetration test before every release; although the goal of the penetration test is valuable, the activity itself and its place in the process need to change. The increasingly popular approach of bug bounties is a potential replacement for penetration tests. These challenges that security teams are now facing are the same ones that operations teams faced at the birth of DevOps in the early 2000s.

It's crucial to set the context, as it leads to the right conversations, ideas, problems, and solutions to achieve the right outcomes. As you can see, the engineering and cultural principles needed to allow companies to merely survive today forces wide-scale changes in security, the reality of which is what the industry calls *DevSecOps*.

Two of the seminal texts in DevOps, *The Phoenix Project* (by Gene Kim et al., IT Revolution Press) and *The Unicorn Project* (by Gene Kim, IT Revolution Press), elaborate "the Three Ways" and "the Five Ideals" as underlying principles. I'll examine them briefly here as they also underpin DevSecOps.

The Three Ways

These are the Three Ways:

Flow and Systems Thinking
> The first way tells us that you need to optimize for the whole system, not simply for one component. Local optimization can often come at the expense of the system as a whole, which leads us to the realization that the most secure system is not necessarily in the best interests of the business. Delaying a critical feature because of a vulnerability is a trade-off that needs to be made on a case-by-case basis.

Amplify Feedback Loops
> The second way tells us that feedbacks loops are the mechanisms that allow for correction; the shorter they are, the faster you can correct. This leads us to the potential value of the short-term embedding of security specialists in teams, and also adopting tooling that allows for rapid feedback on changes, such as in IDE SAST tooling.

Culture of Continual Experimentation and Learning

The third way is how you need to embrace risk, and only by taking and learning from risks can you achieve mastery. This leads us to the realization that the technology domain is moving forward ever more rapidly, and you need to move with it, not fight against it. Dogma leads to ruin.

The Five Ideals

These are the Five Ideals:

Locality and Simplicity

The first ideal around locality means that you should enable autonomous teams; changes should be able to happen without approval from many people and teams. Teams should own their entire value stream, which is a significant shift from the siloed approach of the past, where handoffs reduced accountability and added waste.

Focus, Flow, and Joy

The second ideal means that you should be looking to enable teams to focus on their objectives and find flow, as working in a state of flow brings joy. Rather than getting in each other's way and working in the gatekeeper functions of the past, you need to find how you can help people and teams achieve flow and make the passage of work easy and enjoyable.

Improvement of Daily Work

Historically, the rush for features has drowned systems and teams in seas of technical debt. Instead, you need to be mindful and enable teams to pay down their technical debt. There may be systems that are in need of decommissioning, systems that have started to struggle to scale, or decisions that have proved less than optimal over time.

Psychological Safety

People should feel secure and safe to express themselves and should not be blamed for mistakes, which instead are used as opportunities for learning. Through rigorous and meticulous study, Google found that psychological safety is one of the key properties of high-performing teams.

Customer Focus

Systems fall into one of two categories: core and context. Core generates a durable competitive advantage for the business; context is everything else. Security for most businesses is context; it exists to enable core but is not core itself, as it is not generally a source of competitive advantage. This is shown by the fact that security operates as an enablement team and is there to support core in delivering the greatest value.

What Is DevSecOps?

DevSecOps is the natural extension of DevOps into the security domain. You are now charged with a goal of enabling business agility *securely*. Within that shift comes people, process, and tool changes, but it is important to understand that it is, at its core, a shift in culture. Simply replacing tools in isolation will not allow you to thrive in the new reality, no matter what the vendor might say.

As I said previously, security operates in the domain of risk. As part of the approval and testing processes, for a change, you are trying to build confidence that you are not introducing a large amount of risk. This is analogous to functional testing of software: you cannot prove the nonexistence of bugs, but you can pass a confidence threshold, meaning that you can release into production. Proving that a change contains no security issues is impossible; being confident that a major issue is not introduced is possible. This brings us to the following two properties of a change that impact risk:

Size of the change
> Size is the most critical property of a change to consider when looking at risk. The more you change, the more risk is involved. This is something that is hard to definitively measure, as most things in security unfortunately are. But as a base, heuristic lines of code are effective more often than not. You want many small changes as opposed to fewer large ones. This allows you to more easily understand which change caused an adverse impact and to more effectively peer-review the change, and it means that one bad change does not block all other changes.

Lead time for changes
> Based on our shared understanding that changes with security vulnerabilities are inevitable, the speed with which you can resolve introduced issues becomes crucial. The total risk posed by a change is capped by the length of time it is exposed and live. When an issue is discovered in production, the lower the lead time, the less the exposure. In reality, the teams that pose the greatest challenge when first embarking on DevSecOps, the pioneers moving the fastest, have the highest potential for security. The days of "move fast and break things" are behind us; today's mantra is "Better Value, Sooner, *Safer*, Happier" (*https://soonersaferhappier.com*).

Resolving issues with roll forward versus roll back

Upon discovery of an issue, in an ideal world you want to *roll forward*—introduce a new change to resolve the issue—rather than *roll back* and revert all changes. An operationally mature team has more options—the same processes and tools that allow them to deploy many times a day give them a scalpel to target and resolve issues. Teams early in their DevOps journey often only have sledgehammers, meaning that the business impact of resolving an issue is much worse.

Continuous integration and continuous delivery

Continuous integration (CI) and *continuous delivery* (CD) are two foundational patterns that enable DevOps; they are how system change happens. Teams possess a CI/CD pipeline which takes their code changes and applies them to environments. Security teams possessing their own pipelines can rapidly enact change, while hooking into all pipelines in the organization allows them to enact change at scale.

Before I discuss what exactly continuous integration and continuous delivery are, let's segue briefly into how code is stored.

Version Control

Version control is the process of maintaining many versions of code in parallel. There is a base branch, often called *trunk* or *main*, which has a full history of every change that has ever happened. When a team member wishes to make a change, they make a new branch, make their changes independently, and merge them back into the base branch.

Companies will have at least one version control system they use, most commonly GitHub, GitLab, or BitBucket. Becoming familiar with how version control operates is a required skill for the modern security engineer.

What is continuous integration?

Continuous integration is the practice of regularly testing, at least daily, against the base branch. Its primary purpose is to check that the proposed changes are compatible with the common code. Often, a variety of checks and tests are run against the code before it is allowed to be merged back into the base branch, including a human peer review.

As this process allows for barring changes, you can embed security tooling that analyzes code and dependencies to stop known issues from being merged and ever reaching a live environment.

What is continuous delivery?

Continuous delivery is the practice of having the common code maintained in a deployable state; i.e., the team is able to perform a production release at any time. The intent is to make releasing a business decision rather than a technical one. As the code exists to fulfill a business need, it makes sense for this decision to be purely business driven.

This approach runs in opposition to significant human oversight on changes. A mandatory human-operated penetration test before release means that continuous delivery cannot be achieved, and the business loses agility as its ability to react is constrained.

What is continuous deployment?

Continuous delivery and deployment are often confused, as they are very closely related. *Continuous deployment* is the practice of performing an automated production release when new code is merged into the shared common code. By building the apparatus around this, teams can be elite and release tens to hundreds of times a day.

The level of automation required shifts almost 100% of quality control onto tooling, with the sole human interaction being the peer review. Teams reaching for this goal introduces a need for a mature, fully automated DevSecOps tool chain.

CI/CD pipelines

As mentioned previously, teams possess CI/CDs, which is how change is applied to environments. These pipelines are the only way to make production changes, and provide the vector for embedding practices across all teams in an organization. As long as you can automate something, it can become part of a pipeline and can be run against every change as it makes its way to production and even after. Pipelines become the bedrock for the technical aspects of the DevSecOps cultural shift.

Want to start running dependency checks of imported packages? Embed it into the pipeline. Want to run static code analysis before allowing the code to be merged? Embed it into the pipeline. Want to check infrastructure configuration before it's live in the cloud? Embed it into the pipeline.

Additionally, these pipelines operate as information radiators. As all change goes through them, they become the obvious choice for where to surface information from. As I am now broaching the topic of measuring the impact of security, many of the metrics are observed from the pipelines themselves.

1.6 How to Measure the Impact of Security

I often find myself quoting Peter Drucker: "What gets measured, gets managed." With that in mind, how can you tackle measuring the impact of security? This has often proved to be a vexing question for many chief information security officers (CISOs), as security is only ever top of mind when something has gone wrong. While I do not believe I have the one true answer, let's discuss some ideas and heuristics that are often used.

Time to Notify for Known Vulnerabilities

As modern systems are built on the shoulders of giants—i.e., software is built depending on frameworks and libraries from innumerable developers and companies —we need an ability to notify teams when one of their dependencies is known to have a potential vulnerability.

For example, I'm building a serverless function in Python, and I have used the latest version of a library. Two days after that code is deployed into production, a vulnerability is identified and raised against the library. How long a wait is acceptable before my team is notified of the vulnerability?

Time to Fix a Known Vulnerability

Coupled to the notification time, what is an acceptable wait time for the vulnerability to be fixed? Fixing in this context can take a few different guises, the simplest being deploying a new version of the function with a patched, updated library; slightly more complicated is the decommissioning of the function until a patch is available, and potentially most complicated is self-authoring the library fix.

The selection of the solution is context specific, but the metric will help drive maturity and will produce concrete examples around what risk is truly tolerable from the business.

Service Impacts Incurred Through Security Vulnerabilities

Often the quickest way to close a potential security threat is to turn something off, whether literally flicking a switch or making something inaccessible. As an organization operationally matures, the service impact of fixing a security issue should be negligible. As talked about previously, you want to roll forward fixes, thereby not impacting service availability, but there will be cases along the journey where it is better to place the service in a degraded state while the fix is applied. Improvements in this metric are correlated with increased operational maturity.

Attempted Breaches Prevented

Modern tooling is sophisticated enough to identify breaches being attempted or retroactively identify past breach attempts. To make the impact of investment in security more tangible, understanding how many potential incidents have been prevented is a powerful metric to obtain. It is important, however, that there is nuance in the measurement. Being able to drill down to the component level is crucial; for example, reducing your attack surface by decommissioning infrastructure will make the aggregate count decrease but could be misconstrued as a loss in tooling efficacy, or it could simply be that fewer attempts are being made.

Compliance Statistics

Having a robust set of controls that define compliant cloud resource configurations is crucial in a scalable security approach, as you will see in greater detail later in the book. For now, consider an AWS organization with hundreds of S3 buckets spread across tens of accounts—you should be able to track and report on how many of them have sufficient levels of server-side encryption enabled. By tracking this metric across many resource types and configuration options, you can understand our baseline security posture at scale and show the impact of security initiatives.

Percentage of Changes Rejected

As part of a security team's enablement objective, over time you need to determine efficacy. Over time, teams should understand the security context they operate within, and doing things securely should be the default. A metaphor I like for this is that developers are like lightning—they pursue the path of least resistance. If you can make the secure path the one of least resistance, you will observe the percentage of changes rejected on security grounds decrease over time.

1.7 The Principles of Security

By establishing principles, a common set of beliefs, and embedding them through action, you make significant progress on two pivotal goals. First, you strengthen a culture that takes security seriously. Second, you build the foundations for autonomy. Fundamentally, scaling is achieved by giving people the tools and mental models required to make the correct decisions. It is not enough for people to be able to parrot answers back; they need to be able to arrive at the same answer independently. To that end, let's look at a starting set of principles.

Least Privilege

Often the first principle that comes to mind when discussing security, the principle of least privilege is that actors in the system, both human and robot, have enough privilege to perform their jobs and no more. For example, a human cannot make changes to production environments without using the CI/CD pipeline, or a system cannot provision infrastructure in regions that are not needed for the application.

Currently this is hard to achieve and maintain. As I have already discussed, the business needs to be agile, which means that the scope of permissions someone requires can rapidly change. The most common issue I've seen is that although getting extended permissions is normally streamlined and fairly trivial, permissions are rarely revoked or challenged. Often what was least privileged in the past is now overly privileged due to a decrease in scope. We'll evaluate recipes later in the book around both the initial creation of permission sets and their ongoing maintenance.

Only as Strong as Your Weakest Link

Your security posture is not determined by your strongest point but by your weakest. Having a castle doesn't help keep you safe if you leave the gate unlocked and open. When you look at how to implement cloud native security, you need to make sure you're focusing on the weak points, not reinforcing areas of strength.

There's no value in investing significant time in finely tuned identity and access management (IAM) policies, if users are not ubiquitously using multifactor authentication (MFA).

Defense in Depth

This principle is closely related to the concept of weakest links. To have a robust security posture, you need layered solutions. For example, company systems are often only accessible over a virtual private network (VPN), and the intent is that the VPN is only accessible by authenticated users; however, you should not implicitly trust that all users coming from the VPN address space have been authenticated. Otherwise, a compromise in one system cascades, and the potential impact of a breach is magnified.

Another example is when designing networking, as discussed in Chapter 5. Applications in the cloud have distinct identities that define access, beneath that should be additional firewall rules that use IP address ranges to allow groups of systems to communicate, and beneath that are the routes which dictate where traffic can flow. These combine to iteratively reduce the blast radius of a breach: a compromise in one layer does not completely negate all controls.

Security Is Job Zero

A phrase initially coined by Amazon, this principle speaks to how security is the first step in the process. Although I have already discussed how not everyone can be security experts, everyone must become security conscious, literate, and cognizant. Allowing people to look through a security lens is the most critical aspect of a security team, which we'll discuss as part of the enablement strategies in Chapter 4.

Culturally, security has to be the basis from which both technical and social systems are built. An insecure foundation will undermine anything built on top of it. Bad password management undoes password complexity requirements. Unencrypted traffic can make encryption at rest pointless.

You can't out-engineer a culture that doesn't value security at its core.

Quality Is Built In

This principle goes hand in hand with security as job zero. Historically, security was a "bolt-on"—once the functionality was built, it was then made secure, to varying levels of efficacy. In a world centered around the need for business agility, it is hard to see how this "bolt-on" approach, even if it was effective in preventing incidents, allowed teams to be agile and effective. Security is an aspect of system quality. In the preceding principle, it is the alpha quality; without a secure foundation the change should never see the light of day. Code, architectures, and systems need to be designed to allow for security, meaning that security is something that needs to be prioritized and invested in from day one.

Businesses can often be myopic in the pursuit of new functionality, and under pressure to hit release dates, security is often deprioritized. This technical debt accrues over time and becomes incredibly expensive to pay back, orders of magnitude more than was initially required to build in at the start.

DevSecOps initiatives, tooling, and processes like threat modeling make security a first-class initiative from before a line of code is written. By enforcing security standards from the beginning, it is no longer work that can be dropped when there is schedule pressure. It's part of the standard operating procedure.

Chapter Summary

Let's review the learning objectives.

Modern life means that ever more value is being created digitally, and with that come more incentives for cyber criminals and worse damages as regulation increases. As the attacks grow in sophistication, so must our defenses. Cloud native security is security principles applied in true symbiosis with the cloud, ensuring that you are building fit-for-purpose processes, using the right tools, and making sure our people understand the new reality.

Security is an enablement function in a modern organization, as opposed to the gatekeeper position it often previously occupied. It needs to allow for change to flow quickly, easily, and safely. Security exists to manage risk, both at the macro and micro levels. Risk is introduced through change, so being able to understand change at scale is critical in managing risk. Smaller, more frequent change is far less risky than bigger, less frequent change.

DevSecOps is a cultural shift that transforms how security works in concert with delivery teams. You cannot achieve DevSecOps by buying a new tool; instead, it is a deep-rooted change that starts and ends with people. I talked about a few quantitative measures that could be used together to understand how security is maturing at your organization, such as the percentage of compliant infrastructure, the speed with which the issues are rectified, and the number of potential breaches negated.

The fundamental principles of security have not changed in decades; instead it is their application that has changed. From least privilege to defense in depth, understanding these principles enables you to form a security strategy and understand how the recipes in this book stem from a strong, principled foundation.

With the introduction done, we'll now look at the recipes that allow you to establish a solid foundation in the cloud. As with a shaky foundation, everything built on top will quickly come crashing down around you.

CHAPTER 2

Setting Up Accounts and Users

In Chapter 1, you saw the principles that underly modern security and, specifically, how security functions as cloud native becomes the dominant paradigm in the industry. Now, let's move on to the initial configuration of your cloud estate. Investing in a scalable, programmatic approach will let you move with the business, allowing teams to rapidly onboard and innovate and allowing you to focus your energies and efforts on higher-value activities.

You'll see how to do the following:

- Create the fundamental building blocks of cloud estates
- Deploy a region-based guardrail to constrain teams to only approved regions
- Centralize and create users to allow people to access your estate in a manageable way

2.1 Scalable Project Structures on GCP

Problem

You need to deploy the projects required to rapidly onboard a new team in to your organization.

Solution

In this recipe, you will deploy a new folder for a team, with the four required projects underneath, as shown in Figure 2-1.

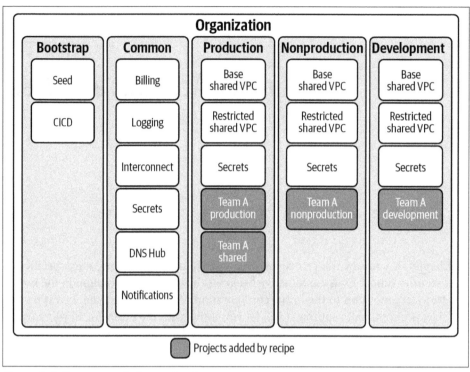

Figure 2-1. Recommended organization structure

If you haven't already done so, familiarize yourself with Terraform and the different authentication mechanisms in Chapter 11.

Create a *variables.tf* file and copy the following contents:

```
variable "production_folder_name" {
  type        = string
  description = "The name of the production folder"
}

variable "nonproduction_folder_name" {
  type        = string
  description = "The name of the nonproduction folder"
}

variable "development_folder_name" {
  type        = string
  description = "The name of the development folder"
}

variable "project_prefix" {
  type        = string
  description = "Used to prefix the project names to ensure global uniqueness"
```

```
  }

variable "team_name" {
  type        = string
  description = "The name of the team to be onboarded"
}
```

Then fill out the corresponding *terraform.tfvars* file:

```
production_folder_name    = ""
nonproduction_folder_name = ""
development_folder_name   = ""
project_prefix            = ""
team_name                 = ""
```

Create the following *provider.tf* file and run `terraform init`:

```
provider "google" {}

terraform {
  required_providers {
    google = {
      source  = "hashicorp/google"
      version = "~> 3"
    }
  }
}
```

Create the following *main.tf* file and run `terraform plan`:

```
data "google_folder" "production" {
  folder = var.production_folder_name
}

data "google_folder" "nonproduction" {
  folder = var.nonproduction_folder_name
}

data "google_folder" "development" {
  folder = var.development_folder_name
}

resource "google_project" "production" {
  name       = "${var.team_name}Production"
  project_id = "${var.project_prefix}-${var.team_name}-prod"
  folder_id  = data.google_folder.production.name
}

resource "google_project" "preproduction" {
  name       = "${var.team_name}PreProduction"
  project_id = "${var.project_prefix}-${var.team_name}-preprod"
  folder_id  = data.google_folder.nonproduction.name
}
```

```
resource "google_project" "development" {
  name       = "${var.team_name}Development"
  project_id = "${var.project_prefix}-${var.team_name}-dev"
  folder_id  = data.google_folder.development.name
}

resource "google_project" "shared" {
  name       = "${var.team_name}Shared"
  project_id = "${var.project_prefix}-${var.team_name}-shared"
  folder_id  = data.google_folder.production.name
}
```

Review the resources that are going to be created, and then run `terraform apply` to make the changes.

Discussion

On Google Cloud Platform (GCP), you have a three-tier resource hierarchy that allows you to define your organizational structure, as shown in Figure 2-2.

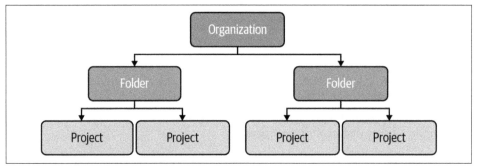

Figure 2-2. The organization hierarchy in GCP

Through a GCP organization, you are able to centrally manage identity (see Recipe 2.7), apply policies (see Recipe 2.4), and get visibility of security issues at scale (see Recipe 3.1).

 It is highly recommended that you have two organizations set up. This allows you to test and measure the impact of changes made at the organization level, e.g., enabling a new organization policy for the entire organization.

Core folders

Google best practice recommends five core folders you should have underneath your organization:

- Common, which contains the centralized and shared resources for the entire organization. It can include the following projects:
  — Billing, which gives centralized management of billing logs.

  — Logging, where you store an immutable copy of all logs for audit and investigation purposes.

  — Interconnect, where you deploy the Cloud Interconnect and related resources for hybrid networking.

  — Secrets, for housing the organization-wide secrets allowing for centralized access, management, and rotation.

  — DNS Hub, for configuring peered DNS between Google Cloud and on-premise.

  — Notifications, where you centrally configure alerting from a Security Command Center (see Recipe 3.1).
- Production, which holds all the projects containing production resources. In addition to one or more projects for each production application, it can include the following projects:
  — Base Shared VPC, which hosts the base production shared VPC.

  — Restricted Shared VPC, which hosts the restricted production shared VPC.

  — Secrets, for housing the shared production secrets.
- NonProd, which holds all the projects containing nonproduction resources. It will have a nonproduction copy of all production projects.
- Dev, which holds all the projects containing development resources. It will have a development copy of all production projects.
- Bootstrap, which contains the projects used to create the resource hierarchy. It will contain these two projects:
  — CI/CD, which houses the CI/CD pipeline to deploy the resource hierarchy.

  — Seed, which contains the Terraform state and service account required for the CI/CD pipeline to operate.

To create the `Bootstrap` folder and move the current project underneath it, copy and apply the following Terraform. The current project then becomes the `Seed` project outlined previously.

```
resource "google_folder" "bootstrap" {
  display_name = "Bootstrap"
  parent       = data.google_organization.this.name
}

resource "null_resource" "move_initial_project" {
  provisioner "local-exec" {
    command = "gcloud beta --quiet projects move ${var.project_id}" +
    "--folder ${split("/", google_folder.bootstrap.id)[1]}"
  }
}
```

Per workload projects

This recipe created the following four projects for the team onboarding to your GCP organization:

- Production, which holds all the resources for the production instance of the service:
  — User access to this project should be disabled by default.

  — All change should happen via infrastructure as code and CI/CD pipelines.

  — In an emergency, user access can be reenabled.

- Preproduction, which holds a full copy of production without production data.
  — This project is used to test changes before promoting them to production.

  — Access to this project should be identical to production, by default through automation.

  — User changes result in differences between nonproduction and production, which decreases testing efficacy, resulting in more production issues.

- Development, which is for developers to rapidly experiment against.
  — Developers should have direct access to this project.

  — By allowing developers direct access, they are able to iterate much faster.

  — Ideally, changes are made through locally executed infrastructure as code.

- Shared, which holds the shared infrastructure for the application.
  — For example, DNS infrastructure and artifact repositories.

  — Changes here should be done via infrastructure as code through CI/CD pipelines.

  — If the CI/CD pipelines fail, then user access will be required to recover them.

Strategies for converging organizations

Over time, it often becomes necessary to migrate projects between GCP organizations. This can be due to mergers and acquisitions, business requirements necessitating multiple organizations, or pulling together business unit–owned organizations under centralized IT management.

To enable this, two folders are often used temporarily when migrating projects between organizations: *Import* and *Export*. These folders are used during the onboarding and offboarding process, respectively, and allow you to test that the workloads in the projects operate as expected when moved. This also means that you can explicitly only allow for the migration of projects that are contained within these folders, allowing you to more closely observe the principle of least privilege.

As of the time of writing, migrating projects between organizations is an alpha feature, whereas historically it required a support ticket to action. As this process is becoming increasingly common among companies, let's discuss the potential strategies that exist:

Migrate projects
> Depending on the nature of the resources within a project, this can vary in difficulty from trivial to requiring significant amounts of planning. Using Cloud Asset Inventory allows you to understand all the resources within a project, the details of which can be exported to BigQuery, allowing you to run queries to determine the required approach.

Migrate workloads
> into fresh accounts. If the workload has been created with infrastructure as code and its data is not cost prohibitive to move, it can be easier to simply stand the workload up in a new project within the new organization. For a lot of development and test workloads that do not have full production databases, this can be an easy solution to test that the new organization is configured to support production.

Upgrade the existing foundation
> It is possible to maintain multiple organizations such that they function similarly with high levels of infrastructure as code. This should only be selected as the enduring option when it proves too complex or expensive to bring all workloads under a single organization.

Maintain all organizations
> Not considered an enduring option, based on business priorities, it can make sense to allow two organizations to coexist and not make short-term investments into merging them together. However, over the long term, this can prove very

expensive as significant amounts of engineering effort must be expended to maintain both to a sufficient standard.

Summarizing the Recipe

Let's summarize what was covered in this recipe:

- GCP organizations are built from a root organization node, with folders and projects underneath.
- A set of core folders suffice for the requirements of most organizations:
  - Bootstrap, where the initial project goes and the organization is modified from.
  - Common, where the core infrastructure pieces such as shared networking exist.
  - Production, where delivery teams are able to deploy their production workloads.
  - NonProduction, where delivery teams are able to deploy their nonproduction workloads.
  - Development, where delivery teams are able to deploy their development workloads.
- There are additional folders which organizations often use, and you learned about having explicit Import and Export folders for managing moving projects between organizations.

2.2 Scalable Account Structures on AWS

Problem

You need to deploy the accounts required to rapidly onboard a new team into your organization.

Solution

This recipe builds out four accounts, as shown in Figure 2-3.

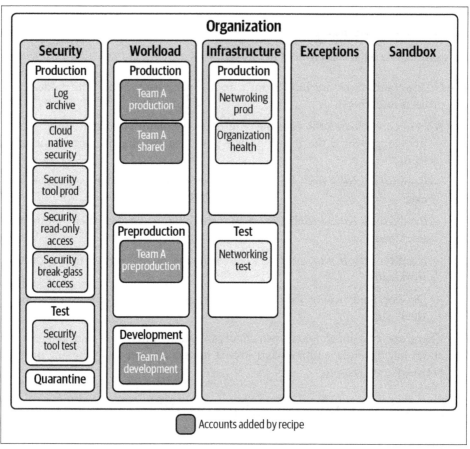

Figure 2-3. Recommended organization structure

If you haven't already done so, familiarize yourself with Terraform and the different authentication mechanisms in Chapter 11.

Create a *variables.tf* file and copy the following contents:

```
variable "production_ou_id" {
  type        = string
  description = "The ID of the production OU"
}

variable "preproduction_ou_id" {
  type        = string
  description = "The ID of the preproduction OU"
}

variable "development_ou_id" {
  type        = string
```

```
      description = "The ID of the development OU"
    }

    variable "team_name" {
      type        = string
      description = "The name of the team to be onboarded"
    }

    variable "production_account_email" {
      type        = string
      description = "The production root account email"
    }

    variable "preproduction_account_email" {
      type        = string
      description = "The preproduction root account email"
    }

    variable "development_account_email" {
      type        = string
      description = "The development root account email"
    }

    variable "shared_account_email" {
      type        = string
      description = "The shared root account email"
    }
```

Then fill out the corresponding *terraform.tfvars* file:

```
production_ou_id             = ""
preproduction_ou_id          = ""
development_ou_id            = ""
team_name                    = ""
production_account_email     = ""
preproduction_account_email = ""
development_account_email    = ""
shared_account_email         = ""
```

Create the following *provider.tf* file and run `terraform init`:

```
provider "aws" {}

terraform {
  required_providers {
    aws = {
      source  = "hashicorp/aws"
      version = "~> 3"
    }
  }
}
```

Create the following *main.tf* file and run `terraform plan`:

```
resource "aws_organizations_organizational_unit" "team" {
  name      = var.team_name
  parent_id = var.organizational_unit_parent_id
}

resource "aws_organizations_account" "production" {
  name      = "${var.team_name}-production"
  email     = var.production_account_email
  parent_id = aws_organizations_organizational_unit.team.id
}

resource "aws_organizations_account" "preproduction" {
  name      = "${var.team_name}-preproduction"
  email     = var.preproduction_account_email
  parent_id = aws_organizations_organizational_unit.team.id
}

resource "aws_organizations_account" "development" {
  name      = "${var.team_name}-development"
  email     = var.development_account_email
  parent_id = aws_organizations_organizational_unit.team.id
}

resource "aws_organizations_account" "shared" {
  name      = "${var.team_name}-shared"
  email     = var.shared_account_email
  parent_id = aws_organizations_organizational_unit.team.id
}
```

Review the resources that are going to be created, and then run `terraform apply` to make the changes.

Discussion

On AWS, cloud estates are built from three foundational resources—organizations, organizational units, and accounts—which create the hierarchy shown in Figure 2-4.

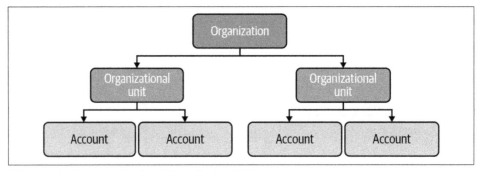

Figure 2-4. The organization hierarchy in AWS

The organization works as the root of the entire estate, and a number of security activities are done at the organizational level, as it allows you to look holistically across all accounts. Both Recipes 3.2 and 3.8 aggregate data from across the organization.

 It is highly recommended that you have two AWS organizations. This allows you to test and measure the impact of changes made at the organization level, e.g., enabling a new service control policy (SCP) for the entire organization, such as in Recipe 2.5.

The organizational units you should have

Organization units (OUs) are a way of grouping accounts, and other organizational units together. In this recipe, you created one for a specific team, but when initially creating your organization, there are a number of AWS-recommended OUs and accounts to create based on function and ownership:

The Security OU
This houses the centralized security resources and facilitates cross-account access. It should contain both production and test OUs to allow for the proper management of workloads. Under the Security OU should be the following accounts and OUs:

- The log archive account, which serves as the central log aggregation location, allowing users to review immutable logs from across the entire estate. See Recipe 3.5.

- The cloud native security tooling account, which acts as the centralized aggregator for AWS security services for the organization. These include Amazon GuardDuty (see Recipe 3.8) and AWS Security Hub (see Recipe 3.2).

- A production and test account for each self-hosted security tool, such as Splunk or HashiCorp Vault.

- The security read-only account, which serves as a gateway to read-only access in all accounts across the estate for incident investigation and threat hunting.

- The security break-glass account, which serves as a privileged gateway to accounts within the estate in case of an emergency.

- The quarantine OU, which locks down accounts that have potentially been compromised.

The Workload OU

This is the parent of delivery team–specific OUs and accounts as created in this recipe.

The Infrastructure OU

This can contain the following accounts:

- A production and a preproduction transit or networking account, which serves to enable centralized, secure North-South connectivity to on-premise workloads and East-West connectivity between AWS Accounts.

- An organization health account, which serves as a central, operations-focused, single pane of glass for the entire organization. Commonly, services such as AWS Systems Manager Explorer, seen in Recipe 8.5, are managed and viewed from this account.

There are also some additional OUs that can be helpful in specific scenarios, including the following:

The Exceptions OU

Sometimes you have accounts that house workloads that are particularly unusual or hard to fit within your guardrails. In these cases, you can create an exceptions OU that allows them to run in the cloud.

The Transitional OU

At times you may need to merge disparate AWS organizations, and the accounts being moved will need to be retrofitted to work in the new organization. This OU can be used as a temporary holder while the required changes are made to the accounts.

The Suspended OU

This houses accounts that are awaiting decommissioning or have been suspended.

The Policy Staging OU

This is recommended by AWS for the testing and promotion of policies such as service control policies (SCPs). In general, this is better served by a full secondary organization, as it provides a higher signal testing approach.

The Sandbox OU

This houses accounts with minimal guardrails, which allows users to experiment with the full breadth of what AWS has to offer. They are often completely removed from the shared infrastructure, and should regularly have all resources deleted to control costs.

The Individual Business Owners OU
> This houses resources that do not constitute a full workload, such as a public S3 bucket holding certain public assets.

Per workload accounts

This recipe created four accounts to house the workload of the onboarding team:

Production
> This holds all the required production resources.
>
> - Human access to this account should be disabled by default.
> - All change should happen via infrastructure as code and CI/CD pipelines.
> - In an emergency, user access can be reenabled.

Preproduction
> This holds a full copy of production resources but not production data.
>
> - This account is used to test changes before promoting to production.
> - Access to this account should be identical to production, by default through automation.
> - User changes result in differences between nonproduction and production, which decreases testing efficacy, resulting in more production issues.

Development
> This account is for developers to rapidly experiment against.
>
> - Developers should have direct access to this account.
> - Direct access lets developers iterate much faster.
> - Ideally, changes are made through locally executed infrastructure as code.

Shared
> This account holds the shared infrastructure for the application.
>
> - This might include DNS infrastructure and artifact repositories.
> - Changes here should be done via infrastructure as code through CI/CD pipelines.
> - If the CI/CD pipelines fail, then user access will be required to recover them.

Strategies for converging organizations

It might be that after reading this recipe and others further in the book, your existing AWS organization needs reworking or potentially recreating. With that in mind, let's quickly talk through the options that exist for handling multiple organizations.

Migrate accounts

Depending on the complexity of the workloads hosted in the accounts, this can range from easy to nearly impossible. Workloads that are running self-sufficiently from a connectivity and infrastructure perspective can be moved with a reasonable amount of effort. If they are dependent on resources from many other accounts in the organization, the effort grows exponentially.

Migrate workloads

If the workload has been created with infrastructure as code, then there is potential to easily recreate the workloads in a new account. The complexity here is often due to two factors: the cost to potentially extricate the data and move it into the new account and the service outage necessitated by this movement.

Upgrade the existing organizations

This is where you invest effort to bring the organizations into feature and implementation parity. This enables workloads to be housed where they currently reside and ideally look to move all new workloads to one organization over the other. This can be a large effort depending on the differences between the two organizations.

Maintain all organizations

This should not be considered as a realistic, enduring option, as you commit to duplicating effort on an ongoing basis. However, due to prioritization and budget constraints, this can be the chosen option for the short to medium term. In this case, ensure that all new workloads go to the organization which would become enduring if the call was made.

Summarizing the Recipe

Let's review what was covered as part of this recipe:

- Within an AWS organization, you have organizational units and accounts.
- Organizational units allow you to group accounts and other organizational units together
- Thea recommended set of core organizational units includes the following:
  — Security, which houses the accounts for security activities
  — Workloads, where all the business workloads are housed
  — Infrastructure, where common shared infrastructure pieces live, like Transit Gateway
- To fully test organization structure changes, it is recommended to have a second organization as a preproduction mirror of the production organization.
- Organization structures can be created through code.

2.3 Scalable Subscription Structures on Azure

Problem

You need to deploy the subscriptions required to rapidly onboard a new team into your organization.

Solution

This recipe builds out four subscriptions, as shown in Figure 2-5.

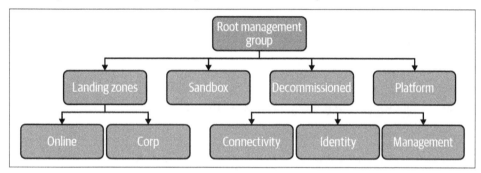

Figure 2-5. Recommended tenant structure

If you haven't already done so, familiarize yourself with Terraform and the different authentication mechanisms in Chapter 11.

Create a *variables.tf* file and copy the following contents:

```
variable "management_group_parent_id" {
  type        = string
  description = "The ID of the parent for the team's management group"
}

variable "billing_account_name" {
  type        = string
  description = "The name of the Azure billing account"
}

variable "enrollment_account_name" {
  type        = string
  description = "The name of the Azure enrollment account"
}

variable "team_name" {
  type        = string
  description = "The name of the team to be onboarded"
}
```

Then fill out the corresponding *terraform.tfvars* file:

```
management_group_parent_id = ""
billing_account_name       = ""
enrollment_account_name    = ""
team_name                  = ""
```

Create the following *provider.tf* file and run `terraform init`:

```
provider "azurerm" {
  features {}
}

terraform {
  required_providers {
    azurerm = {
      source  = "hashicorp/azurerm"
      version = "~> 2"
    }
  }
}
```

Create the following *main.tf* file and run `terraform plan`:

```
resource "azurerm_management_group" "team" {
  display_name             = var.team_name
  parent_management_group_id = var.management_group_parent_id

  subscription_ids = [
    azurerm_subscription.production.subscription_id,
    azurerm_subscription.preproduction.subscription_id,
    azurerm_subscription.development.subscription_id,
    azurerm_subscription.shared.subscription_id
  ]
}

data "azurerm_billing_enrollment_account_scope" "root" {
  billing_account_name    = var.billing_account_name
  enrollment_account_name = var.enrollment_account_name
}

resource "azurerm_subscription" "production" {
  billing_scope_id  = data.azurerm_billing_enrollment_account_scope.root[0].id
  subscription_name = "${var.team_name}Production"
}

resource "azurerm_subscription" "preproduction" {
  billing_scope_id  = data.azurerm_billing_enrollment_account_scope.root[0].id
  subscription_name = "${var.team_name}Preproduction"
}

resource "azurerm_subscription" "development" {
  billing_scope_id  = data.azurerm_billing_enrollment_account_scope.root[0].id
  subscription_name = "${var.team_name}Development"
}
```

```
resource "azurerm_subscription" "shared" {
  billing_scope_id   = data.azurerm_billing_enrollment_account_scope.root[0].id
  subscription_name = "${var.team_name}Shared"
}
```

Review the resources that are going to be created, and then run terraform apply to make the changes.

Discussion

In Azure, there is a three-tier hierarchy for creating your estate: management groups, subscriptions, and resource groups, as shown in Figure 2-6.

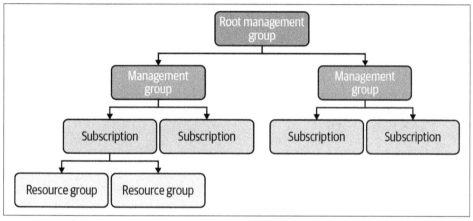

Figure 2-6. The tenant hierarchy in Azure

At the top level you have a root management group, and underneath that you can have subscriptions and other management groups. You can apply policies at the management group level, so you can apply guardrails high up your hierarchy to simplify management at scale.

> It is highly recommended that you create two tenants. This allows you to test and measure the impact of changes made at the tenant level, e.g., making core networking changes, such as in Recipe 5.9.

The management groups you should have

Underneath the root management group, there are a series of management groups you should have to enable different parts of the business:

Sandbox

This management group gives users a space to experiment with Azure. You should not allow production workloads to be run from here; instead, they should be in the outlined landing zones management group. This also gives you a management group to automatically assign new subscriptions if not specified; otherwise they are created under the root management group.

Platform

This management group exists for the creation and management of platform level resources and other shared services. Underneath this management group, you should look to create three more:

- Identity, a management group to hold all the subscriptions required for identity management, containing resources such as Active Directory Domain Services

- Management, a management group to cater to platform-level monitoring and logging

- Connectivity, a management group to hold all the central networking components, such as the Hub VNet at the center of your networking topology, as seen in Recipe 5.9

Decommissioned

This management group is for subscriptions that are being decommissioned or retired. Subscriptions self-delete 90 days after being cancelled or can be force deleted after 72 hours have passed.

Landing zones

This management group allows you to create areas that are preconfigured to support teams with a particular application architecture. Underneath this management group, two common landing zone flavors are Online, which are externally accessible applications, and Corp, for applications only reachable from the internal network. As your estate scales, you'll need to create landing zones to cater to different requirements and architectures.

Per workload subscriptions

This recipe created four subscriptions to house the workload of the onboarding team:

Production

This holds all the required production resources.

- User access to this subscription should be disabled by default.

- All change should happen via infrastructure as code and CI/CD pipelines.

- In an emergency, user access can be reenabled.

Preproduction
This holds a full copy of production resources but not production data.

- This subscription is used to test changes before promoting to production.
- Access to this subscription should be identical to production, by default through automation.
- User changes result in differences between nonproduction and production, which decreases testing efficacy, resulting in more production issues.

Development
This subscription is for developers to rapidly experiment against.

- Developers should have direct access to this subscription.
- Direct access allows developers to iterate much faster.
- Ideally, changes are made through locally executed infrastructure as code.

Shared
This subscription holds the shared infrastructure for the application.

- This may include DNS infrastructure and artifact repositories.
- Changes here should be done via infrastructure as code through CI/CD pipelines.
- If the CI/CD pipelines themselves fail, then user access will be required to recover them.

Considerations for subscriptions

Subscriptions in Azure are a unit of management, billing, and scale. You can apply Azure policies directly to subscriptions. Taking the example of personally identifiable information (PII), you can apply required policies to those subscriptions without needing a dedicated management group. This allows you to have coarse-grained controls at the management group layer and to use subscriptions to be able to apply fine-grained controls.

Furthering on that governance theme, subscriptions should be used to segment production and nonproduction environments. Often, access controls are tighter for production resources, but to enable teams to move and experiment rapidly, development controls are relaxed.

The important thing with subscriptions is to be flexible; as more teams move into the cloud, they will often have unique or new requirements that must be catered to. As these new requirements surface, you can build out further subscriptions and policies to achieve your governance objectives without producing too much friction for teams.

Summarizing the Recipe

Let's summarize what you learned and deployed in this recipe:

- Azure organizations are built from management groups, subscriptions, and resource groups.
- They are centered around a root management group.
- There are four core recommended management groups:
  — Sandbox, where users can experiment with Azure.

  — Platform, where centralized services are created. Underneath this management group, you should have further management groups based on what service is being provided.

  — Decommissioned, where subscriptions that are pending decommission are stored.

  — Landing zones, where teams are onboarded. Underneath this management group, you should have further management group applications based on infrastructure requirements.

2.4 Region Locking on GCP

Problem

You are setting up your initial GCP organization, and you need to ensure that teams are only able to deploy resources into Australian regions for data sovereignty and limit the blast radius in case of a breach.

Solution

If you haven't already done so, familiarize yourself with Terraform and the different authentication mechanisms in Chapter 11.

Create a *variables.tf* file and copy the following contents:

```
variable "organization_domain" {
  type        = string
  description = "The domain for your Organization"
}

variable "allowed_location" {
  type        = string
  description = "The allowed location for resources"
}
```

Then fill out the corresponding *terraform.tfvars* file:

```
organization_domain = ""
allowed_location    = ""
```

Create the following *provider.tf* file and run `terraform init`:

```
provider "google" {}

terraform {
  required_providers {
    google = {
      source  = "hashicorp/google"
      version = "~> 3"
    }
  }
}
```

Create the following *main.tf* file and run `terraform plan`:

```
data "google_organization" "this" {
  domain = var.organization_domain
}

resource "google_organization_policy" "region_lock" {
  org_id     = data.google_organization.this.org_id
  constraint = "constraints/gcp.resourceLocations"

  list_policy {
    allow {
      values = ["in:${var.allowed_location}"]
    }
  }
}
```

Review the resources that are going to be created, and then run `terraform apply` to make the changes.

Discussion

On GCP, to enact region locking, you should use organization policies. You can use these to region lock your entire organization as in the preceding solution, or you can apply them directly to folders or even specific projects. The policies are implicitly inherited down your organization hierarchy but can be overruled by an explicit assignment further down.

For example, to apply a policy that also allows access to Singapore (asia-southeast-1), you can use the same `google_project_organization_policy` and apply it directly to a given project:

```
resource "google_project_organization_policy" "region_lock_policy" {
  project    = ""
  constraint = "constraints/gcp.resourceLocations"
```

```
list_policy {
  allow {
    values = ["in:australia-locations", "in:asia-southeast1-locations"]
  }
}
}
```

 Region locking on GCP only applies to resource creation; it will not impact running resources unless they themselves create resources. Also, some GCP services store and process data in different regions from where the resource is actually created. Consult the service documentation directly when there are data sovereignty concerns.

The different kinds of locations

Within GCP there are three levels of locations: multiregion, region, and zone. You can use all of these in organization policies to restrict resource creation.

Multiregion
These locations are backed by hardware across multiple regions; typically this only applies for storage-based resources. Examples include global, asia, europe.

Region
These locations are geographically isolated from each other. Examples include australia-southeast1, europe-west4, and us-central1.

Zone
These locations are isolated failure domains, i.e., data centers, within a region. Examples include australia-southeast1-a, europe-west4-b, and us-central1-c.

Value groups
Value groups are Google-curated lists that allow for selecting locations that will naturally expand as new locations are added. For example, you can select to allow regions and zones within the European Union by using the selector in: eu-locations. This allows for simplified policies, with minimal management overhead due to regulatory or data sovereignty requirements.

 Some resources in GCP are global and therefore are unaffected by the resource locations' organization policies.

For example, to create a secret in the Secrets Manager with automatic replication, the global region must be allowed.

Summarizing the recipe

Let's summarize what was learned and deployed in this recipe:

- Organization policies allow you to implement region locking in GCP.
- They are automatically inherited down your organization structure, but you can override from down the hierarchy, so start with the maximum restriction at the top level.
- Certain resources are global and are automatically exempted from being affected by the policy.
- The recipe creates an organization policy that locks resource creation specifically to the specified regions.

2.5 Region Locking on AWS

Problem

You are setting up your initial AWS organization, and you need to ensure that teams are only able to deploy resources into Australian regions for data sovereignty and limit the blast radius in case of a breach.

Solution

If you haven't already done so, familiarize yourself with Terraform and the different authentication mechanisms in Chapter 11.

Create a *variables.tf* file and copy the following contents:

```
variable "allowed_regions" {
  type        = list(string)
  description = "The allowed regions for resources"
}
```

Then fill out the corresponding *terraform.tfvars* file:

```
allowed_regions = []
```

Create a *locals.tf* file and copy the following contents:

```
locals {
  service_exemptions = [
    "a4b:*",
    "acm:*",
    "aws-marketplace-management:*",
    "aws-marketplace:*",
    "aws-portal:*",
    "awsbillingconsole:*",
    "budgets:*",
    "ce:*",
    "chime:*",
    "cloudfront:*",
    "config:*",
```

```
        "cur:*",
        "directconnect:*",
        "ec2:DescribeRegions",
        "ec2:DescribeTransitGateways",
        "ec2:DescribeVpnGateways",
        "fms:*",
        "globalaccelerator:*",
        "health:*",
        "iam:*",
        "importexport:*",
        "kms:*",
        "mobileanalytics:*",
        "networkmanager:*",
        "organizations:*",
        "pricing:*",
        "route53:*",
        "route53domains:*",
        "s3:GetAccountPublic*",
        "s3:ListAllMyBuckets",
        "s3:PutAccountPublic*",
        "shield:*",
        "sts:*",
        "support:*",
        "trustedadvisor:*",
        "waf-regional:*",
        "waf:*",
        "wafv2:*",
        "wellarchitected:*"
    ]
}
```

Create the following *provider.tf* file and run `terraform init`:

```
provider "aws" {}

terraform {
  required_providers {
    aws = {
      source  = "hashicorp/aws"
      version = "~> 3"
    }
  }
}
```

Create the following *main.tf* file and run `terraform plan`:

```
data "aws_organizations_organization" "this" {}

resource "aws_organizations_policy_attachment" "root" {
  policy_id = aws_organizations_policy.top_level_region_lock.id
  target_id = data.aws_organizations_organization.this.roots[0].id
}
```

```
resource "aws_organizations_policy" "top_level_region_lock" {
  name    = "region-lock"
  content = data.aws_iam_policy_document.region_lock_policy.json
}

data "aws_iam_policy_document" "region_lock_policy" {
  statement {
    effect      = "Deny"
    not_actions = local.service_exemptions
    resources   = ["*"]
    condition {
      test     = "StringNotEquals"
      values   = var.allowed_regions
      variable = "aws:RequestedRegion"
    }
  }
}
```

Review the resources that are going to be created, and then run `terraform apply` to make the changes.

Discussion

To implement region locking on AWS, you need to use SCPs. They can be applied at any point of your organization hierarchy, be that at the organization root, as per the solution, or against an organizational unit or individual account.

 SCPs do not apply to the management account. This is one of the reasons it is recommended to minimize the amount of infrastructure deployed in the management account.

You will have noticed, as part of the solution, a long list of API calls that are exempted from the lock. This is due to one of the following reasons:

- The service is global in nature and therefore needs to be exempted, such as a web application firewall.
- The service has a hard requirement on a particular region, such as CloudFront.

To dive a bit further into the hard requirement on a particular region, for certain AWS services, the control plane for that service exists only in one region. In the case of CloudFront, as noted, the certificate to be used for TLS must be in us-east-1. Unfortunately, the only way to find these is to read the service documentation.

The exemption list is unfortunately not provided as an artifact that can be referenced. However, the SCP example documentation is routinely updated with the most recent list.

What you can also do as part of the SCP is allow certain principals to circumnavigate the restrictions. The SCP defined in the solution stops you not only from creating resources in unapproved regions but also from deleting, listing, or describing them. By adding a condition to the IAM policy, you can allow particular roles to operate in all regions so you can more readily react in case of a breach or incident. To achieve this, you can add a condition as shown in the following Terraform. You will need to fill the `role_exemptions` local variable with the Amazon Resource Names (ARNs) of the required roles.

```
locals {
  role_exemptions = []
}

data "aws_iam_policy_document" "sydney_region_lock_policy" {
  statement {
    effect      = "Deny"
    not_actions = local.service_exemptions
    resources   = ["*"]
    condition {
      test     = "StringNotEquals"
      values   = ["ap-southeast-2"]
      variable = "aws:RequestedRegion"
    }
    condition {
      test = "ArnNotLike"
      values = local.role_exemptions
      variable = "aws:PrincipalARN"
    }
  }
}
```

 IAM principals acting from outside your organization, for example, an IAM user that has cross-account S3 bucket access, are not affected by SCPs.

Instead, if they must assume a role in the account, then they are beholden to the SCPs in place.

Summarizing the recipe

Let's summarize what was learned and deployed in this recipe:

- SCPs allow you to implement region locking in AWS.

- They are automatically inherited down your organization structure, so you should start with the most permissive and narrow as required.
- You can also add conditions to allow certain users, often security personnel, to subvert the region locking when needed.
- Certain resources require `us-east-1` to function, so you need to maintain a service exception list.
- Your organization management account is unaffected by SCPs, so you should look to minimize the resources deployed into that account.
- IAM principals acting from outside your organization are not affected by SCPs.

2.6 Region Locking on Azure

Problem

You are setting up your initial Azure tenancy, and you need to ensure that teams are only able to deploy resources into Australian regions for data sovereignty and limit the blast radius in the case of a breach.

Solution

If you haven't already done so, familiarize yourself with Terraform and the different authentication mechanisms in Chapter 11.

Create a *variables.tf* file and copy the following contents:

```
variable "root_management_group_uuid" {
  type = string
  description = "The UUID for the root management group"
}

variable "allowed_locations" {
  type        = list(string)
  description = "The locations to allow resources"
}
```

Then fill out the corresponding *terraform.tfvars* file:

```
root_management_group_uuid = ""
allowed_locations          = []
```

Create the following *provider.tf* file and run `terraform init`:

```
provider "azurerm" {
  features {}
}

terraform {
  required_providers {
```

```
    azurerm = {
      source  = "hashicorp/azurerm"
      version = "~> 2"
    }
  }
}
```

Create the following *main.tf* file and run `terraform plan`:

```
data "azurerm_management_group" "root" {
  name = var.root_management_group_uuid
}

resource "azurerm_policy_assignment" "root_region_lock" {
  name                 = "root-region-lock"
  scope                = data.azurerm_management_group.root.id
  policy_definition_id = join("", [
    "providers/Microsoft.Authorization/policyDefinitions/",
    "e56962a6-4747-49cd-b67b-bf8b01975c4c"
  ])

  parameters = <<PARAMETERS
{
  "listOfAllowedLocations": {
    "value": ${var.allowed_locations}
  }
}
PARAMETERS

}
```

Review the resources that are going to be created, and then run `terraform apply` to make the changes.

Discussion

To enable region locking on Azure, you use Azure Policy. Azure provides a built-in policy that allows you to restrict resources to particular regions but has a built-in escape hatch for global resources as required. These policies can be applied at the management group, subscription, and resource group level, which allows you to explicitly control the restrictions at any point in your hierarchy.

Summarizing the recipe

Let's summarize what you learned and deployed in this recipe:

- Azure Policy allows you to implement region locking in Azure.
- Polies are automatically inherited down your organization structure, so you should start with the most permissive and narrow as required.
- The built-in Azure Policy maintains a list of required exceptions for global resources.

2.7 Centralizing Users on GCP

Problem

You have a new team looking to onboard into your GCP organization. You need to be able to give them access that follows the principle of least privilege and will be maintainable in the long term.

Solution

If you haven't already done so, familiarize yourself with Terraform and the different authentication mechanisms in Chapter 11.

You need to create a service account to interact with the Google Workspace APIs.

Create a *variables.tf* file and copy the following contents:

```
variable "identity_project_id" {
  type        = string
  description = "The project ID for your centralized Identity project"
}
```

Then fill out the corresponding *terraform.tfvars* file:

```
identity_project_id = ""
```

Create the following *provider.tf* file and run `terraform init`:

```
provider "google" {
  project = var.identity_project_id
}

terraform {
  required_providers {
    google = {
      source  = "hashicorp/google"
      version = "~> 3"
    }
    local = {
```

```
        source  = "hashicorp/local"
        version = "~> 2"
      }
    }
  }
}
```

Create the following *main.tf* file and run `terraform plan`:

```
resource "google_project_service" "admin" {
  service = "admin.googleapis.com"
}

resource "google_service_account" "workspace_admin" {
  account_id   = "workspace-admin"
  display_name = "Workspace Admin"
}

resource "google_service_account_key" "workspace_admin" {
  service_account_id = google_service_account.workspace_admin.name
  public_key_type    = "TYPE_X509_PEM_FILE"
}

resource "local_file" "workspace_admin" {
  content  = base64decode(google_service_account_key.workspace_admin.private_key)
  filename = "workspace_admin.json"
}
```

Review the resources that are going to be created, and then run `terraform apply` to make the changes.

With the service account now created, you need to authorize it to perform the required operations against your Google Workspace account. The instructions for this can be found in the Google Workspace for Developers documentation (*https://oreil.ly/uR1tf*). Ensure that the service account has the following scopes when configuring the domain-wide delegation:

- _https://www.googleapis.com/auth/admin.directory.user_
- _https://www.googleapis.com/auth/admin.directory.group_

In a new directory, create a *variables.tf* file and copy the following contents:

```
variable "service_account_key_path" {
  type        = string
  description = "Path to where the service account key is located"
}

variable "customer_id" {
  type        = string
  description = <<DESCRIPTION
Customer ID for your Google Workspace account
Can be found at https://admin.google.com/ac/accountsettings
```

```
DESCRIPTION
}

variable "impersonated_user_email" {
  type        = string
  description = "The email address of a privileged user in your Google Workspace"
}

variable "identity_project_id" {
  type        = string
  description = "The project ID for your centralized Identity project"
}

variable "target_project_id" {
  type        = string
  description = "The project ID to give the group read-only access"
}

variable "users" {
  type        = map(map(any))
  description = "A list of user data objects"
}

variable "team_name" {
  type        = string
  description = "The name of the team"
}

variable "team_description" {
  type        = string
  description = "The description of the team"
}

variable "team_email" {
  type        = string
  description = "The email address for the team"
}
```

Then fill out the corresponding *terraform.tfvars* file:

```
service_account_key_path = ""
customer_id              = ""
impersonated_user_email  = ""
identity_project_id      = ""
target_project_id        = ""
users = {
  "jane.doe@example.com" = {
    given_name  = "Jane"
    family_name = "Doe"
  }
}
team_name            = ""
```

```
team_email       = ""
team_description = ""
```

Create the following *provider.tf* file and run `terraform init`:

```
provider "google" {
  project = var.identity_project_id
}

provider "googleworkspace" {
  credentials             = var.service_account_key_path
  customer_id             = var.customer_id
  impersonated_user_email = var.impersonated_user_email
  oauth_scopes            = [
    "https://www.googleapis.com/auth/admin.directory.user",
    "https://www.googleapis.com/auth/admin.directory.group"
  ]
}

terraform {
  required_providers {
    google = {
      source  = "hashicorp/google"
      version = "~> 3"
    }
    googleworkspace = {
      source  = "hashicorp/googleworkspace"
      version = "~> 0.3"
    }
    random = {
      source  = "hashicorp/random"
      version = "~> 3"
    }
  }
}
```

Create the following *main.tf* file and run `terraform plan`:

```
resource "random_password" "password" {
  for_each = var.users
  length   = 16
  special  = true
}

resource "googleworkspace_user" "user" {
  for_each = var.users
  name {
    family_name = each.value.family_name
    given_name  = each.value.given_name
  }
  change_password_at_next_login = true
  password                      = random_password.password[each.key].result
  primary_email                 = each.key
```

```
}

resource "googleworkspace_group" "team" {
  email       = var.team_email
  name        = var.team_name
  description = var.team_description
}

resource "googleworkspace_group_member" "team" {
  for_each = var.users
  group_id = googleworkspace_group.team.id
  email    = googleworkspace_user.user[each.key].primary_email
}

resource "google_project_iam_binding" "target_project_access" {
  project = var.target_project_id
  role    = "roles/viewer"
  members = [
    "group:${googleworkspace_group.team.email}",
  ]
}

output "passwords" {
  sensitive = true
  value     = [
    for user in googleworkspace_user.user :
      {(user.primary_email) = user.password}
  ]
}
```

Review the resources that are going to be created, and then run `terraform apply` to make the changes.

To get the passwords for the created users, run `terraform output passwords` to print out all the initial passwords set for the users. They will be forced to change their password as soon as they log in.

Discussion

Identity in native GCP environments is managed between Cloud IAM and Google Workspaces. By creating users and groups in Google Workspaces, you have centralized authentication which can be used for not only GCP, but also for managing other Google services like Drive and Docs.

As you scale your organization to hundreds, or maybe even thousands, of users, writing wrapper code to simplify the assignments of users to teams will be required. As the relationship between teams and users is many to many, this can lead to an explosion in the amount of data captured in the variables, which becomes unmaintainable. This is also why in the solution, permissions were applied using groups, not individual users, as that simplifies access management at scale.

In this solution, you applied the permissions directly at the project level. In practice, you would often apply permissions as high in the hierarchy as possible. Due to the nature of how Google IAM functions, you want to apply minimal permissions and then explicitly allow permissions as low as possible. For example, if you have a folder containing all the projects for a team, then you can apply the same roles/viewer to the folder to allow the team read access but then add roles/editor directly on the Development project to allow for rapid experimentation in a safe environment.

Summarizing the recipe

Let's summarize what you've learned and created through this recipe:

1. User access on GCP is managed between Google Workspaces and Cloud IAM.

2. Google Workspaces gives you a centralized directory to manage users and groups for all Google services.

3. To interact programmatically with Google Workspaces, you need to create a service account and assign it the requisite permissions.

4. Cloud IAM is responsible for assigning users permissions, and it is recommended that you do this through groups to allow for simplified management at scale.

2.8 Centralizing Users on AWS

Problem

You have a new team looking to onboard into your AWS organization. You need to be able to give them access that follows the principle of least privilege and will be maintainable in the long term.

Solution

If you haven't already done so, familiarize yourself with Terraform and the different authentication mechanisms in Chapter 11.

Create a *variables.tf* file and copy the following contents:

```
variable "target_account_id" {
  type        = string
  description = "The account to give the users access to"
}

variable "auth_account_id" {
  type        = string
  description = "The account to create the users in"
}
```

```
variable "cross_account_role" {
  type        = string
  description = "The name of the role for the target and auth accounts"
}

variable "users" {
  type        = list(string)
  description = "A list of user email addresses"
}
```

Then fill out the corresponding *terraform.tfvars* file:

```
target_account_id  = ""
auth_account_id    = ""
cross_account_role = ""
users              = [""]
```

Create the following *provider.tf* file and run `terraform init`:

```
provider "aws" {
  alias = "auth_account"
  assume_role {
    role_arn = join("" , [
      "arn:aws:iam::",
      var.auth_account_id,
      ":role/",
      var.cross_account_role
    ])
  }
}

provider "aws" {
  alias = "target_account"
  assume_role {
    role_arn = join("" , [
      "arn:aws:iam::",
      var.target_account_id,
      ":role/",
      var.cross_account_role
    ])
  }
}

terraform {
  required_providers {
    aws = {
      source  = "hashicorp/aws"
      version = "~> 3"
    }
  }
}
```

Create the following *main.tf* file and run `terraform plan`:

```
resource "aws_iam_role" "target_read_only" {
  provider = aws.target_account

  assume_role_policy  = data.aws_iam_policy_document.assume_policy.json
  managed_policy_arns = ["arn:aws:iam::aws:policy/ReadOnlyAccess"]
}

data "aws_iam_policy_document" "assume_policy" {
  statement {
    effect = "Allow"

    principals {
      type        = "AWS"
      identifiers = ["arn:aws:iam::${var.auth_account_id}:root"]
    }

    actions = ["sts:AssumeRole"]
  }
}

resource "aws_iam_user" "user" {
  provider = aws.auth_account
  for_each = toset(var.users)

  name          = each.value
  force_destroy = true
}

resource "aws_iam_group" "group" {
  provider = aws.auth_account
  name     = "read_only"
  path     = "/${var.target_account_id}/"
}

resource "aws_iam_group_membership" "group" {
  provider = aws.auth_account
  name     = "${var.target_account_id}_read_only"

  users = [for user in var.users : user]

  group = aws_iam_group.group.name
}

resource "aws_iam_group_policy" "target_read_only" {
  provider = aws.auth_account

  name  = "${var.target_account_id}_read_only"
  group = aws_iam_group.group.name

  policy = data.aws_iam_policy_document.target_read_only.json
}
```

```
data "aws_iam_policy_document" "target_read_only" {
  statement {
    actions = [
      "sts:AssumeRole"
    ]

    effect = "Allow"

    resources = [
      aws_iam_role.target_read_only.arn
    ]
  }
}
```

Review the resources that are going to be created, and then run `terraform apply` to make the changes.

Discussion

In AWS, you should centralize all IAM users into a single AWS account that exists solely for this purpose. This allows you to simplify management and monitoring of your users at scale, and there is even an AWS Config managed rule for detecting the presence of IAM users in an account. For more on AWS Config managed rules, see Recipe 7.5.

For tooling deployed into your AWS accounts that require privileged access to AWS APIs, there are a few options.

For an external software-as-a-service (SaaS) tool, leverage cross-account roles with an external ID to obtain the required permissions in your account. The following is an example assume role policy.

```
data "aws_iam_policy_document" "assume_policy" {
  statement {
    effect = "Allow"

    principals {
      type        = "AWS"
      identifiers = ["arn:aws:iam::${var.external_account_id}:root"]
    }

    actions = ["sts:AssumeRole"]

    condition {
      test     = "StringEquals"
      variable = "sts:ExternalId"

      values = [
        var.external_id
      ]
    }
```

```
    }
  }
```

If deployed within your AWS environment, users should be able to leverage the roles or profiles attached to their resources, e.g., the attached AWS Lambda execution role or the attached instance profile on the EC2 machine. Unfortunately, there are still older tools that require explicit IAM users to be created, but this should be a last resort as the user credentials are inherently long-lived compared to the routinely rotated credentials used by the other options. This increases the chance of a sustained compromise.

When it comes to assuming roles in AWS, a bidirectional trust must be created, the user must be allowed to call `sts:AssumeRole` on the role, and the assume role policy on the target role must allow the user to assume the role. This gives you options such as allowing one user to assume a read-only role in an account while allowing another to assume the read-only role but additionally a privileged role.

Summarizing the recipe

Let's summarize what was learned and deployed in this recipe:

- AWS users should all exist in a dedicated account for this purpose.
- Assuming roles in other accounts requires bidirectional trust.
  — The `AssumeRolePolicy` on the target should explicitly allow the user.
  — The user should be able to invoke `sts:assumerole` on the target.

2.9 Centralizing Users on Azure

Problem

You have a new team looking to onboard into your Azure tenant. You need to be able to give them access that follows the principle of least privilege and will be maintainable in the long term.

Solution

If you haven't already done so, familiarize yourself with Terraform and the different authentication mechanisms in Chapter 11.

Create a *variables.tf* file and copy the following contents:

```
variable "target_subscription_id" {
  type        = string
  description = "The subscription ID to give the users access to"
}
```

```
variable "users" {
  type        = map(map(any))
  description = "A map of read-only users to create"
}
```

Then fill out the corresponding *terraform.tfvars* file:

```
target_subscription_id = ""

users = {
  "jane.doe@example.com" = {
    display_name = "Jane Doe"
  }
}
```

Create the following *provider.tf* file and run `terraform init`:

```
provider "azuread" {}

provider "azurerm" {
  features {}
}

provider "random" {}

terraform {
  required_providers {
    azuread = {
      source  = "hashicorp/azuread"
      version = "~> 1"
    }
    azurerm = {
      source  = "hashicorp/azurerm"
      version = "~> 2"
    }
    random = {
      source  = "hashicorp/random"
      version = "~> 3"
    }
  }
}
```

Create the following *main.tf* file and run `terraform plan`:

```
resource "random_password" "password" {
  for_each = var.users
  length   = 16
  special  = true
}

resource "azuread_user" "this" {
  for_each              = var.users
  force_password_change = true
  display_name          = each.value.display_name
```

```
    password             = random_password.password[each.key].result
    user_principal_name  = each.key
  }

  resource "azuread_group" "target_read_only" {
    display_name = "${data.azurerm_subscription.target.display_name}ReadOnly"
    members = [
      for user in azuread_user.this : user.object_id
    ]
  }

  data "azurerm_subscription" "target" {
    subscription_id = var.target_subscription_id
  }

  resource "azurerm_role_assignment" "target_read_only" {
    scope                = data.azurerm_subscription.target.id
    role_definition_name = "Reader"
    principal_id         = azuread_group.target_read_only.object_id
  }

  output "passwords" {
    sensitive = true
    value     = [
      for user in azuread_user.this : {(user.user_principal_name) = user.password}
    ]
  }
}
```

Review the resources that are going to be created, and then run `terraform apply` to make the changes.

To retrieve a user's initial password, run `terraform output passwords` to print out a list of all initial passwords. When the user logs in, they will be forced to change their password and configure two-factor authentication, so the only time the password is known by more than just the user is from user creation and first sign-in.

Discussion

Managing users on Azure is centered around Azure Active Directory (Azure AD). When managing the loud infrastructure for an organization, you should ideally have one production Azure AD tenancy and one testing Azure AD tenancy. As Azure AD becomes the focal point for identity, it also becomes your source for Single Sign On (SSO), device management, and licensing, amongst others.

Permissions should only be assigned directly to users in truly exceptional cases, but standard permissions should be defined by a user's group memberships. This is the approach taken in the solution, as when the number of users grows into the hundreds or thousands, managing permissions on an individual basis becomes nearly impossible. Even if the group only had a single member, you retain a more readily understood and extensible identity architecture by creating the group.

 The user principal name for members of your Azure AD tenant must be from a tenant-approved domain. You can easily add new domains through the Azure AD console and by adding some DNS records to verify domain ownership.

Unfortunately, the Azure AD Terraform provider and the Azure AD APIs do not give Azure the ability to automatically generate initial passwords; hence, in this instance you use the Terraform Random Provider to set the initial passwords. As was mentioned in the solution, the initial password will only exist until first sign-in, so it is critical that as a security team you ensure that users log in soon after their accounts are created in Azure AD to mitigate the risk of compromised credentials.

Summarizing the recipe

Let's summarize what was learned and deployed in this recipe:

- Production identity and access management on Azure should be managed through a single centralized Azure AD tenant.
- It is recommended to have a second Azure AD tenant for testing.
- As creating users requires an initial password for the user, you need to be mindful of how that password is created and stored.
  — By using the Terraform Random Provider, you can create unique random passwords that fit basic security requirements.
  — You can use Terraform Outputs to retrieve the initial password.
- Authorization is best handled using Azure AD groups rather than assigning to particular users, as it is more manageable at scale.

CHAPTER 3

Getting Security Visibility at Scale

When looking at security, an often-referenced framework for looking at how teams can operate during incidents is John Boyd's OODA loop, shown in Figure 3-1.

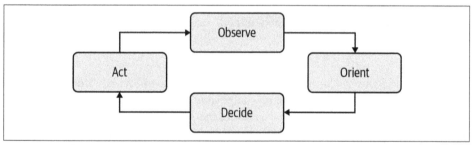

Figure 3-1. The OODA loop

What this model implies is that the quicker you can cycle through this loop, the more you will outmaneuver and outperform your competitors and adversaries. John himself was a decorated US Air Force fighter pilot and Pentagon consultant who was dubbed "Forty-Second Boyd" for his standing bet that he would beat any other pilot from a state of disadvantage in 40 seconds. Applied in a security context, it means that during an incident, you need to able to rapidly cycle through this loop to be able to react and act proactively.

With this model in mind, this chapter focuses on visibility, building the ability for you to observe your estate at scale. Without the right infrastructure in place, you will be stuck fumbling around in the dark or having to invest too much time trying to see what's going on to be able to take control of the situation and act.

In this chapter, you will learn how to accomplish the following:

- Build a lightweight cloud native Security Operations Center
- Centralize your logs into a secure location for analysis and investigations
- Leverage the automated log anomaly detection available from your CSP to detect common threat vectors
- Build an asset registry so you can understand what infrastructure has been deployed across your entire estate

3.1 Building a Cloud Native Security Operations Center on GCP

Problem

You need to create a centralized Security Operations Center (SOC) to allow you to understand your security posture at scale across your estate. You also wish to be notified as soon as high-level threats are identified.

Solution

First, to enable Security Command Center (SCC), browse to Security Command Center Initial Set Up (*https://console.cloud.google.com/security/command-center/welcome*) and complete the wizard. Once that is done, the management of all GCP resources will be enabled for your subscription level; see "Discussion" on page 70 for more details.

Next, you need to build the architecture shown in Figure 3-2, which provides real-time alerting of identified threats.

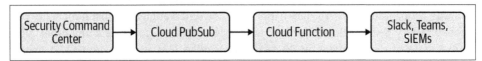

Figure 3-2. Security Command Center notification architecture

Interacting with Security Command Center APIs must be done via a service account.

If you haven't already done so, familiarize yourself with Terraform and the different authentication mechanisms in Chapter 11.

Create and enter an *auth* folder in your working directory.

Then create a *variables.tf* file and copy the following contents:

```
variable "project_id" {
  type        = string
  description = "The project ID to create the resources"
}

variable "organization_domain" {
  type        = string
  description = "The organization domain of your Google Cloud estate"
}
```

And fill out the corresponding *terraform.tfvars* file:

```
project_id          = ""
organization_domain = ""
```

Create the following *provider.tf* file and run `terraform init`:

```
provider "google" {
  project = var.project_id
}

terraform {
  required_providers {
    google = {
      source  = "hashicorp/google"
      version = "~> 3"
    }
    local = {
      source  = "hashicorp/local"
      version = "~> 2"
    }
  }
}
```

Create the following *main.tf* file and run `terraform plan`:

```
resource "google_project_service" "scc" {
  service = "securitycenter.googleapis.com"
}

data "google_organization" "this" {
  domain = var.organization_domain
}

resource "google_service_account" "scc_admin" {
  account_id   = "scc-admin"
  display_name = "SCC Admin"
}

resource "google_organization_iam_binding" "scc_admin" {
  role   = "roles/securitycenter.notificationConfigEditor"
  org_id = data.google_organization.this.org_id

  members = [
```

```
      "serviceAccount:${google_service_account.scc_admin.email}",
    ]
}

resource "google_service_account_key" "scc_admin" {
  service_account_id = google_service_account.scc_admin.name
  public_key_type    = "TYPE_X509_PEM_FILE"
}

resource "local_file" "scc_admin" {
  content  = base64decode(google_service_account_key.scc_admin.private_key)
  filename = "scc_admin.json"
}
```

Review the resources that are going to be created, and then run `terraform apply` to make the changes.

With the service account created, and the access key stored locally, you can now create the notification mechanism for SCC findings.

Move back to the parent folder.

Install `google-cloud-securitycenter==1.3.0` into your local Python environment.

Create a *variables.tf* file and copy the following contents:

```
variable "project_id" {
  type        = string
  description = "The project to create the resources in"
}

variable "region" {
  type        = string
  description = "The region to create the resources in"
}

variable "organization_domain" {
  type        = string
  description = "The organization domain of your Google Cloud estate"
}

variable "python_path" {
  type        = string
  description = "Path to a python instance with required libraries"
  default     = "python"
}
```

Then fill out the corresponding *terraform.tfvars* file:

```
project_id          = ""
region              = ""
organization_domain = ""
python_path         = ""
```

Create the following *provider.tf* file and run `terraform init`:

```
provider "google" {
  project = var.project_id
  region  = var.region
}

terraform {
  required_providers {
    google = {
      source  = "hashicorp/google"
      version = "~> 3"
    }
    null = {
      source  = "hashicorp/null"
      version = "~> 3"
    }
    archive = {
      source  = "hashicorp/archive"
      version = "~> 2"
    }
  }
}
```

Create the following *main.py*:

```
import base64


def handle(event, _):
    if "data" in event:
        print(base64.b64decode(event["data"]).decode("utf-8"))
```

And the following *create_notification_config.py*:

```
import sys

from google.cloud import securitycenter

client = securitycenter.SecurityCenterClient.from_service_account_json(
    "auth/scc_admin.json"
)


def run(org_id, project_id, topic_id):
    org_name = f"organizations/{org_id}"

    created_notification_config = client.create_notification_config(
        request={
            "parent": org_name,
            "config_id": f"{project_id}-scc",
            "notification_config": {
                "description": "Notification for active findings",
                "pubsub_topic": topic_id,
```

```
                        "streaming_config": {"filter": 'state = "ACTIVE"'},
                },
            }
        )

        print(created_notification_config)


    if __name__ == "__main__":
        run(sys.argv[1], sys.argv[2], sys.argv[3])
```

Create the following *main.tf* file and run `terraform plan`:

```
data "google_organization" "this" {
  domain = var.organization_domain
}

resource "null_resource" "create_notification_config" {
  provisioner "local-exec" {
    command = join(" ", [
      var.python_path,
      "create_notification_config.py",
      data.google_organization.this.org_id,
      var.project_id,
      google_pubsub_topic.scc.id
    ])
  }
}

resource "google_pubsub_topic" "scc_findings" {
  name = "scc-findings"
}

resource "google_pubsub_subscription" "scc_findings" {
  name  = "scc-findings"
  topic = google_pubsub_topic.scc_findings.name
}

resource "google_pubsub_topic_iam_binding" "scc-admin" {
  project = google_pubsub_topic.scc.project
  topic   = google_pubsub_topic.scc.name
  role    = "roles/pubsub.admin"
  members = [
    "serviceAccount:scc-admin@${var.project_id}.iam.gserviceaccount.com",
  ]
}

resource "google_project_service" "cloudfunctions" {
  service = "cloudfunctions.googleapis.com"
}

resource "google_project_service" "cloudbuild" {
  service = "cloudbuild.googleapis.com"
```

```
}

resource "google_storage_bucket" "bucket" {
  name = "${split(".", var.organization_domain)[0]}-scc-notifications"
}

data "archive_file" "code" {
  type        = "zip"
  source_dir  = "${path.module}/src"
  output_path = "${path.module}/main.zip"
}

resource "google_storage_bucket_object" "code" {
  name   = "index.zip"
  bucket = google_storage_bucket.bucket.name
  source = data.archive_file.code.output_path
}

resource "google_cloudfunctions_function" "function" {
  name    = "scc_findings"
  runtime = "python39"

  available_memory_mb   = 128
  source_archive_bucket = google_storage_bucket.bucket.name
  source_archive_object = google_storage_bucket_object.code.name
  entry_point           = "handle"

  event_trigger {
    event_type = "google.pubsub.topic.publish"
    resource   = google_pubsub_topic.scc_findings.name
  }

  depends_on = [
    google_project_service.cloudfunctions,
    google_project_service.cloudbuild
  ]
}
```

Review the resources that are going to be created, and then run `terraform apply` to make the changes.

The deployed Cloud Function will now be automatically triggered whenever there is a new finding in the SCC. This can now be extended to integrate into your wide tool-chain by extending the *main.py* file.

For more details on Cloud Functions, see Recipe 6.4.

Discussion

On GCP, your cloud native SOC is centered around SCC. It summarizes all your findings from a variety of sources, allowing you to understand your security posture and threats at scale. The SCC comes in two editions: Standard and Premium.

Standard Edition, which comes free, includes the following:

- Security Health Analytics, which analyzes resources for common misconfigurations such as open ports, multifactor authentication not being enforced, or logs not being exported.

- Web Security Scanner custom scans, which find common security issues in public-facing applications such as OWASP top 10 vulnerabilities.

- Integration with Google Cloud services such as
  — Cloud Data Loss Prevention, which protects your sensitive data

  — Google Cloud Armor, which protects your applications against external web threats such as distributed denial-of-service (DDoS) attacks

  — Anomaly Detection, which discovers usage anomalies in your projects and Virtual Machines

Premium Edition, which costs a percentage of your Google Cloud bill, includes the following on top of everything in Standard Edition:

- Event Threat Detection; for more information, see Recipe 3.7.

- Container Threat Detection, which identifies issues in your running containers.

- Security Health Analytics, which performs compliance monitoring for the following standards:
  — CIS 1.1

  — CIS 1.0

  — PCI DSS v3.2.1

  — NIST 800-53

  — ISO 27001

- Web Security Scanner managed scans, which continually scan your applications for issues.

The SCC comes preconfigured when you enable it through the console, which is currently the only method. This recipe focused on giving you a framework to turn findings into actionable insights by allowing you to integrate the notifications into whatever tooling you choose. A common problem that undermines the usefulness of these single panes of glass is that since they become falling trees with no one around to hear them fall, it is critical that the findings from tooling such as the SCC become embedded in your processes.

Without real-time alerts that are low noise and high signal, it becomes impossible for your team to react to the active security incidents, or even be aware that breaches occurred.

Summarizing the Recipe

Let's review what you learned and created during this recipe:

- The central hub for understanding your security on Google Cloud is the SCC.
- It comes in two editions, Standard and Premium.
  — Standard Edition is free with every Google Cloud organization.

  — Premium Edition is charged based on your total Cloud Bill.
- Once enrolled through the console, all available GCP services are automatically enrolled.
- You created the requisite infrastructure to allow you to build SCC notifications into your internal processes.
  — As the SCC APIs are service account only, you created a minimally privileged service account for this purpose.

  — You created a Pub/Sub topic, with a target Cloud Function, as a target for Findings.

  — Last, you ran a Python script that links the Pub/Sub topic with your SCC installation.

3.2 Building a Cloud Native Security Operations Center on AWS

Problem

You need to create a centralized Security Operations Center to allow you to understand your security posture at scale across your estate.

Solution

First, you will need to assume a privileged role in your organization root account, i.e., the account that has access to the organizations APIs.

If you haven't already done so, familiarize yourself with Terraform and the different authentication mechanisms in Chapter 11.

Create a *variables.tf* file and copy the following contents:

```
variable "delegated_admin_account" {
  type        = string
  description = "The account ID for the account to be the delegated admin"
}

variable "cross_account_role" {
  type        = string
  description = "The cross account role to assume"
}
```

Then fill out the corresponding *terraform.tfvars* file:

```
delegated_admin_account = ""
cross_account_role      = ""
```

Create the following *provider.tf* file and run `terraform init`:

```
provider "aws" {}

provider "aws" {
  alias = "delegated_admin_account"
  assume_role {
    role_arn = join("", [
      "arn:aws:iam::",
      var.delegated_admin_account,
      ":role/${var.cross_account_role}"
    ]
  }
}

terraform {
  required_providers {
    aws = {
      source  = "hashicorp/aws"
      version = "~> 3"
    }
  }
}
```

 Your `aws_organizations_organization` resource should only exist in one location. The following Terraform shows an example of that resource. You need to add securityhub.amazonaws.com to your `aws_service_access_principals` list and create the other resources outlined in the following file.

Create the following *main.tf* file and run `terraform plan`:

```
resource "aws_organizations_organization" "this" {
  aws_service_access_principals = [
    "cloudtrail.amazonaws.com",
    "guardduty.amazonaws.com",
```

```
      "ram.amazonaws.com",
      "config-multiaccountsetup.amazonaws.com",
      "config.amazonaws.com",
      "member.org.stacksets.cloudformation.amazonaws.com",
      "securityhub.amazonaws.com",
      "sso.amazonaws.com"
  ]
  enabled_policy_types = [
    "SERVICE_CONTROL_POLICY",
    "TAG_POLICY",
  ]
}

resource "aws_securityhub_organization_admin_account" "this" {
  depends_on = [aws_organizations_organization.this]

  admin_account_id = var.delegated_admin_account
}

resource "aws_securityhub_organization_configuration" "this" {
  auto_enable = true
}
```

Review the resources that are going to be created, and then run `terraform apply` to make the changes.

Discussion

On AWS, the service that provides a summarized view of security across your estate is AWS Security Hub. It aggregates data from the following sources:

- Amazon GuardDuty, seen in Recipe 3.8
- AWS Systems Manager, seen in Recipe 8.5
- Amazon Inspector, which provides rules for keeping your EC2 machines secure
- AWS Firewall Manager, which allows for centralized firewall management across your estate
- IAM Access Analyzer, which helps protect against the unintended sharing of resources
- Amazon Macie, which scans your S3 buckets for PII data
- An ever-increasing array of third-party solutions

It also provides the option to provide automated reporting against industry-standard benchmarks such as the CIS AWS Benchmarks and PCI DSS.

By centralizing administration into a dedicated account, you can see your security posture at scale with a glance. This allows you to more quickly and easily triage and prioritize active security issues. This recipe does not automatically handle existing accounts in your organization. The following *create_members.py* Python file resolves this issue:

```python
import sys

import boto3

delegated_admin_account = sys.argv[1]
role_name = sys.argv[2]

organizations = boto3.client("organizations")
credentials = boto3.client("sts").assume_role(
    RoleArn=f"arn:aws:iam::{delegated_admin_account}:role/{role_name}",
    RoleSessionName="SecurityHubDelegatedAdmin",
)["Credentials"]
securityhub = boto3.Session(
    aws_access_key_id=credentials["AccessKeyId"],
    aws_secret_access_key=credentials["SecretAccessKey"],
    aws_session_token=credentials["SessionToken"],
).client("securityhub")

account_paginator = organizations.get_paginator("list_accounts")
for page in account_paginator.paginate(PaginationConfig={"MaxItems": 50}):
    accounts = page["Accounts"]
    securityhub.create_members(
        AccountDetails=[
            {"AccountId": account["Id"], "Email": account["Email"]}
            for account in accounts
        ],
    )
```

To execute the Python file, run python create_members.py <delega ted_admin_account_id> <cross_account_role>, filling in the two parameters.

Summarizing the Recipe

Let's summarize what was learned and deployed in this recipe:

- Security Hub is your centralized, single pane of glass for understanding your security on AWS.
- You should delegate Security Hub administration to a dedicated security account, as specified in Recipe 2.2.
- Security Hub should be enabled at the organization level to automatically enroll new accounts.
- You used Terraform to elect your delegated administrator account.
- Python can be used to enable Security Hub across all existing accounts in an organization.

3.3 Building a Cloud Native Security Operations Center on Azure

Problem

You need to create a centralized Security Operations Center to allow you to understand your security posture at scale across your estate. You want to ensure that your SOC reports on common threats in your estate.

Solution

If you haven't already done so, familiarize yourself with Terraform and the different authentication mechanisms in Chapter 11.

Create a *variables.tf* file and copy the following contents:

```
variable "root_management_group_uuid" {
  type        = string
  description = "The UUID of your Root Management Group"
}

variable "location" {
  type        = string
  description = "The location to deploy your resource into"
}
```

Then fill out the corresponding *terraform.tfvars* file:

```
root_management_group_uuid = ""
location                   = ""
```

Create the following *provider.tf* file and run `terraform init`:

```
terraform {
  required_providers {
    azurerm = {
      source  = "hashicorp/azurerm"
      version = "~> 2"
    }
  }
}

provider "azurerm" {
  features {}
}
```

Create the following *main.tf* file and run `terraform plan`:

```
resource "azurerm_resource_group" "sentinel" {
  name     = "sentinel"
  location = "Australia East"
```

```
}

resource "azurerm_log_analytics_workspace" "sentinel" {
  name                = "sentinel"
  location            = azurerm_resource_group.sentinel.location
  resource_group_name = azurerm_resource_group.sentinel.name
  sku                 = "PerGB2018"
}

resource "azurerm_log_analytics_solution" "sentinel" {
  solution_name         = "SecurityInsights"
  location              = azurerm_resource_group.sentinel.location
  resource_group_name   = azurerm_resource_group.sentinel.name
  workspace_resource_id = azurerm_log_analytics_workspace.sentinel.id
  workspace_name        = azurerm_log_analytics_workspace.sentinel.name
  plan {
    publisher = "Microsoft"
    product   = "OMSGallery/SecurityInsights"
  }
}

resource "azurerm_sentinel_data_connector_azure_security_center" "this" {
  name                      = "security_center"
  log_analytics_workspace_id = azurerm_log_analytics_workspace.sentinel.id
}

resource "azurerm_sentinel_data_connector_threat_intelligence" "this" {
  name                      = "threat_intelligence"
  log_analytics_workspace_id = azurerm_log_analytics_workspace.sentinel.id
}
```

Review the resources that are going to be created, and then run `terraform apply` to make the changes.

Discussion

On Azure, your cloud native SOC is Azure Sentinel. This service brings together data from across your Azure estate, your on-premise infrastructure, and other clouds into a fully managed, cloud native Security Incident and Event Management (SIEM) solution.

Some integrations, such as Azure Security Center and Microsoft Threat Intelligence, are natively supported by Terraform. For other integrations, you may need to reverse engineer the specifics of the resources to be configured. For example, the following Terraform enables the Key Vault operations connector:

```
data "azurerm_management_group" "root" {
  name = var.root_management_group_uuid
}

resource "azurerm_policy_assignment" "key_vault_sentinel" {
```

```
name                    = "key_vault_sentinel"
location                = azurerm_resource_group.sentinel.location
scope                   = data.azurerm_management_group.root.id
policy_definition_id = join("", [
  "/providers/Microsoft.Authorization/policyDefinitions/",
  "951af2fa-529b-416e-ab6e-066fd85ac459"
])

identity {
  type = "SystemAssigned"
}

parameters = <<PARAMETERS
{
  "logAnalytics": {
    "value": "${azurerm_log_analytics_workspace.sentinel.name}"
  }
}
PARAMETERS

}

data "azurerm_sentinel_alert_rule_template" "sensitive_key_vault" {
  log_analytics_workspace_id = azurerm_log_analytics_workspace.sentinel.id
  display_name               = "Sensitive Azure Key Vault operations"
}

locals {
  key_vault = data.azurerm_sentinel_alert_rule_template.sensitive_key_vault
}

resource "azurerm_sentinel_alert_rule_scheduled" "sensitive_key_vault" {
  name                       = "sensitive_key_vault"
  log_analytics_workspace_id = azurerm_log_analytics_workspace.sentinel.id
  display_name               = local.key_vault.display_name
  severity                   = local.key_vault.scheduled_template[0].severity
  query                      = local.key_vault.scheduled_template[0].query
}
```

To configure Azure Sentinel to detect incidents, you need to use analytics rules. There are currently five built-in types of rules:

Microsoft Security

These rules automatically create Sentinel alerts when other Microsoft products alert. By default, Sentinel records that the alerts happened but does not generate an alert itself.

Fusion

These rules are machine learning–based and correlate low-fidelity events across many systems to generate high-fidelity events and alerts.

Machine Learning Behavioral Analytics

These rules are built on top of proprietary Microsoft machine learning algorithms, operating as black boxes.

Anomaly

These rules use configurable machine learning models to generate alerts. You can configure them yourself, running in parallel to ensure they provide alerts that are signal, not noise.

Scheduled

These rules are written by Microsoft security experts, and the query within can be customized. The alerts from scheduled rules are key data points that enable several of the Fusion rules to operate.

By understanding the types of rules that exist and how they are modified and extended, you can ensure Azure Sentinel reports with a high signal-to-noise ratio. By only being alerted on findings that are both relevant and actionable, you prevent security teams from suffering alert fatigue, where they begin to ignore incoming alerts as they are likely to be redundant.

Summarizing the Recipe

Let's review what you learned and created through this recipe:

- Azure Sentinel is a managed service that provides SOC functionality in the cloud.
- For Azure Sentinel to function optimally, you need to configure and enable the data connectors.
- You configured the Azure Security Center and Microsoft Threat Intelligence data connectors.
- You ensured that a high signal-to-noise ratio is maintained for alerts so the team will actively respond.

3.4 Centralizing Logs on GCP

Problem

You need to centralize all audit logs for the organization into a central location so you can perform retrospective analysis and allow for alerting of potential security incidents in real-time.

Solution

If you haven't already done so, familiarize yourself with Terraform and the different authentication mechanisms in Chapter 11.

The ideal project for this recipe is the Logging project under the *Common* folder, as explained in Recipe 2.1.

Create a *variables.tf* file and copy the following contents:

```
variable "project" {
  type        = string
  description = "The ID of the project to deploy the resources into"
}

variable "organization_domain" {
  type        = string
  description = "The domain of your Google Organization"
}
```

Then fill out the corresponding *terraform.tfvars* file:

```
project             = ""
organization_domain = ""
```

Create the following *provider.tf* file and run `terraform init`:

```
provider "google" {
  project = var.project
}

terraform {
  required_providers {
    google = {
      source  = "hashicorp/google"
      version = "~> 3"
    }
  }
}
```

Create the following *main.tf* file and run `terraform plan`:

```
data "google_organization" "this" {
  domain = var.organization_domain
}

resource "google_bigquery_dataset" "organization_audit_logs" {
  dataset_id = "organization_audit_logs"
}

resource "google_logging_organization_sink" "organization_sink" {
  name             = "organization_audit"
  org_id           = data.google_organization.this.org_id
  include_children = true
  filter           = "logName:cloudaudit.googleapis.com"
```

```
    destination = join("",[
      "bigquery.googleapis.com/",
      google_bigquery_dataset.organization_audit_logs.id
    ])
}

resource "google_bigquery_dataset_access" "access" {
    dataset_id   = google_bigquery_dataset.organization_audit_logs.dataset_id
    role         = "OWNER"
    user_by_email = split(
      ":",
      google_logging_organization_sink.organization_sink.writer_identity
    )[1]
}
```

Review the resources that are going to be created, and then run `terraform apply` to make the changes.

Discussion

This recipe elects to store the logs directly in BigQuery instead of Cloud Storage as the data storage costs for hot data are identical. This has the benefit of the logs being immediately queryable in BigQuery. For long term archival storage, you will want to configure an organizational sink that pushes directly into a coldline archival cloud storage bucket.

The sink you created has an active filter, meaning only cloud audit logs are captured. Cloud audit logs capture *who*, is doing *what*, *where*, and *when* against any GCP API within your estate. This data is critical to being able to proactively and retrospectively act when a breach occurs, as it is your source of truth for what happened in and to your estate.

It is also possible to capture application logs on a per-project basis. Although this can be achieved through an organizational sink, as a cost control measure, you often need to enable this explicitly on a per project basis.

The following Terraform deploys a project sink into the list of projects identified in the local `projects` variable. Currently, it selects all active projects within the organization; however, you can modify it to filter for selected projects.

```
data "google_projects" "active" {
    filter = "lifecycleState:ACTIVE"
}

locals {
    projects = toset([
      for project in data.google_projects.active.projects : project.project_id
    ])
}
```

```
resource "google_bigquery_dataset" "oal" {
  dataset_id = "organization_application_logs"
}

resource "google_logging_project_sink" "project_sink" {
  for_each              = local.projects
  name                  = "${each.value}_application_logs"
  project               = each.value
  unique_writer_identity = true
  exclusions {
    name   = "no_audit_logs"
    filter = "logName:cloudaudit.googleapis.com"
  }

  destination = join("",[
    "bigquery.googleapis.com/",
    google_bigquery_dataset.oal.id
  ])
}

resource "google_bigquery_dataset_access" "project_access" {
  for_each      = local.projects
  dataset_id    = google_bigquery_dataset.oal.dataset_id
  role          = "OWNER"
  user_by_email = split(
    ":",
    google_logging_project_sink.project_sink[each.value].writer_identity
  )[1]
}
```

There is also a third sink option, a *folder sink*. This works as you would expect from the name, allowing you to collect logs from all projects within a folder. Depending on how your organization is structured, this can be a useful tool.

Summarizing the Recipe

Let's summarize what you learned and created through this recipe:

- Logs on GCP come in two dominant flavors: audit logs and application logs.
- Audit logs are a record of every API call done against the Google Cloud control plane.
- Application logs are created through workloads running in your organization.
- There are two kinds of log sinks:
    - *Organization sinks*, as the name implies, pull logs indiscriminately from your entire organization. You configured an organization sink to forward only audit logs to a purpose-built BigQuery dataset.

— *Project sinks* forward logs from a project to another destination. You config‐
ured a project sink for every project in your organization to forward logs to a
centralized BigQuery dataset.

- By storing logs in BigQuery, you can leverage its tremendous querying power to
quickly crunch your logs in case of a security incident.

3.5 Centralizing Logs on AWS

Problem

You need to centralize all audit logs for the organization into a central location so you
can perform retrospective analysis and allow for alerting of potential security inci‐
dents in real-time.

Solution

This recipe needs to be run in the organization root account.

If you haven't already done so, familiarize yourself with Terraform and the different
authentication mechanisms in Chapter 11.

Create a *variables.tf* file and copy the following contents:

```
variable "logging_account_id" {
  type        = string
  description = "The account ID to deploy resources into"
}

variable "cross_account_role" {
  type        = string
  description = "The name of the role that is assumable in the logging account"
}

variable "bucket_name" {
  type        = string
  description = "The name of the centralized storage bucket"
}
```

Then fill out the corresponding *terraform.tfvars* file:

```
logging_account_id = ""
cross_account_role = ""
bucket_name        = ""
```

Create the following *provider.tf* file and run `terraform init`:

```
provider "aws" {}

provider "aws" {
  alias = "logging"
```

```
      assume_role {
        role_arn = join("", [
          "arn:aws:iam::",
          var.logging_account_id,
          ":role/",
          var.cross_account_role
        ])
      }
    }

    terraform {
      required_providers {
        aws = {
          source  = "hashicorp/aws"
          version = "~> 3"
        }
      }
    }
  }
```

Create the following *main.tf* file and run `terraform plan`:

```
data "aws_organizations_organization" "current" {}

resource "aws_cloudtrail" "organizational_trail" {
  name                          = "organizational_trail"
  s3_bucket_name                = aws_s3_bucket.centralized_audit_logs.id
  include_global_service_events = true
  is_multi_region_trail         = true
  is_organization_trail         = true
  enable_log_file_validation    = true

  depends_on = [
    aws_s3_bucket_policy.cloudtrail_access,
  ]
}

resource "aws_s3_bucket" "centralized_audit_logs" {
  provider = aws.logging
  bucket   = var.bucket_name
}

resource "aws_s3_bucket_policy" "cloudtrail_access" {
  provider = aws.logging
  bucket = aws_s3_bucket.centralized_audit_logs.id
  policy = <<POLICY
{
    "Version": "2012-10-17",
    "Statement": [
        {
            "Sid": "AWSCloudTrailAclCheck",
            "Effect": "Allow",
            "Principal": {
                "Service": "cloudtrail.amazonaws.com"
```

```
            },
            "Action": "s3:GetBucketAcl",
            "Resource": "${aws_s3_bucket.centralized_audit_logs.arn}"
        },
        {
            "Sid": "AWSCloudTrailWrite",
            "Effect": "Allow",
            "Principal": {
              "Service": "cloudtrail.amazonaws.com"
            },
            "Action": "s3:PutObject",
            "Resource": join("/", [
              aws_s3_bucket.centralized_audit_logs.arn,
              "AWSLogs",
              var.logging_account_id,
              "*"
            ])
            "Condition": {
                "StringEquals": {
                    "s3:x-amz-acl": "bucket-owner-full-control"
                }
            }
        },
        {
            "Sid": "AWSCloudTrailWriteOrgWrite",
            "Effect": "Allow",
            "Principal": {
                "Service": [
                    "cloudtrail.amazonaws.com"
                ]
            },
            "Action": "s3:PutObject",
            "Resource": join("/", [
              aws_s3_bucket.centralized_audit_logs.arn,
              "AWSLogs",
              data.aws_organizations_organization.current.id,
              "*"
            ])
            "Condition": {
                "StringEquals": {
                    "s3:x-amz-acl": "bucket-owner-full-control"
                }
            }
        }
    ]
}
POLICY
}
```

Review the resources that are going to be created, and then run `terraform apply` to make the changes.

Discussion

Capturing audit logs from across the entire organization is critical to maintaining a solid security posture in AWS. They contain critical data for both proactively and retrospectively responding to breaches as they provide a full history of what has happened across your estate.

By configuring an organizational trail, you don't allow teams to disable that trail in their accounts. This prevents the loss of audit logs and allows the teams to create and manage their own distinct trails.

 If operating with accounts that already have CloudTrail enabled, it is recommended to leave the account trail enabled for up to a day once the organizational-level trail is enabled to ensure that events are not lost. Once that day has passed, ensure that account-level trails are disabled, as they can attract significant cost at high volumes.

Once the recipe is deployed, it can be extended in a number of ways:

- You can write the logs directly to CloudWatch to be able to leverage its analytical capabilities.
- You can trigger notifications via Simple Notification Service (SNS) upon log file delivery to alert users and other systems.
- You can attach Lambda functions to S3 to perform bespoke actions.
- You can set up S3 bucket Lifecycle policies to automatically archive older logs to save on storage costs.

Capturing application logs

The core service used to capture application logs is AWS CloudWatch. Unfortunately, to date, there is no method of turning on log centralization at an organization level; instead the solution shown in Figure 3-3 has to be deployed.

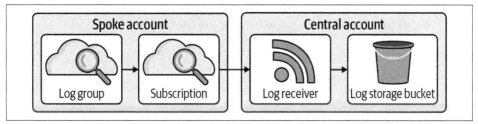

Figure 3-3. Centralized CloudWatch logs architecture

The solution can be extended to perform automated analysis on the logs with Lambda functions or fire logs directly into Elasticsearch or Splunk.

The following Terraform deploys the centralized components on the solution:

```
data "aws_caller_identity" "c" {}

data "aws_organizations_organization" "current" {}

resource "aws_s3_bucket" "centralized_application_logs" {
  force_destroy = true
}

resource "aws_iam_role" "kinesis_firehose_role" {
  assume_role_policy = <<POLICY
{
  "Statement":
    {
      "Effect": "Allow",
      "Principal":
        {
          "Service": "firehose.amazonaws.com"
        },
      "Action": "sts:AssumeRole",
      "Condition":
        {
          "StringEquals": {
            "sts:ExternalId": ${data.aws_caller_identity.c.account_id}
          }
        }
    }
}
POLICY
}

resource "aws_kinesis_firehose_delivery_stream" "log_delivery_stream" {
  name = "log_delivery_stream"
  destination = "s3"

  s3_configuration {
    role_arn   = aws_iam_role.kinesis_firehose_role.arn
    bucket_arn = aws_s3_bucket.centralized_application_logs.arn
  }
}

resource "aws_iam_role" "cloudwatch_logs_role" {
  assume_role_policy = <<POLICY
{
  "Statement": {
    "Effect": "Allow",
    "Principal": { "Service": "logs.amazonaws.com" },
    "Action": "sts:AssumeRole"
```

```
    }
}
POLICY

  inline_policy {
    policy = <<POLICY
{
    "Statement":[
      {
        "Effect":"Allow",
        "Action":["firehose:*"],
        "Resource":[
          "arn:aws:firehose:region:${data.aws_caller_identity.c.account_id}:*"
        ]
      }
    ]
}
POLICY
  }
}

resource "aws_cloudwatch_log_destination" "kinesis_firehose" {
  name       = "firehose_destination"
  role_arn   = aws_iam_role.cloudwatch_logs_role.arn
  target_arn = aws_kinesis_firehose_delivery_stream.log_delivery_stream.arn
}

resource "aws_cloudwatch_log_destination_policy" "policy" {
  for_each = toset(data.aws_organizations_organization.current.accounts[*].id)
  destination_name = aws_cloudwatch_log_destination.kinesis_firehose.name
  access_policy    = <<POLICY
{
  "Version" : "2012-10-17",
  "Statement" : [
    {
      "Sid" : "",
      "Effect" : "Allow",
      "Principal" : {
        "AWS" : "${each.value}"
      },
      "Action" : "logs:PutSubscriptionFilter",
      "Resource" : "${aws_cloudwatch_log_destination.kinesis_firehose.arn}"
    }
  ]
}
POLICY
}
```

Summarizing the Recipe

Let's summarize what you learned and created through this recipe:

- Logs on AWS come in two dominant flavors: audit logs and application logs.
- Audit logs record all actions done against the AWS Control Plane.
  — They are managed via CloudTrail.
- Application logs are created through workloads running in your organization.
  — They are managed via CloudWatch.
- You configured CloudTrail at an organization level to automatically centralize logs into a selected account.
- You then configured a solution using Amazon Kinesis Data Firehose to centralize all your application logs.

3.6 Centralizing Logs on Azure

Problem

You need to centralize all activity logs for the tenant into a central location so you can perform retrospective analysis and allow for alerting of potential security incidents in real time.

Solution

If you haven't already done so, familiarize yourself with Terraform and the different authentication mechanisms in Chapter 11.

Create a *variables.tf* file and copy the following contents:

```
variable "location" {
  type        = string
  description = "The location to create the resources in"
}

variable "storage_account_name" {
  type        = string
  description = "The name of the storage account"
}
```

Then fill out the corresponding *terraform.tfvars* file:

```
location             = ""
storage_account_name = ""
```

Create the following *provider.tf* file and run `terraform init`:

```
terraform {
  required_providers {
    azurerm = {
      source  = "hashicorp/azurerm"
      version = "~> 2"
    }
  }
}

provider "azurerm" {
  features {}
}
```

Create the following *main.tf* file and run `terraform plan`:

```
data "azurerm_subscriptions" "available" {}

locals {
  log_categories = toset([
    "Administrative",
    "Security",
    "ServiceHealth",
    "Alert",
    "Recommendation",
    "Policy",
    "Autoscale",
    "ResourceHealth"
  ])
}

resource "azurerm_resource_group" "activity-log-archive" {
  name     = "activity-log-archive"
  location = var.location
}

resource "azurerm_storage_account" "activity-logs" {
  name                     = var.storage_account_name
  resource_group_name      = azurerm_resource_group.activity-log-archive.name
  location                 = azurerm_resource_group.activity-log-archive.location
  account_tier             = "Standard"
  account_replication_type = "GRS"
}

resource "azurerm_storage_container" "activity-logs" {
  name                  = "activity-logs"
  storage_account_name  = azurerm_storage_account.activity-logs.name
  container_access_type = "private"
}

resource "azurerm_log_analytics_workspace" "activity-logs" {
  name                = "activity-logs"
  location            = azurerm_resource_group.activity-log-archive.location
  resource_group_name = azurerm_resource_group.activity-log-archive.name
```

```
  sku                       = "PerGB2018"
  retention_in_days         = 30
}

resource "azurerm_monitor_diagnostic_setting" "activity-to-storage" {
  for_each                  = {
    for subscription in data.azurerm_subscriptions.available.subscriptions :
    subscription.subscription_id => subscription
  }
  name                      = "activity-${each.value.subscription_id}"
  target_resource_id        = each.value.id
  log_analytics_workspace_id = azurerm_log_analytics_workspace.activity-logs.id
  storage_account_id        = azurerm_storage_account.activity-logs.id

  dynamic "log" {
    for_each = local.log_categories
    content {
      category = log.value
    }
  }
}
```

Review the resources that are going to be created, and then run `terraform apply` to make the changes.

Discussion

On Azure, the central pieces of the puzzle when it comes to logging are *Log Analytics workspaces* and Diagnostic Settings. Log Analytics workspaces allow you to dynamically query logs streamed from many locations, allowing you to build out specific workspaces for teams and use cases. Diagnostic Settings are how you define log destinations such as Log Analytics workspaces, storage accounts, and event hubs.

The two key log types in Azure are activity logs and resource logs. *Activity logs* record all Azure control plane interactions, including API calls, resource health notifications, and policy enforcements. *Resource logs* are generated through the running of a service, such as application logs, system logs, and container runtime logs.

Activity logs are critical to understanding your security posture at scale. Being able to see who did what where against the Azure APIs is fundamental in both proactive and reactive response to security incidents. By default, in an Azure tenant, activity logs are collected across all management groups and subscriptions; what you did in the solution is bring them to a central location that allows you to turn them into actionable insights.

Currently, for Subscription Activity logs, eight types of logs can be captured:

- Administrative
- Security

- ServiceHealth
- Alert
- Recommendation
- Policy
- Autoscale
- ResourceHealth

As these continue to get added to over time, you will need to extend the log_cate gories local variable to include them.

 In the next section, you will see an example of using Terraform to dynamically discover the different log types for a particular resource. Unfortunately, that lookup does not support subscriptions at the current time.

Resource logs

For application logs in Azure, you again want to make use of Log Analytics workspaces; however, you will need to deploy infrastructure into each subscription. For examples of how to do this, see Recipes 6.3 and 6.12.

The following Terraform does three things:

- Creates an Azure Web App from a demo Docker container in the delivery team subscription
- Creates a Log Analytics workspace in a central subscription
- Sets up the Diagnostic Settings so that logs are automatically streamed from the delivery team subscription to the central Log Analytics workspace

Create a *variables.tf* file and copy the following contents:

```
variable "location" {
  type        = string
  description = "The location to create the resources in"
}

variable "delivery_subscription_id" {
  type        = string
  description = "The delivery team subscription ID"
}

variable "central_subscription_id" {
  type        = string
  description = "The centralized team subscription ID"
}
```

Then fill out the corresponding *terraform.tfvars* file:

```
location                  = ""
delivery_subscription_id = ""
central_subscription_id  = ""
```

Create the following *provider.tf* file and run `terraform init`:

```
terraform {
  required_providers {
    azurerm = {
      source  = "hashicorp/azurerm"
      version = "~> 2"
    }
  }
}

provider "azurerm" {
  alias = "delivery"
  features {}
  subscription_id = var.delivery_subscription_id
}

provider "azurerm" {
  alias = "central"
  features {}
  subscription_id = var.central_subscription_id
}
```

Create the following *main.tf* file and run `terraform plan`:

```
resource "azurerm_resource_group" "cal" {
  provider = azurerm.central
  name     = "centralized-application-logs"
  location = var.location
}

resource "azurerm_log_analytics_workspace" "application-logs" {
  provider            = azurerm.central
  name                = "application-logs"
  location            = azurerm_resource_group.cal.location
  resource_group_name = azurerm_resource_group.cal.name
  sku                 = "PerGB2018"
  retention_in_days   = 30
}

resource "azurerm_resource_group" "delivery" {
  provider = azurerm.delivery
  name     = "delivery-rg"
  location = var.location
}

resource "azurerm_app_service_plan" "delivery" {
  provider            = azurerm.delivery
```

```
  name                 = "delivery-service-plan"
  location             = azurerm_resource_group.delivery.location
  resource_group_name = azurerm_resource_group.delivery.name
  kind                 = "Linux"
  reserved             = true

  sku {
    tier = "Standard"
    size = "S1"
  }
}

resource "azurerm_app_service" "delivery" {
  provider = azurerm.delivery
  name     = "delivery-${var.delivery_subscription_id}"

  site_config {
    linux_fx_version = "DOCKER|appsvcsample/static-site:latest"
    always_on        = true
  }

  location             = azurerm_resource_group.delivery.location
  resource_group_name = azurerm_resource_group.delivery.name
  app_service_plan_id = azurerm_app_service_plan.delivery.id
}

data "azurerm_monitor_diagnostic_categories" "delivery_app_service" {
  provider    = azurerm.delivery
  resource_id = azurerm_app_service.delivery.id
}

resource "azurerm_monitor_diagnostic_setting" "delivery_central_log_forwarding" {
  provider                   = azurerm.delivery
  name                       = "central_log_forwarding"
  target_resource_id         = azurerm_app_service.delivery.id
  log_analytics_workspace_id = azurerm_log_analytics_workspace.application-logs.id

  dynamic "log" {
    for_each = data.azurerm_monitor_diagnostic_categories.delivery_app_service.logs
    content {
      category = log.value
      enabled  = true

      retention_policy {
        days    = 0
        enabled = false
      }
    }
  }

  metric {
    category = "AllMetrics"
```

```
      enabled  = false

      retention_policy {
        days     = 0
        enabled = false
      }
    }
  }
}
```

Review the resources that are going to be created, and then run `terraform apply` to make the changes.

 Unlike with subscriptions, for other resources you can use `azurerm_monitor_diagnostic_categories` data provider to allow for the dynamic gathering of all log categories to forward, rather than having to retrospectively update the Terraform over time.

Summarizing the Recipe

Let's summarize what you learned and created through this recipe:

- Logs on Azure come in two main varieties: audit logs and resource logs.
- Diagnostic Settings allow for the forwarding of logs to target locations.
- You set up a Log Analytics workspace and Azure Storage Account in a dedicated subscription to simplify querying and storage.
- Then you set up a Diagnostic Setting to automatically route all audit logs.
- Every resource in Azure has its own log categories.
- You then created a simple container app service that automatically routed logs to a centralized Log Analytics workspace.

3.7 Log Anomaly Alerting on GCP

Problem

You want to ensure that all the relevant logs are collected and automatically processed by Google tooling to alert if anomalous or unusual activity is detected.

Solution

If you haven't already done so, familiarize yourself with Terraform and the different authentication mechanisms in Chapter 11.

Create a *variables.tf* file and copy the following contents:

```
variable "project" {
  type        = string
  description = "The ID of the project to deploy the infrastructure"
}

variable "region" {
  type        = string
  description = "The region to deploy the infrastructure in"
}

variable "organization_domain" {
  type        = string
  description = "The domain of your GCP organization"
}
```

Then fill out the corresponding *terraform.tfvars* file:

```
project_id          = ""
region              = ""
organization_domain = ""
```

Create the following *provider.tf* file and run `terraform init`:

```
provider "google" {
  project = var.project_id
  region  = var.region
}

terraform {
  required_providers {
    google = {
      source  = "hashicorp/google"
      version = "~> 3"
    }
  }
}
```

Create the following *main.tf* file and run `terraform plan`:

```
resource "google_compute_network" "this" {
  name = "flow-log-example"
}

resource "google_compute_subnetwork" "subnet" {
  name          = "flow-log-subnet"
  ip_cidr_range = "10.0.0.0/24"
  network       = google_compute_network.this.id

  log_config {
    aggregation_interval = "INTERVAL_5_SEC"
    flow_sampling        = 1
    metadata             = "INCLUDE_ALL_METADATA"
  }
}
```

```
data "google_organization" "this" {
  domain = var.organization_domain
}

resource "google_organization_iam_audit_config" "organization" {
  org_id  = data.google_organization.this.org_id
  service = "allServices"
  audit_log_config {
    log_type = "ADMIN_READ"
  }
  audit_log_config {
    log_type = "DATA_READ"
  }
  audit_log_config {
    log_type = "DATA_WRITE"
  }
}

resource "google_dns_policy" "logging" {
  name = "logging"

  enable_logging = true

  networks {
    network_url = google_compute_network.this.id
  }
}

resource "google_compute_firewall" "rule" {
  name    = "log-firewall"
  network = google_compute_network.this.name

  deny {
    protocol = "icmp"
  }

  log_config {
    metadata = "INCLUDE_ALL_METADATA"
  }
}

resource "google_compute_router" "router" {
  name    = "router"
  network = google_compute_network.this.id
}

resource "google_compute_router_nat" "nat" {
  name                               = "logging-nat"
  router                             = google_compute_router.router.name
  nat_ip_allocate_option             = "AUTO_ONLY"
  source_subnetwork_ip_ranges_to_nat = "ALL_SUBNETWORKS_ALL_IP_RANGES"
```

```
    log_config {
      enable = true
      filter = "ALL"
    }
  }
```

Review the resources that are going to be created, and then run `terraform apply` to make the changes.

Discussion

As the automated collecting and processing of logs is done by Event Threat Detection, this recipe focused on how to enable logging on key resource types. By combining this recipe with Recipe 6.1, you ensure that the logs are enabled on all infrastructure deployed by teams. The following log types were enabled in the recipe:

- Virtual Private Cloud (VPC) flow logs
- Cloud audit logs
  — Admin Write and Read Activity logs

  — Data Write and Read Access logs
- Cloud DNS logs
- Firewall rules logs
- Cloud NAT logs

Event Threat Detection comes bundled and fully enabled with Security Command Center Premium. When it detects a potential threat, Event Threat Detection raises a finding in Security Command Center and a Cloud Logging Project. The only log types it analyzes not covered by the solution are host-based secure shell (SSH) logs and syslog, both of which need to be configured on hosts and are outside the scope of this recipe.

VPC flow log considerations

VPC flow logs sample and record the network flows on the VPCs in your organization. To understand more about how VPCs are best architected on GCP, see Recipe 5.1.

In the preceding solution, the sampling rate for logs was set at 100% and at the smallest interval. This means that you will not drop any logs; however, it comes with a cost trade-off, in that this is the most expensive option. Depending on the scale of your network traffic, you will need to evaluate what cost benefit ratio makes the most sense for your use case.

Cloud audit data logs

Admin Write Activity logs are automatically captured on GCP and cannot be disabled, so there are three kinds of audit logs you need to enable:

- DATA_WRITE
- DATA_READ
- ADMIN_READ

Similarly to VPC flow logs, you need to consider the cost implications of enabling every type of audit log, as enabling all of these will incur significant costs to process and store.

Summarizing the Recipe

So let's review what you learned and created as part of this recipe:

- Event Threat Detection automatically registers findings based on anomalous log activity.
- It is included as part of Security Command Center Premium Edition.
- It ingests and parses logs from six main sources:
  — SSH logs/syslog

  — VPC flow logs

  — Cloud audit logs

  — Cloud DNS logs

  — Firewall rules logs

  — Cloud NAT logs
- Apart from Cloud Audit Admin Write logs, none of these logs are enabled by default.
- You saw how to enable all the types of logs apart from SSH/syslog, which are out of scope.
- You learned that there is a trade-off to be made between cost and the amount and types of logs to capture.

3.8 Log Anomaly Alerting on AWS

Problem

You want to ensure that all the relevant logs are collected and automatically processed by AWS tooling to alert if anomalous or unusual activity is detected.

Solution

If you haven't already done so, familiarize yourself with Terraform and the different authentication mechanisms in Chapter 11.

Create a *variables.tf* file and copy the following contents:

```
variable "delegated_admin_account" {
  type        = string
  description = "The target account ID"
}

variable "cross_account_role" {
  type        = string
  description = "The name of the role to assume"
}
```

Then fill out the corresponding *terraform.tfvars* file:

```
delegated_admin_account = ""
cross_account_role      = ""
```

Create the following *provider.tf* file and run `terraform init`:

```
provider "aws" {}

provider "aws" {
  alias = "delegated_admin_account"
  assume_role {
    role_arn = join("", [
      "arn:aws:iam::",
      var.delegated_admin_account,
      ":role/",
      var.cross_account_role
    ])
  }
}

terraform {
  required_providers {
    aws = {
      source  = "hashicorp/aws"
      version = "~> 3"
    }
  }
}
```

> Your `aws_organizations_organization` resource should only exist in one location. The following Terraform shows an example of that resource. You need to add `guardduty.amazonaws.com` to your `aws_service_access_principals` list and create the other resources outlined in the following file.

Create the following *main.tf* file and run `terraform plan`:

```
resource "aws_organizations_organization" "this" {
  aws_service_access_principals = [
    "cloudtrail.amazonaws.com",
    "guardduty.amazonaws.com",
    "ram.amazonaws.com",
    "config-multiaccountsetup.amazonaws.com",
    "config.amazonaws.com",
    "member.org.stacksets.cloudformation.amazonaws.com",
    "securityhub.amazonaws.com",
    "sso.amazonaws.com"
  ]
  enabled_policy_types = [
    "SERVICE_CONTROL_POLICY",
    "TAG_POLICY",
  ]
}

resource "aws_guardduty_organization_admin_account" "this" {
  admin_account_id = var.delegated_admin_account
}

resource "aws_guardduty_organization_configuration" "delegated_admin" {
  provider    = aws.delegated_admin_account
  auto_enable = true
  detector_id = aws_guardduty_detector.delegated_admin.id

  datasources {
    s3_logs {
      auto_enable = true
    }
  }

  depends_on = [
    aws_guardduty_organization_admin_account.this,
  ]
}

resource "aws_guardduty_detector" "delegated_admin" {
  provider = aws.delegated_admin_account
  enable   = true
}
```

Review the resources that are going to be created, and then run `terraform apply` to make the changes.

Discussion

Amazon GuardDuty provides intelligent threat detection, parsing CloudTrail management events, CloudTrail S3 data events, VPC flows logs, and Route53 DNS logs to identify potential issues. It automatically integrates in AWS Security Hub, as covered in Recipe 3.2. It is consistently updated with the latest trends and data from AWS, giving you an ever better view of your security posture.

GuardDuty generates findings, which are then enriched by Amazon Detective, giving you as much information about the potential breach as possible. Additionally, findings are classified as high, medium, and low risk, allowing you to focus your efforts on the more important incidents. You can also optionally enable S3 protection on the account to alert you when potentially malicious actors are accessing your data.

Unfortunately, the solution automatically enrolls new accounts as they are created but does not act on existing accounts within the organization. To fill this gap, the following *create_members.py* file is a Python solution that enables GuardDuty in every existing account simultaneously. You will need boto3 installed in your local Python environment (the code was developed against boto3 version 1.17.62).

```python
import sys

import boto3


delegated_admin_account = sys.argv[1]
role_name = sys.argv[2]

organizations = boto3.client("organizations")
credentials = boto3.client("sts").assume_role(
    RoleArn=f"arn:aws:iam::{delegated_admin_account}:role/{role_name}",
    RoleSessionName="GuardDutyDelegatedAdmin",
)["Credentials"]
guardduty = boto3.Session(
    aws_access_key_id=credentials["AccessKeyId"],
    aws_secret_access_key=credentials["SecretAccessKey"],
    aws_session_token=credentials["SessionToken"],
).client("guardduty")

detector_paginator = guardduty.get_paginator("list_detectors")
detectors = []
for page in detector_paginator.paginate():
    detectors.extend(page["DetectorIds"])
detector_id = detectors[0]

account_paginator = organizations.get_paginator("list_accounts")
for page in account_paginator.paginate(PaginationConfig={"MaxItems": 50}):
    accounts = page["Accounts"]
    guardduty.create_members(
        DetectorId=detector_id,
        AccountDetails=[
            {"AccountId": account["Id"], "Email": account["Email"]}
            for account in accounts
        ],
    )
```

To execute the Python, run python create_members.py <delegated_admin_ account_id> <cross_account_role>, filling in the two parameters.

Summarizing the Recipe

Let's summarize what you learned and created through this recipe:

- Automated threat detection on AWS is done by GuardDuty.
- As part of best practice, you should assign a delegated administrator for GuardDuty.
- By enabling GuardDuty at the organizational level, you can automatically enroll new accounts.
- You first assigned your delegated administrator for your organization.
- Then you wrote some Python to properly enroll all the existing accounts.

3.9 Log Anomaly Alerting on Azure

Problem

You want to ensure that all the relevant logs are collected and automatically processed by Azure tooling to alert if anomalous or unusual activity is detected.

Solution

If you haven't already done so, familiarize yourself with Terraform and the different authentication mechanisms in Chapter 11.

Create a *variables.tf* file and copy the following contents:

```
variable "location" {
  type        = string
  description = "The location in which to deploy the resource"
}

variable "target_management_group_uuid" {
  type        = string
  description = "The UUID of the target management group"
}
```

Then fill out the corresponding *terraform.tfvars* file:

```
location                     = ""
target_management_group_uuid = ""
```

Create the following *provider.tf* file and run terraform init:

```
terraform {
  required_providers {
    azurerm = {
      source  = "hashicorp/azurerm"
      version = "~> 2"
    }
  }
}

provider "azurerm" {
  features {}
}
```

Create the following *main.tf* file and run `terraform plan`:

```
data "azurerm_management_group" "target" {
  name = var.target_management_group_uuid
}

data "azurerm_subscription" "current" {}

resource "azurerm_resource_group" "security_center" {
  name     = "security-center"
  location = var.location
}

resource "azurerm_log_analytics_workspace" "security_center" {
  name                = "security-center"
  location            = azurerm_resource_group.security_center.location
  resource_group_name = azurerm_resource_group.security_center.name
  sku                 = "PerGB2018"
}

resource "azurerm_security_center_workspace" "security_center" {
  scope        = data.azurerm_subscription.current.id
  workspace_id = azurerm_log_analytics_workspace.security_center.id
}

resource "azurerm_security_center_auto_provisioning" "this" {
  auto_provision = "On"
}

locals {
  resource_types = toset([
    "AppServices",
    "ContainerRegistry",
    "KeyVaults",
    "KubernetesService",
    "SqlServers",
    "SqlServerVirtualMachines",
    "StorageAccounts",
    "VirtualMachines",
    "Arm",
```

```
    "Dns"
  ])
}

resource "azurerm_security_center_subscription_pricing" "this" {
  for_each      = local.resource_types
  tier          = "Standard"
  resource_type = each.value
}

resource "azurerm_policy_assignment" "sc_auto_enable" {
  name                 = "security_center"
  location             = azurerm_resource_group.security_center.location
  scope                = data.azurerm_management_group.target.id
  policy_definition_id = join("", [
    "/providers/Microsoft.Authorization/policyDefinitions/",
    "ac076320-ddcf-4066-b451-6154267e8ad2"
  ])

  identity {
    type = "SystemAssigned"
  }
}

resource "azurerm_policy_remediation" "sc_auto_enable" {
  name                 = "security_center"
  scope                = azurerm_policy_assignment.sc_auto_enable.scope
  policy_assignment_id = azurerm_policy_assignment.sc_auto_enable.id
}
```

Review the resources that are going to be created, and then run terraform apply to make the changes.

Discussion

On Azure, your centralized log anomaly alerting is Azure Security Center. It provides a single pane of glass to monitor your security posture in the cloud, as well as covering on premise and even infrastructure in other clouds. To enable a robust security posture, and take advantage of all the tools Azure has to offer, you should enable Azure Defender across all subscriptions. Azure Defender can be configured to automatically analyze a list of resource types, including the following:

- App services
- Container registry
- Key vaults
- Kubernetes service
- SQL servers

- SQL server virtual machines
- Storage accounts
- Virtual machines
- ARM templates
- DNS

 This list is continually growing, and the `resource_types` local variable in the recipe will need updating as new capabilities are added.

In this recipe, you used an Azure Policy to report compliance for where Security Center is currently enabled and then created a remediation task to fix noncompliant subscriptions. The remediation task for that policy enables Security Center but does not configure Azure Defender; you should combine this with Recipe 6.12 to ensure that it is configured exactly to your specifications in every subscription in your Azure tenant.

With a sufficiently privileged user account, you can bring together the security findings from across many subscriptions in your tenant. Security Center is centrally organized, but what a user can see is constrained by their own permissions.

Additionally, Azure Security Center also includes Cloud Connectors, which allow you to use it to monitor and manage both GCP and AWS environments as well. In a multicloud world, bringing threat intelligence to a centralized location becomes critical to avoid being overwhelmed by different and disparate telemetry.

Summarizing the Recipe

So let's review what you learned and created as part of this recipe:

- Azure Security Center processes multiple log streams from across Azure to find anomalous activity.
- Azure Security Center can be enabled at scale through the use of Azure Policy.
- To get the best value out of Azure Security Center, you need to enable Azure Defender across all subscriptions in your tenant.
- Azure Defender automatically scans and analyzes a variety of resource types on Azure.
- Azure Defender needs to be configured directly on the subscription.
- By using Recipe 6.12, you can apply your required configuration at scale.

3.10 Building an Infrastructure Registry on GCP

Problem

You need to understand what infrastructure is deployed across your estate so you can understand where to invest your time to best protect your estate.

Solution

If you haven't already done so, familiarize yourself with Terraform and the different authentication mechanisms in Chapter 11.

Create a *variables.tf* file and copy the following contents:

```
variable "project_id" {
  type        = string
  description = "The project to create the resources in"
}

variable "region" {
  type        = string
  description = "The region to create the resources in"
}

variable "organization_domain" {
  type        = string
  description = "The organization domain of your Google Cloud estate"
}
```

Then fill out the corresponding *terraform.tfvars* file:

```
project_id          = ""
region              = ""
organization_domain = ""
```

Create the following *provider.tf* file and run `terraform init`:

```
provider "google" {
  project = var.project_id
  region  = var.region
}

terraform {
  required_providers {
    google = {
      source  = "hashicorp/google"
      version = "~> 3"
    }
  }
}
```

Create the following *main.tf* file and run `terraform plan`:

```
data "google_organization" "this" {
  domain = var.organization_domain
}

data "google_project" "current" {}

resource "null_resource" "create_assets_service_account" {
  provisioner "local-exec" {
    command = join(" ", [
      "gcloud beta services identity create",
      "--service=cloudasset.googleapis.com"
    ])
  }
}

resource "google_project_service" "assets_api" {
  service  = "cloudasset.googleapis.com"
}

resource "google_cloud_asset_organization_feed" "networking_changes" {
  billing_project = data.google_project.current.name
  org_id          = data.google_organization.this.org_id
  feed_id         = "network-changes"
  content_type    = "RESOURCE"

  asset_types = [
    "compute.googleapis.com/Subnetwork",
    "compute.googleapis.com/Network",
    "compute.googleapis.com/Router",
    "compute.googleapis.com/Route",
    "compute.googleapis.com/ExternalVpnGateway"
  ]

  feed_output_config {
    pubsub_destination {
      topic = google_pubsub_topic.network_changes.id
    }
  }

  depends_on = [
    google_pubsub_topic_iam_member.cloud_asset_writer,
    google_project_service.assets_api
  ]
}

resource "google_pubsub_topic" "network_changes" {
  name     = "network-changes"
}

resource "google_pubsub_topic_iam_member" "cloud_asset_writer" {
  topic  = google_pubsub_topic.network_changes.id
  role   = "roles/pubsub.publisher"
```

```
member  = join("",[
  "serviceAccount:service-",
  data.google_project.current.number,
  "@gcp-sa-cloudasset.iam.gserviceaccount.com"
])

depends_on = [
  null_resource.create_assets_service_account
]
}
```

Review the resources that are going to be created, and then run `terraform apply` to make the changes.

Discussion

This recipe creates a Pub/Sub topic that gets triggered every time network resources are changed in your estate. Understanding the changes that occur in your estate is critical for maintaining a robust security posture and threat hunting. By configuring Cloud Asset Inventory feeds, you can operate in a *trust but verify* model.

Users are allowed to make the changes they need to support their system; however, the security team can review changes they deem pertinent. This is a paradigm shift from working on premises, where changes often have to pass a series of manual reviews before they are actioned.

In the solution, you used an organizational feed, but you can also configure both project- and folder-level feeds, enabling you to set up notifications for segments of your organization. It may be that you care far more about a certain type of resource changing in production, but you do not wanted to be notified when it changes in development or preproduction environments.

This recipe focused on networking resources, as they are generally less volatile, meaning changes are less expected, and they have a direct impact on your security posture. Each change can be sorted into one of three mutually exclusive, collectively exhaustive buckets:

- Required changes required by systems within the estate
- Accidental changes made in error
- A malicious change made by bad actors within your estate, key data when threat hunting

With this in mind, how can you improve the signal-to-noise ratio of the events? The following Terraform shows how to apply conditions to the feeds to be more selective over the alerts. Specifically, it shows how to filter explicitly for resource creation events.

```
locals {
  does_not_exist = join(".", [
    "google.cloud.asset.v1",
    "TemporalAsset.PriorAssetState",
    "DOES_NOT_EXIST"
  ])
}
resource "google_cloud_asset_organization_feed" "networking_changes" {
  billing_project = data.google_project.current.name
  org_id          = data.google_organization.this.org_id
  feed_id         = "network-changes"
  content_type    = "RESOURCE"

  asset_types = [
    "compute.googleapis.com/Subnetwork",
    "compute.googleapis.com/Network",
    "compute.googleapis.com/Router",
    "compute.googleapis.com/Route",
    "compute.googleapis.com/ExternalVpnGateway"
  ]

  condition {
    expression = <<-CONDITION
    !temporal_asset.deleted &&
    temporal_asset.prior_asset_state == local.does_not_exist
    CONDITION
    title = "created"
    description = "Filter for created resources only"
  }

  feed_output_config {
    pubsub_destination {
      topic = google_pubsub_topic.network_changes.id
    }
  }

  depends_on = [
    google_pubsub_topic_iam_member.cloud_asset_writer,
    google_project_service.assets_api
  ]
}
```

Summarizing the Recipe

So let's review what you learned and created as part of this recipe:

- Cloud Asset Inventory comes preconfigured in your GCP organization.

- You can create notifications based on particular resource types changing, allowing you to "trust but verify."

- "Trust but verify" allows you to enable teams to be empowered to make changes without compromising your security posture.

- You can use conditions to filter for only particular events, such as creation or deletion.

3.11 Building an Infrastructure Registry on AWS

Problem

You need to understand what infrastructure is deployed across your estate so you can understand where to invest your time to best protect your estate.

Solution

If you haven't already done so, familiarize yourself with Terraform and the different authentication mechanisms in Chapter 11.

This recipe assumes you are using a privileged role within the organization root account and have the `boto3` library installed and available on your Python path, which can be done via `pip install boto3`.

Create a *variables.tf* file and copy the following contents:

```
variable "delegated_admin_account" {
  type        = string
  description = "The account ID for the account to be the Config delegated admin"
}

variable "cross_account_role" {
  type        = string
  description = "The cross account role to assume"
}
```

Then fill out the corresponding *terraform.tfvars* file:

```
delegated_admin_account = ""
cross_account_role      = ""
```

Create the following *provider.tf* file and run `terraform init`:

```
provider "aws" {}

provider "aws" {
  alias = "delegated_admin_account"
  assume_role {
    role_arn = join("", [
      "arn:aws:iam::",
      var.delegated_admin_account,
      ":role/:",
      var.cross_account_role
```

```
    ])
  }
}

terraform {
  required_providers {
    aws = {
      source  = "hashicorp/aws"
      version = "~> 3"
    }
  }
}
```

Create the following *set_delegated_admin.py* file:

```
import sys

import boto3


delegated_admin_account = sys.argv[1]

organizations = boto3.client("organizations")

for principal in [
    "config-multiaccountsetup.amazonaws.com",
    "config.amazonaws.com",
]:
    delegated_admins = organizations.list_delegated_administrators(
        ServicePrincipal=principal,
    )["DelegatedAdministrators"]

    if len(delegated_admins) == 0:
        organizations.register_delegated_administrator(
            AccountId=delegated_admin_account,
            ServicePrincipal=principal,
        )
```

 Your aws_organizations_organization resource should only exist in one location. The following Terraform shows an example of that resource. Add config-multiaccountsetup.amazonaws.com and config.amazonaws.com to your aws_service_access_princi pals list and create the other resources outlined in the following file.

Create the following *main.tf* file and run terraform plan:

```
resource "aws_organizations_organization" "this" {
  aws_service_access_principals = [
    "cloudtrail.amazonaws.com",
    "guardduty.amazonaws.com",
```

```
      "ram.amazonaws.com",
      "config-multiaccountsetup.amazonaws.com",
      "config.amazonaws.com",
      "member.org.stacksets.cloudformation.amazonaws.com",
      "securityhub.amazonaws.com",
      "sso.amazonaws.com"
    ]
    enabled_policy_types = [
      "SERVICE_CONTROL_POLICY",
      "TAG_POLICY",
    ]
  }

  resource "null_resource" "set_delegated_admin" {
    provisioner "local-exec" {
      command = join(" ",[
        "python",
        "set_delegated_admin.py",
        var.delegated_admin_account
      ])
    }
  }

  resource "aws_config_configuration_aggregator" "organization" {
    provider = aws.delegated_admin_account
    depends_on = [
      aws_iam_role_policy_attachment.organization,
      null_resource.set_delegated_admin
    ]

    name = "org_aggregator"

    organization_aggregation_source {
      all_regions = true
      role_arn    = aws_iam_role.organization.arn
    }
  }

  resource "aws_iam_role" "organization" {
    provider = aws.delegated_admin_account

    name = "org-config-role"

    assume_role_policy = <<EOF
  {
    "Version": "2012-10-17",
    "Statement": [
      {
        "Sid": "",
        "Effect": "Allow",
        "Principal": {
          "Service": "config.amazonaws.com"
```

```
      },
        "Action": "sts:AssumeRole"
      }
    ]
  }
}
EOF
}

resource "aws_iam_role_policy_attachment" "organization" {
  provider = aws.delegated_admin_account

  role       = aws_iam_role.organization.name
  policy_arn = join("", [
    "arn:aws:iam::aws:policy/service-role/","AWSConfigRoleForOrganizations"
  ])
}
```

Review the resources that are going to be created, and then run `terraform apply` to make the changes.

Discussion

This recipe configured a delegated administrator account for AWS Config and an organization-level aggregator which allows for the collation of data from all the enrolled accounts.

AWS Config is a core service not only for resource inventories but also for managing compliance at scale across your AWS estate. This recipe forms the basis of further recipes such as Recipes 7.2, 7.5, and 7.11.

Although the aggregator is configured centrally, the recipe does not handle the configuration of AWS Config on a per-account basis. The following Terraform, combined with Recipe 6.11, handles the per-account configuration.

The required variables are as follows:

```
variable "central_account" {
  type        = string
  description = "The account ID for the centralized Config account"
}

variable "target_account" {
  type        = string
  description = "The account ID to configure the Delivery Channel in"
}

variable "cross_account_role" {
  type        = string
  description = "The cross account role to assume"
}
```

```
variable "bucket_name" {
  type        = string
  description = "The name of the bucket to store AWS Config data"
}
```

It requires the following providers to be configured:

```
provider "aws" {
  alias = "central"
  assume_role {
    role_arn = join("", [
      "arn:aws:iam::",
      var.central_account,
      ":role/",
      var.cross_account_role
    ])
  }
}

provider "aws" {
  alias = "target"
  assume_role {
    role_arn = join("", [
      "arn:aws:iam::",
      var.target_account,
      ":role/",
      var.cross_account_role
    ])
  }
}

terraform {
  required_providers {
    aws = {
      source  = "hashicorp/aws"
      version = "~> 3"
    }
  }
}
```

And the following resources, which handle the per-account configuration, create a centralized S3 bucket and an SNS topic for data aggregation and triggering workflows from compliance events:

```
data "aws_organizations_organization" "this" {}

resource "aws_config_delivery_channel" "this" {
  provider       = aws.target
  name           = "delivery_channel"
  s3_bucket_name = aws_s3_bucket.central_config.bucket
  sns_topic_arn  = aws_sns_topic.config.arn
  depends_on     = [
    aws_config_configuration_recorder.this,
```

```
      aws_s3_bucket_policy.config
  ]
}

resource "aws_s3_bucket" "central_config" {
  provider = aws.central
  bucket   = var.bucket_name
}

resource "aws_s3_bucket_policy" "config" {
  provider = aws.central
  bucket = aws_s3_bucket.central_config.id

  policy = data.aws_iam_policy_document.bucket_policy.json
}

data "aws_iam_policy_document" "bucket_policy" {
  statement {
    actions = [
      "S3:GetBucketAcl",
      "S3:ListBucket",
      "S3:PutObject",
    ]

    effect = "Allow"

    principals {
      type        = "AWS"
      identifiers = [aws_iam_role.config.arn]
    }

    resources = [
      aws_s3_bucket.central_config.arn,
      "${aws_s3_bucket.central_config.arn}/*"
    ]
  }
}

resource "aws_sns_topic" "config" {
  name = "central_config"
}

resource "aws_sns_topic_policy" "default" {
  arn = aws_sns_topic.config.arn

  policy = data.aws_iam_policy_document.allow_config.json
}

data "aws_iam_policy_document" "allow_config" {
  statement {
    actions = [
      "SNS:Publish"
```

```
    ]

    effect = "Allow"

    principals {
      type        = "AWS"
      identifiers = [aws_iam_role.config.arn]
    }

    resources = [
      aws_sns_topic.config.arn,
    ]
  }
}

resource "aws_config_configuration_recorder" "this" {
  provider = aws.target
  name     = "recorder"
  role_arn = aws_iam_role.config.arn
}

resource "aws_iam_role" "config" {
  provider = aws.target
  name     = "config-delivery"

  assume_role_policy = data.aws_iam_policy_document.assume_role.json
}

data "aws_iam_policy_document" "assume_role" {
  statement {
    actions = [
      "sts:AssumeRole"
    ]

    effect = "Allow"

    principals {
      type        = "Service"
      identifiers = ["config.amazonaws.com"]
    }
  }
}

resource "aws_iam_role_policy" "config" {
  provider = aws.target
  name     = "config-delivery"
  role     = aws_iam_role.config.id
  policy   = data.aws_iam_policy_document.config_role.json
}

data "aws_iam_policy_document" "config_role" {
  statement {
```

```
    actions = [
      "SNS:Publish"
    ]

    effect = "Allow"

    resources = [
      aws_sns_topic.config.arn,
    ]
  }
  statement {
    actions = [
      "S3:GetBucketAcl",
      "S3:ListBucket",
      "S3:PutObject",
      "S3:PutObjectAcl"
    ]

    effect = "Allow"

    resources = [
      aws_s3_bucket.central_config.arn,
      "${aws_s3_bucket.central_config.arn}/*"
    ]
  }
}
```

Once AWS Config recorders are properly configured in all accounts, you can then use the advanced query functionality within AWS Config to run ad hoc queries against the infrastructure across your estate. The delivery channel ensures that a copy of all configuration data is stored in the S3 bucket, where you can query it with external tooling or Athena. The SNS topic means you can send notifications, send emails, or trigger AWS Lambda functions when there are infrastructure changes.

Summarizing the Recipe

So let's review what you learned and created as part of this recipe:

- With AWS Config, it is possible to build a centralized asset inventory on AWS.
- AWS Config should be set up with a delegated administrator account.
- By creating an AWS Config Aggregator, you can easily pull all data centrally.
- To be able to understand when particular changes are being made, you need to deploy delivery channels out to every account in your organization.
- By combining this recipe with Recipe 6.11, you can easily manage deployment of AWS Config at scale.

3.12 Building an Infrastructure Registry on Azure

Problem

You need to understand what infrastructure is deployed across your estate so you can understand where to invest your time to best protect your estate.

Solution

To achieve this, you're going to deploy an Azure Monitor workbook that allows you to dynamically query what resources exist in your estate.

If you haven't already done so, familiarize yourself with Terraform and the different authentication mechanisms in Chapter 11.

Create a *variables.tf* file and copy the following contents:

```
variable "location" {
  type        = string
  description = "The location to deploy your resource into"
}
```

Then fill out the corresponding *terraform.tfvars* file:

```
location = ""
```

Create the following *provider.tf* file and run `terraform init`:

```
terraform {
  required_providers {
    azurerm = {
      source  = "hashicorp/azurerm"
      version = "~> 2"
    }
  }
}
```

```
}

provider "azurerm" {
  features {}
}
```

Download the *workbook_data.json* file into your working directory from the book's accompanying GitHub repository (*https://oreil.ly/hV4aC*).

Create the following *main.tf* file and run `terraform plan`:

```
resource "azurerm_resource_group" "resource_inventory" {
  name     = "resource_inventory"
  location = var.location
}

resource "azurerm_resource_group_template_deployment" "resource_inventory" {
  name                = "resource_inventory"
  resource_group_name = azurerm_resource_group.resource_inventory.name
  deployment_mode     = "Complete"
  template_content    = <<TEMPLATE
{
  "contentVersion": "1.0.0.0",
  "parameters": {
    "workbookDisplayName": {
      "type": "string",
      "defaultValue": "Resource Inventory",
      "metadata": {
        "description": "The friendly name for the workbook."
      }
    },
    "workbookType": {
      "type": "string",
      "defaultValue": "workbook",
      "metadata": {
        "description": "The gallery that the workbook will be shown under.""
      }
    },
    "workbookSourceId": {
      "type": "string",
      "defaultValue": "Azure Monitor",
      "metadata": {
        "description": "The id of resource instance"
      }
    },
    "workbookId": {
      "type": "string",
      "defaultValue": "[newGuid()]",
      "metadata": {
        "description": "The unique guid for this workbook instance"
      }
    }
  },
```

```
    "resources": [
      {
        "name": "[parameters('workbookId')]",
        "type": "microsoft.insights/workbooks",
        "location": "[resourceGroup().location]",
        "apiVersion": "2018-06-17-preview",
        "dependsOn": [],
        "kind": "shared",
        "properties": {
          "displayName": "[parameters('workbookDisplayName')]",
          "serializedData": ${jsonencode(data.local_file.workbook.content)},
          "version": "1.0",
          "sourceId": "[parameters('workbookSourceId')]",
          "category": "[parameters('workbookType')]"
        }
      }
    ],
    "outputs": {
      "workbookId": {
        "type": "string",
        "value": "[
          resourceId('microsoft.insights/workbooks',
          parameters('workbookId'))
        ]"
      }
    },
    "$schema": join("", [
      "http://schema.management.azure.com/",
      "schemas/2015-01-01/deploymentTemplate.json#"
    ])
}
TEMPLATE
}

output "workbooks_url" {
  value = join("", [
    "https://portal.azure.com/#blade/",
    "Microsoft_Azure_Monitoring/AzureMonitoringBrowseBlade/",
    "workbooks"
  ])
}
```

Review the resources that are going to be created, and then run `terraform apply` to make the changes.

Discussion

By browsing to the `workbooks_url` output and selecting the *Resource Inventory* workbook, you will see an interface that allows you to query the resources from across the tenant. It will also have preconfigured filters, enabling you to easily narrow by resource type, parent subscription, and resource group.

In this recipe, you used Terraform to deploy an Azure Resource Manager (ARM) template, as opposed to directly deploying a resource. ARM templates are Microsoft's first-class infrastructure-as-code approach. This book has focused on Terraform as it provides a common language, syntax, and interface to all three major clouds; however, there are resources the providers do not cover. As of the time of writing, the Azure Terraform provider did not yet support workbooks.

A common pattern for working around missing resources is to use ARM templates initially and migrate to the native Terraform resources once they are supported.

Azure provides the Azure Resource Graph as the engine that drives resource exploration in your tenant. You can actively query it yourself, and it is the same service that powers the Azure Portal. It comes with a sophisticated query language that allows you to ask it almost any question about your resources. For example, the query that generates the body of the workbook is relatively simple:

```
where type in~({ResourceTypes})
| project Resource = id,
  Type = type,
  Subscription = subscriptionId,
  ['Resource group'] = strcat(
    '/subscriptions/',
    subscriptionId,
    '/resourceGroups/',
    resourceGroup
  ),
  Location = location
```

This query grabs the resource ID, type, subscription, resource group, and location, filtering for only the resource types that are specified in the workbook parameters. By extending this query, you can have the workbook report on any data you wish to see, including changes in resource properties over time.

Azure Monitor is the centralized observability tool with the Azure ecosystem. Here are some of the common outcomes it drives:

- Understanding your application health through Application Insights
- Gaining visibility into your infrastructure with VM and Container Insights
- Performing bespoke reporting and visualizations with workbooks and dashboards
- Centralizing your monitoring with Azure Monitor Metrics
- Creating alerts and automated remediation

Additionally, in recipes such as Recipes 3.3 and 3.6 in this chapter alone, you used Log Analytics workspaces, which fall under the banner of Azure Monitor.

Summarizing the Recipe

So let's review what you learned and created as part of this recipe:

- Azure Monitor is your centralized observability solution.
- Azure Resource Graph allows you to write bespoke queries against all the resources in your tenant.
- Azure Monitor workbooks allow you to build reports based on Resource Graph queries.
- Workbooks are not available as a native Terraform resource.
- By deploying ARM templates with Terraform, you can access unsupported resource types.

CHAPTER 4

Protecting Your Data

The crown jewel in your cloud estate is the data that you store and process. As crafting and scaling a data security strategy is at least one book in and of itself, in this chapter you'll be seeing how to implement the fundamental building blocks on which such a strategy would rest. In Chapter 1, you learned that you are only as strong as your weakest link. By embedding these recipes into the infrastructure fabric of your cloud estate, you can ensure that insufficient data encryption is not what will cause a data breach.

When talking of data, it can be in one of two states: at rest or in transit. The first nine recipes show how you should handle data in both states. The last three recipes are about data loss prevention, how you find where your valuable data is, and how you verify it has the level of warranted protection. When you have a cloud estate actively leveraged by hundreds of teams and thousands of engineers, it is beyond the scope of any one unaided human to be able to stay on top of what data is where. Instead, you'll see how to use tooling as the needed force multiplier to manage data at scale.

Envelope Encryption

Envelope encryption is the process of encrypting keys with other keys. The three major cloud providers all use envelope encryption and key hierarchies to keep data safe (Figure 4-1).

At the simplest level, there are two different kinds of keys.

Data encryption keys, DEKs, are used to actually encrypt the data. They are usually stored near the data they have encrypted and must be encrypted at rest.

Key encryption keys, KEKs, are used to encrypt DEKs or other KEKs. They need to be stored centrally and rotated regularly.

Figure 4-1. Envelope encryption

By using different cryptographic algorithms for the keys, you remove the ability of a single compromise to unravel all the layers of encryption.

So let's dive into the wonderful world of encrypting your data in the cloud.

4.1 Encrypting Data at Rest on GCP

Problem

As part of securely hosting data on GCP, you need to be able to encrypt data at rest on the most common storage options available.

Solution

If you haven't already done so, familiarize yourself with Terraform and the different authentication mechanisms in Chapter 11.

Create a *variables.tf* file and copy the following contents:

```
variable "project_id" {
  type        = string
  description = "The project to create the resources in"
}

variable "region" {
  type        = string
  description = "The region to create the resources in"
}
```

Then fill out the corresponding *terraform.tfvars* file:

```
project_id = ""
region     = ""
```

Create the following *provider.tf* file and run `terraform init`:

```
provider "google" {
  project = var.project_id
  region  = var.region
}

provider "google-beta" {
  project = var.project_id
```

```
    region  = var.region
  }

  terraform {
    required_providers {
      google = {
        source  = "hashicorp/google"
        version = "~> 3"
      }
      google-beta = {
        source  = "hashicorp/google-beta"
        version = "~> 3"
      }
      null = {
        source  = "hashicorp/null"
        version = "~> 3"
      }
    }
  }
}
```

Create the following *main.tf* file:

```
resource "google_project_service" "cloud_kms" {
  service = "cloudkms.googleapis.com"
}

resource "google_kms_key_ring" "keyring" {
  name       = "sensitive-data-keyring"
  location   = var.region
  depends_on = [google_project_service.cloud_kms]
}

resource "google_kms_crypto_key" "key" {
  name     = "sensitive-data-key"
  key_ring = google_kms_key_ring.keyring.id
}
```

To create an encrypted Cloud Compute Disk, add the following resources to *main.tf*:

```
resource "google_service_account" "sensitive" {
  account_id   = "sensitive-data-service-account"
  display_name = "Sensitive Data Handler"
}

resource "google_service_account_iam_policy" "sensitive" {
  service_account_id = google_service_account.sensitive.name
  policy_data        = data.google_iam_policy.sa.policy_data
}

data "google_client_openid_userinfo" "me" {}

data "google_iam_policy" "sa" {
  binding {
    role = "roles/iam.serviceAccountUser"
```

```
    members = [
      "user:${data.google_client_openid_userinfo.me.email}",
    ]
  }
}

resource "google_kms_crypto_key_iam_member" "service_account_use" {
  crypto_key_id = google_kms_crypto_key.key.id
  role          = "roles/cloudkms.cryptoKeyEncrypterDecrypter"
  member        = "serviceAccount:${google_service_account.sensitive.email}"
}

resource "google_compute_disk" "encrypted" {
  name = "encrypted"
  size = "10"
  type = "pd-standard"
  zone = "${var.region}-a"
  disk_encryption_key {
    kms_key_self_link       = google_kms_crypto_key.key.id
    kms_key_service_account = google_service_account.sensitive.email
  }

  depends_on = [google_kms_crypto_key_iam_member.service_account_use]
}
```

To create an encrypted Cloud SQL database, add the following resources to *main.tf*:

```
resource "google_compute_network" "vpc_network" {
  name = "vpc-network"
}

resource "google_sql_database_instance" "encrypted" {
  provider            = google-beta
  name                = "encrypted-instance"
  database_version    = "POSTGRES_13"
  region              = var.region
  deletion_protection = false
  encryption_key_name = google_kms_crypto_key.key.id
  settings {
    tier = "db-f1-micro"
    ip_configuration {
      private_network = google_compute_network.vpc_network.id
    }
  }

  depends_on = [google_kms_crypto_key_iam_member.sql_binding]
}

resource "google_kms_crypto_key_iam_member" "sql_binding" {
  crypto_key_id = google_kms_crypto_key.key.id
  role          = "roles/cloudkms.cryptoKeyEncrypterDecrypter"
  member        = join("", [
```

```
      "serviceAccount:service-",
      data.google_project.current.number,
      "@gcp-sa-cloud-sql.iam.gserviceaccount.com"
    ])

    depends_on = [null_resource.create_database_service_account]
  }

  resource "null_resource" "create_database_service_account" {
    provisioner "local-exec" {
      command = join(" ", [
        "gcloud beta services identity create",
        "--project=${var.project_id}",
        "--service=sqladmin.googleapis.com"
      ])
    }
  }
}
```

To create an encrypted Cloud Storage bucket, add the following resources to *main.tf*:

```
data "google_project" "current" {}

resource "google_storage_bucket" "encrypted" {
  name          = "${data.google_project.current.project_id}-encrypted"
  force_destroy = true
  location      = var.region
  encryption {
    default_kms_key_name = google_kms_crypto_key.key.id
  }

  depends_on = [google_kms_crypto_key_iam_member.storage_binding]
}

data "google_storage_project_service_account" "this" {}

resource "google_kms_crypto_key_iam_member" "storage_binding" {
  crypto_key_id = google_kms_crypto_key.key.id
  role          = "roles/cloudkms.cryptoKeyEncrypterDecrypter"
  member        = join("",[
    "serviceAccount:",
    data.google_storage_project_service_account.this.email_address
  ])
}
```

Review the resources to be created by running `terraform plan`, and then run `terra
form apply` to make the changes.

Discussion

In this recipe, you saw how to deploy the following resources with the data encrypted
at rest:

- Cloud compute volumes
- Cloud SQL databases
- Cloud storage buckets

 This recipe used a single, shared Cloud KMS key to secure all the resources deployed. In a normal scenario, you should be using multiple keys to enable finely grained access control and limit the blast radius of a breach.

As you can see in the recipe, in order to use a key with a particular resource, you need to give the correct service account the permissions to leverage the key. You will find that most resources will automatically leverage a default key for the project to encrypt resources when you do not specify what key to use. However, it is best to create distinct keys so you can segment resources within a project, allowing you to maintain the principle of least privilege.

When you create a key, the principal you use retains editor writes so you can continue to administer the key. Additionally, all keys belong to a *key ring*, which is a logical group that allows for managing groups of keys simultaneously, which has a distinct set of permissions compared to the keys. For example, you can allow someone to create new keys that they manage without giving them access to manage preexisting keys in the ring.

When defining IAM permissions for the keys in Terraform, you are given the following three types of resources:

google_kms_crypto_key_iam_policy
> The *policy* resource allows for the authoritative setting of the IAM access to the key; by applying this resource all other preexisting assignments are removed. For example, use this resource if you wish the policies to be the only ones for the key.

google_kms_crypto_key_iam_binding
> The *binding* resource allows for the authoritative setting of IAM access to a key for a particular role. All other assignments for a given role are removed. For example, use this resource to give cryptoKeyEncrypterDecrypter access to only the defined members.

google_kms_crypto_key_iam_member
> The *member* resource allows for nonauthoritative setting of permissions on the key. In the recipe, you used this resource to allow for setting the required permissions individually for each use case, without overwriting the previous access.

Between the three resource types, you saw three different methods for using service accounts with KMS keys.

To create the Compute Disk, you needed to create a bespoke service account and assign that when creating the resources.

To create the Cloud SQL database, you needed to use a `null_resource` to invoke `gcloud beta` to create a specific service account not natively supported by Terraform.

To create the Cloud Storage bucket, there is a Terraform data provider that gives you the details of the project-specific Service Account you need to use.

To know what service account you need for each resource type, refer to the service documentation. However, by using Recipe 6.1, you make it possible to produce reusable artifacts that make it simple for every team to enable encryption at rest.

Summary

Let's summarize what was learned and deployed in this recipe:

- On GCP, Cloud KMS gives you the ability to encrypt resources at rest.
- Although GCP will encrypt many resources by default with an automatically generated key, you should look to create distinct keys that you can control.
- Keys are created under a key ring, which allows for managing keys by logical groupings.
- In order for a resource to leverage a key, the `cloudkms.cryptoKeyEncrypterDe crypter` role needs to be given to the appropriate service account.
- Depending on the resource type, what service account to use and how to create it varies.
- You saw examples of how to encrypt Compute Engine disks, Cloud SQL databases, and Cloud Storage buckets, which all require different approaches for having the correct service account.

4.2 Encrypting Data at Rest on AWS

Problem

As part of securely hosting data on AWS, you need to be able to encrypt data at rest on the most common storage options available.

Solution

If you haven't already done so, familiarize yourself with Terraform and the different authentication mechanisms in Chapter 11.

Create a *variables.tf* file and copy the following contents:

```
variable "key_administrator_role" {
  type        = string
  description = "The role used to administer the key"
}

variable "database_subnets_ids" {
  type        = string
  description = "The IDs of the subnets to host the database"
}
```

Then fill out the corresponding *terraform.tfvars* file:

```
key_administrator_role = ""
database_subnets_ids   = [""]
```

Create the following *provider.tf* file and run `terraform init`:

```
provider "aws" {}

terraform {
  required_providers {
    aws = {
      source  = "hashicorp/aws"
      version = "~> 3"
    }
    random = {
      source  = "hashicorp/random"
      version = "~> 3"
    }
  }
}
```

Create the following *main.tf* file:

```
resource "aws_kms_key" "key" {
  policy = data.aws_iam_policy_document.key_policy.json
}

data "aws_iam_policy_document" "key_policy" {
  statement {
    sid = "Allow access for Key Administrators"
    actions = [
      "kms:Create*",
      "kms:Describe*",
      "kms:Enable*",
      "kms:List*",
      "kms:Put*",
      "kms:Update*",
      "kms:Revoke*",
      "kms:Disable*",
      "kms:Get*",
      "kms:Delete*",
```

```
        "kms:TagResource",
        "kms:UntagResource",
        "kms:ScheduleKeyDeletion",
        "kms:CancelKeyDeletion"
      ]
      effect = "Allow"
      principals {
        type        = "AWS"
        identifiers = [var.key_administrator_role]
      }
      resources = ["*"]
    }

    statement {
      sid = "Allow use of the key"
      actions = [
        "kms:Encrypt",
        "kms:Decrypt",
        "kms:ReEncrypt*",
        "kms:GenerateDataKey*",
        "kms:DescribeKey"
      ]
      effect = "Allow"
      principals {
        type        = "AWS"
        identifiers = ["*"]
      }
      resources = ["*"]
    }

    statement {
      sid     = "Allow attachment of persistent resources"
      effect = "Allow"
      principals {
        type        = "AWS"
        identifiers = ["*"]
      }
      actions = [
        "kms:CreateGrant",
        "kms:ListGrants",
        "kms:RevokeGrant"
      ]
      resources = ["*"]
      condition {
        test     = "Bool"
        variable = "kms:GrantIsForAWSResource"
        values   = [true]
      }
    }
  }
}
```

To create an encrypted Elastic Block Store (EBS) volume, enable EBS encryption by default, and set the default EBS encryption key by adding the following resources to *main.tf*:

```
data "aws_region" "current" {}

resource "aws_ebs_default_kms_key" "this" {
  key_arn = aws_kms_key.key.arn
}

resource "aws_ebs_encryption_by_default" "this" {
  enabled = true

  depends_on = [
    aws_ebs_default_kms_key.this
  ]
}

resource "aws_ebs_volume" "this" {
  availability_zone = "${data.aws_region.current.name}a"
  size              = 1
  type              = "gp3"
  depends_on = [
    aws_ebs_encryption_by_default.this
  ]
}
```

To create an encrypted RDS database, add the following resources to *main.tf*:

```
resource "random_password" "database" {
  length           = 16
  special          = true
  override_special = "_%@"
}

resource "aws_db_instance" "default" {
  allocated_storage      = 10
  db_subnet_group_name   = aws_db_subnet_group.default.name
  engine                 = "postgres"
  engine_version         = "13.2"
  instance_class         = "db.t3.micro"
  name                   = "encrypteddatabase"
  kms_key_id             = aws_kms_key.this.arn
  username               = "postgres"
  password               = random_password.database.result
  parameter_group_name   = "default.postgres13"
  skip_final_snapshot    = true
  storage_encrypted      = true
  vpc_security_group_ids = [aws_security_group.database.id]
}

resource "aws_db_subnet_group" "default" {
  subnet_ids = var.database_subnet_ids
```

```
}

resource "aws_security_group" "database" {
  vpc_id = var.vpc_id
}

output "database_password" {
  value = aws_db_instance.default.password
}
```

To create an encrypted S3 bucket, add the following resources to *main.tf*:

```
resource "aws_s3_bucket" "encrypted_bucket" {
  server_side_encryption_configuration {
    rule {
      apply_server_side_encryption_by_default {
        kms_master_key_id = aws_kms_key.this.arn
        sse_algorithm     = "aws:kms"
      }
    }
  }
}
```

Review the resources to be created by running `terraform plan`, and then run `terra
form apply` to make the changes.

Discussion

In this recipe, you saw how to deploy the following resources with the data encrypted
at rest:

- EBS volumes
- RDS databases
- S3 buckets

This recipe used a single, shared AWS KMS key to secure all the
resources deployed. In a normal scenario, you should be using
multiple keys to enable finely grained access control and limit the
blast radius of a breach.

The service that lives at the core of AWS encryption is AWS Key Management Service
(KMS). For many services, AWS will provision a KMS key for that service that you
can leverage for encryption, known as an AWS customer managed key (CMK). However, although this potentially simplifies things, it now gives a single point of failure
or compromise shared across many resources.

Instead, you should create your own KMS keys, known as *customer-managed keys*, and apply them explicitly to resources. By doing this, you have the ability to be explicit about who can use what key where, and control potential privilege escalation.

Three different kinds of KMS policies

When looking at KMS policies, there are generally three kinds of users who need to be able to interact with a key:

- Administrators, allowing them to control usage of the key but not use the key
- Users, allowing them to use the key but not change how it can be used
- AWS services, allowing them to temporarily leverage the key as required

Setting up the policy to enable administrators and users is relatively trivial. However, to set up access that AWS services can leverage, you need the permission to create *grants*. Grants are a way to give temporary permission to AWS principals to use a CMK. They only allow the principal to use the minimum subset of required KMS operations: encrypting and decrypting data, creating grants, and retiring or revoking grants.

Encrypting data at rest on EBS

With EBS, you need to ensure that both volumes and snapshots are encrypted. When a volume is encrypted, any snapshots taken from it will be encrypted as well. If you have unencrypted volumes, you cannot then encrypt them on demand; it can only be done on creation. To move the data to encrypted storage, you need to take a snapshot and restore it, which can be done with the following Terraform:

```
data "aws_ebs_volume" "unencrypted" {
  filters {
    name   = "volume-id"
    values = [var.volume_id]
  }
}

resource "aws_ebs_snapshot" "conversion" {
  volume_id = var.volume_id
}

resource "aws_ebs_volume" "encrypted" {
  availability_zone = data.aws_ebs_volume.unencrypted.type.availability_zone
  encrypted         = true
  snapshot_id       = aws_ebs_snapshot.conversion.id
  type              = data.aws_ebs_volume.unencrypted.type
}
```

If you have unencrypted snapshots, you can copy them to encrypt them, like so:

```
data "aws_region" "current" {}

resource "aws_ebs_snapshot_copy" "snapshot" {
  source_snapshot_id = var.snapshot_id
  source_region      = data.aws_region.current.name
  encrypted          = true
}
```

Encrypting data at rest on RDS

With databases on RDS, the rules for enabling encryption are similar to EBS. To encrypt an existing database, you need to take a snapshot and restore it, and to encrypt an existing snapshot, you need to copy it. The following two code snippets show how to perform each of these operations.

The following Terraform encrypts an existing database by creating and then restoring from a snapshot:

```
resource "aws_db_snapshot" "conversion" {
  db_instance_identifier = var.database_id
  db_snapshot_identifier = "encryption_conversion"
}

resource "aws_db_instance" "default" {
  allocated_storage     = 10
  db_subnet_group_name  = aws_db_subnet_group.default.name
  engine                = "postgres"
  engine_version        = "13.2"
  instance_class        = "db.t3.micro"
  name                  = "encrypteddatabase"
  kms_key_id            = aws_kms_key.rds.arn
  username              = var.username
  password              = var.password
  parameter_group_name  = "default.postgres13"
  skip_final_snapshot   = true
  snapshot_identifier   = aws_db_snapshot.conversion.id
  storage_encrypted     = true
  vpc_security_group_ids = [aws_security_group.database.id]
}
```

The following Terraform uses a null resource to create an encrypted copy of an existing database snapshot:

```
resource "null_resource" "create_encrypted_copy" {
  provisioner "local-exec" {
    command = join(" ", [
      "aws rds copy-db-snapshot",
      "--source-db-snapshot-identifier ${var.snapshot_arn}",
      "--target-db-snapshot-identifier encryptedsnapshot",
      "--kms-key-id ${aws_kms_key.rds.arn}"
    ])
```

```
        }
    }
```

Encrypting data at rest on S3

With S3, there are four options for encryption:

- AWS-managed CMKs
- Customer-managed CMKs
- S3-managed encryption keys
- Customer-provided encryption keys

To continue with the theme of using customer-provided CMKs to retain control of how the keys are used, this recipe focused on the second option. To see the last option in action, see Recipe 4.5. Depending on your use case, you also need to look into how objects stored in your bucket are encrypted. Imagine a case where some highly sensitive objects need to be encrypted with a specific KMS key, not the bucket default. By using bucket policies, you can force users to conform to certain encryption standards. Let's look at two examples, enforcing that KMS is used for the objects, and enforcing that a specific KMS key is used.

The following bucket policy enforces that a KMS key must be used:

```
data "aws_iam_policy_document" "kms_enforcement" {
  statement {
    effect = "Deny"

    actions = ["s3:PutObject"]

    resources = ["${aws_s3_bucket.kms_enforcement.arn}/*"]

    principals {
      type        = "*"
      identifiers = ["*"]
    }

    condition {
      test     = "StringNotEquals"
      values   = ["aws:kms"]
      variable = "s3:x-amz-server-side-encryption"
    }
  }
}
```

The following bucket policy enforces that a specific KMS key be used:

```
data "aws_iam_policy_document" "specific_kms_enforcement" {
  statement {
    effect = "Deny"
```

```
    actions = ["s3:PutObject"]

    resources = ["${aws_s3_bucket.specific_kms_enforcement.arn}/*"]

    principals {
      type        = "*"
      identifiers = ["*"]
    }

    condition {
      test     = "StringNotEquals"
      values   = [aws_kms_key.s3.arn]
      variable = "s3:x-amz-server-side-encryption-aws-kms-key-id"
    }
  }
}
```

Summary

Let's summarize what was learned and deployed in this recipe:

- On AWS, your core service for encryption is KMS.
- AWS provides AWS-managed KMS keys that are used for default encryption of resources.
- KMS allows you to create customer-managed keys.
- By creating customer-managed CMKs, you can explicitly control and audit usage.
- Many resources on AWS need to be recreated to enable data-at-rest encryption.
- Some resources allow you to set specific policies governing how users interact with them, allowing you to enforce encryption standards.

4.3 Encrypting Data at Rest on Azure

Problem

As part of securely hosting data on Azure, you need to be able to encrypt data at rest on the most common storage options available.

Solution

If you haven't already done so, familiarize yourself with Terraform and the different authentication mechanisms in Chapter 11.

Create a *variables.tf* file and copy the following contents:

```
variable "location" {
  type        = string
  description = "The location to deploy your resource into"
}

variable "storage_account_name" {
  type        = string
  description = "The name of the storage account"
}
```

Then fill out the corresponding *terraform.tfvars* file:

```
location             = ""
storage_account_name = ""
```

Create the following *provider.tf* file and run `terraform init`:

```
terraform {
  required_providers {
    azurerm = {
      source  = "hashicorp/azurerm"
      version = "~> 2"
    }
    random = {
      source  = "hashicorp/random"
      version = "~> 3"
    }
  }
}

provider "azurerm" {
  features {}
}
```

Create the following *main.tf* file:

```
resource "random_string" "key_vault" {
  length  = 16
  special = false
}

data "azurerm_client_config" "current" {}

resource "azurerm_resource_group" "encrypted" {
  name     = "encrypted"
  location = var.location
}

resource "azurerm_key_vault" "keys" {
  name                     = random_string.key_vault.result
  location                 = azurerm_resource_group.encrypted_blobs.location
  resource_group_name      = azurerm_resource_group.encrypted_blobs.name
  tenant_id                = data.azurerm_client_config.current.tenant_id
  enabled_for_disk_encryption = true
```

```
  soft_delete_retention_days  = 7
  purge_protection_enabled    = true
  sku_name                    = "standard"
}

resource "azurerm_key_vault_key" "key" {
  name         = "key"
  key_vault_id = azurerm_key_vault.keys.id
  key_type     = "RSA"
  key_size     = 2048
  key_opts     = ["decrypt", "encrypt", "sign", "unwrapKey", "verify", "wrapKey"]
}

resource "azurerm_key_vault_access_policy" "client" {
  key_vault_id = azurerm_key_vault.keys.id
  tenant_id    = data.azurerm_client_config.current.tenant_id
  object_id    = data.azurerm_client_config.current.object_id

  key_permissions    = ["get", "create", "delete"]
  secret_permissions = ["get"]
}
```

To create an encrypted managed disk, add the following resources to *main.tf*:

```
resource "azurerm_disk_encryption_set" "des" {
  name                = "des"
  resource_group_name = azurerm_resource_group.encrypted_blobs.name
  location            = azurerm_resource_group.encrypted_blobs.location
  key_vault_key_id    = azurerm_key_vault_key.blob.id

  identity {
    type = "SystemAssigned"
  }
}

resource "azurerm_key_vault_access_policy" "disk" {
  key_vault_id = azurerm_key_vault.keys.id

  tenant_id = azurerm_disk_encryption_set.des.identity.0.tenant_id
  object_id = azurerm_disk_encryption_set.des.identity.0.principal_id

  key_permissions = [
    "Get",
    "WrapKey",
    "UnwrapKey"
  ]
}

resource "azurerm_managed_disk" "encrypted" {
  name                = "encryption-test"
  location            = azurerm_resource_group.encrypted_blobs.location
  resource_group_name = azurerm_resource_group.encrypted_blobs.name
  storage_account_type = "Standard_LRS"
```

```
      create_option         = "Empty"
      disk_size_gb           = "1"
      disk_encryption_set_id = azurerm_disk_encryption_set.des.id
    }
```

To create an encrypted database, add the following resources to *main.tf*:

```
    resource "azurerm_postgresql_server" "database" {
      name                    = "encrypted-database"
      location                = azurerm_resource_group.encrypted_blobs.location
      resource_group_name     = azurerm_resource_group.encrypted_blobs.name

      administrator_login          = "postgres"
      administrator_login_password = random_password.database.result

      sku_name   = "GP_Gen5_2"
      version    = "11"
      storage_mb = 5120

      ssl_enforcement_enabled = true

      threat_detection_policy {
        disabled_alerts     = []
        email_account_admins = false
        email_addresses     = []
        enabled             = true
        retention_days      = 0
      }

      identity {
        type = "SystemAssigned"
      }
    }
```

To create an encrypted storage account, add the following resources to *main.tf*:

```
    resource "azurerm_key_vault_access_policy" "storage" {
      key_vault_id = azurerm_key_vault.keys.id
      tenant_id    = data.azurerm_client_config.current.tenant_id
      object_id    = azurerm_storage_account.sensitive.identity.0.principal_id

      key_permissions    = ["get", "unwrapkey", "wrapkey"]
      secret_permissions = ["get"]
    }

    resource "azurerm_storage_account" "sensitive" {
      name                     = var.storage_account_name
      resource_group_name      = azurerm_resource_group.encrypted_blobs.name
      location                 = azurerm_resource_group.encrypted_blobs.location
      account_tier             = "Standard"
      account_replication_type = "LRS"

      identity {
        type = "SystemAssigned"
```

```
    }
  }

  resource "azurerm_storage_account_customer_managed_key" "sensitive" {
    storage_account_id = azurerm_storage_account.sensitive.id
    key_vault_id       = azurerm_key_vault.keys.id
    key_name           = azurerm_key_vault_key.blob.name
  }
```

Review the resources to be created by running `terraform plan`, and then run `terraform apply` to make the changes.

Discussion

In this recipe, you saw how to deploy the following resources with the data encrypted at rest:

- Managed disks
- PostgreSQL databases
- Storage accounts

 This recipe used a single, shared key within the Key Vault to secure all the resources deployed. In a normal scenario, you should be using multiple keys to enable finely grained access control and limit the blast radius of a breach.

This brings us to the topic of how IAM is applied in the context of Key Vaults in Azure. In this recipe, you defined multiple different access policies which enabled the specific required usage of the different principals. First was the `0_key_vault_access_policy` `client` resource, ensuring that the principal who created the vault retained the ability to create and delete keys as required.

Then as you created the workload resources, each time in turn you needed to apply a distinct access policy to allow the managed identity to perform the required operations with the key. In all three cases, the identity can only perform the `get`, `unwrap key`, and `wrapkey` operations, the minimum set of permissions required. As a further step, you could extend the recipe to not leverage `SystemAssigned` identities, instead defining your own to further segment who can leverage what keys. Rather than having a shared system identity between resources, by them having distinct identities with access to different keys, you can handle different levels of data sensitivity.

It's one thing to enable encryption on the resources that you own and control. The next step is understanding where other people are not conforming to the same approach. How can you know when people are not correctly using CMKs? For that, you need to turn to Azure Policy. Let's look at how you can apply policies to subscriptions that hold sensitive data and identify where CMKs have not been used for the three resources looked at in this recipe.

You can extend this recipe with the following variable:

```
variable "sensitive_subscription_ids" {
  type        = list(string)
  description = "The IDs of the sensitive data subscriptions"
}
```

And then add the following data provider and resources to apply the policy to the selected subscriptions:

```
data "azurerm_subscription" "subscription" {
  for_each        = toset(var.sensitive_subscription_ids)
  subscription_id = each.value
}

resource "azurerm_policy_assignment" "storage_cmk" {
  for_each = toset(var.sensitive_subscription_ids)
  name     = "storage-cmk-${each.value}"
  scope    = data.azurerm_subscription.subscription[each.value].id
  policy_definition_id = join("", [
    "/providers/Microsoft.Authorization/policyDefinitions/",
    "b5ec538c-daa0-4006-8596-35468b9148e8"
  ])
}

resource "azurerm_policy_assignment" "postgres_cmk" {
  for_each = toset(var.sensitive_subscription_ids)
  name     = "postgres-cmk-${each.value}"
  scope    = data.azurerm_subscription.subscription[each.value].id
  policy_definition_id = join("", [
    "/providers/Microsoft.Authorization/policyDefinitions/",
    "18adea5e-f416-4d0f-8aa8-d24321e3e274"
  ])
}

resource "azurerm_policy_assignment" "disk_cmk" {
  for_each = toset(var.sensitive_subscription_ids)
  name     = "disk-cmk-${each.value}"
  scope    = data.azurerm_subscription.subscription[each.value].id
  policy_definition_id = join("", [
    "/providers/Microsoft.Authorization/policyDefinitions/",
    "702dd420-7fcc-42c5-afe8-4026edd20fe0"
  ])
}
```

Summary

Let's summarize what was learned and deployed in this recipe:

- On Azure, for key management, you create keys within Key Vaults.

- By applying access policies to your vaults, you can control who has access to keys.

- You should have separate identities for managing keys and using keys.

- Giving access to resources to leverage customer-managed keys involves giving their identity access.

- You can either give access to the `SystemAssigned` identity or create and manage identities yourself.

- You created an encrypted storage account, PostgreSQL database, and disk.

- By assigning Azure Policies to subscriptions, you can detect where people are not leveraging CMKs when required.

4.4 Encrypting Data on GCP with Your Own Keys

Problem

Compliance requirements dictate that particular data on GCP be stored with encryption keys created and managed by the internal systems.

Solution

If you haven't already done so, familiarize yourself with Terraform and the different authentication mechanisms in Chapter 11.

Create a *variables.tf* file and copy the following contents:

```
variable "project_id" {
  type        = string
  description = "The project to create the resources in"
}

variable "region" {
  type        = string
  description = "The region to create the resources in"
}
```

Then fill out the corresponding *terraform.tfvars* file:

```
project_id = ""
region     = ""
```

Create the following *provider.tf* file and run `terraform init`:

```
provider "google" {
  project = var.project_id
  region  = var.region
}
```

```
terraform {
  required_providers {
    google = {
      source  = "hashicorp/google"
      version = "~> 3"
    }
  }
}
```

Create the following *main.tf* file and run `terraform plan`:

```
data "google_project" "current" {}

resource "google_storage_bucket" "csek" {
  name          = "${data.google_project.current.project_id}-csek"
  force_destroy = true
  location      = var.region
}

output "storage_bucket_name" {
  value = google_storage_bucket.csek.name
}
```

Review the resources that are going to be created, and then run `terraform apply` to make the changes.

Install the pycryptodomex and `google-cloud-storage` libraries by running `pip install pycryptodomex google-cloud-storage`.

This code is just demonstrative for the recipe. You should use specialized software for the creation and management of your keys.

Create the following *generate_data_key.py* file and run `python generate_data_key.py` to create a local *key* file.

```
import base64

from Cryptodome.Random import get_random_bytes

key = get_random_bytes(32)
print(key)
with open("key", "w") as file:
    file.write(str(base64.b64encode(key), "utf-8"))
```

Copy a file you wish to store encrypted into your working directory.

Create the following *upload_file.py* file:

```
import base64
import sys
from subprocess import run

from google.cloud import storage


def upload(file_name):
    storage_client = storage.Client()
    bucket_name = (
        run(
            "terraform output storage_bucket_name",
            capture_output=True,
            check=True,
            shell=True,
        )
        .stdout.decode("utf-8")
        .split('"')[1]
    )
    bucket = storage_client.bucket(bucket_name)

    with open("key", "r") as file:
        encryption_key = base64.b64decode(file.read())
        blob = bucket.blob(file_name, encryption_key=encryption_key)

        blob.upload_from_filename(file_name)


if __name__ == "__main__":
    upload(sys.argv[1])
```

To upload your file to the Cloud Storage bucket, run `python upload_file.py` with
the name of your file. For example, run `python upload_file.py message.txt`.

Discussion

The following Python *download_file.py* file will download your file to your local
directory:

```
import base64
import sys
from subprocess import run

from google.cloud import storage


def download(file_key, file_name):
    storage_client = storage.Client()
    bucket_name = (
        run(
            "terraform output storage_bucket_name",
            capture_output=True,
```

```
            check=True,
            shell=True,
        )
        .stdout.decode("utf-8")
        .split('"')[1]
    )
    bucket = storage_client.bucket(bucket_name)

    with open("key", "r") as file:
        encryption_key = base64.b64decode(file.read())
        blob = bucket.blob(file_key, encryption_key=encryption_key)

        blob.download_to_filename(file_name)


if __name__ == "__main__":
    download(sys.argv[1], sys.argv[2])
```

To execute the code, run `python download_file.py` with the name of the file you uploaded, and the filename to use for the copy. For example, run `python download_file.py message.txt message_copy.txt`.

> Files stored with this encryption mechanism cannot be uploaded or downloaded through the console.

Managing your own keys quickly becomes a laborious practice. The burden of rotating, securing, and providing access to keys is something that should only be shouldered when explicitly required. For the vast majority of use cases, Cloud KMS should suffice, or potentially use Cloud Hardware Security Module (HSM), which allows you to leverage fully managed FIPS 140-2 Level 3 certified HSMs.

If it is required that key material exist outside GCP, then use the Cloud External Key Manager (Cloud EKM). This allows you to leverage third-party key management services from vendors such as the following:

- Fortanix
- Ionic
- Thales
- Equinix SmartKey
- Unbound Tech

This offering is only supported on a small subset of services, including the following:

- Compute Engine
- Secrets Manager
- Cloud SQL

Summary

Let's summarize what was learned and deployed in this recipe:

- On GCP you can create and use your own encryption keys, known as customer-supplied encryption keys, or CSEKs.
- They can be used with Cloud Storage to encrypt objects, so only those who hold the key can decrypt them; even GCP cannot do so.
- You wrote Python for generating a key, and then using the key to upload and download files securely.
- CSEKs should only be used when absolutely required, as the maintenance burden is high.
- Other options other than Cloud KMS for encrypting data include Cloud HSM and Cloud EKM.

4.5 Encrypting Data on AWS with Your Own Keys

Problem

Compliance requirements dictate that particular data on AWS be stored with encryption keys created and managed by the business's internal systems.

Solution

If you haven't already done so, familiarize yourself with Terraform and the different authentication mechanisms in Chapter 11.

Create the following *provider.tf* file and run `terraform init`:

```
provider "aws" {}

terraform {
  required_providers {
    aws = {
      source  = "hashicorp/aws"
      version = "~> 3"
    }
```

```
  }
}
```

Create the following *main.tf* file and run `terraform plan`:

```
resource "aws_s3_bucket" "bucket" {}

output "bucket_name" {
  value = aws_s3_bucket.bucket.bucket
}
```

Review the resources that are going to be created, and then run `terraform apply` to make the changes.

Install the `pycryptodomex` and `boto3` libraries by running `pip install pycryptodo mex boto3`.

Create the following *generate_data_key.py* file and run `python generate_data_key.py` to create a local *key* file.

 This code is just demonstrative for the recipe. You should use specialized software for the creation and management of your keys.

```
import base64

from Cryptodome.Random import get_random_bytes

key = get_random_bytes(32)
print(key)
with open("key", "w") as file:
    file.write(str(base64.b64encode(key), "utf-8"))
```

Copy a file you wish to store encrypted into your working directory.

Create the following *put_object.py* file:

```
import base64
import subprocess
import sys

import boto3

filename = sys.argv[1]

bucket_name = (
    subprocess.run(
        "terraform output bucket_name",
        shell=True,
        check=True,
```

```
            capture_output=True,
        )
        .stdout.decode("utf-8")
        .split('"')[1]
)

with open("key", "r") as file:
    key = base64.b64decode(file.read())

s3 = boto3.client("s3")
with open(filename, "r") as file:
    s3.put_object(
        Body=file.read(),
        Bucket=bucket_name,
        Key=filename,
        SSECustomerAlgorithm="AES256",
        SSECustomerKey=key,
    )
```

To upload your file to the S3 bucket, run python put_object.py with the name of
your file. For example, run python put_object.py message.txt.

Discussion

The following Python *get_object.py* file will download your file to your local
directory:

```
import base64
import subprocess
import sys

import boto3

filename = sys.argv[1]

with open("key", "r") as file:
    key = base64.b64decode(file.read())

s3 = boto3.client("s3")
bucket_name = (
    subprocess.run(
        "terraform output bucket_name",
        shell=True,
        check=True,
        capture_output=True,
    )
    .stdout.decode("utf-8")
    .split('"')[1]
)
print(
    s3.get_object(
        Bucket=bucket_name,
```

```
        Key=filename,
        SSECustomerAlgorithm="AES256",
        SSECustomerKey=key,
    )["Body"]
    .read()
    .decode()
)
```

To execute the code, run python get_object.py with the name of the file you uploaded, and the filename to use for the copy. For example, run python get_object.py message.txt message_copy.txt.

 Objects stored with this encryption mechanism cannot be uploaded or downloaded through the console.

Customer-supplied encryption keys should only be used when it is necessary that the key material be created, managed, and owned outside of AWS. Where possible, you should look to leverage AWS KMS to create and manage keys. By creating them yourself, you take on a much larger burden of responsibility. The processes of protecting, serving, and rotating keys all become areas where you need to invest significant time.

In "Encrypting data at rest on S3" on page 136, you saw a bucket policy that enforced that consumers use a KMS key to encrypt their objects. Following is a Terraform data provider snippet that configures a similar policy that ensures that users encrypt objects with an AES256 key:

```
data "aws_iam_policy_document" "kms_enforcement" {
  statement {
    effect = "Deny"

    actions = ["s3:PutObject"]

    resources = ["${aws_s3_bucket.kms_enforcement.arn}/*"]

    principals {
      type        = "*"
      identifiers = ["*"]
    }

    condition {
      test     = "StringNotEquals"
      values   = ["AES256"]
      variable = "s3:x-amz-server-side-encryption"
    }
  }
}
```

Because AWS does not store any information related to the customer-supplied key, there is no policy that allows you to enforce that a specific key is used, as there is with KMS managed keys.

Summary

Let's summarize what was learned and deployed in this recipe:

- On AWS, you can supply your own encryption keys to store objects in S3, known as customer-supplied keys.
- As the keys are not stored on AWS, you prevent anyone without direct access to the keys from accessing the objects.
- By adopting this technique, you shoulder the large burden of key rotation, access, and creation.
- In order to use a customer-supplied key, you will need to provide it for both storing and retrieving objects.
- It is possible to enforce the use of encryption keys with bucket policies.

4.6 Encrypting Data on Azure with Your Own Keys

Problem

Compliance requirements dictate that particular data on Azure be stored with encryption keys created and managed by the businesses internal systems.

Solution

If you haven't already done so, familiarize yourself with Terraform and the different authentication mechanisms in Chapter 11.

Create a *variables.tf* file and copy the following contents:

```
variable "location" {
  type        = string
  description = "The location to deploy your resource into"
}

variable "storage_account_name" {
  type        = string
  description = "The name of the storage account"
}
```

Then fill out the corresponding *terraform.tfvars* file:

```
location             = ""
storage_account_name = ""
```

Create the following *provider.tf* file, and run `terraform init`:

```
terraform {
  required_providers {
    azurerm = {
      source  = "hashicorp/azurerm"
      version = "~> 2"
    }
  }
}

provider "azurerm" {
  features {}
}
```

Create the following *main.tf* file and run `terraform plan`:

```
resource "azurerm_resource_group" "csks" {
  name     = "csks"
  location = var.location
}

resource "azurerm_storage_account" "csk" {
  name                     = var.storage_account_name
  resource_group_name      = azurerm_resource_group.csks.name
  location                 = azurerm_resource_group.csks.location
  account_tier             = "Standard"
  account_replication_type = "LRS"
}

resource "azurerm_storage_container" "csk" {
  name                  = "csk"
  storage_account_name  = azurerm_storage_account.csk.name
  container_access_type = "private"
}

output "connection_string" {
  value     = azurerm_storage_account.csk.primary_connection_string
  sensitive = true
}

output "container_name" {
  value = azurerm_storage_container.csk.name
}
```

Review the resources that are going to be created, and then run `terraform apply` to make the changes.

Install the `pycryptodomex`, `azure-storage-blob`, and `azure-identity` libraries by running `pip install pycryptodomex azure-storage-blob azure-identity`.

This code is just demonstrative for the recipe. You should use specialized software for the creation and management of your keys.

Create the following *generate_data_key.py* file and run python generate_data_key.py to create a local *key* file.

```python
import base64

from Cryptodome.Random import get_random_bytes

key = get_random_bytes(32)
print(key)
with open("key", "w") as file:
    file.write(str(base64.b64encode(key), "utf-8"))
```

Copy a file you wish to store encrypted into your working directory.

Create the following *upload_blob.py* file:

```python
import base64
import sys
from hashlib import sha256
from subprocess import run

from azure.identity import AzureCliCredential
from azure.storage.blob import BlobClient, CustomerProvidedEncryptionKey

conn_str = (
    run(
        "terraform output connection_string",
        shell=True,
        check=True,
        capture_output=True,
    )
    .stdout.decode("utf-8")
    .split('"')[1]
)

container_name = (
    run(
        "terraform output container_name",
        shell=True,
        check=True,
        capture_output=True,
    )
    .stdout.decode("utf-8")
    .split('"')[1]
)

credential = AzureCliCredential()
```

```
blob = BlobClient.from_connection_string(
    conn_str=conn_str, container_name=container_name, blob_name=sys.argv[1]
)

with open("key", "r") as file:
    key = file.read()
    hash = sha256(base64.b64decode(key))

with open(sys.argv[1], "rb") as file:
    blob.upload_blob(
        file,
        cpk=CustomerProvidedEncryptionKey(
            key, str(base64.b64encode(hash.digest()), "utf-8")
        ),
    )
```

To upload your file to the S3 bucket, run python upload_blob.py with the name of
your file. For example, run python upload_blob.py message.txt.

Discussion

The following Python *download_blob.py* file will download your file to your local
directory:

```
import base64
import sys
from hashlib import sha256
from subprocess import run

from azure.identity import AzureCliCredential
from azure.storage.blob import BlobClient, CustomerProvidedEncryptionKey

conn_str = (
    run(
        "terraform output connection_string",
        shell=True,
        check=True,
        capture_output=True,
    )
    .stdout.decode("utf-8")
    .split('"')[1]
)

container_name = (
    run(
        "terraform output container_name",
        shell=True,
        check=True,
        capture_output=True,
    )
    .stdout.decode("utf-8")
    .split('"')[1]
```

```
)

credential = AzureCliCredential()
blob = BlobClient.from_connection_string(
    conn_str=conn_str, container_name=container_name, blob_name=sys.argv[1]
)

with open("key", "r") as file:
    key = file.read()
    hash = sha256(base64.b64decode(key))

with open(f"{sys.argv[1]}_copy", "wb") as file:
    data = blob.download_blob(
        cpk=CustomerProvidedEncryptionKey(
            key, str(base64.b64encode(hash.digest()), "utf-8")
        )
    )
    data.readinto(file)
```

To execute the code, run python download_blog.py with the name of the file you uploaded and the filename to use for the copy. For example, run python down load_blog.py message.txt message_copy.txt.

> Blobs stored with this encryption mechanism cannot be uploaded or downloaded through the console.

This recipe is needed due to internal requirements at some businesses. However, if you do not explicitly need to use keys created and managed outside of Azure, you should look to leverage customer-managed keys wherever possible. In using customer-supplied keys, as in this recipe, you take on the nontrivial burden of key management, security, rotation, and provisioning.

Another option is uploading your externally created keys to Azure, so you can leverage them through the normal Azure APIs the same way you would a customer-managed key. That allows you to use your own keys with services outside of storage, as customer-supplied keys as shown in this recipe cannot be used with the majority of services.

Summary

Let's summarize what was learned and deployed in this recipe:

- On Azure, you can use what are known as customer-supplied keys for encrypting data at rest.

- The keys are securely discarded when used through API calls and are never persisted in Azure.

- The main service that can use these keys is storage.

- By using customer-supplied keys, you accept a large burden of responsibility and effort.

- You should only use this approach when it is explicitly required.

4.7 Enforcing In-Transit Data Encryption on GCP

Problem

As delivery teams are rapidly standing up infrastructure across your estate, you need to ensure that, wherever possible, data is encrypted in transit.

Solution

If you haven't already done so, familiarize yourself with Terraform and the different authentication mechanisms in Chapter 11.

Create a *variables.tf* file and copy the following contents:

```
variable "project_id" {
  type        = string
  description = "The project to create the resources in"
}

variable "region" {
  type        = string
  description = "The region to create the resources in"
}

variable "organization_domain" {
  type        = string
  description = "The organization domain of your Google Cloud estate"
}
```

Then fill out the corresponding *terraform.tfvars* file:

```
project_id          = ""
region              = ""
organization_domain = ""
```

Create the following *provider.tf* file and run `terraform init`:

```
provider "google" {
  project = var.project_id
  region  = var.region
}
```

```
terraform {
  required_providers {
    google = {
      source  = "hashicorp/google"
      version = "~> 3"
    }
    null = {
      source  = "hashicorp/null"
      version = "~> 3"
    }
  }
}
```

Create the following *main.tf* file and run `terraform plan`:

```
data "google_organization" "current" {
  domain = var.organization_domain
}

data "google_project" "current" {}

resource "google_project_service" "cloud_asset" {
  service = "cloudasset.googleapis.com"
}

resource "null_resource" "cloudasset_service_account" {
  provisioner "local-exec" {
    command = join(" ", [
      "gcloud beta services identity create",
      "--service=cloudasset.googleapis.com",
      "--project=${var.project_id}"
    ])
  }

  depends_on = [
    google_project_service.cloud_asset
  ]
}

resource "google_bigquery_dataset" "assets" {
  dataset_id                = "assets"
  delete_contents_on_destroy = true
}

resource "google_project_iam_member" "asset_sa_editor_access" {
  role   = "roles/bigquery.dataEditor"
  member = join("",[
    "serviceAccount:service-",
    data.google_project.current.number,
    "@gcp-sa-cloudasset.iam.gserviceaccount.com"
  ])

  depends_on = [
```

```
        null_resource.cloudasset_service_account
  ]
}

resource "google_project_iam_member" "asset_sa_user_access" {
  role   = "roles/bigquery.user"
  member = join("",[
    "serviceAccount:service-",
    data.google_project.current.number,
    "@gcp-sa-cloudasset.iam.gserviceaccount.com"
  ])

  depends_on = [
    null_resource.cloudasset_service_account
  ]
}

resource "null_resource" "run_export" {
  provisioner "local-exec" {
    command = join(" ", [
      "gcloud asset export --content-type resource",
      "--project ${data.google_project.current.project_id},",
      "--bigquery-table ${google_bigquery_dataset.assets.id}/tables/assets,",
      "--output-bigquery-force --per-asset-type"
    ])
  }

  depends_on = [
    google_project_iam_member.asset_sa_editor_access,
    google_project_iam_member.asset_sa_user_access
  ]
}
```

Review the resources that are going to be created, and then run `terraform apply` to make the changes.

Discussion

This recipe created a BigQuery dataset with a table per resource for all the projects in your organization. With that dataset created, you are now able to query details of resource configurations to find where unencrypted traffic is possible.

Recipe 3.10 introduced Cloud Asset registry and built out a mechanism for alerting you when particular resources changed. This recipe extended that to add an ability to retroactively ask questions about your estate. This allows you to determine non-compliant resources as your control set grows and matures.

Finding firewall rules with insecure ports

Following is a BigQuery query which will find all firewall rules that allow access on the following three unencrypted ports:

- 21, unencrypted FTP traffic
- 80, unencrypted HTTP traffic
- 3306, unencrypted MySQL traffic

```
SELECT * FROM
(
    SELECT name, allowed.ports as ports FROM
    `<project-id>.assets.assets_compute_googleapis_com_Firewall`
    as firewall
    JOIN UNNEST(firewall.resource.data.allowed) as allowed
)
WHERE ARRAY_TO_STRING(ports, "") = "20"
OR ARRAY_TO_STRING(ports, "") = "21"
OR ARRAY_TO_STRING(ports, "") = "3306"
```

Finding load balancers accepting HTTP traffic

As a general rule, web load balancers should be configured to accept HTTPS traffic, not HTTP traffic. The following query identifies the load balancer target proxies that are configured for HTTP traffic:

```
SELECT resource.data.name, updateTime, resource.parent FROM
`<project-id>.assets.assets_compute_googleapis_com_TargetHttpProxy`
```

As you can see from these examples, you can write queries to determine what resources match a particular state and return when they were last modified and what project they are under. Unfortunately, the export cannot be configured to automatically run on a schedule, but by using Cloud Functions, as shown in Recipe 6.4, you can build a simple scheduler to run the export. This, coupled with BigQuery scheduled queries, enables you to determine when resources fall outside of your encryption requirements.

Summary

Let's summarize what was learned and deployed in this recipe:

- On GCP, you can use Cloud Asset Inventory and BigQuery to dynamically understand how resources are configured.
- This combines with the automated notification component of Recipe 3.10.
- However, it allows you to look at all current resources, as opposed to only acting when a resource is changed.

- You created a BigQuery dataset and exported all resources in your estate into distinct tables.
- Then you saw some example queries of determining when resources are allowing insecure traffic.
- By adding scheduled Cloud Functions and scheduled BigQuery queries, you can build a solution to alert on any configuration you desire.

4.8 Enforcing In-Transit Data Encryption on AWS

Problem

As delivery teams are rapidly standing up infrastructure across your estate, you need to ensure that, wherever possible, data is encrypted in transit.

Solution

If you haven't already done so, familiarize yourself with Terraform and the different authentication mechanisms in Chapter 11.

If you have not previously completed Recipe 3.11, go and do that first so that AWS Config is enabled in your accounts.

Create the following *provider.tf* file and run `terraform init`:

```
provider "aws" {}

terraform {
  required_providers {
    aws = {
      source  = "hashicorp/aws"
      version = "~> 3"
    }
  }
}
```

Create the following *main.tf* file and run `terraform plan`:

```
locals {
  rules_to_deploy = [
    "ALB_HTTP_TO_HTTPS_REDIRECTION_CHECK",
    "API_GW_SSL_ENABLED",
    "ELB_TLS_HTTPS_LISTENERS_ONLY",
    "REDSHIFT_REQUIRE_TLS_SSL",
    "RESTRICTED_INCOMING_TRAFFIC",
    "S3_BUCKET_SSL_REQUESTS_ONLY",
    "VPC_SG_OPEN_ONLY_TO_AUTHORIZED_PORTS"
  ]
}
```

```
resource "aws_config_config_rule" "rule" {
  for_each = toset(local.rules_to_deploy)
  name = each.value

  source {
    owner = "AWS"
    source_identifier = each.value
  }
}
```

Review the resources that are going to be created, and then run `terraform apply` to make the changes.

Discussion

This recipe deployed the following series of Managed AWS Config rules to the account that detect when resources are configured to allow certain kinds of unencrypted traffic:

ALB_HTTP_TO_HTTPS_REDIRECTION_CHECK
> Checks whether Application Load Balancers allow straight HTTP traffic; ideally they automatically redirect clients to HTTPs.

API_GW_SSL_ENABLED
> Checks whether an SSL certificate has been configured for the API Gateway. Without one, you cannot handle encrypted traffic.

ELB_TLS_HTTPS_LISTENERS_ONLY
> Checks whether Elastic Load Balancers have listeners for HTTP traffic.

REDSHIFT_REQUIRE_TLS_SSL
> Checks whether your Redshift data warehouse only accepts SSL/TLS-based traffic.

RESTRICTED_INCOMING_TRAFFIC
> Checks whether security groups allow traffic on ports that have secure variants; by default, they are 20, 21, 3389, 3306, and 4333. But this rule can be configured to check for specific ports.

S3_BUCKET_SSL_REQUESTS_ONLY
> Checks whether S3 buckets allow direct HTTP traffic.

VPC_SG_OPEN_ONLY_TO_AUTHORIZED_PORTS
> Checks whether any security groups with inbound traffic from 0.0.0.0/0 have any ports configured outside an approved list that you control.

Analyzing VPC flow logs is another way to solve the problem of detecting unencrypted traffic. However, to automate the process would require a third-party application or an internal development effort.

In Recipe 7.8, you'll see what options exist for actively preventing people from being able to deploy noncompliant infrastructure, but the strategies are not foolproof. This necessitates the ability for you to operate in the same "trust but verify" posture that is a common theme across recipes. In this case, the verification stems from the rules, creating a feedback loop that allows you to understand when teams are in need of support and enablement.

Summary

Let's summarize what was learned and deployed in this recipe:

- AWS provides a selection of managed Config rules that identify when resources allow for unencrypted traffic.
- They do not cover all resources; however, they do target common culprits.
- Actively preventing noncompliant infrastructure is never foolproof, but by configuring AWS Config rules, you have a feedback loop that allows you to understand when infrastructure doesn't meet the required controls.
- By combining this recipe with Recipe 7.8, you'll be able to deploy these rules across all accounts in the organization, allowing you to see into every account.

4.9 Enforcing In-Transit Data Encryption on Azure

Problem

As delivery teams are rapidly standing up infrastructure across your estate, you need to ensure that, wherever possible, data is encrypted in transit.

Solution

If you haven't already done so, familiarize yourself with Terraform and the different authentication mechanisms in Chapter 11.

Create the following *provider.tf* file and run `terraform init`:

```
terraform {
  required_providers {
    azurerm = {
      source  = "hashicorp/azurerm"
      version = "~> 2"
```

```
      }
    }
  }

  provider "azurerm" {
    features {}
  }
```

Create the following *main.tf* file and run `terraform plan`:

```
data "azurerm_subscription" "current" {}

locals {
  policy_ids = [
    "b7ddfbdc-1260-477d-91fd-98bd9be789a6",
    "e802a67a-daf5-4436-9ea6-f6d821dd0c5d",
    "d158790f-bfb0-486c-8631-2dc6b4e8e6af",
    "399b2637-a50f-4f95-96f8-3a145476eb15",
    "4d24b6d4-5e53-4a4f-a7f4-618fa573ee4b",
    "9a1b8c48-453a-4044-86c3-d8bfd823e4f5",
    "6d555dd1-86f2-4f1c-8ed7-5abae7c6cbab",
    "22bee202-a82f-4305-9a2a-6d7f44d4dedb",
    "404c3081-a854-4457-ae30-26a93ef643f9",
    "8cb6aa8b-9e41-4f4e-aa25-089a7ac2581e",
    "f9d614c5-c173-4d56-95a7-b4437057d193",
    "f0e6e85b-9b9f-4a4b-b67b-f730d42f1b0b",
    "a4af4a39-4135-47fb-b175-47fbdf85311d",
  ]
  policy_assignments = azurerm_subscription_policy_assignment.transit
}

resource "azurerm_subscription_policy_assignment" "transit" {
  count              = length(local.policy_ids)
  name               = "transit${count.index}"
  policy_definition_id = join("", [
    "/providers/Microsoft.Authorization/policyDefinitions/",
    local.policy_ids[count.index]
  ])
  subscription_id    = data.azurerm_subscription.current.id
}

resource "azurerm_policy_remediation" "transit" {
  count              = length(local.policy_ids)
  name               = "transit${count.index}"
  scope              = data.azurerm_subscription.current.id
  policy_assignment_id = local.policy_assignments[count.index].id
}
```

Review the resources that are going to be created, and then run `terraform apply` to make the changes.

Discussion

In Security Center, the following list of recommendations specifically target encrypted data in transit:

- API App should only be accessible over HTTPS.
- Enforce SSL connection should be enabled for MySQL database servers.
- Enforce SSL connection should be enabled for PostgreSQL database servers.
- FTPS should be required in your API App.
- FTPS should be required in your Functions App.
- FTPS should be required in your Web App.
- Functions App should only be accessible over HTTPS.
- Only secure connections to your Redis Cache should be enabled.
- Secure transfer to storage accounts should be enabled.
- TLS should be updated to the latest version for your API App.
- TLS should be updated to the latest version for your Functions App.
- TLS should be updated to the latest version for your Web App.
- Web App should only be accessible over HTTPS.

In this recipe, the `local.policy_ids` variable contains the IDs for each of these recommendations. As Azure Policy is naturally extended over time, this recipe will need updating to be exhaustive for what policies are available. Additionally, with the automated remediation actions here, you can end up in a position where the infrastructure as code is no longer reflective of the reality on Azure. Remediating in this way should be a last resort; instead, by using Recipe 6.3, you will see how to support teams in deploying infrastructure that encrypts data in transit by default. You also run the risk of potentially breaking systems by changing active configurations, which can be politically challenging and erode trust.

By using these policies, you target common misconfigurations for encryption, but these policies alone are not sufficient for ensuring data encryption across your entire estate. Performing training sessions with delivery teams, running threat modelling sessions, and migrating to more cloud native services, such as containers and Recipe 6.6, will make it easier to understand how data moves around your estate, as Azure is more heavily leveraged to perform the heavy lifting when it comes to encryption.

Summary

Let's summarize what was learned and deployed in this recipe:

- Azure Security Center provides a series of recommendations on encryption in transit.
- By using the Azure Policies that underpin these recommendations, you can identify and remediate problematic infrastructure.
- Automated remediation actions, while powerful, can undermine infrastructure-as-code usage and potentially erode trust.
- These policies are a great starting point, but ensuring encryption in transit across the entire estate involves the following:
  — Training teams in the how and why of encryption in transit

  — Running threat modelling sessions

  — Providing teams with secure-by-default infrastructure patterns
- By migrating to more cloud native infrastructure such as Recipe 6.6, you can make it simpler to understand how encryption is implemented across your estate.

4.10 Preventing Data Loss on GCP

Problem

As more data is stored in your GCP organization, you need to identify where sensitive and PII data is stored and ensure that the correct controls are applied.

Solution

If you haven't already done so, familiarize yourself with Terraform and the different authentication mechanisms in Chapter 11.

You need to create a service account to interact with the Google Workspace APIs.

Create a *variables.tf* file and copy the following contents:

```
variable "project_id" {
  type        = string
  description = "The project to create the resources in"
}

variable "region" {
  type        = string
  description = "The region to create the resources in"
}

variable "organization_domain" {
  type        = string
  description = "The organization domain of your Google Cloud estate"
}
```

Then fill out the corresponding *terraform.tfvars* file:

```
project_id          = ""
region              = ""
organization_domain = ""
```

Create the following *provider.tf* file and run `terraform init`:

```
provider "google" {
  project = var.project_id
  region  = var.region
}

terraform {
  required_providers {
    google = {
      source  = "hashicorp/google"
      version = "~> 3"
    }
    local = {
      source  = "hashicorp/local"
      version = "~> 2"
    }
  }
}
```

Create the following *main.tf* file and run `terraform plan`:

```
data "google_organization" "current" {
  domain = var.organization_domain
}

resource "google_project_service" "dlp" {
  service = "dlp.googleapis.com"
}

resource "google_service_account" "dlp_admin" {
  account_id   = "dlp-admin"
  display_name = "Data Loss Prevention Configuration"
}

resource "google_organization_iam_member" "dlp_access" {
  org_id = data.google_organization.current.org_id
  role   = "roles/dlp.admin"
  member = "serviceAccount:${google_service_account.dlp_admin.email}"
}

resource "google_project_iam_member" "viewer" {
  role   = "roles/viewer"
  member = "serviceAccount:${google_service_account.dlp_admin.email}"
}

resource "google_project_iam_member" "dataset_owner" {
  role   = "roles/bigquery.dataOwner"
```

```
    member = "serviceAccount:${google_service_account.dlp_admin.email}"
}

resource "google_service_account_key" "dlp_admin" {
  service_account_id = google_service_account.dlp_admin.name
  public_key_type    = "TYPE_X509_PEM_FILE"
}

resource "local_file" "service_account" {
  content  = base64decode(google_service_account_key.dlp_admin.private_key)
  filename = "service_account.json"
}
```

Review the resources that are going to be created, and then run `terraform apply` to make the changes.

In a new directory, create a *variables.tf* file and copy the following contents:

```
variable "service_account_key_path" {
  type        = string
  description = "Path to where the service account key is located"
}

variable "project_id" {
  type        = string
  description = "The project to create the resources in"
}

variable "region" {
  type        = string
  description = "The region to create the resources in"
}

variable "bucket_path" {
  type        = string
  description = "The bucket path to inspect with DLP"
}
```

Then fill out the corresponding *terraform.tfvars* file:

```
service_account_key_path = ""
project_id               = ""
region                   = ""
bucket_path              = ""
```

Create the following *provider.tf* file and run `terraform init`:

```
provider "google" {
  project     = var.project_id
  region      = var.region
  credentials = var.service_account_key_path
}

terraform {
```

```
    required_providers {
      google = {
        source  = "hashicorp/google"
        version = "~> 3"
      }
    }
  }
}
```

Create the following *main.tf* file and run `terraform plan`:

```
data "google_project" "current" {}

resource "google_data_loss_prevention_inspect_template" "basic" {
  parent = data.google_project.current.id
}

resource "google_bigquery_dataset" "findings" {
  dataset_id                = "findings"
  delete_contents_on_destroy = true
}

resource "google_data_loss_prevention_job_trigger" "basic" {
  parent       = data.google_project.current.id
  display_name = "Scan ${var.bucket_path}"

  triggers {
    schedule {
      recurrence_period_duration = "86400s"
    }
  }

  inspect_job {
    inspect_template_name = google_data_loss_prevention_inspect_template.basic.id

    actions {
      save_findings {
        output_config {
          table {
            project_id = data.google_project.current.project_id
            dataset_id = google_bigquery_dataset.findings.dataset_id
          }
        }
      }
    }

    storage_config {
      cloud_storage_options {
        file_set {
          url = "gs://${var.bucket_path}/**"
        }
      }
      timespan_config {
        enable_auto_population_of_timespan_config = true
```

```
            timestamp_field {
              name = "timestamp"
            }
          }
        }
      }
    }
  }
}
```

Review the resources that are going to be created, and then run `terraform apply` to make the changes.

Discussion

This recipe configured GCP's Data Loss Prevention (DLP) solution and created a daily DLP that scans the created Cloud Storage bucket.

DLP on GCP is a multifaceted service that can integrate into a variety of applications and architectures to ensure that your data is classified and handled appropriately. In this instance, you have set up a scheduled job that scans a particular storage bucket. You may wonder why the recipe does not start scanning all the buckets that exist, and that is because DLP can quickly become an expensive service to operate. This recipe is a way of dipping your toe in the water without the risk of a scary bill arriving at the end of the month. Another option to explore when productionizing your DLP configuration is to sample data. This is where you make determinations on a random sample of the data, rather than having to process and pay for it all.

For the scanning of static data, DLP can also run jobs directly against BigQuery datasets and Datastore kinds, as well as Cloud Storage buckets, allowing you to understand where the most valuable data lies. Additionally, by automatically forwarding the findings into BigQuery, it is possible to dynamically query the output of DLP to ensure you can find and triage the highest-priority findings.

The service comes with over 140 preconfigured infoType detectors, allowing you to automatically identify common forms of PII, from Australian Medicare numbers, to US Social Security numbers, and everything in between. You can also construct your own detectors to classify data that is unique to your business.

In addition to identifying sensitive data, DLP also provides pseudonymization capabilities, allowing for the replacement of sensitive data with nonidentifying tokens, preserving the data utility while minimizing the data risk when it is used. You can also configure it to do automatic redaction, ensuring the PII is not allowed to cross security boundaries.

Common solutions in the space, although outside of the remit of the security function, are automatic data classifiers, where data is placed into a staging bucket before being processed and segregated into sensitive and nonsensitive data. Another option is constructing a Dataflow pipeline that automatically redacts and pseudonymizes data as it flows through in real time.

Summary

Let's summarize what was learned and deployed in this recipe:

- Google's Data Loss Prevention (DLP) service is critical to managing sensitive data at scale.
- You can leverage DLP to routinely scan storage locations to automatically classify data and report findings.
- The findings can be automatically forwarded into BigQuery, allowing you to query your data.
- DLP can get expensive at scale, so focusing your scans on particularly risky areas, using sampling and ensuring you only scan modified data, can keep it under control.
- DLP also provides other services, such as pseudonymization and redaction, allowing you to ensure that data can still be utilized but with significantly reduced risk.
- You created a DLP inspection template and a job trigger to automatically scan a Cloud Storage bucket every day.

4.11 Preventing Data Loss on AWS

Problem

As more data is stored in your AWS organization, you need to identify where sensitive and PII data is stored and ensure that the correct controls are applied.

Solution

If you haven't already done so, familiarize yourself with Terraform and the different authentication mechanisms in Chapter 11.

Create a *variables.tf* file and copy the following contents:

```
variable "delegated_admin_account" {
  type        = string
  description = "The account ID for the account to be the Config delegated admin"
}

variable "cross_account_role" {
  type        = string
```

```
    description = "The cross account role to assume"
}
```

Then fill out the corresponding *terraform.tfvars* file:

```
delegated_admin_account = ""
cross_account_role      = ""
```

Create the following *provider.tf* file and run `terraform init`:

```
provider "aws" {}

provider "aws" {
  alias = "delegated_admin_account"
  assume_role {
    role_arn = join("", [
      "arn:aws:iam::",
      var.delegated_admin_account,
      ":role/",
      var.cross_account_role
    ])
  }
}

terraform {
  required_providers {
    aws = {
      source  = "hashicorp/aws"
      version = "~> 3"
    }
  }
}
```

Create the following *main.tf* file and run `terraform plan`:

```
data "aws_organizations_organization" "this" {}

resource "aws_macie2_account" "payer" {}

resource "aws_macie2_organization_admin_account" "this" {
  admin_account_id = var.delegated_admin_account
  depends_on       = [aws_macie2_account.payer]
}

resource "aws_macie2_member" "account" {
  provider = aws.delegated_admin_account
  for_each = {
    for account in data.aws_organizations_organization.this.accounts :
    account.id => account if account.id != var.delegated_admin_account
  }
  account_id = each.value.id
  email      = each.value.email
  depends_on = [aws_macie2_organization_admin_account.this]
}
```

Review the resources that are going to be created, and then run `terraform apply` to make the changes.

Discussion

This recipe configured Amazon Macie, giving you a single view on PII data in S3 buckets across your organization.

Amazon Macie is a service focused on making the mass of objects in S3, in many cases terabytes to petabytes of data, understandable from a sensitivity perspective. One of the main features is the evaluation of S3 bucket configuration, looking at the following:

- Which buckets are publicly accessible for read or write operations
- Whether buckets have default encryption that is enforced by bucket policies
- Where buckets are shared, both within the organization and with external parties

On top of this, Amazon provides a variety of *managed data identifiers* that detect sensitive data, such as PII, PHI, and financial. Additionally, you create *custom data identifiers* to detect sensitive data that is unique to your organization or business domain. In doing so, you can cross-reference what is being stored with how it is being stored, ensuring that appropriate levels of protection are applied to your most sensitive assets.

Whenever Macie detects a potential issue, it raises a *finding*. Each finding provides a severity rating, information about the affected resource, and metadata about when and how Macie discovered the issue. These findings can be sent directly into AWS Security Hub, as was configured in Recipe 3.2. They are also automatically loaded on Amazon EventBridge, which allows you to create and trigger bespoke workflows upon certain findings being raised.

All this data is brought into a dashboard, giving you a simple visual way of identifying issues in your environment. By enabling Macie across the entire organization, this recipe allows you to review findings across all accounts from one central location.

In order for Macie to be able to read the data in buckets, where restrictive bucket policies are applied, you will need to ensure that a Macie service role exception is applied. For example, given a bucket policy that only allows a certain role to access the bucket, you need to add an extra condition for the Macie service role, like so:

```
data "aws_caller_identity" "current" {}

data "aws_iam_policy_document" "restricted" {
  statement {
    effect = "Deny"

    actions = ["s3:*"]
```

```
      resources = [
        "${aws_s3_bucket.bucket.arn}/*",
        aws_s3_bucket.bucket.arn
      ]

      principals {
        type        = "*"
        identifiers = ["*"]
      }

      condition {
        test     = "StringNotLike"
        values   = ["aws:PrincipalArn"]
        variable = join("", [
          "arn:aws:iam::",
          data.aws_caller_identity.account_id,
          ":role/RestrictedBucketAccessRole"
        ])
      }

      condition {
        test     = "StringNotLike"
        values   = ["aws:PrincipalArn"]
        variable = join("", [
          "arn:aws:iam::",
          data.aws_caller_identity.account_id,
          ":role/aws-service-role/macie.amazonaws.com/AWSServiceRoleForAmazonMacie"
        ])
      }
    }
  }
}
```

Summary

Let's summarize what was learned and deployed in this recipe:

- To prevent the loss of sensitive data in your estate, it is critical to know where the data is.
- Amazon Macie allows for the identification of sensitive data across your estate.
- Macie provides a variety of managed data identifiers that automatically classify data.
- It also looks at the configuration of the S3 buckets to identify potential issues.
- Issues discovered in configuration or data protection are raised as findings.
- This recipe configured Macie centrally, so all findings can be triaged and actioned from a single location.
- To get the best value from Macie, you may need to update bucket policies, allowing its service role to access the objects in the buckets.

4.12 Preventing Data Loss on Azure

Problem

As more data is stored in your Azure tenant, you need to identify where sensitive and PII data is stored and ensure that the correct controls are applied.

Solution

If you haven't already done so, familiarize yourself with Terraform and the different authentication mechanisms in Chapter 11.

Create a *variables.tf* file and copy the following contents:

```
variable "location" {
  type        = string
  description = "The location to deploy your resource into"
}

variable "purview_account_name" {
  type        = string
  description = "The name for the Purview account"
}

variable "storage_account_name" {
  type        = string
  description = "The name for the storage account"
}
```

Then fill out the corresponding *terraform.tfvars* file:

```
location             = ""
purview_account_name = ""
storage_account_name = ""
```

Create the following *provider.tf* file and run `terraform init`:

```
terraform {
  required_providers {
    azurerm = {
      source  = "hashicorp/azurerm"
      version = "~> 2"
    }
    local = {
      source  = "hashicorp/local"
      version = "~> 2"
    }
    null = {
      source  = "hashicorp/null"
      version = "~> 3"
    }
  }
}
```

```
}

provider "azurerm" {
  features {}
}
```

Install the `purviewcli` from the `purviewcli` GitHub (*https://github.com/tayganr/
purviewcli*). This recipe was developed against version 0.1.31, so it may require modification if you install a later version.

Create the following *main.tf* file and run `terraform plan`:

```
data "azurerm_client_config" "current" {}

data "azurerm_subscription" "current" {}

resource "azurerm_resource_group" "purview" {
  name     = "purview-resources"
  location = var.location
}

resource "azurerm_purview_account" "purview" {
  name                = var.purview_account_name
  resource_group_name = azurerm_resource_group.purview.name
  location            = azurerm_resource_group.purview.location
  sku_name            = "Standard_4"
}

resource "azurerm_role_assignment" "data_curator" {
  scope                = azurerm_purview_account.purview.id
  role_definition_name = "Purview Data Curator"
  principal_id         = data.azurerm_client_config.current.object_id
}

resource "azurerm_role_assignment" "data_source_admin" {
  scope                = azurerm_purview_account.purview.id
  role_definition_name = "Purview Data Source Administrator"
  principal_id         = data.azurerm_client_config.current.object_id
}

resource "azurerm_storage_account" "purview" {
  name                     = var.storage_account_name
  resource_group_name      = azurerm_resource_group.purview.name
  location                 = azurerm_resource_group.purview.location
  account_tier             = "Standard"
  account_replication_type = "GRS"

  identity {
    type = "SystemAssigned"
  }
}

resource "azurerm_storage_container" "purview" {
```

```
  name                = "purview"
  storage_account_name = azurerm_storage_account.purview.name
  container_access_type = "private"
}

resource "azurerm_role_assignment" "reader" {
  scope                = azurerm_storage_account.purview.id
  role_definition_name = "Storage Blob Data Reader"
  principal_id         = azurerm_purview_account.purview.identity[0].principal_id
}

resource "local_file" "storage_account" {
  filename = "blob_storage.json"
  content  = <<CONTENT
{
    "id": "datasources/AzureStorage",
    "kind": "AzureStorage",
    "name": "AzureStorage",
    "properties": {
        "collection": null,
        "endpoint": "${azurerm_storage_account.purview.primary_blob_endpoint}",
        "location": "${azurerm_resource_group.purview.location}",
        "parentCollection": null,
        "resourceGroup": "${azurerm_resource_group.purview.name}",
        "resourceName": "${azurerm_storage_account.purview.name}",
        "subscriptionId": "${data.azurerm_subscription.current.subscription_id}"
    }
}
CONTENT
}

resource "local_file" "scan" {
  filename = "scan.json"
  content  = <<CONTENT
{
    "kind": "AzureStorageMsi",
    "properties": {
        "scanRulesetName": "AzureStorage",
        "scanRulesetType": "System"
    }
}
CONTENT
}

resource "null_resource" "add_data_source" {
  provisioner "local-exec" {
    command = join(" ", [
      "pv scan putDataSource",
      "--dataSourceName=AzureStorage",
      "--payload-file=${local_file.storage_account.filename}",
      "--purviewName ${azurerm_purview_account.purview.name}"
    ])
```

```
    }
  }

  resource "null_resource" "create_scan" {
    provisioner "local-exec" {
        command = join(" ", [
        "pv scan putScan",
        "--dataSourceName=AzureStorage",
        "--scanName=storage",
        "--payload-file=${local_file.scan.filename}",
        "--purviewName ${azurerm_purview_account.purview.name}"
      ])
    }

    depends_on = [
      null_resource.add_data_source
    ]
  }

  resource "null_resource" "run_scan" {
    provisioner "local-exec" {
      command = join(" ", [
        "pv scan runScan",
        "--dataSourceName=AzureStorage",
        "--scanName=storage",
        "--purviewName ${azurerm_purview_account.purview.name}"
      ])
    }

    depends_on = [
      null_resource.create_scan
    ]
  }
```

Review the resources that are going to be created, and then run `terraform apply` to make the changes.

Discussion

This recipe created a Purview application and used it to scan a storage account for PII data.

Azure Purview is a unified data governance service. By leveraging its capabilities, you are able to classify the data across your estate automatically against a collection of default rules that Microsoft provides. With the potential scale and sprawl that Azure allows you to achieve, having the right tools in place to understand where data is and how it is protected is critical.

The default rules detect many kinds of PII, such as

- US/UK passport numbers
- Australian bank account numbers
- IP addresses

In order for Purview to be able to access the data, you need to give Purview managed identity access to the resources in your estate, which you did in the recipe through the creation of the `azurerm_role_assignment.reader` resource. By giving the identity the required permissions at high-level scopes, you can have the access filter down rather than directly applying it to every resource.

Additionally, as your use with Purview matures and scales, use collections to keep your data map manageable and enable more nuanced and flexible identity and access management. Here, you simply registered the resource under the default collection, but a common pattern includes segmenting by business unit. This also allows you to apply only relevant scans to each collection, ensuring performance and cost-effectiveness.

In this recipe, you executed an ad hoc scan, but for full production use, you need to decide how frequently to schedule the scans based on cost, risk, and value. To manage the cost aspect, it is also possible to run incremental scans so you focus on the new and the changed rather than redundantly scanning old data. Additionally, it is possible to build your own rules to classify data using RegEx and Bloom Filters, so you can identify the data that is specifically critical to your business.

Azure Purview also provides many integrations that allow it to operate in both a multicloud and hybrid cloud environment. Connectors already exist for services such as

- SAP HANA
- On-premise SQL server
- Amazon S3
- Google BigQuery

By supporting data sources outside of Azure as first-class citizens, Purview has the potential to be the centralized data governance tooling for any business with an Azure presence, ensuring that you can have a single pane of glass, a single classification engine, and no redundant effort when managing a suite of tools for a heterogeneous environment.

Summary

Let's summarize what was learned and deployed in this recipe:

- At scale, the hardest thing about data is understanding what you have and where it lives.
- Azure Purview is a centralized data governance platform that allows you to classify data.
- You deployed a Purview application and an Azure storage account to hold some sensitive data.
- By programmatically running scans, you can ensure that your data is classified.
- Scans can be configured to run on a schedule and against collections of resources.
- Azure Purview has first-class support for resources outside of Azure, allowing it to become a truly unified data governance tool and approach.

CHAPTER 5

Secure Networking

When designing networks in the cloud, the topologies are defined by software rather than the physical structure within the data centers. All three cloud providers allow you to define your own private networks, which you can then share or connect together to enable connectivity between disparate teams and applications. You can then subdivide these private networks into subnetworks, often shortened to subnets. Once the subnets are defined, how the clouds allow you to implement networking begins to vary, as you will see in the recipes in this chapter.

Building scalable, enterprise-level network topologies is possible on all three CSPs, and they all provide a variety of on-premises connectivity options. In this chapter, you will see how to build base networks that enable your traffic flow patterns, allow engineers to SSH and remote desktop protocol (RDP) onto machines using IAM for authentication rather than long-lived keys, build estate-wide network topologies to enable east-west and north-south traffic, build patterns for exposing applications to the internet, and provide private access to services.

> The wider technology industry is currently converging on the idea of zero-trust networking, which is where identity, not network address, is the primary currency for determining visibility and access.
>
> Using IP addresses as the base of your network security is useful as a coarse-grained, defense-in-depth approach, but you should use higher-level resources such as service accounts on GCP, security groups on AWS, or application security groups on Azure as the basis of your rules where possible.

Using route tables, you can also define different types of subnetworks, nominally public, private, and internal. Public subnets allow traffic from the outside world, private subnets allow traffic from within the internal network, and internal subnets allow traffic from within the local network.

5.1 Networking Foundations on GCP

Problem

For teams to be able to securely deploy workloads into GCP, they need to deploy a secure-by-default Virtual Private Cloud (VPC) for hosting the required resources.

Solution

This recipe creates a VPC that spans multiple regions, with firewall rules that mean resources are deployed with no access by default. The high-level architecture is shown in Figure 5-1.

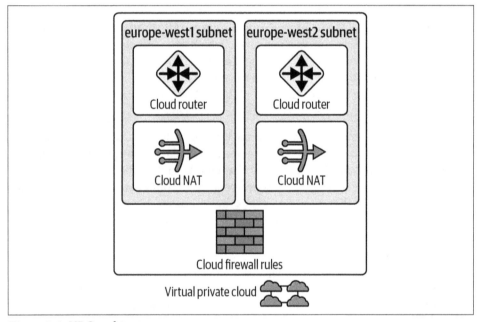

Figure 5-1. VPC architecture

If you haven't already done so, familiarize yourself with Terraform and the different authentication mechanisms in Chapter 11.

First, create the following *variables.tf* file:

```
variable "project" {
  type        = string
  description = "The project to deploy the resources into"
```

```
}

variable "region_subnets" {
  type        = map(any)
  description = "A map of region subnet pairings"
}
```

Then fill out the corresponding *terraform.tfvars* file:

```
project = ""
region_subnets = {
  "europe-west1": "10.0.0.0/24",
  ...
}
```

Create the following *provider.tf* file and run `terraform init`:

```
provider "google" {
  project = var.project
}

terraform {
  required_providers {
    google = {
      source  = "hashicorp/google"
      version = "~> 3"
    }
  }
}
```

Create the following *main.tf* file and run `terraform plan`:

```
resource "google_project_service" "compute_api" {
  service = "compute.googleapis.com"
}

resource "google_compute_network" "this" {
  name                            = "network"
  auto_create_subnetworks         = false
  delete_default_routes_on_create = true

  depends_on = [
    google_project_service.compute_api,
  ]
}

resource "google_compute_subnetwork" "subnet" {
  for_each      = var.region_subnets
  name          = each.key
  ip_cidr_range = each.value
  network       = google_compute_network.this.id
  region        = each.key
}
```

```
resource "google_compute_router" "r" {
  for_each = var.region_subnets
  name     = "router-${each.key}"
  network  = google_compute_network.this.id
  region   = each.key
}

resource "google_compute_router_nat" "nat" {
  for_each                           = var.region_subnets
  name                               = "nat-${each.key}"
  router                             = google_compute_router.r[each.key].name
  nat_ip_allocate_option             = "AUTO_ONLY"
  source_subnetwork_ip_ranges_to_nat = "ALL_SUBNETWORKS_ALL_IP_RANGES"
  region                             = each.key
}

resource "google_compute_route" "internet_route" {
  name             = "internet"
  dest_range       = "0.0.0.0/0"
  network          = google_compute_network.this.name
  next_hop_gateway = "default-internet-gateway"
}

resource "google_compute_firewall" "default_ingress_deny" {
  name      = "default-ingress-deny"
  network   = google_compute_network.this.name
  direction = "INGRESS"
  priority  = 65533
  deny {
    protocol = "all"
  }
}

resource "google_compute_firewall" "default_egress_deny" {
  name      = "default-egress-deny"
  network   = google_compute_network.this.name
  direction = "EGRESS"
  priority  = 65533
  deny {
    protocol = "all"
  }
}

resource "google_compute_firewall" "internet_egress" {
  name      = "allow-internet-egress"
  network   = google_compute_network.this.name
  direction = "EGRESS"
  priority  = 1000
  allow {
    protocol = "all"
  }
```

```
    target_tags = ["external-egress"]
}

resource "google_compute_firewall" "internet_ingress" {
  name      = "allow-internet-ingress"
  network   = google_compute_network.this.name
  direction = "INGRESS"
  priority  = 1000
  allow {
    protocol = "all"
  }

  target_tags = ["external-ingress"]
}
```

Review the resources that are going to be created, and then run `terraform apply` to make the changes.

Discussion

With the resources successfully created, you now have a VPC that can scale with your requirements. The firewall rules make resources inaccessible by default, forcing consumers to think about how they need to allow access. With the recipe here, you deployed two firewall rules that allow you to tag resources to enable them to either be accessed from the internet or access the internet themselves.

For example, the following Terraform resource deploys a Compute Engine instance that can access the internet but cannot be accessed directly itself:

```
resource "google_compute_instance" "default" {
  name         = "test"
  machine_type = "f1-micro"
  zone         = "europe-west1-b"

  tags = ["external-egress"]

  boot_disk {
    initialize_params {
      image = "debian-cloud/debian-9"
    }
  }

  network_interface {
    subnetwork = google_compute_subnetwork.subnet["europe-west1"].name

    access_config {}
  }
}
```

Compute Engine instances being directly accessible over the internet should be a last resort. See Recipe 5.10 for how to securely handle incoming internet traffic on GCP.

Networking on GCP is built on top of zero-trust networking fundamentals. Although you can deploy multiple subnets within a particular region, preference should be given to access based on *identity*, not *network address*. When looking at firewall rules, you are given an option of three targets:

- All instances in the network
- Specified target tags
- Specified service account

There is no option allowing you to specify all instances within a given subnet.

Wherever possible, using service accounts as the determiner of access should be the preferred option. Not only does it allow for more cloud native firewall rules, but the ability to give a particular Service Account to a resource can be locked down as required. The following are four resources that, when combined, create a firewall rule that allows specific access between resources over the default PostgreSQL port:

```
resource "google_service_account" "application" {
  account_id   = "application"
  display_name = "application"
}

resource "google_service_account" "database" {
  account_id   = "database"
  display_name = "database"
}

resource "google_compute_firewall" "service_account_ingress" {
  name      = join("-", [
    "allow",
    google_service_account.application.account_id,
    "to",
    google_service_account.database.account_id,
    "ingress"
  ])
  network   = google_compute_network.this.name
  direction = "INGRESS"
  priority  = 1000
  allow {
    protocol = "TCP"
    ports    = ["5432"]
  }
```

```
    source_service_accounts = [google_service_account.application.email]

    target_service_accounts = [google_service_account.database.email]
}

resource "google_compute_firewall" "service_account_egress" {
  name       = join("-", [
    "allow-",
    google_service_account.application.account_id,
    "to",
    google_service_account.database.account_id,
    "egress"
  network    = google_compute_network.this.name
  direction = "EGRESS"
  priority  = 1000
  allow {
    protocol = "TCP"
    ports    = ["5432"]
  }

  target_service_accounts = [google_service_account.application.email]
}
```

In Recipe 5.7, you'll see how to use Shared VPCs to enable a scalable networking approach. When using this approach, you can reference service accounts in other projects to maintain this optimal method of managing your firewall rules.

Summary

Let's summarize what was learned and deployed in this recipe:

- To build private networks on GCP, you create VPCs.
  — VPCs span globally by design, whereas subnets are region specific.
- You created a VPC that can be extended to cover as many regions as required.
- The default level of network access for any resource should be minimized.
- By creating tag-based firewall rules, you enable external access as needed.
- When communicating between services within Google Cloud, service accounts should be used to determine connectivity.
  — When using Shared VPCs, as in Recipe 5.7, you can reference service accounts in other projects.

5.2 Networking Foundations on AWS

Problem

For teams to securely deploy workloads into AWS, they need to deploy a secure-by-default VPC for hosting the required resources.

Solution

This recipe creates a three-tier VPC across multiple availability zones, as shown in Figure 5-2.

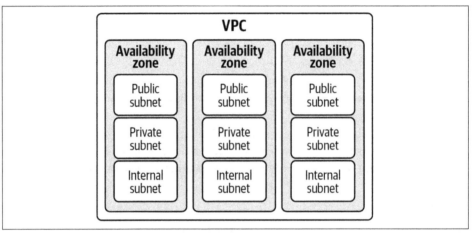

Figure 5-2. Three-tier VPC in AWS

If you haven't already done so, familiarize yourself with Terraform and the different authentication mechanisms in Chapter 11.

Create a *variables.tf* file and copy the following contents:

```
variable "vpc_cidr" {
  type        = string
  description = "The CIDR range for the entire VPC"
}

variable "public_cidrs" {
  type        = list(any)
  description = "A list of CIDRs for the public subnets"
}

variable "private_cidrs" {
  type        = list(any)
  description = "A list of CIDRs for the private subnets"
}
```

```
variable "internal_cidrs" {
  type        = list(any)
  description = "A list of CIDRs for the internal subnets"
}
```

Then fill out the corresponding *terraform.tfvars* file:

```
vpc_cidr       = ""
public_cidrs   = [""]
private_cidrs  = [""]
internal_cidrs = [""]
```

Create the following *provider.tf* file and run `terraform init`:

```
provider "aws" {}

terraform {
  required_providers {
    aws = {
      source  = "hashicorp/aws"
      version = "~> 3"
    }
  }
}
```

Create the following *main.tf* file and run `terraform plan`:

```
data "aws_region" "current" {}

locals {
  availability_zones = ["a", "b", "c", "d", "e", "f"]
}

resource "aws_vpc" "this" {
  cidr_block           = var.vpc_cidr
  enable_dns_support   = true
  enable_dns_hostnames = true
}

resource "aws_subnet" "public" {
  count             = length(var.public_cidrs)
  availability_zone = join("", [
    data.aws_region.current.name,
    local.availability_zones[count.index]
  ])
  vpc_id            = aws_vpc.this.id
  cidr_block        = var.public_cidrs[count.index]
}

resource "aws_subnet" "private" {
  count             = length(var.private_cidrs)
  availability_zone = join("", [
    data.aws_region.current.name,
    local.availability_zones[count.index]
```

```
  ])
  vpc_id            = aws_vpc.this.id
  cidr_block        = var.private_cidrs[count.index]
}

resource "aws_subnet" "internal" {
  count             = length(var.internal_cidrs)
  availability_zone = join("", [
    data.aws_region.current.name,
    local.availability_zones[count.index]
  ])
  vpc_id            = aws_vpc.this.id
  cidr_block        = var.internal_cidrs[count.index]
}

resource "aws_default_security_group" "default" {
  vpc_id = aws_vpc.this.id
}

resource "aws_network_acl" "public" {
  vpc_id     = aws_vpc.this.id
  subnet_ids = [for subnet in aws_subnet.public : subnet.id]
}

resource "aws_network_acl_rule" "public_ingress" {
  network_acl_id = aws_network_acl.public.id
  rule_number    = 200
  egress         = false
  protocol       = "-1"
  rule_action    = "allow"
  cidr_block     = "0.0.0.0/0"
}

resource "aws_network_acl_rule" "public_egress" {
  network_acl_id = aws_network_acl.public.id
  rule_number    = 200
  egress         = true
  protocol       = "-1"
  rule_action    = "allow"
  cidr_block     = "0.0.0.0/0"
}

resource "aws_network_acl_rule" "local_private_egress" {
  count          = length(var.private_cidrs)
  network_acl_id = aws_network_acl.public.id
  rule_number    = 100 + count.index
  egress         = true
  protocol       = "-1"
  rule_action    = "allow"
  cidr_block     = var.private_cidrs[count.index]
}
```

```
resource "aws_network_acl_rule" "local_private_ingress" {
  count         = length(var.private_cidrs)
  network_acl_id = aws_network_acl.public.id
  rule_number   = 100 + count.index
  egress        = false
  protocol      = "-1"
  rule_action   = "allow"
  cidr_block    = var.private_cidrs[count.index]
}

resource "aws_network_acl_rule" "block_private_network_egress" {
  network_acl_id = aws_network_acl.public.id
  rule_number   = 150
  egress        = true
  protocol      = "-1"
  rule_action   = "deny"
  cidr_block    = "10.0.0.0/8"
}

resource "aws_network_acl_rule" "block_private_network_ingress" {
  network_acl_id = aws_network_acl.public.id
  rule_number   = 150
  egress        = false
  protocol      = "-1"
  rule_action   = "deny"
  cidr_block    = "10.0.0.0/8"
}

resource "aws_network_acl" "private" {
  vpc_id     = aws_vpc.this.id
  subnet_ids = [for subnet in aws_subnet.private : subnet.id]
}

resource "aws_network_acl_rule" "private_network_ingress" {
  network_acl_id = aws_network_acl.private.id
  rule_number   = 150
  egress        = false
  protocol      = "-1"
  rule_action   = "allow"
  cidr_block    = "0.0.0.0/0"
}

resource "aws_network_acl_rule" "private_network_egress" {
  network_acl_id = aws_network_acl.private.id
  rule_number   = 150
  egress        = true
  protocol      = "-1"
  rule_action   = "allow"
  cidr_block    = "0.0.0.0/0"
}

resource "aws_network_acl" "internal" {
```

```
  vpc_id     = aws_vpc.this.id
  subnet_ids = [for subnet in aws_subnet.internal : subnet.id]
}

resource "aws_network_acl_rule" "internal_network_ingress" {
  count           = length(var.private_cidrs)
  network_acl_id  = aws_network_acl.internal.id
  rule_number     = 100 + count.index
  egress          = true
  protocol        = "-1"
  rule_action     = "allow"
  cidr_block      = var.private_cidrs[count.index]
}

resource "aws_network_acl_rule" "internal_network_egress" {
  count           = length(var.private_cidrs)
  network_acl_id  = aws_network_acl.internal.id
  rule_number     = 100 + count.index
  egress          = false
  protocol        = "-1"
  rule_action     = "allow"
  cidr_block      = var.private_cidrs[count.index]
}

resource "aws_internet_gateway" "gw" {
  vpc_id = aws_vpc.this.id
}

resource "aws_eip" "nat" {
  count = length(var.private_cidrs)
}

resource "aws_nat_gateway" "gw" {
  count = length(var.private_cidrs)
  allocation_id = aws_eip.nat[count.index].id
  subnet_id     = aws_subnet.private[count.index].id
  depends_on = [aws_internet_gateway.gw]
}

resource "aws_default_route_table" "example" {
  default_route_table_id = aws_vpc.this.default_route_table_id

  route {
    cidr_block = "0.0.0.0/0"
    gateway_id = aws_internet_gateway.gw.id
  }
}
```

Review the resources that are going to be created, and then run `terraform` `apply` to make the changes.

Discussion

The fundamental construct for networking on AWS is the VPC. A VPC is locked to a region, but can span multiple availability zones. The first line of control for allowing and denying traffic is the security group. If a security group does not explicitly allow the traffic, it is implicitly denied. Additionally, it is critical to understand that security groups are *stateful*. For example, your internal database will need ingress rules to allow it to be communicated, but it doesn't need a reciprocal egress rule to allow the traffic back.

When handling network access within a VPC, you should always look first to use security groups as the identity to allow or deny traffic. Your database security group should allow traffic from your workload security group, not just the entire private IP range. This is a step along the journey to zero-trust networking, as discussed at the start of this chapter, where identity, not network location, becomes the source of access.

When you create a new AWS account, it comes with a default VPC. Although this allows you to get up and running quickly, it shouldn't be used for production workloads, as they are all deployed with identical Classless Inter-Domain Routing (CIDR) ranges, and the subnets are not configured correctly to achieve your security objectives.

In this recipe, you built a three-tier VPC based around the need to support a variety of connectivity and security requirements:

Public subnets
> These allow ingress from the internet. Workloads often need to be accessible externally, but we want only those resources that need to be directly accessible to be so. This subnet will allow resources such as load balancers and network address translation (NAT) gateways. For a deeper dive, see Recipe 5.11.

Private subnets
> These allow east-west communication across the business. As your estate grows, there will be requirements to allow systems to connect without traversing the public internet. Common examples include shared services like Active Directory, SAP systems, and shared developer tooling.

Internal subnets
> These allow for internal resources only accessible from your local network. Databases and other data storage systems should only be accessible from the local network. Having a database directly accessible from outside your local network is a potential threat vector for malicious actors.

New VPCs in AWS come with a default security group that allows unrestricted external access and everything with the security group to communicate—not something you want to allow as a default. The `aws_default_security_group` resource automatically removes the permissions, forcing users to create their own security groups specific for their purpose.

Enforce the following rules to meet the requirements:

- The public subnets are accessible from the public internet, and can only access the private subnets.
- The private subnets are accessible from the public subnet, the wider private network, and can access the internal subnets and the outside world.
- The internal subnets can only be accessed from the private subnets.

To achieve this level of control, and enact defense in-depth underneath the security groups, you configured network access control lists (NACLs). These are *stateless* rules that define traffic flow between subnets. Through these you can enforce common rules, such as those outlined previously, that cannot be circumvented with a misconfigured security group.

Let's quickly discuss routing within the VPC. By default, every route table has a local route that allows for intra-VPC routing. For each tier of the subnet, in this recipe, you configured a bespoke route table that handled external routing, the public subnet's route to the internet via the internet gateway, and the private subnet's route via the NAT gateway. The internal subnets cannot route externally at all. With security groups, NACLs, and route tables, you can construct a layered defense in-depth approach that allows you to robustly achieve your security objectives.

This recipe forms the backbone of the following recipes:

- Recipe 5.5
- Recipe 5.8
- Recipe 5.11

Summary

Let's summarize what was learned and deployed in this recipe:

- Although AWS provides default VPCs in an account, they should be deleted as standard practice.
- To enable highly available architectures, the VPCs should span multiple availability zones.

- To retain flexibility to secure your network, you need the following three tiers of subnets:

Public
Houses the resources that need to be accessed directly from the internet

Private
Houses the resources that can be accessed from across the business, and the public subnets

Internal
Houses the resources that can only be accessed from the private subnets

- You created a VPC with these three tiers.
- NACLs are stateless rules for allowing traffic between subnets.
- Security groups are stateful rules for allowing traffic between network interfaces.
- By defining custom route tables for each tier, as well as adopting security groups and NACLs, you can build out a defense in-depth approach to network security.

5.3 Networking Foundations on Azure

Problem

For teams to be able to securely deploy workloads into Azure, they need to deploy a secure-by-default Virtual Network (VNet) for hosting the required resources.

Solution

This recipe creates a three-tier Virtual Network that routes all external-bound traffic through an Azure Firewall. The high-level architecture is shown in Figure 5-3.

For a production use case, having both Azure Firewall and DDoS protection enabled is recommended. However, the static running cost of both is around $4,000 per month.

To prevent bill shock, the recipe by default does not deploy either but can be toggled via the `enable_firewall` and `enable_ddos_protection` variables.

Azure DDoS protection should be purchased centrally for the tenant and shared.

Azure Firewall should be centrally managed via Recipe 5.9.

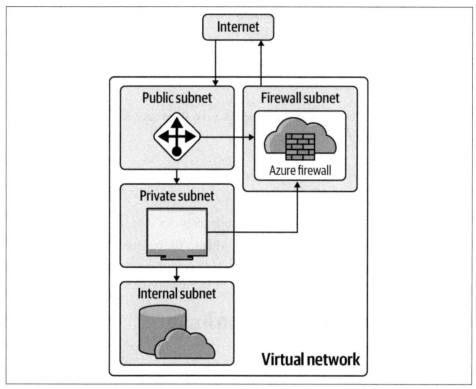

Figure 5-3. Virtual Network architecture

If you haven't already done so, familiarize yourself with Terraform and the different authentication mechanisms in Chapter 11.

Create a *variables.tf* file and copy the following contents:

```
variable "vnet_cidr" {
  type        = string
  description = "The CIDR range for the Virtual Network"
}

variable "public_cidr" {
  type        = string
  description = "The CIDR range for the Public Subnet"
}

variable "private_cidr" {
  type        = string
  description = "The CIDR range for the Private Subnet"
}

variable "internal_cidr" {
  type        = string
```

```
    description = "The CIDR range for the Internal Subnet"
  }

  variable "firewall_cidr" {
    type        = string
    description = "The CIDR range for the Firewall Subnet"
    default     = ""
  }

  variable "enable_firewall" {
    type        = bool
    description = "Enable Azure firewall (approx $1k per month)"
    default     = false
  }

  variable "enable_ddos_protection" {
    type        = bool
    description = "Enable Azure firewall (approx $3k per month)"
    default     = false
  }
```

Then fill out the corresponding *terraform.tfvars* file:

```
vnet_cidr     = ""
public_cidr   = ""
private_cidr  = ""
internal_cidr = ""
```

Create the following *provider.tf* file and run `terraform init`:

```
terraform {
  required_providers {
    azurerm = {
      source  = "hashicorp/azurerm"
      version = "~> 2"
    }
  }
}

provider "azurerm" {
  features {}
}
```

Create the following *main.tf* file and run `terraform plan`:

```
locals {
  fw    = azurerm_firewall.this[0]
  fw_ip = local.fw.ip_configuration[0].private_ip_address
}

resource "azurerm_resource_group" "n" {
  name     = "network"
  location = var.location
}
```

```
resource "azurerm_public_ip" "nat_gateway" {
  name                = "nat-gateway"
  location            = azurerm_resource_group.n.location
  resource_group_name = azurerm_resource_group.n.name
  allocation_method   = "Static"
  sku                 = "Standard"
  availability_zone   = "1"
}

resource "azurerm_nat_gateway_public_ip_association" "this" {
  nat_gateway_id       = azurerm_nat_gateway.this.id
  public_ip_address_id = azurerm_public_ip.nat_gateway.id
}

resource "azurerm_nat_gateway" "this" {
  name                    = "this"
  location                = azurerm_resource_group.n.location
  resource_group_name     = azurerm_resource_group.n.name
  sku_name                = "Standard"
  idle_timeout_in_minutes = 10
}

resource "azurerm_virtual_network" "n" {
  name                = "this"
  address_space       = [var.vnet_cidr]
  location            = azurerm_resource_group.n.location
  resource_group_name = azurerm_resource_group.n.name
}

resource "azurerm_subnet" "public" {
  name                 = "public"
  resource_group_name  = azurerm_resource_group.n.name
  virtual_network_name = azurerm_virtual_network.n.name
  address_prefixes     = [var.public_cidr]
}
resource "azurerm_subnet" "private" {
  name                 = "private"
  resource_group_name  = azurerm_resource_group.n.name
  virtual_network_name = azurerm_virtual_network.n.name
  address_prefixes     = [var.private_cidr]
}

resource "azurerm_subnet_nat_gateway_association" "private" {
  subnet_id      = azurerm_subnet.private.id
  nat_gateway_id = azurerm_nat_gateway.this.id
}

resource "azurerm_subnet" "internal" {
  name                 = "internal"
  resource_group_name  = azurerm_resource_group.n.name
  virtual_network_name = azurerm_virtual_network.n.name
```

```
  address_prefixes    = [var.internal_cidr]
}

resource "azurerm_route_table" "this" {
  name                = "this"
  location            = azurerm_resource_group.n.location
  resource_group_name = azurerm_resource_group.n.name
}

resource "azurerm_route" "local" {
  name                = "local"
  resource_group_name = azurerm_resource_group.n.name
  route_table_name    = azurerm_route_table.this.name
  address_prefix      = var.vnet_cidr
  next_hop_type       = "VnetLocal"
}

resource "azurerm_route" "internet_via_firewall" {
  count                  = var.enable_firewall ? 1 : 0
  name                   = "internet"
  resource_group_name    = azurerm_resource_group.n.name
  route_table_name       = azurerm_route_table.this.name
  address_prefix         = "0.0.0.0/0"
  next_hop_type          = "VirtualAppliance"
  next_hop_in_ip_address = local.fw_ip
}

resource "azurerm_route" "internet_via_nat" {
  count               = var.enable_firewall ? 0 : 1
  name                = "internet"
  resource_group_name = azurerm_resource_group.n.name
  route_table_name    = azurerm_route_table.this.name
  address_prefix      = "0.0.0.0/0"
  next_hop_type       = "VirtualNetworkGateway"
}

resource "azurerm_network_ddos_protection_plan" "this" {
  count               = var.enable_ddos_protection ? 1 : 0
  name                = "this"
  location            = azurerm_resource_group.n.location
  resource_group_name = azurerm_resource_group.n.name
}

resource "azurerm_subnet" "firewall" {
  count                = var.enable_firewall ? 1 : 0
  name                 = "AzureFirewallSubnet"
  resource_group_name  = azurerm_resource_group.n.name
  virtual_network_name = azurerm_virtual_network.n.name
  address_prefixes     = [var.firewall_cidr]
}

resource "azurerm_public_ip" "firewall" {
```

```
  count               = var.enable_firewall ? 1 : 0
  name                = "firewall"
  location            = azurerm_resource_group.n.location
  resource_group_name = azurerm_resource_group.n.name
  allocation_method   = "Static"
  sku                 = "Standard"
}

resource "azurerm_firewall" "this" {
  count               = var.enable_firewall ? 1 : 0
  name                = "this"
  location            = azurerm_resource_group.n.location
  resource_group_name = azurerm_resource_group.n.name

  ip_configuration {
    name                 = "configuration"
    subnet_id            = azurerm_subnet.firewall[0].id
    public_ip_address_id = azurerm_public_ip.firewall[0].id
  }
}

resource "azurerm_network_security_group" "public" {
  name                = "public"
  location            = azurerm_resource_group.n.location
  resource_group_name = azurerm_resource_group.n.name
}

resource "azurerm_subnet_network_security_group_association" "public" {
  subnet_id                 = azurerm_subnet.public.id
  network_security_group_id = azurerm_network_security_group.public.id
}

resource "azurerm_network_security_group" "private" {
  name                = "private"
  location            = azurerm_resource_group.n.location
  resource_group_name = azurerm_resource_group.n.name
}

resource "azurerm_subnet_network_security_group_association" "private" {
  subnet_id                 = azurerm_subnet.private.id
  network_security_group_id = azurerm_network_security_group.private.id
}

resource "azurerm_network_security_group" "internal" {
  name                = "internal"
  location            = azurerm_resource_group.n.location
  resource_group_name = azurerm_resource_group.n.name
}

resource "azurerm_subnet_network_security_group_association" "internal" {
  subnet_id                 = azurerm_subnet.internal.id
```

```
    network_security_group_id = azurerm_network_security_group.internal.id
}
```

Review the resources that are going to be created and then run `terraform apply` to make the changes.

Discussion

By default, when creating a network security group in Azure, it contains a collection of default rules. For ingress rules, it allows VNet traffic and load balancer traffic by default and denies everything else. For egress rules, it allows VNet traffic and internet traffic by default and denies everything else. In this recipe, you added a specific rule to the public subnet to allow all traffic, whereas the private and internal subnets will block public traffic.

Also for the internal subnet, the route table automatically forwards internet-bound traffic to a black hole, whereas for the public and private subnets, it is routed directly via the firewall. The firewall is configured with no rules, meaning that in its current state it blocks all outbound traffic.

In Table 5-1, you can see the three default Azure Policy network compliance checks. As noted earlier in the recipe, the second and third policies can be toggled on when required.

Table 5-1. Virtual Network policies

Policy	Details
Network Watcher should be enabled.	Network Watcher collects data and logs from your networks, allowing for debugging and understanding of potential security threats.
All internet traffic should be routed via your deployed Azure Firewall.	The route table should be configured to route external traffic via the Azure Firewall.
Azure DDoS Protection Standard should be enabled.	The base level of Azure DDoS should be enabled on your networks.

Let's have a look at Network Watcher. Network Watcher is a network monitoring service which captures flow logs and provides guided diagnosis for connectivity issues. It is your first port of call when looking to debug network issues within your tenant.

It is deployed on a per-region, per-subscription basis, so it should be deployed independently of the virtual network, hence why it's not included in the recipe. The following Terraform creates Network Watcher, and a Log Analytics workspace where the flow logs for each network security group are collected. You will need to update the name of the storage account to something globally unique.

```
resource "azurerm_resource_group" "watcher" {
  name     = "watcher"
  location = var.location
```

```
}

resource "azurerm_network_watcher" "this" {
  name                = "this"
  location            = azurerm_resource_group.watcher.location
  resource_group_name = azurerm_resource_group.watcher.name
}

resource "azurerm_storage_account" "watcher" {
  name                = ""
  resource_group_name = azurerm_resource_group.watcher.name
  location            = azurerm_resource_group.watcher.location

  account_tier             = "Standard"
  account_kind             = "StorageV2"
  account_replication_type = "LRS"
  enable_https_traffic_only = true
}

resource "azurerm_log_analytics_workspace" "watcher" {
  name                = "watcher"
  location            = azurerm_resource_group.watcher.location
  resource_group_name = azurerm_resource_group.watcher.name
  sku                 = "PerGB2018"
}

resource "azurerm_network_watcher_flow_log" "this" {
  for_each = toset([
    azurerm_network_security_group.public.id,
    azurerm_network_security_group.private.id,
    azurerm_network_security_group.internal.id,
  ])

  network_watcher_name = azurerm_network_watcher.this.name
  resource_group_name  = azurerm_resource_group.watcher.name

  network_security_group_id = each.value
  storage_account_id        = azurerm_storage_account.watcher.id
  enabled                   = true

  retention_policy {
    enabled = true
    days    = 7
  }

  traffic_analytics {
    enabled              = true
    workspace_id         = azurerm_log_analytics_workspace.watcher.workspace_id
    workspace_region     = azurerm_log_analytics_workspace.watcher.location
    workspace_resource_id = azurerm_log_analytics_workspace.watcher.id
  }
}
```

Summary

Let's summarize what was learned and deployed in this recipe:

- Virtual Networks (VNets) are the base networking construct in Azure.
- You can divide a VNet into disparate subnetworks.
- Each subnetwork should have its own network security group attached.
- It should also have a specific route table attached.
- The recipe deploys four subnets: public, private, internal, and firewall.
- All internet-bound traffic is routed via an Azure Firewall.
- Applications, where possible, should use application security groups.
- To monitor and debug VNet connectivity issues, use Network Watcher.

5.4 Enabling External Access on GCP

Problem

As part of the operation and development of services, engineers need to access machines within a VPC.

Solution

This recipe deploys a Compute Engine instance, as shown in Figure 5-4, that cannot access the internet but can be privately accessed using SSH and an Identity-Aware Proxy (IAP).

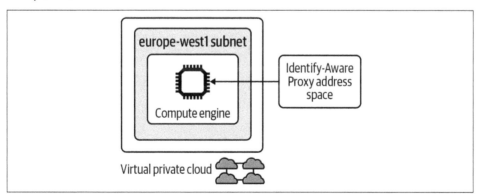

Figure 5-4. SSH over IAP

First, complete Recipe 5.1 and open the working directory.

Add the following variable definition to your *variables.tf* file:

```
...
variable "instance_zone" {
  type        = string
  description = "The zone for the Compute Engine instance"
}
```

And to your *terraform.tfvars* file:

```
...
instance_zone = ""
```

Create the following *instance.tf* file and run `terraform plan`:

```
locals {
  compute_region = join("-", [
    split("-", var.instance_zone)[0],
    split("-", var.instance_zone)[1]
  ])
}

resource "google_service_account" "ssh" {
  account_id   = "allow-ssh"
  display_name = "allow-ssh"
}

resource "google_compute_firewall" "ssh-ingress" {
  name      = "ssh-ingress"
  network   = google_compute_network.this.name
  direction = "INGRESS"
  priority  = 1000
  allow {
    protocol = "TCP"
    ports    = ["22"]
  }

  source_ranges = [
    "35.235.240.0/20"
  ]

  target_service_accounts = [
    google_service_account.ssh.email
  ]
}

resource "google_compute_instance" "default" {
  name         = "test"
  machine_type = "f1-micro"
  zone         = var.instance_zone

  boot_disk {
    initialize_params {
      image = "debian-cloud/debian-9"
```

```
    }
  }

  network_interface {
    subnetwork = google_compute_subnetwork.subnet[local.compute_region].name
  }

  service_account {
    email  = google_service_account.ssh.email
    scopes = ["cloud-platform"]
  }
}
```

Review the resources that are going to be created, and then run `terraform apply` to make the changes.

Discussion

With the instance deployed, if you now run `gcloud compute ssh test`, you will be dropped into an SSH session on the instance.

On Google Cloud, that native way to establish SSH or RDP sessions is tunneling via IAP. This allows you to manage machine access via IAM, rather than having to manage, secure, and rotate keys yourself. Helpfully, the `gcloud` CLI abstracts the IAP from you, meaning that you are able to simply connect to a private machine that has a port open for the IAP address range (35.235.240.0/20).

The instance cannot be accessed from anywhere other than the IAP address range and cannot, by default, connect to any other resources on the network. Now let's look at extending the recipe to be able to tunnel connections to internal resources.

A common request is being able to directly interact with a database from a local development machine to assist in debugging. The following Terraform creates a PostgreSQL instance in the VPC, adds the required firewall rules, and prints out the SSH tunnel command.

Add the following *database.tf* file to your working directory:

```
resource "google_project_service" "service_networking" {
  service            = "servicenetworking.googleapis.com"
  disable_on_destroy = false
}

resource "google_compute_firewall" "service_account_ingress" {
  name      = join("-", [
    "allow"
    google_service_account.ssh.account_id,
    "to-database-ingress"
  ])
  network   = google_compute_network.this.name
```

```
  direction = "INGRESS"
  priority  = 1000
  allow {
    protocol = "TCP"
    ports    = ["5432"]
  }

  source_service_accounts = [google_service_account.ssh.email]

  target_service_accounts = [
    google_sql_database_instance.postgres.service_account_email_address
  ]
}

resource "google_compute_global_address" "private_ip_address" {
  name          = "private-ip-address"
  purpose       = "VPC_PEERING"
  address_type  = "INTERNAL"
  prefix_length = 16
  network       = google_compute_network.this.id
}

resource "google_service_networking_connection" "private_vpc_connection" {
  network                 = google_compute_network.this.id
  service                 = "servicenetworking.googleapis.com"
  reserved_peering_ranges = [
    google_compute_global_address.private_ip_address.name
  ]

  depends_on = [
    google_project_service.service_networking
  ]
}

resource "google_compute_firewall" "service_account_egress" {
  name      = join("-". [
    "allow",
    google_service_account.ssh.account_id,
    "to-database-egress"
  ])
  network   = google_compute_network.this.name
  direction = "EGRESS"
  priority  = 1000
  allow {
    protocol = "TCP"
    ports    = ["5432"]
  }

  destination_ranges = [
    google_sql_database_instance.postgres.private_ip_address
  ]
```

```
      target_service_accounts = [google_service_account.ssh.email]
    }

    resource "google_sql_database_instance" "postgres" {
      name                = "postgres"
      database_version    = "POSTGRES_13"
      deletion_protection = false
      region              = local.compute_region
      settings {
        tier = "db-f1-micro"
        ip_configuration {
          ipv4_enabled    = false
          private_network = google_compute_network.this.id
        }
      }

      depends_on = [
        google_project_service.service_networking,
        google_service_networking_connection.private_vpc_connection
      ]
    }

    output "tunnel" {
      value = join("", [
        "gcloud compute ssh test ",
        "--ssh-flag '-L 5432:",
        google_sql_database_instance.postgres.private_ip_address,
        ":5432'"
      ])
    }
```

Once you have run `terraform apply` and created the resources, the `tunnel` output will give you the required command to tunnel to the database.

This pattern can be used to access any internal resource. When accessing Cloud SQL instances, Google provides the Cloud SQL Auth proxy, which is the recommended way of accessing private databases from applications as it manages the encryption in transit and enables IAM-based access, as opposed to native database users.

Summary

Let's summarize what was learned and deployed in this recipe:

- Opening sessions to instances on Google Cloud should be done via the Identity-Aware Proxy (IAP):
  — By using IAP, you use IAM as the source of your authentication and authorization.
  — This is both more secure and operationally efficient than managing keys and certificates.

- By opening up instances to purely the IAP address range, you can enable secure SSH and RDP access.
- The gcloud command line abstracts the configuration of IAP for you.
- You can also use this approach to tunnel to private resources within your VPCs.

5.5 Enabling External Access on AWS

Problem

As part of the operation and development of services, engineers need to access machines within a VPC.

Solution

This recipe deploys an EC2 instance, as shown in Figure 5-5, that cannot access the internet but can be privately accessed via SSH and AWS Systems Manager.

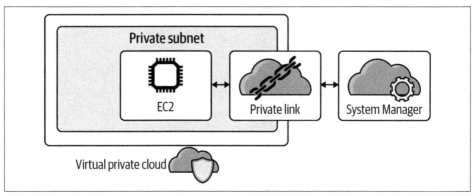

Figure 5-5. Private SSH with Systems Manager

First, complete Recipe 5.2 and open the working directory.

 Although connecting to the EC2 instance directly doesn't require SSH keys, in order to tunnel through the instance, you need an SSH public key to be uploaded. As this can only be done when the instance is created, the recipe requires that the keys be specified.

Add the following variable definition to your *variables.tf* file:

```
...

variable "public_key_path" {
    type        = string
```

```
    description = "The absolute path to your public key"
}

variable "private_key_path" {
  type        = string
  description = "The absolute path to your private key"
}
```

And to your *terraform.tfvars* file:

```
...
public_key_path  = ""
private_key_path = ""
```

Update the *provider.tf* file to contain only the following contents, and run `terraform init`:

```
provider "aws" {}

terraform {
  required_providers {
    aws = {
      source  = "hashicorp/aws"
      version = "~> 3"
    }
    random = {
      source  = "hashicorp/random"
      version = "~> 3"
    }
    local = {
      source  = "hashicorp/local"
      version = "~> 2"
    }
  }
}
```

Create the following *instance.tf* file and run `terraform plan`:

```
resource "aws_vpc_endpoint" "ssm" {
  vpc_id              = aws_vpc.this.id
  service_name        = "com.amazonaws.eu-west-1.ssm"
  vpc_endpoint_type   = "Interface"
  private_dns_enabled = true
  subnet_ids          = [for subnet in aws_subnet.private : subnet.id]

  security_group_ids = [
    aws_security_group.endpoint_sg.id,
  ]
}

resource "aws_vpc_endpoint" "ssmmessages" {
  vpc_id              = aws_vpc.this.id
  service_name        = "com.amazonaws.eu-west-1.ssmmessages"
  vpc_endpoint_type   = "Interface"
```

```
    private_dns_enabled = true
    subnet_ids          = [for subnet in aws_subnet.private : subnet.id]

    security_group_ids = [
      aws_security_group.endpoint_sg.id,
    ]
}

resource "aws_vpc_endpoint" "ec2messages" {
  vpc_id              = aws_vpc.this.id
  service_name        = "com.amazonaws.eu-west-1.ec2messages"
  vpc_endpoint_type   = "Interface"
  private_dns_enabled = true
  subnet_ids          = [for subnet in aws_subnet.private : subnet.id]

  security_group_ids = [
    aws_security_group.endpoint_sg.id,
  ]
}

resource "aws_security_group" "endpoint_sg" {
  vpc_id = aws_vpc.this.id

  ingress {
    from_port   = 443
    to_port     = 443
    protocol    = "tcp"
    cidr_blocks = [aws_vpc.this.cidr_block]
  }
}

data "aws_ami" "ubuntu" {
  most_recent = true

  filter {
    name   = "name"
    values = ["ubuntu/images/hvm-ssd/ubuntu-focal-20.04-amd64-server-*"]
  }

  filter {
    name   = "virtualization-type"
    values = ["hvm"]
  }

  owners = ["099720109477"] # Canonical
}

data "local_file" "ssh_public" {
  filename = var.public_key_path
}

resource "aws_key_pair" "key" {
```

```
  public_key = data.local_file.ssh_public.content
}

resource "aws_instance" "web" {
  ami                  = data.aws_ami.ubuntu.id
  instance_type        = "t3.micro"
  iam_instance_profile = aws_iam_instance_profile.ssm_profile.name
  key_name             = aws_key_pair.key.key_name
  security_groups      = [aws_security_group.instance.id]
  subnet_id            = aws_subnet.private[0].id
}

resource "aws_security_group" "instance" {
  vpc_id = aws_vpc.this.id
}

resource "aws_security_group_rule" "ssh_ingress" {
  type                     = "ingress"
  from_port                = 22
  to_port                  = 22
  protocol                 = "tcp"
  source_security_group_id = aws_security_group.endpoint_sg.id
  security_group_id        = aws_security_group.instance.id
}

resource "aws_security_group_rule" "endpoint_egress" {
  type                     = "egress"
  from_port                = 443
  to_port                  = 443
  protocol                 = "tcp"
  source_security_group_id = aws_security_group.endpoint_sg.id
  security_group_id        = aws_security_group.instance.id
}

resource "aws_iam_instance_profile" "ssm_profile" {
  name = "ssm_profile"
  role = aws_iam_role.role.name
}

resource "aws_iam_role" "role" {
  name = "ssm_role"
  path = "/"

  managed_policy_arns = ["arn:aws:iam::aws:policy/AmazonSSMManagedInstanceCore"]

  assume_role_policy = <<EOF
{
    "Version": "2012-10-17",
    "Statement": [
        {
            "Action": "sts:AssumeRole",
            "Principal": {
```

```
                    "Service": "ec2.amazonaws.com"
                },
                "Effect": "Allow",
                "Sid": ""
            }
        ]
    }
}
EOF
}

output "start_session" {
  value = "aws ssm start-session --target ${aws_instance.web.id}"
}
```

Review the resources that are going to be created and then run `terraform apply` to make the changes.

Discussion

When the resources are created, the `start_session` output will contain the command needed to create an SSH on the instance.

 As the AWS CLI does not natively support the Session Manager plug-in, you will need to install it by following the documentation (*https://oreil.ly/sr0mq*).

In this recipe, you used VPC endpoints to allow access to the AWS APIs through private networking alone. To explore the topic further, see Recipe 5.14.

Although you are now able to SSH onto a private Linux EC2 instance in your VPC, often engineers need to tunnel through a machine to access a database or similar resource. Let's look at the extra steps required to achieve this.

 The `random_password` resource used to generate the password for the database is a convenience measure. Ideally, database passwords should be generated out of Terraform to avoid the result being stored in state.

Let's create a Postgres database to query directly from your laptop, by creating a *database.tf* file with the following contents.

```
resource "random_password" "database" {
  length  = 16
  special = false
}
```

```
resource "aws_db_instance" "default" {
  allocated_storage      = 10
  db_subnet_group_name   = aws_db_subnet_group.default.name
  engine                 = "postgres"
  engine_version         = "13.2"
  instance_class         = "db.t3.micro"
  name                   = "mydb"
  username               = "postgres"
  password               = random_password.database.result
  parameter_group_name   = "default.postgres13"
  skip_final_snapshot    = true
  vpc_security_group_ids = [aws_security_group.database.id]
}

resource "aws_security_group_rule" "database_egress" {
  type                    = "egress"
  from_port               = 5432
  to_port                 = 5432
  protocol                = "tcp"
  source_security_group_id = aws_security_group.database.id
  security_group_id       = aws_security_group.instance.id
}

resource "aws_db_subnet_group" "default" {
  subnet_ids = [for subnet in aws_subnet.internal : subnet.id]
}

resource "aws_security_group" "database" {
  vpc_id = aws_vpc.this.id

  ingress {
    from_port       = 5432
    to_port         = 5432
    protocol        = "tcp"
    security_groups = [aws_security_group.instance.id]
  }
}

output "db_password" {
  value     = random_password.database.result
  sensitive = true
}

output "tunnel_command" {
  value = join(" ", [
    "ssh",
    "-i ${var.private_key_path}",
    "ubuntu@${aws_instance.web.id}",
    "-L",
    "5432:${aws_db_instance.default.address}:5432",
  ])
}
```

Once you have run `terraform apply` to create the resources, you can run `terraform output db_password` to get the administrator password.

To tunnel through the instance to RDS, you will need to configure your SSH client to leverage Session Manager to handle the connection. To do this, follow the instructions in the AWS documentation (*https://oreil.ly/derBK*).

Once your client is configured, you can run the `tunnel_command` output, which will start an SSH session that allows you to connect to your database through `127.0.0.1:5432`. You can then use your full array of local tooling to interact with the database.

Summary

Let's summarize what was learned and deployed in this recipe:

- On AWS, you can leverage AWS Systems Manager to access instances.
- By using VPC Endpoints, you can allow private instances to talk to AWS APIs.
- After creating the required endpoints, you then created an EC2 that had these elements:
  — The SSM agent preinstalled on the AMI

  — An instance profile with the required permissions

  — A security group that allowed for incoming SSH and outgoing connections to AWS APIs
- Then you added the Session Manager plug-in to your AWS CLI and connected to the instance.
- Session Manager also enables tunneling to resources.
- You created a database and used the EC2 instance and Session Manager to create a connection from your local machine.

5.6 Enabling External Access on Azure

Problem

As part of the operation and development of services, engineers need to access machines within a VPC.

Solution

This recipe deploys an Azure Bastion host, as shown in Figure 5-6, to enable SSH and RDP access driven directly through the Azure Portal.

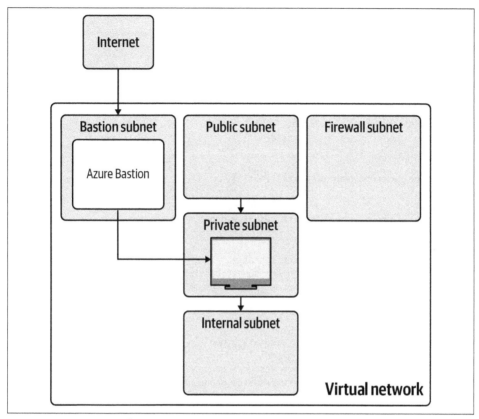

Figure 5-6. Bastion architecture

First, complete Recipe 5.3 and open the working directory.

Add the following variable definition to your *variables.tf* file:

```
...

variable "bastion_cidr" {
  type        = string
  description = "The CIDR for the Bastion Subnet"
}
```

And to your *terraform.tfvars* file:

```
...
bastion_cidr  = ""
```

Create the following *bastion.tf* file and run `terraform plan`:

```
resource "azurerm_subnet" "bastion" {
  name                = "AzureBastionSubnet"
  resource_group_name = azurerm_resource_group.network.name
```

```
  virtual_network_name = azurerm_virtual_network.this.name
  address_prefixes     = [var.bastion_cidr]
}

resource "azurerm_public_ip" "bastion" {
  name                = "bastion"
  location            = azurerm_resource_group.network.location
  resource_group_name = azurerm_resource_group.network.name
  allocation_method   = "Static"
  sku                 = "Standard"
}

resource "azurerm_bastion_host" "this" {
  name                = "this"
  location            = azurerm_resource_group.network.location
  resource_group_name = azurerm_resource_group.network.name

  ip_configuration {
    name                 = "configuration"
    subnet_id            = azurerm_subnet.bastion.id
    public_ip_address_id = azurerm_public_ip.bastion.id
  }
}

resource "azurerm_application_security_group" "s" {
  name                = "ssh_example"
  location            = azurerm_resource_group.network.location
  resource_group_name = azurerm_resource_group.network.name
}

resource "azurerm_network_security_rule" "bastion_ingress" {
  name                        = "bastion-private-ingress"
  priority                    = 100
  direction                   = "Inbound"
  access                      = "Allow"
  protocol                    = "Tcp"
  source_port_range           = "*"
  destination_port_range      = "22"
  source_address_prefixes     = azurerm_subnet.bastion.address_prefixes
  destination_application_security_group_ids = [
    azurerm_application_security_group.ssh_example.id
  ]
  resource_group_name         = azurerm_resource_group.network.name
  network_security_group_name = azurerm_network_security_group.private.name
}
```

Review the resources that are going to be created and then run `terraform apply` to make the changes.

Discussion

In this recipe, you created an application security group that remains unattached. This can then be associated to resources to enable identity-based connectivity. The following is a Terraform that creates a minimal Linux virtual machine for testing the bastion host:

```
resource "azurerm_network_interface_application_security_group_association" "s" {
  network_interface_id        = azurerm_network_interface.ssh_example.id
  application_security_group_id = azurerm_application_security_group.s.id
}

resource "azurerm_linux_virtual_machine" "ssh_example" {
  name                = "ssh-example"
  resource_group_name = azurerm_resource_group.network.name
  location            = azurerm_resource_group.network.location
  size                = "Standard_B1s"
  admin_username      = "adminuser"
  network_interface_ids = [
    azurerm_network_interface.ssh_example.id,
  ]

  admin_ssh_key {
    username   = "adminuser"
    public_key = file("~/.ssh/id_rsa.pub")
  }

  os_disk {
    caching              = "ReadWrite"
    storage_account_type = "Standard_LRS"
  }

  source_image_reference {
    publisher = "Canonical"
    offer     = "UbuntuServer"
    sku       = "16.04-LTS"
    version   = "latest"
  }
}

resource "azurerm_network_interface" "ssh_example" {
  name                = "ssh_example"
  location            = azurerm_resource_group.network.location
  resource_group_name = azurerm_resource_group.network.name

  ip_configuration {
    name                          = "internal"
    subnet_id                     = azurerm_subnet.private.id
    private_ip_address_allocation = "Dynamic"
  }
}
```

When using Azure Bastion, you need to use key material to connect over SSH. Although access to Azure Bastion is IAM based, as it runs agentless on the host, authentication is host OS based.

Rather than host key material locally, Azure Bastion natively supports using private keys stored in Azure Key Vault. This means that key access is also IAM based, allows you to rotate keys by updating the secrets, and means that you are no longer machine bound. To configure a Key Vault in Terraform, see the following resources. You will need to configure an explicit `access_policy` on the vault, manage IAM to control access, and update the vault name to something globally unique:

```
data "azurerm_client_config" "current" {}

resource "azurerm_key_vault" "ssh_keys" {
  name                = "ssh-keys"
  location            = azurerm_resource_group.network.location
  resource_group_name = azurerm_resource_group.network.name

  sku_name  = "standard"
  tenant_id = data.azurerm_client_config.current.tenant_id
}

resource "azurerm_key_vault_secret" "id_rsa" {
  name         = "ssh-private-key"
  value        = file("~/.ssh/id_rsa")
  key_vault_id = azurerm_key_vault.ssh_keys.id
}
```

At the moment, there is no way to leverage Azure Bastion from outside the Azure Portal. You cannot augment your SSH configuration to perform tunneling via the bastion host. To achieve this, you can configure temporary virtual machines to act as bastions for tunneling purposes, or look at leveraging Azure Virtual Desktops to get your local tools hosted seamlessly in Azure.

Summary

Let's summarize what was learned and deployed in this recipe:

- Azure offers Azure Bastion, a fully managed bastion host service.
- It runs in a distinct subnet alongside your virtual network.
- By using application security groups for controlling traffic, you can make your firewall identity based.
- As Azure Bastion is agentless, although accessing the bastion host is controlled via IAM, authentication to the host is with classic methods, such as Lightweight Directory Access Protocol (LDAP) or SSH keys.

- Rather than rely on SSH keys being locally available, you can store them in Azure Key Vault; this has numerous security and operational benefits.

5.7 Allowing Access to Internal Resources on GCP

Problem

As your estate has grown, there is now a need to enable traffic to and from disparate GCP projects in the organization and also to on-premises resources.

Solution

This recipe deploys a Shared VPC, as shown in Figure 5-7, that connects to a central hub VPC that contains the VPN endpoint for on-premises connectivity.

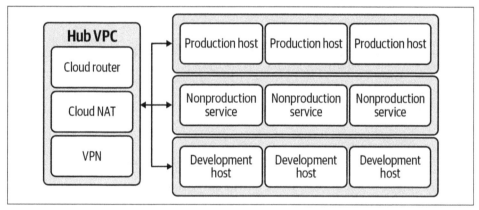

Figure 5-7. Shared VPC architecture

First, complete Recipe 5.1, and open the working directory.

Add the following variable definition to your *variables.tf* file:

```
...

variable "region" {
  type        = string
  description = "The region to deploy the hub subnet into"
}

variable "hub_project" {
  type        = string
  description = "The project ID for the central hub"
}

variable "service_projects" {
  type        = list(string)
```

```
    description = "The projects to have share the VPC"
  }
```

And to your *terraform.tfvars* file:

```
...
region          = ""
hub_project     = ""
service_projects = [""]
```

Add the following provider definition to *provider.tf*:

```
provider "google" {
  alias   = "hub"
  region  = var.region
  project = var.hub_project
}
```

Create the following *sharing.tf* file:

```
data "google_project" "current" {}

resource "google_compute_shared_vpc_host_project" "host" {
  project = data.google_project.current.project_id

  depends_on = [
    google_project_service.compute_api
  ]
}

resource "google_compute_shared_vpc_service_project" "service" {
  for_each      = toset(var.service_projects)
  host_project  = google_compute_shared_vpc_host_project.host.project
  service_project = each.value
}
```

Create the following *hub.tf* file and run `terraform plan`:

```
resource "google_project_service" "hub_compute_api" {
  provider          = google.hub
  service           = "compute.googleapis.com"
  disable_on_destroy = false
}

resource "google_compute_network" "hub" {
  provider                        = google.hub
  name                            = "network"
  auto_create_subnetworks         = false
  delete_default_routes_on_create = true

  depends_on = [
    google_project_service.hub_compute_api,
  ]
}
```

```
resource "google_compute_subnetwork" "hub_subnet" {
  provider      = google.hub
  name          = var.region
  ip_cidr_range = "10.0.255.0/24"
  network       = google_compute_network.hub.id
}

resource "google_compute_router" "hub_router" {
  provider = google.hub
  name     = "router"
  network  = google_compute_network.hub.id
}

resource "google_compute_router_nat" "hub_nat" {
  provider                           = google.hub
  name                               = "nat"
  router                             = google_compute_router.hub_router.name
  nat_ip_allocate_option             = "AUTO_ONLY"
  source_subnetwork_ip_ranges_to_nat = "ALL_SUBNETWORKS_ALL_IP_RANGES"
}

resource "google_compute_firewall" "hub_ingress_deny" {
  provider  = google.hub
  name      = "default-ingress-deny"
  network   = google_compute_network.hub.name
  direction = "INGRESS"
  priority  = 65533
  deny {
    protocol = "all"
  }
}

resource "google_compute_firewall" "hub_egress_deny" {
  provider  = google.hub
  name      = "default-egress-deny"
  network   = google_compute_network.hub.name
  direction = "EGRESS"
  priority  = 65533
  deny {
    protocol = "all"
  }
}

resource "google_compute_network_peering" "hub_to_base" {
  name         = "hub-to-base"
  network      = google_compute_network.this.id
  peer_network = google_compute_network.hub.id
}

resource "google_compute_network_peering" "base_to_hub" {
  name         = "base-to-hub"
  network      = google_compute_network.hub.id
```

```
    peer_network = google_compute_network.this.id
}

resource "google_compute_ha_vpn_gateway" "on-premises" {
  provider = google.hub
  name      = "on-premises"
  network  = google_compute_network.hub.id
}
```

Review the resources that are going to be created, and then run `terraform apply` to make the changes.

Discussion

This recipe at first glance seems unnecessarily complicated: you created a hub VPC with resources that could have easily been placed within the Shared VPC. For full-scale production usage, having only one Shared VPC is not recommended: at least three will be required depending on your data sensitivity requirements.

You will notice that you added internet routing directly to the Shared VPC with its own Cloud NAT and Cloud Router. If you are looking to route all external traffic first through a centrally hosted network appliance, then by defining a custom route in the hub, all external traffic will be routed there, and the Cloud NAT and Router become redundant. In this recipe, there is no centralized appliance, so GCP will not allow you to route over the peering connection as there is no value and indeed an increased cost to do so.

The recommended approach on GCP is to have a Shared VPC for production, non-production, and development, all peered into the hub, as shown in Figure 5-7. This allows them to share the centralized connections, such as on premises and routing via security network appliances. As transitive routing is not supported across peering connections, you cannot route from between the VPCs via the hub. Environments are completely segmented and share centralized resources for ease of management and cost-effectiveness.

VPC Service Controls allow for the definition and enforcement of fine-grained perimeter controls. If you need extra controls to combat data exfiltration threats, control multitenant services, or isolate environments by levels of trust, then VPC Service Controls will enable you to do that.

When using Shared VPCs, the power to create firewall rules exists only in the host project. Users in the service projects cannot create their own firewall rules. As such, a lean and efficient lifecycle should be built around firewall rules to enable users to rapidly develop their application. If the friction of the process becomes too great, users will be driven to create wider and more permissive rules to avoid the process, resulting in a worse security posture. In Chapter 6, the recipes show approaches to enable this rapid feedback.

When using Shared VPCs on Google Cloud, there are three organization policies that allow you to control the administration of Shared VPCs. The first policy restricts what projects are allowed to act as Shared VPC hosts. The second policy restricts the removal of liens from projects by users who do not have the permission at an organizational level. A lien is a special lock that prevents the project from being deleted. The last policy restricts a service project to only using certain subnetworks from the Shared VPC. The following Terraform configures these three policies:

```
data "google_organization" "current" {
  domain = var.organization_domain
}

resource "google_organization_policy" "shared_vpc_projects" {
  org_id     = data.google_organization.current.org_id
  constraint = "constraints/compute.restrictSharedVpcHostProjects"

  list_policy {
    allow {
      values = ["projects/${var.hub_project}"]
    }
  }
}

resource "google_organization_policy" "shared_vpc_lien_removal" {
  org_id     = data.google_organization.current.org_id
  constraint = "constraints/compute.restrictXpnProjectLienRemoval"

  boolean_policy {
    enforced = true
  }
}

resource "google_organization_policy" "shared_vpc_subnetworks" {
  org_id     = data.google_organization.current.org_id
  constraint = "constraints/compute.restrictSharedVpcSubnetworks"

  list_policy {
    allow {
      values = [
        for subnet in google_compute_subnetwork.subnet : subnet.id
      ]
    }
  }
}
```

In this recipe, you created a VPN gateway to enable connecting on premises. The recipe was left without all the resources defined, as VPN configuration is highly contextual.

 When using highly available VPN configurations, if you configure Active/Active routing, you will get higher bandwidth, but the impact of losing an endpoint will be a sudden bandwidth drop of 50%. By using Active/Passive routing, you will get a stable throughput after a failover.

If a VPN will not be performant enough either in bandwidth or latency, then GCP offers two options of Cloud Interconnect. Dedicated Interconnect is a direct physical connection between your on-premises data center and a Google Cloud location, and Partner Interconnect is routing via a supported service provider. Dedicated Interconnect provides higher potential speeds but requires integrating directly into the Google data center, whereas service providers are available in a much larger number of locations. Both offer significantly improved bandwidth options over VPNs: 10 Gbps for Partner Interconnect and up to 200 Gbps for Dedicated Interconnect.

Summary

Let's summarize what was learned and deployed in this recipe:

- To provide a scalable networking approach on GCP, you should use Shared VPCs.
- You should look to create a Shared VPC per environment, i.e., production, non-production, and development.
- With Shared VPCs, firewall rule management is centralized, so care should be taken to ensure it doesn't become a bottleneck.
- Shared VPCs should be peered into a hub VPC where you can deploy centralized networking resources.
- To begin communicating on premises, a VPN provides a lower-cost option.
- You should look to use either Dedicated or Partner Interconnect if
  — the VPN bandwidth or latency is insufficient

    — you want your traffic to only traverse private networking between on premises and Google Cloud

5.8 Allowing Access to Internal Resources on AWS

Problem

As your estate has grown, there is now a need to enable traffic to and from disparate AWS accounts in the organization and also to on-premises resources.

Solution

This recipe configures an AWS Transit Gateway as a central networking hub and enables centralized on-premises connectivity, as shown in Figure 5-8.

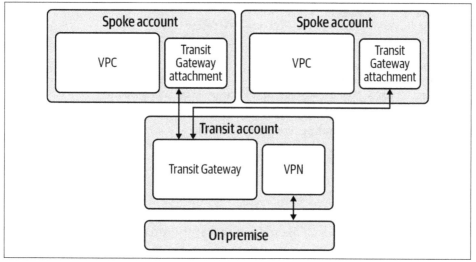

Figure 5-8. Transit Gateway architecture

This recipe should be run from the account where you are deploying the Transit Gateway itself.

 The recipe deploys minimal spoke VPCs for illustrative purposes. This approach would not scale as the number of VPCs grows. The important aspects are the creation of the route and the `aws_ec2_transit_gateway_vpc_attachment` resource.

If you haven't already done so, familiarize yourself with Terraform and the different authentication mechanisms in Chapter 11.

Create a *variables.tf* file and copy the following contents:

```
variable "spoke1_account_id" {
    type        = string
```

```
  description = "The Account ID of the first spoke account"
}

variable "spoke2_account_id" {
  type        = string
  description = "The Account ID of the second spoke account"
}

variable "cross_account_role" {
  type        = string
  description = "The role that can be assumed in each spoke"
}

variable "vpn_asn" {
  type        = number
  description = "The ASN you wish the VPN to use"
}

variable "vpn_ip_address" {
  type        = string
  description = "The IP address of the on-premises VPN endpoint"
}
```

Then fill out the corresponding *terraform.tfvars* file:

```
spoke1_account_id  = ""
spoke2_account_id  = ""
cross_account_role = ""
vpn_asn            = ""
vpn_ip_address     = ""
```

Create the following *provider.tf* file and run `terraform init`:

```
provider "aws" {
  alias = "transit"
}

provider "aws" {
  alias = "spoke1"
  assume_role {
    role_arn = join("", [
      "arn:aws:iam::",
      var.spoke1_account_id,
      ":role/",
      var.cross_account_role
    ])
  }
}

provider "aws" {
  alias = "spoke2"
  assume_role {
    role_arn = join("", [
```

```
            "arn:aws:iam::",
            var.spoke2_account_id,
            ":role/",
            var.cross_account_role
        ])
      }
    }

    terraform {
      required_providers {
        aws = {
          source  = "hashicorp/aws"
          version = "~> 3"
        }
      }
    }
```

Create the following *main.tf* file:

```
data "aws_organizations_organization" "current" {}

resource "aws_ec2_transit_gateway" "this" {
  provider = aws.transit
}

resource "aws_ram_resource_share" "transit_gateway" {
  provider = aws.transit
  name     = "transit_gateway"
}

resource "aws_ram_resource_association" "transit_gateway" {
  provider           = aws.transit
  resource_arn       = aws_ec2_transit_gateway.this.arn
  resource_share_arn = aws_ram_resource_share.transit_gateway.arn
}

resource "aws_ram_principal_association" "org_share" {
  provider           = aws.transit
  principal          = data.aws_organizations_organization.current.arn
  resource_share_arn = aws_ram_resource_share.transit_gateway.arn
}

resource "aws_ec2_transit_gateway_vpc_attachment_accepter" "spoke1" {
  provider                      = aws.transit
  transit_gateway_attachment_id = aws_ec2_transit_gateway_vpc_attachment.s1.id
}

resource "aws_ec2_transit_gateway_vpc_attachment_accepter" "spoke2" {
  provider                      = aws.transit
  transit_gateway_attachment_id = aws_ec2_transit_gateway_vpc_attachment.s2.id
}

resource "aws_customer_gateway" "this" {
```

```
    provider    = aws.transit
    bgp_asn     = var.vpn_asn
    ip_address = var.vpn_ip_address
    type        = "ipsec.1"
}

resource "aws_vpn_connection" "this" {
    provider            = aws.transit
    customer_gateway_id = aws_customer_gateway.this.id
    transit_gateway_id  = aws_ec2_transit_gateway.this.id
    type                = aws_customer_gateway.this.type
}
```

Create the following *spoke1.tf* file:

```
resource "aws_vpc" "spoke1" {
    provider            = aws.spoke1
    cidr_block          = "10.0.0.0/24"
    enable_dns_support  = true
    enable_dns_hostnames = true
}

resource "aws_subnet" "spoke1_private" {
    provider          = aws.spoke1
    availability_zone = "eu-west-1a"
    vpc_id            = aws_vpc.spoke1.id
    cidr_block        = aws_vpc.spoke1.cidr_block
}

resource "aws_default_route_table" "spoke1" {
    provider              = aws.spoke1
    default_route_table_id = aws_vpc.spoke1.default_route_table_id

    route {
        cidr_block         = "10.0.0.0/8"
        transit_gateway_id = aws_ec2_transit_gateway.this.id
    }
}

resource "aws_ec2_transit_gateway_vpc_attachment" "s1" {
    provider           = aws.spoke1
    subnet_ids         = [aws_subnet.spoke1_private.id]
    transit_gateway_id = aws_ec2_transit_gateway.this.id
    vpc_id             = aws_vpc.spoke1.id

    depends_on = [
        aws_ram_resource_association.transit_gateway,
        aws_ram_principal_association.org_share
    ]
}
```

Create the following *spoke2.tf* file and run `terraform plan`:

```
resource "aws_vpc" "spoke2" {
  provider            = aws.spoke2
  cidr_block          = "10.0.1.0/24"
  enable_dns_support  = true
  enable_dns_hostnames = true
}

resource "aws_subnet" "spoke2_private" {
  provider          = aws.spoke2
  availability_zone = "eu-west-1b"
  vpc_id            = aws_vpc.spoke2.id
  cidr_block        = aws_vpc.spoke2.cidr_block
}

resource "aws_default_route_table" "spoke2" {
  provider              = aws.spoke2
  default_route_table_id = aws_vpc.spoke2.default_route_table_id

  route {
    cidr_block         = "10.0.0.0/8"
    transit_gateway_id = aws_ec2_transit_gateway.this.id
  }
}

resource "aws_ec2_transit_gateway_vpc_attachment" "s2" {
  provider           = aws.spoke2
  subnet_ids         = [aws_subnet.spoke2_private.id]
  transit_gateway_id = aws_ec2_transit_gateway.this.id
  vpc_id             = aws_vpc.spoke2.id

  depends_on = [
    aws_ram_resource_association.transit_gateway,
    aws_ram_principal_association.org_share
  ]
}
```

Review the resources that are going to be created, and then run `terraform apply` to make the changes.

Discussion

By centralizing all traffic through Transit Gateway, you unlock a variety of options for securing your network. East-west routing happens purely at your discretion, as disparate accounts have no direct knowledge of each other's networking; they can talk over the private network only because the routes exist in the Transit Gateway. Effectively, all the spoke VPCs know is that the rest of the private network exists over the Transit Gateway attachment, putting the onus on Transit Gateway to make sure the traffic ends up in the right place.

The recipe expects that routes from on premises will be advertised over Border Gateway Protocol (BGP), but if needed, you can extend it to explicitly create static routes.

To make the Transit Gateway available across the organization, you used Resource Access Manager (RAM), which allows the sharing of specific types of resources across accounts and organizations. You can use this to onboard accounts and VPCs outside of your organization onto a Transit Gateway located within your organization.

You can also have all traffic, when onboarding to the Transit Gateway, be passed through a network appliance, such as a firewall, an IDS, or an IPS system. This saves you the effort of deploying these appliances in multiple locations throughout the estate. The Gateway Load Balancer service is specifically designed to facilitate this pattern with third-party network appliances, and AWS Network Firewall is a first-party offering in this space.

In this example, you provisioned a VPN tunnel to handle traffic destined for on-premises. Although VPNs are often how people get started with bringing their cloud and on-premises estates together, at significant scale, AWS Direct Connect is used for significantly higher bandwidth and a much higher service-level agreement (SLA). It comes at a cost premium and is not something that can be easily experimented with as it involves negotiating with third parties and Amazon.

There are other options for allowing VPCs in different AWS accounts to communicate with each other; the two that are most notable are VPC peering and VPC sharing. Peering connections build direct networking pathways between VPCs. While useful in smaller-scale scenarios, they rapidly become unmanageable at scale due to the sheer number that need provisioning as routing is not transitive, and you lose the centralized location to apply networking controls. Shared VPCs are a more recent offering on AWS and can make sense when the application suite is used to fairly open and permissive networking. However, as your estate matures and becomes cloud native first, the hub-and-spoke model of Transit Gateway is more scalable and puts more power in the hands of the delivery teams.

Summary

Let's summarize what was learned and deployed in this recipe:

- On AWS, to allow on-premises connectivity, use a centralized Transit Gateway.
- The Transit Gateway also operates as a hub allowing traffic between VPCs.
- To connect on premises, you can use either a VPN or Direct Connect.
  — VPNs are simple to configure but have bandwidth and uptime limitations.

— Direct Connect is more scalable than VPN connections but is significantly more expensive.

- In the recipe, you created
  — a centralized Transit Gateway with a VPN endpoint

  — two VPCs in two spoke accounts that were connected back the Transit Gateway

5.9 Allowing Access to Internal Resources on Azure

Problem

As your estate has grown, there is now a need to enable traffic to and from disparate Azure subscriptions in the tenant and also to on-premises resources.

Solution

This recipe deploys a hub-and-spoke network topology, as shown in Figure 5-9, with an ExpressRoute for on-premises connectivity.

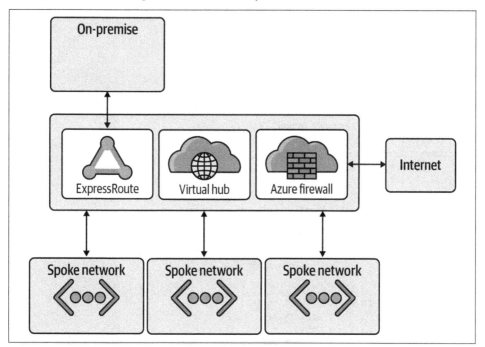

Figure 5-9. Hub-and-spoke architecture

First, complete Recipe 5.3 and open the working directory.

Add the following variable definition to your *variables.tf* file:

```
...

variable "hub_subscription_id" {
  type        = string
  description = "The subscription for the Hub Network"
}

variable "hub_cidr" {
  type        = string
  description = "The CIDR range for the Hub Network"
}
```

And to your *terraform.tfvars* file:

```
...
hub_subscription_id = ""
hub_cidr            = ""
```

Add the following provider definition to *provider.tf*:

```
...

provider "azurerm" {
  alias           = "hub"
  subscription_id = var.hub_subscription_id

  features {}
}
```

Create the following *hub.tf* file and run `terraform plan`:

```
resource "azurerm_resource_group" "hub" {
  provider = azurerm.hub
  name     = "hub"
  location = var.location
}

resource "azurerm_virtual_wan" "this" {
  provider            = azurerm.hub
  name                = "this"
  resource_group_name = azurerm_resource_group.hub.name
  location            = azurerm_resource_group.hub.location
}

resource "azurerm_virtual_hub" "this" {
  provider            = azurerm.hub
  name                = "this"
  resource_group_name = azurerm_resource_group.hub.name
  location            = azurerm_resource_group.hub.location
  virtual_wan_id      = azurerm_virtual_wan.this.id
  sku                 = "Standard"
  address_prefix      = var.hub_cidr
}
```

```
}

resource "azurerm_virtual_hub_connection" "spoke" {
  provider                 = azurerm.hub
  name                     = "spoke"
  virtual_hub_id           = azurerm_virtual_hub.this.id
  remote_virtual_network_id = azurerm_virtual_network.this.id
}

resource "azurerm_express_route_gateway" "this" {
  name                = "this"
  resource_group_name = azurerm_resource_group.hub.name
  location            = azurerm_resource_group.hub.location
  virtual_hub_id      = azurerm_virtual_hub.this.id
  scale_units         = 1
}

resource "azurerm_firewall" "hub" {
  name                = "hub"
  resource_group_name = azurerm_resource_group.hub.name
  location            = azurerm_resource_group.hub.location
  sku_name            = "AZFW_Hub"
  threat_intel_mode   = ""

  virtual_hub {
    virtual_hub_id  = azurerm_virtual_hub.this.id
    public_ip_count = 1
  }
}
```

The creation of the ExpressRoute gateway can take significant time to provision; 20 minutes is not unusual. Do not be worried if Terraform seems to be taking a while to create these resources.

Review the resources that are going to be created, and then run `terraform apply` to make the changes.

Discussion

Through the configuration of the Virtual Hub, you bring together a centralized point to manage your network security posture at scale. With the Border Gateway Protocol (BGP) propagating routes throughout your infrastructure, you can have a robust, highly resilient network topology that moves with you. With the transitive routing, you now have the ability to facilitate east-west traffic across your tenant. Speaking of routing, let's look at a few common patterns and how you can implement them.

This recipe configures the ExpressRoute gateway but not the ExpressRoute circuits. This is to maintain some brevity, especially as the configuration of ExpressRoutes can be highly contextual. You can also utilize VPN Gateways if ExpressRoute is too expensive or over-engineering. This trade-off is covered in more depth in the following discussion.

First, let's look at the concept of isolated virtual networks. Often you will be hosting sensitive workloads, and need to manage data exfiltration risks. In that case, you need the ability to lock down particular virtual networks, from both ingress and egress perspectives. When creating Virtual Hub connections, it is possible to assign custom route tables to the connection to ensure that once traffic is onboarded onto the hub, it is treated appropriately.

The way to design your Virtual Hub routing is to draw up a table containing the different connections and create a route table for each row in the table. This is easiest shown with an example, as in Table 5-2. Let's assume you have a virtual network that needs to communicate on premises but should not be accessible from anywhere within your Azure tenancy; you also have shared service VNets that should be accessible from everywhere. Connections such as ExpressRoute and VPNs are known as *branches* on Azure, to distinguish them from VNets.

Table 5-2. Isolated virtual network connection table

From	To	Standard VNets	Shared VNets	Branches
Standard VNet			Direct	Direct
Shared VNet	Direct		Direct	Direct
Branches	Direct		Direct	Direct

What you can see from the table is that branches and Shared VNets are treated the same, whereas standard VNets have a different connection profile. This shows that you will need two route tables to implement the required routing. Let's look at the Terraform that would allow you to configure this. Note that this only uses the `connection` resources and doesn't include a full ExpressRoute configuration. You will also see that this does not leverage the default route table that is provisioned with the hub. The default routes configured in most cases do not cater to the principle of least privilege and are instead focused on getting traffic flowing as soon as possible:

```
resource "azurerm_virtual_network" "isolated" {
  name                = "isolated"
  address_space       = ["10.2.0.0/24"]
  location            = azurerm_resource_group.network.location
  resource_group_name = azurerm_resource_group.network.name
}
```

```
resource "azurerm_virtual_network" "shared" {
  name                = "shared"
  address_space       = ["10.3.0.0/24"]
  location            = azurerm_resource_group.network.location
  resource_group_name = azurerm_resource_group.network.name
}

resource "azurerm_virtual_hub_route_table" "isolation" {
  provider      = azurerm.hub
  name          = "isolation"
  virtual_hub_id = azurerm_virtual_hub.this.id
}

resource "azurerm_virtual_hub_route_table" "shared" {
  provider      = azurerm.hub
  name          = "shared"
  virtual_hub_id = azurerm_virtual_hub.this.id
}

resource "azurerm_virtual_hub_connection" "isolated" {
  provider                  = azurerm.hub
  name                      = "isolated"
  virtual_hub_id            = azurerm_virtual_hub.this.id
  remote_virtual_network_id = azurerm_virtual_network.isolated.id

  routing {
    associated_route_table_id = azurerm_virtual_hub_route_table.isolation.id

    propagated_route_table {
      route_table_ids = [
        azurerm_virtual_hub_route_table.shared.id
      ]
    }
  }
}

resource "azurerm_virtual_hub_connection" "shared" {
  provider                  = azurerm.hub
  name                      = "shared"
  virtual_hub_id            = azurerm_virtual_hub.this.id
  remote_virtual_network_id = azurerm_virtual_network.shared.id

  routing {
    associated_route_table_id = azurerm_virtual_hub_route_table.shared.id

    propagated_route_table {
      route_table_ids = [
        azurerm_virtual_hub_route_table.isolation.id,
        azurerm_virtual_hub_route_table.shared.id
      ]
    }
  }
}
```

```
  }

  resource "azurerm_express_route_connection" "this" {
    name                          = "this"
    express_route_gateway_id      = azurerm_express_route_gateway.this.id
    express_route_circuit_peering_id = azurerm_express_route_circuit_peering.t.id

    routing {
      associated_route_table_id = azurerm_virtual_hub_route_table.shared.id

      propagated_route_table {
        route_table_ids = [
          azurerm_virtual_hub_route_table.isolation.id,
          azurerm_virtual_hub_route_table.shared.id
        ]
      }
    }
  }
}
```

Summary

Let's summarize what was learned and deployed in this recipe:

- By using an Azure Virtual Hub, you can create a hub-and-spoke networking topology.
- With a central location to provision shared networking resources, you can more readily manage and scale your networking infrastructure.
- To connect with on-premises resources, you can use VPNs or ExpressRoutes.
  — VPNs are lower cost, with lower bandwidth.
  — ExpressRoutes allow for low-latency, ultra-high bandwidth but at a significant ongoing cost.
  — Generally, start with VPNs and upgrade to ExpressRoute when required.
- By mindfully planning out your transit connectivity requirements, you can implement any number of different routing patterns.
- You saw an example of creating the resources required for isolated and shared virtual networks.

5.10 Controlling External Network Connectivity on GCP

Problem

Delivery teams are asking for secure patterns to expose applications to the internet.

Solution

This recipe deploys the architecture shown in Figure 5-10, an NGINX container exposed to the internet over HTTPS.

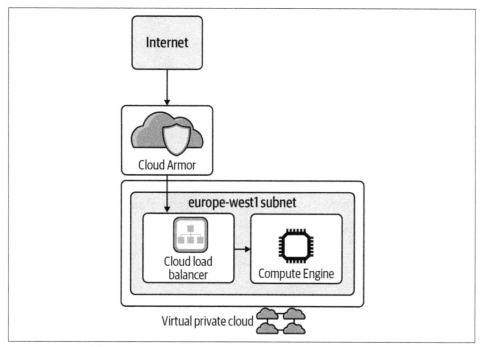

Figure 5-10. Public applications on GCP

 This recipe requires a public DNS zone on GCP to be available to create the DNS record and provision the SSL certificate.

First, complete Recipe 5.1 and open the working directory.

Add the following variable definition to your *variables.tf* file:

```
...

variable "application_region" {
  type        = string
  description = "The region to deploy the application"
}

variable "application_zone" {
  type        = string
  description = "The zone to deploy into, e.g., a, b or c"
```

```
}

variable "hosted_zone_domain" {
  type        = string
  description = "The name of your hosted zone resource"
}

variable "dns_record" {
  type        = string
  description = "The DNS record for your application"
}
```

And to your *terraform.tfvars* file:

```
...
application_region = ""
application_zone   = ""
hosted_zone_domain = ""
dns_record         = ""
```

Create the following *application.tf* file and run `terraform plan`:

```
data "google_dns_managed_zone" "target" {
  name = var.hosted_zone_domain
}

resource "google_dns_record_set" "set" {
  name         = var.dns_record
  type         = "A"
  ttl          = 3600
  managed_zone = data.google_dns_managed_zone.target.name
  rrdatas = [
    google_compute_global_forwarding_rule.default.ip_address
  ]
}

resource "google_compute_managed_ssl_certificate" "prod" {
  name = "production"

  managed {
    domains = [
      var.dns_record
    ]
  }
}

resource "google_compute_global_forwarding_rule" "default" {
  name       = "global-rule"
  target     = google_compute_target_https_proxy.nginx.id
  port_range = "443"
}

resource "google_compute_target_https_proxy" "nginx" {
```

```
  name    = "nginx"
  url_map = google_compute_url_map.nginx.id
  ssl_certificates = [
    google_compute_managed_ssl_certificate.prod.id
  ]
}

resource "google_compute_url_map" "nginx" {
  name            = "url-map-target-proxy"
  description     = "a description"
  default_service = google_compute_backend_service.nginx.id

  host_rule {
    hosts        = [var.dns_record]
    path_matcher = "allpaths"
  }

  path_matcher {
    name            = "allpaths"
    default_service = google_compute_backend_service.nginx.id

    path_rule {
      paths   = ["/*"]
      service = google_compute_backend_service.nginx.id
    }
  }
}

resource "google_service_account" "nginx" {
  account_id   = "nginx-workers"
  display_name = "nginx-workers"
}

resource "google_compute_backend_service" "nginx" {
  name        = "backend"
  port_name   = "http"
  protocol    = "HTTP"
  timeout_sec = 10

  backend {
    group = google_compute_instance_group.nginx.id
  }

  health_checks = [google_compute_http_health_check.nginx.id]
}

resource "google_compute_http_health_check" "nginx" {
  name               = "check-backend"
  request_path       = "/"
  check_interval_sec = 1
  timeout_sec        = 1
}
```

```
resource "google_compute_instance_group" "nginx" {
  name = "nginx"

  instances = [
    google_compute_instance.nginx.id,
  ]

  named_port {
    name = "http"
    port = "80"
  }

  zone = "europe-west1-b"
}
resource "google_compute_firewall" "http-ingress" {
  name      = "http-ingress"
  network   = google_compute_network.this.name
  direction = "INGRESS"
  priority  = 1000
  allow {
    protocol = "TCP"
    ports    = ["80"]
  }

  source_ranges = [
    "130.211.0.0/22",
    "35.191.0.0/16"
  ]

  target_service_accounts = [
    google_service_account.nginx.email
  ]
}

resource "google_compute_firewall" "internet_egress" {
  name      = "allow-internet-egress"
  network   = google_compute_network.this.name
  direction = "EGRESS"
  priority  = 1000
  allow {
    protocol = "all"
  }

  target_service_accounts = [
    google_service_account.nginx.email
  ]
}
resource "google_compute_instance" "nginx" {
  name                   = "nginx"
```

```
  machine_type            = "f1-micro"
  zone                    = join("-", [
    var.application_region,
    var.application_zone
  ])
  allow_stopping_for_update = true

  boot_disk {
    initialize_params {
      image = "cos-cloud/cos-stable-89-16108-470-25"
    }
  }

  metadata_startup_script = "docker run -p 80:80 nginx"

  network_interface {
    subnetwork = google_compute_subnetwork.subnet[var.application_region].name
  }

  service_account {
    email  = google_service_account.nginx.email
    scopes = ["cloud-platform"]
  }
}
```

Review the resources that are going to be created, and then run `terraform apply` to make the changes.

The `google_compute_managed_ssl_certificate` resource will return once Google accepts the request to vend the certificate. But the certificate can take up to 24 hours to provision. If you try and browse to the application before this has finished, you will get errors such as SSL_ERROR_NO_CYPHER_OVERLAP.

Discussion

This recipe created an architecture that does SSL offloading, which would normally mean that traffic behind the load balancer is unencrypted. On GCP, depending on the load balancer chosen, Google provides *automatic network-level encryption*, which encrypts your data in transit within the VPC.

Currently, automatic network-level encryption is enabled for

- global external HTTP(S) load balancers
- TCP proxy load balancers
- SSL proxy load balancers

It is not enabled for

- regional external HTTP(S) load balancers
- internal HTTP(S) load balancers
- Traffic Director

To handle other types of traffic, you will need to replace the `google_compute_tar`
`get_https_proxy` resource. If you are looking to handle non-HTTP TCP traffic with
SSL offloading, use the `google_compute_target_ssl_proxy` resource. If you do not
wish to SSL offload, use the `google_compute_target_tcp_proxy` resource.

Having properly managed SSL certificates is only one piece of the puzzle for keeping
your applications safe and secure. For protecting from DDoS attacks and adding a
web application firewall (WAF), Google provides the Cloud Armor service. It comes
in two flavors: Standard and Managed Protection Plus. Standard, as the name implies,
comes built-in to your Google environment and is automatically enabled for workloads. After completing this recipe, the `google_compute_backend_service` resource
is already covered. With this you get preconfigured WAF rules that are targeted predominantly against the OWASP top 10, such as SQL injection, cross-site scripting,
and remote code execution.

With Managed Protection Plus, you can get support from Google during DDoS
attacks and additionally enable Adaptive Protection. Adaptive Protection automatically builds custom machine learning models for each of your applications, allowing
each to understand the difference between normal and anomalous traffic. It then uses
the traffic signatures to generate WAF rules to automatically block the traffic. As
Cloud Armor acts at the network edge, before traffic hits the load balancer, it reduces
the traffic volume in your VPCs and your resource usage.

A common pattern on public clouds is to configure a static site using object storage.
In this case, you will need to update the recipe, replacing the `google_compute_back`
`end_service`, and the references to it, with a `google_compute_backend_bucket`
resource. Following is an example of setting up the required resources for the Cloud
Storage bucket:

```
resource "google_compute_backend_bucket" "static" {
  name        = "${var.project}-static"
  bucket_name = google_storage_bucket.static_site.name
  enable_cdn  = true
}

resource "google_storage_bucket" "static_site" {
  name     = "${var.project}-static"
  location = var.application_region
}
```

Summary

Let's summarize what was learned and deployed in this recipe:

- On GCP, the most common entry pathway for external traffic is via a load balancer.
- Load balancers come in a variety of types:
  - HTTP(s) for web traffic
  - SSL for TCP traffic that needs SSL offloading
  - TCP for TCP traffic that does not need SSL offloading
- You created a simple load-balanced application hosting NGINX served over HTTPS.
- Cloud Armor is DDoS protection and a WAF rolled into one.
  - Cloud Armor is automatically enabled across your estate but comes with a more expensive version, Managed Protection Plus.
  - Managed Protection Plus unlocks Google support for DDoS attacks and Adaptive Protection, where custom machine learning models protect your application.
- To host static sites on GCP, you can use Cloud Storage, but it needs to be routed through a load balancer to serve it over HTTPS.

5.11 Controlling External Network Connectivity on AWS

Problem

Delivery teams are asking for secure patterns to expose applications to the internet.

Solution

This recipe deploys the architecture shown in Figure 5-11. An NGINX container is exposed to the internet over HTTPS.

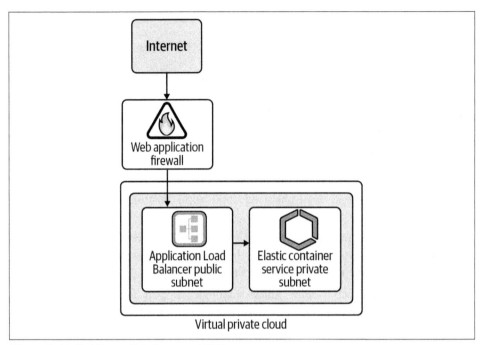

Figure 5-11. Public applications on AWS

 This recipe requires a public Route53-hosted zone in the account to be available to create the DNS record and provision the SSL certificate.

First, complete Recipe 5.2 and open the working directory.

Add the following variable definition to your *variables.tf* file:

```
...

variable "hosted_zone_domain" {
  type        = string
  description = "The name of your hosted zone domain"
}
```

And to your *terraform.tfvars* file:

```
...
hosted_zone_domain = ""
```

Create the following *ecs.tf* file:

```
resource "aws_ecs_cluster" "this" {
  name = "load_balanced_cluster"
```

```
}

resource "aws_ecs_service" "this" {
  name            = "application"
  cluster         = aws_ecs_cluster.this.id
  task_definition = aws_ecs_task_definition.this.arn
  desired_count   = 1
  launch_type     = "FARGATE"

  load_balancer {
    target_group_arn = aws_lb_target_group.application.arn
    container_name   = "nginx"
    container_port   = 80
  }

  network_configuration {
    subnets         = [for subnet in aws_subnet.private : subnet.id]
    security_groups = [aws_security_group.application.id]
  }
}

resource "aws_security_group" "application" {
  name   = "ecs-task-sg"
  vpc_id = aws_vpc.this.id
}

resource "aws_security_group_rule" "alb_ingress" {
  type                     = "ingress"
  from_port                = 80
  to_port                  = 80
  protocol                 = "tcp"
  source_security_group_id = aws_security_group.alb.id
  security_group_id        = aws_security_group.application.id
}

resource "aws_security_group_rule" "application_public_egress" {
  type              = "egress"
  from_port         = 0
  to_port           = 0
  protocol          = "-1"
  cidr_blocks       = ["0.0.0.0/0"]
  security_group_id = aws_security_group.application.id
}

resource "aws_ecs_task_definition" "this" {
  family = "service"
  cpu    = "256"
  memory = "512"
  container_definitions = jsonencode([
    {
      name  = "nginx"
      image = "nginx"
```

```
        essential = true
        portMappings = [
          {
            containerPort = 80
            hostPort      = 80
          }
        ]
      }
    ])
    network_mode            = "awsvpc"
    requires_compatibilities = ["FARGATE"]
  }
```

Create the following *alb.tf* file and run `terraform plan`:

```
resource "aws_lb" "application" {
  name               = "application-load-balanced-ecs"
  internal           = false
  load_balancer_type = "application"
  security_groups    = [aws_security_group.alb.id]
  subnets            = [for subnet in aws_subnet.public : subnet.id]
}

resource "aws_lb_listener" "application" {
  load_balancer_arn = aws_lb.application.arn
  port              = "443"
  protocol          = "HTTPS"
  ssl_policy        = "ELBSecurityPolicy-2016-08"
  certificate_arn   = aws_acm_certificate.nginx.arn

  default_action {
    type             = "forward"
    target_group_arn = aws_lb_target_group.application.arn
  }
}

resource "aws_security_group" "alb" {
  vpc_id = aws_vpc.this.id
}

resource "aws_security_group_rule" "public_ingress" {
  type              = "ingress"
  from_port         = 443
  to_port           = 443
  protocol          = "tcp"
  cidr_blocks       = ["0.0.0.0/0"]
  security_group_id = aws_security_group.alb.id
}

resource "aws_security_group_rule" "alb_to_ecs" {
  type              = "egress"
  from_port         = 80
  to_port           = 80
```

```
    protocol                = "tcp"
    source_security_group_id = aws_security_group.application.id
    security_group_id       = aws_security_group.alb.id
}

resource "aws_lb_target_group" "application" {
    port        = 80
    protocol    = "HTTP"
    target_type = "ip"
    vpc_id      = aws_vpc.this.id
}

resource "aws_route53_record" "application" {
    name    = "application.${var.hosted_zone_domain}"
    type    = "A"
    zone_id = data.aws_route53_zone.this.zone_id

    alias {
        name                   = aws_lb.application.dns_name
        zone_id                = aws_lb.application.zone_id
        evaluate_target_health = true
    }
}

data "aws_route53_zone" "this" {
    name = var.hosted_zone_domain
}

resource "aws_acm_certificate" "nginx" {
    domain_name       = "*.${var.hosted_zone_domain}"
    validation_method = "DNS"

    lifecycle {
        create_before_destroy = true
    }
}

resource "aws_route53_record" "certificate_validation" {
    for_each = {
        for dvo in aws_acm_certificate.nginx.domain_validation_options :
            dvo.domain_name => {
                name   = dvo.resource_record_name
                record = dvo.resource_record_value
                type   = dvo.resource_record_type
            }
    }

    allow_overwrite = true
    name            = each.value.name
    records         = [each.value.record]
    ttl             = 60
    type            = each.value.type
```

```
  zone_id          = data.aws_route53_zone.this.zone_id
}

resource "aws_wafv2_web_acl" "firewall" {
  name  = "load-balancer-firewall"
  scope = "REGIONAL"

  default_action {
    allow {}
  }

  rule {
    name     = "AWSManagedRulesCommonRuleSet"
    priority = 1

    override_action {
      count {}
    }

    statement {
      managed_rule_group_statement {
        name        = "AWSManagedRulesCommonRuleSet"
        vendor_name = "AWS"
      }
    }

    visibility_config {
      cloudwatch_metrics_enabled = false
      metric_name                = "AWSManagedRulesAdminProtectionRuleSet"
      sampled_requests_enabled   = false
    }
  }

  visibility_config {
    cloudwatch_metrics_enabled = false
    metric_name                = "base-firewall"
    sampled_requests_enabled   = false
  }
}

resource "aws_wafv2_web_acl_association" "load_balancer" {
  resource_arn = aws_lb.application.arn
  web_acl_arn  = aws_wafv2_web_acl.firewall.arn
}

output "alb_url" {
  value = "https://${aws_route53_record.application.name}"
}
```

Review the resources that are going to be created, and then run `terraform apply` to
make the changes.

Discussion

Once Terraform has successfully created the resources, you should be able to browse to the URL in the `alb_url` output and see the NGINX default home page.

This recipe focused on application load balancers with TLS offloading, as they are the most common load balancer type used for applications on AWS. Other options for exposing services to the internet include the following:

- Network load balancers
- CloudFront
- API Gateway
- AppSync

In this section, you will see the Terraform required to stand up both network load balancers and static sites in S3 fronted by CloudFront. But first, let's discuss the purpose and capabilities of Amazon Web Application Firewall (WAF).

What does WAF do?

WAF allows you to use rules to control HTTP and HTTPS traffic before it reaches your applications. You pick from one of three following behaviors:

- Allow all requests except the ones specified in the rules.
- Block all requests except the ones specified in the rules.
- Count the requests that match your specification.

By using WAF, you protect your applications from a variety of web-based threats and filter based on information such as the following:

- The IP addresses the traffic originated from
- The country the traffic originated from
- Request headers
- Filter based on string matching and regexes
- The length of requests
- The presence of SQL statements indicating potential SQL injection attacks
- The presence of potential cross-site scripting attacks

For constructing the rule groups that are applied to your WAF, you can consume groups managed by AWS and groups from the AWS marketplace, and you can create your own as required.

Network Load Balancer

If you're handling traffic that is not HTTP based, or you are operating at a scale beyond what an Application Load Balancer (ALB) can provide, then Network Load Balancer (NLB) might just be the tool you need. Additionally, to maintain encryption through to your application servers, for example, you need the traffic to stay at HTTPS until it hits your application; then you will need to use an NLB, not an ALB.

Following is the Terraform required to stand up an NLB that does TLS offloading. You would need to modify the ECS service to use its target group in the load balancer configuration:

```
resource "aws_lb" "nlb" {
  name               = "network-load-balanced-ecs"
  internal           = false
  load_balancer_type = "network"
  subnets            = [for subnet in aws_subnet.public : subnet.id]
}

resource "aws_lb_listener" "nlb" {
  load_balancer_arn = aws_lb.nlb.arn
  port              = "80"
  protocol          = "TCP"

  default_action {
    type             = "forward"
    target_group_arn = aws_lb_target_group.network.arn
  }
}

resource "aws_lb_target_group" "network" {
  port        = 80
  protocol    = "TCP"
  target_type = "ip"
  vpc_id      = aws_vpc.this.id
}

output "nlb_url" {
  value = "http://${aws_lb.nlb.dns_name}"
}
```

Static sites on AWS

One of the most commonly misconfigured resources in an AWS estate is an S3 bucket. You're going to see now how to host a static site in an S3 bucket securely, using CloudFront to expose it to the internet, and protect it with WAF. Although you can host a site directly from S3, this is less secure and more expensive, and it makes it harder to determine accidental from intentional public buckets.

To allow CloudFront to access the files in your S3 buckets, it uses an IAM concept unique to CloudFront, an origin access identity. By giving that explicit access to the files in your bucket through a bucket policy, you can retain secure buckets while still retaining the ability to serve static sites from them.

For a fully worked example of hosting a static site on S3, refer to the companion GitHub repository (*https://oreil.ly/lnXdE*).

Summary

Let's summarize what was learned and deployed in this recipe:

- On AWS, there are many ways of enabling external connectivity to applications in your estate.
- You learned how to deploy load balanced applications, using a simple NGINX container.
  - You saw the differences between Application Load Balancers (ALBs) and Network Load Balancers (NLBs).
    - ALBs operate at Layer 7 and are for HTTP/HTTPS-based traffic.
    - NLBs operate at Layer 4 and are for all traffic types.
  - You then saw how to do TLS offloading at the load balancers to ensure only secure traffic is allowed.
- Next, you deployed a static site fronted by a Content Delivery Network (CDN), i.e., CloudFront.
- By using Web Application Firewall, you can protect your applications from common threats.

5.12 Controlling External Network Connectivity on Azure

Problem

Delivery teams are asking for secure patterns to expose applications to the internet.

Solution

This recipe deploys the architecture shown in Figure 5-12.

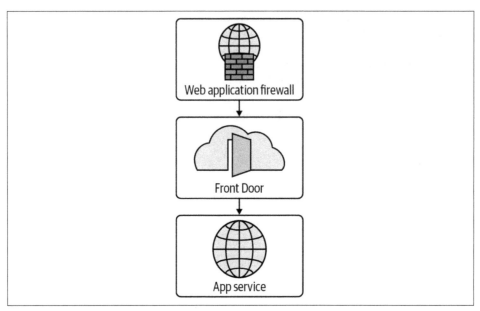

Figure 5-12. Public applications with Azure Front Door

If you haven't already done so, familiarize yourself with Terraform and the different authentication mechanisms in Chapter 11.

Create a *variables.tf* file and copy the following contents:

```
variable "location" {
  type        = string
  description = "The Azure location for resources"
}

variable "application_name" {
  type        = string
  description = "The application name to use as part of the url"
}
```

Then fill out the corresponding *terraform.tfvars* file:

```
location         = ""
application_name = ""
```

Create the following *provider.tf* file and run `terraform init`:

```
terraform {
  required_providers {
    azurerm = {
      source  = "hashicorp/azurerm"
      version = "~> 2"
    }
  }
}
```

```
}

provider "azurerm" {
  features {}
}
```

Create the following *main.tf* file and run `terraform plan`:

```
data "azurerm_subscription" "current" {}

resource "azurerm_resource_group" "a" {
  name     = "application"
  location = var.location
}

locals {
  application_url  = join("-", [
    "application",
    data.azurerm_subscription.current.subscription_id
  ])
}

resource "azurerm_frontdoor" "application" {
  name                                         = var.application_name
  friendly_name                                = var.application_name
  resource_group_name                          = azurerm_resource_group.a.name
  enforce_backend_pools_certificate_name_check = false

  backend_pool {
    name = "backend"
    backend {
      host_header = "${local.application_url}.azurewebsites.net"
      address     = "${local.application_url}.azurewebsites.net"
      http_port   = 80
      https_port  = 443
    }

    load_balancing_name = "application"
    health_probe_name   = "application"
  }

  routing_rule {
    name               = "default"
    accepted_protocols = ["Https"]
    patterns_to_match  = ["/*"]
    frontend_endpoints = ["frontend"]
    forwarding_configuration {
      forwarding_protocol = "HttpsOnly"
      backend_pool_name   = "backend"
    }
  }

  frontend_endpoint {
```

```
    name    = "frontend"
    host_name = "${var.application_name}.azurefd.net"
  }

  backend_pool_health_probe {
    name = "application"
  }

  backend_pool_load_balancing {
    name = "application"
  }
}

resource "azurerm_app_service_plan" "application" {
  name                = "application-service-plan"
  location            = azurerm_resource_group.a.location
  resource_group_name = azurerm_resource_group.a.name
  kind                = "Linux"
  reserved            = true

  sku {
    tier = "Standard"
    size = "S1"
  }
}

resource "azurerm_app_service" "application" {
  name = local.application_url
  https_only = true

  site_config {
    linux_fx_version = "DOCKER|appsvcsample/static-site:latest"
    always_on        = true

    ip_restriction {
      service_tag = "AzureFrontDoor.Backend"

      headers {
        x_azure_fdid = [
          azurerm_frontdoor.application.header_frontdoor_id
        ]
      }
    }
  }

  location            = azurerm_resource_group.a.location
  resource_group_name = azurerm_resource_group.a.name
  app_service_plan_id = azurerm_app_service_plan.application.id
}

resource "azurerm_frontdoor_firewall_policy" "application" {
  name                                = "application"
```

```
    resource_group_name              = azurerm_resource_group.a.name
    enabled                          = true
    mode                             = "Prevention"

    managed_rule {
      type    = "DefaultRuleSet"
      version = "1.0"
    }
}

output "application_url" {
  value = "https://${var.application_name}.azurefd.net"
}
```

Review the resources that are going to be created, and then run `terraform apply` to make the changes.

Discussion

This recipe configured Azure Front Door as a CDN and WAF to globally distribute and protect your application.

In this recipe, with the web application firewall, you configured a base Azure-provided rule set. It is worth evaluating the full suite of Azure-provided rules to understand how you can protect your applications before you embark on a journey of building your own custom rules. At a high level, Azure default rules target the following list of threat vectors, modeled closely around the OWASP Top 10 (*https://owasp.org/Top10*):

- Cross-site scripting
- Java attacks
- Local file inclusion
- PHP injection attacks
- Remote command execution
- Remote file inclusion
- Session fixation
- SQL injection protection
- Protocol attackers

Custom rules are evaluated before any default rules, and if they determine the traffic is legitimate, the traffic is sent on without being appraised by any other rules, custom or default.

The firewall can be configured in either *prevention* or *detection* mode. When introducing new rules, by first enabling them in detection mode, you can assess what the

---

impact of the rule will be: are you going to be incidentally preventing legitimate traffic? Rules also possess an exception facility, allowing you to craft omission rules to allow known legitimate traffic to circumnavigate troublesome rules.

Additionally, when looking at OWASP rules, traditionally they operated on a basis where any rule failure meant the traffic was blocked. More modern configurations operate in an *anomaly score* mode, where depending on the criticality of the rule, ranging from *critical* to *notice*, traffic is scored, and that score determines whether traffic is allowed or blocked. The traditional mode is simpler to reason about but lacks the fidelity to enable more nuanced traffic management, often being overly aggressive and blocking legitimate traffic.

In this recipe, although the App Service itself exposes a public URL, through the usage of *service tag* and *header* filtering, you will notice that if you browse to the URL directly you are rejected, whereas accessing through Front Door works as expected. It is critical that the only access path that functions properly is the path that contains your firewall rules, so they cannot be circumnavigated. As Azure Front Door is a globally shared service, only through the combination of a *service tag*, which restricts to traffic originating from the known Front Door address space, and the x_azure_fdid header, which uniquely identifies your personal Front Door instance, can you be sure that only legitimate traffic reaches your App Service.

To handle external non-HTTP traffic and still retain the global load balancing features of Front Door, use a combination of Azure Traffic Manager and Azure Load Balancers. You can see in Figure 5-13 that the traffic flow is similar to Figure 5-12.

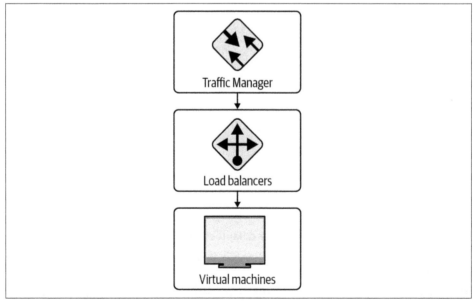

Figure 5-13. Globally load balanced TCP applications with Azure Traffic Manager

Summary

Let's summarize what was learned and deployed in this recipe:

- Azure Front Door handles global HTTP load balancing for your applications.
- Azure Front Door also provides built-in WAF services:
  — Azure provides a variety of WAF rules, predominantly focused on the OWASP top 10.
  — You are able to design and implement custom rules for your applications.
- Additionally, Azure Front Door acts as a CDN, globally caching your website content.
- By using IP and header filtering on your App Services, you can ensure that Front Door cannot be circumnavigated.
- To handle non-HTTP traffic, you can build a similar architecture using Traffic Manager and load balancers.

5.13 Private Application Access on GCP

Problem

You have an internal application you wish to make available directly to GCP projects in your organization without them having to traverse the public internet.

Solution

This recipe deploys the architecture shown in Figure 5-14.

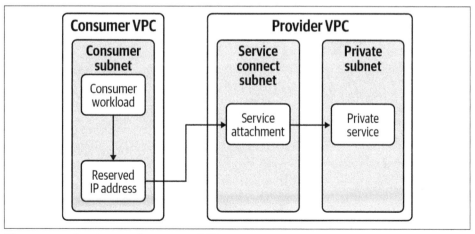

Figure 5-14. Service attachments in GCP

First, complete Recipe 5.1, and open the working directory.

Add the following variable definition to your *variables.tf* file:

```
...
variable "provider_project" {
  type        = string
  description = "The project to deploy the private workload into"
}

variable "region" {
  type        = string
  description = "The region to deploy the application into"
}

variable "application_subnet" {
  type        = string
  description = "The CIDR range for the application"
}

variable "attachment_subnet" {
  type        = string
  description = "The CIDR range for the service attachment"
}
```

And to your *terraform.tfvars* file:

```
...
provider_project   = ""
region             = ""
application_subnet = ""
attachment_subnet  = ""
```

Update *provider.tf* to have the following contents:

```
provider "google" {
  project = var.project
}

terraform {
  required_providers {
    google = {
      source  = "hashicorp/google"
      version = "~> 3"
    }
    null = {
      source  = "hashicorp/null"
      version = "~> 3"
    }
  }
}
```

Create the following *service.tf* file:

```
resource "google_compute_service_attachment" "nginx" {
  provider = google.provider
  name     = "nginx"
  region   = var.region

  enable_proxy_protocol = true
  connection_preference = "ACCEPT_AUTOMATIC"
  nat_subnets           = [google_compute_subnetwork.nat.id]
  target_service        = google_compute_forwarding_rule.nginx.id
}

resource "google_compute_forwarding_rule" "nginx" {
  provider = google.provider
  name     = "producer-forwarding-rule"
  region   = var.region

  load_balancing_scheme = "INTERNAL"
  backend_service       = google_compute_region_backend_service.nginx.id
  all_ports             = true
  network               = google_compute_network.provider.name
  subnetwork            = google_compute_subnetwork.nginx.name
}

resource "google_compute_region_backend_service" "nginx" {
  provider    = google.provider
  name        = "nginx"
  protocol    = "TCP"
  timeout_sec = 10
  region      = var.region

  backend {
    group = google_compute_instance_group.nginx.id
  }

  health_checks = [google_compute_health_check.nginx.id]
}

resource "google_compute_instance_group" "nginx" {
  provider = google.provider
  name     = "nginx"

  instances = [
    google_compute_instance.nginx.id,
  ]

  named_port {
    name = "http"
    port = "80"
  }

  zone = "europe-west1-b"
}
```

```
resource "google_compute_health_check" "nginx" {
  provider = google.provider
  name     = "nginx"

  check_interval_sec = 1
  timeout_sec        = 1
  tcp_health_check {
    port = "80"
  }
}

resource "google_compute_instance" "nginx" {
  provider                  = google.provider
  name                      = "nginx"
  machine_type              = "f1-micro"
  zone                      = "europe-west1-b"
  allow_stopping_for_update = true

  boot_disk {
    initialize_params {
      image = "cos-cloud/cos-stable-89-16108-470-25"
    }
  }

  metadata_startup_script = "docker run -p 80:80 nginx"

  network_interface {
    subnetwork = google_compute_subnetwork.nginx.name
  }

  service_account {
    email  = google_service_account.nginx.email
    scopes = ["cloud-platform"]
  }
}

resource "google_compute_network" "provider" {
  provider                        = google.provider
  name                            = "provider"
  auto_create_subnetworks         = false
  delete_default_routes_on_create = true
}

resource "google_compute_subnetwork" "nginx" {
  provider = google.provider
  name     = "nginx"
  region   = var.region

  network       = google_compute_network.provider.id
  ip_cidr_range = var.application_subnet
}
```

```
resource "google_compute_subnetwork" "nat" {
  provider = google.provider
  name     = "nat"
  region   = var.region

  network       = google_compute_network.provider.id
  purpose       = "PRIVATE_SERVICE_CONNECT"
  ip_cidr_range = var.attachment_subnet
}

resource "google_service_account" "nginx" {
  provider     = google.provider
  account_id   = "nginx-workers"
  display_name = "nginx-workers"
}

resource "google_compute_firewall" "http-provider" {
  provider  = google.provider
  name      = "http-ingress"
  network   = google_compute_network.provider.name
  direction = "INGRESS"
  priority  = 1000
  allow {
    protocol = "TCP"
    ports    = ["80"]
  }

  source_ranges = [
    google_compute_subnetwork.nat.ip_cidr_range
  ]

  target_service_accounts = [
    google_service_account.nginx.email
  ]
}

resource "google_compute_address" "service_attachment" {
  name         = "service-attachment"
  address_type = "INTERNAL"
  subnetwork   = google_compute_subnetwork.subnet[var.region].id
  region       = var.region
}

resource "null_resource" "create_forwarding_rule" {
  provisioner "local-exec" {
    command = join(" ", [
      "gcloud compute forwarding-rules create nginx-service",
      "--region ${var.region}",
      "--network ${google_compute_network.this.id}",
      "--address ${google_compute_address.service_attachment.name}",
      "--target-service-attachment ${google_compute_service_attachment.nginx.id}",
```

```
      "--project ${var.project}"
    ])
  }
}

output "ip_address" {
  value = google_compute_address.service_attachment.address
}
```

As the NGINX container is hosted publicly on Docker Hub, you will need to add resources to allow the compute instance to reach the internet. Add the following resource to *main.tf*, and run `terraform plan`:

```
resource "google_compute_router" "provider" {
  provider = google.provider
  name     = "router"
  network  = google_compute_network.provider.id
  region   = var.region
}

resource "google_compute_router_nat" "provider" {
  provider                           = google.provider
  name                               = "nat"
  router                             = google_compute_router.provider.name
  nat_ip_allocate_option             = "AUTO_ONLY"
  source_subnetwork_ip_ranges_to_nat = "ALL_SUBNETWORKS_ALL_IP_RANGES"
  region                             = var.region
}

resource "google_compute_route" "provider_internet" {
  provider        = google.provider
  name            = "provider-internet"
  dest_range      = "0.0.0.0/0"
  network         = google_compute_network.provider.name
  next_hop_gateway = "default-internet-gateway"
}

resource "google_compute_firewall" "public-egress" {
  provider  = google.provider
  name      = "public-egress"
  network   = google_compute_network.provider.name
  direction = "EGRESS"
  priority  = 1000

  allow {
    protocol = "all"
  }

  target_service_accounts = [
    google_service_account.nginx.email
  ]
}
```

Review the resources that are going to be created, and then run `terraform apply` to make the changes.

Discussion

To test the recipe was successful, you can deploy an instance into your consumer VPC to curl the IP address. To do so, create the following resources, and then ssh onto the box by calling `gcloud compute ssh bastion`:

```
resource "google_service_account" "bastion" {
  account_id   = "bastion"
  display_name = "bastion"
}

resource "google_compute_firewall" "ssh-target" {
  name      = "ssh-ingress-target"
  network   = google_compute_network.this.name
  direction = "INGRESS"
  priority  = 1000
  allow {
    protocol = "TCP"
    ports    = ["22"]
  }

  source_ranges = [
    "35.235.240.0/20"
  ]

  target_service_accounts = [
    google_service_account.bastion.email
  ]
}

resource "google_compute_firewall" "http-target" {
  name      = "http-egress"
  network   = google_compute_network.this.name
  direction = "EGRESS"
  priority  = 1000
  allow {
    protocol = "TCP"
    ports    = ["80"]
  }

  destination_ranges = [
    google_compute_subnetwork.subnet[var.region].ip_cidr_range
  ]

  target_service_accounts = [
    google_service_account.bastion.email
  ]
}
```

```
resource "google_compute_instance" "bastion" {
  name                       = "bastion"
  machine_type               = "f1-micro"
  zone                       = "europe-west1-b"
  allow_stopping_for_update = true

  boot_disk {
    initialize_params {
      image = "cos-cloud/cos-stable-89-16108-470-25"
    }
  }

  network_interface {
    subnetwork = google_compute_subnetwork.subnet[var.region].name
  }

  service_account {
    email  = google_service_account.bastion.email
    scopes = ["cloud-platform"]
  }
}
```

From an accessibility point of view, having an explicit IP address to connect to is not very user friendly. By assigning the service connect endpoint a human-friendly private DNS name, you can more readily operate the connection, as it allows for migrating IP addresses as required.

Although in this instance you created an NGINX container, service attachments can be used to allow any traffic to travel between disparate VPCs, not just HTTP based. For the sake of brevity and simplicity, this recipe does not include the creation and configuration of private certificates, but just because the network traverses only private Google networking, encryption in transit is not something to be forgotten.

When combining this with Recipe 5.7, you can configure the service attachment individually in each Shared VPC. Unfortunately, they cannot be traversed over peered connections, so it is not possible to configure them centrally in the hub at this point in time.

Additionally, they cannot be leveraged directly over VPNs or interconnect attachments, so if you are using this recipe and attempting to access the systems from on premises, you will need to evaluate options for deploying forwarding network devices. In these cases, the simplest option may be to deploy the application directly into the hub VPC. Or you can deploy a proxy to route traffic to the application.

Summary

Let's summarize what was learned and deployed in this recipe:

- Service attachments let you allow access privately hosted systems.
- When using a service attachment, traffic routes purely over private GCP networking.
  - This does not mean that encryption in transit shouldn't be used as appropriate.
- In this recipe, you made an NGINX container accessible between two VPCs in separate projects.
- In the consuming VPC, a local IP address is provisioned that automatically forwards traffic.
- Service attachments do not work over peered connections, so by using Shared VPCs, you can configure a centralized access point.

5.14 Private Application Access on AWS

Problem

You have an internal application you wish to make available directly to AWS accounts in your organization without them having to traverse the public internet.

Solution

This recipe deploys the architecture shown in Figure 5-15. An NGINX container is exposed to the internet over HTTPS.

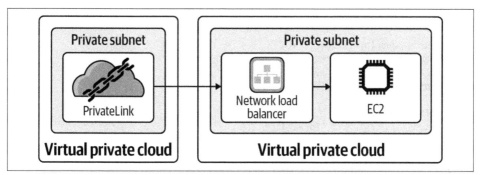

Figure 5-15. AWS PrivateLink

First, complete Recipe 5.2, and open the working directory.

Add the following variable definition to your *variables.tf* file:

```
...

variable "consumer_account_id" {
  type        = string
  description = "The account that wishes to consume the service"
}

variable "cross_account_role" {
  type        = string
  description = "The role to assume in the consumer account"
}
```

And to your *terraform.tfvars* file:

```
...
consumer_account_id = ""
cross_account_role  = ""
```

Create the following *nginx.tf* file and run `terraform plan`:

```
resource "aws_vpc_endpoint_service" "nginx" {
  acceptance_required        = false
  network_load_balancer_arns = [aws_lb.nlb.arn]
}

resource "aws_vpc_endpoint_service_allowed_principal" "consumer" {
  vpc_endpoint_service_id = aws_vpc_endpoint_service.nginx.id
  principal_arn           = "arn:aws:iam::${var.consumer_account_id}:root"
}

resource "aws_lb" "nlb" {
  name               = "network-load-balanced-ecs"
  internal           = false
  load_balancer_type = "network"
  subnets            = [for subnet in aws_subnet.public : subnet.id]
}

resource "aws_lb_listener" "nlb" {
  load_balancer_arn = aws_lb.nlb.arn
  port              = "80"
  protocol          = "TCP"

  default_action {
    type             = "forward"
    target_group_arn = aws_lb_target_group.network.arn
  }
}

resource "aws_lb_target_group" "network" {
  port        = 80
  protocol    = "TCP"
  target_type = "ip"
```

```
  vpc_id       = aws_vpc.this.id
}

resource "aws_ecs_cluster" "this" {
  name = "load_balanced_cluster"
}

resource "aws_ecs_service" "network" {
  name            = "network"
  cluster         = aws_ecs_cluster.this.id
  task_definition = aws_ecs_task_definition.this.arn
  desired_count   = 1
  launch_type     = "FARGATE"

  load_balancer {
    target_group_arn = aws_lb_target_group.network.arn
    container_name   = "nginx"
    container_port   = 80
  }

  network_configuration {
    subnets         = [for subnet in aws_subnet.private : subnet.id]
    security_groups = [aws_security_group.network.id]
  }
}

resource "aws_ecs_task_definition" "this" {
  family = "service"
  cpu    = "256"
  memory = "512"
  container_definitions = jsonencode([
    {
      name      = "nginx"
      image     = "nginx"
      essential = true
      portMappings = [
        {
          containerPort = 80
          hostPort      = 80
        }
      ]
    }
  ])
  network_mode             = "awsvpc"
  requires_compatibilities = ["FARGATE"]
}

resource "aws_security_group" "network" {
  name   = "nlb-ecs-task-sg"
  vpc_id = aws_vpc.this.id
}
```

```
resource "aws_security_group_rule" "network_public_egress" {
  type              = "egress"
  from_port         = 0
  to_port           = 0
  protocol          = "-1"
  cidr_blocks       = ["0.0.0.0/0"]
  security_group_id = aws_security_group.network.id
}

resource "aws_security_group_rule" "nlb_ingress" {
  type              = "ingress"
  from_port         = 80
  to_port           = 80
  protocol          = "tcp"
  cidr_blocks       = ["10.0.0.0/8"]
  security_group_id = aws_security_group.network.id
}

output "service_name" {
  value = aws_vpc_endpoint_service.nginx.service_name
}
```

Review the resources that are going to be created, and then run `terraform apply` to make the changes.

Discussion

With this created, you now need to add a VPC endpoint in the consumer VPC. Add the following Terraform resources to the VPC definition in the consumer account, updating the <service_name> token with the service_name output from the recipe:

```
resource "aws_security_group" "endpoint" {
  vpc_id  = aws_vpc.this.id
}

resource "aws_vpc_endpoint" "nginx" {
  vpc_id              = aws_vpc.this.id
  service_name        = "<service_name>"
  vpc_endpoint_type   = "Interface"
  private_dns_enabled = false

  security_group_ids = [
    aws_security_group.endpoint.id
  ]

  subnet_ids = [
    for subnet in aws_subnet.private : subnet.id
  ]
}

output "endpoint" {
```

```
  value = aws_vpc_endpoint.nginx.dns_entry[0]["dns_name"]
}
```

From a resource in the private subnets of your consumer VPC, if you now curl the endpoint output, you will receive the default NGINX homepage.

Now, although this recipe exposed an application over HTTP to the consumer account, VPC service endpoints can be used to allow access to a wide variety of services using a wide variety of protocols. Commonly, software-as-a-service solutions on the AWS Marketplace use VPC endpoints as their access mechanism, allowing you to more securely communicate with your vendor's tooling.

You may have noticed that in this case, the traffic is operating over an insecure protocol. This choice was made for the sake of recipe brevity. Through the configuration of a private hosted zone and a private certificate authority, you can either do TLS offloading on the NLB, or handle TLS directly within the application itself to enable encryption in transit. The following Terraform configures a two-tier certificate authority using AWS Private Certificate Authority; you will just need to fill out the domain_name parameter on the aws_acm_certificate resource.

 Running a Private CA on AWS costs $400 per month pro rata. To avoid bill shock, when experimenting, ensure you delete the Private CA when you are finished. If you restore a deleted CA, you will be charged for the intervening time.

```
locals {
  ca_root = aws_acmpca_certificate_authority.root
  ca_sub = aws_acmpca_certificate_authority.subordinate
}
resource "aws_acmpca_certificate_authority" "root" {
  certificate_authority_configuration {
    key_algorithm     = "RSA_4096"
    signing_algorithm = "SHA512WITHRSA"

    subject {
      common_name = var.common_name
    }
  }

  type = "ROOT"
}

resource "aws_acmpca_certificate_authority_certificate" "root" {
  certificate_authority_arn = local.ca_root.arn

  certificate       = aws_acmpca_certificate.root.certificate
  certificate_chain = aws_acmpca_certificate.root.certificate_chain
}
```

```
resource "aws_acmpca_certificate" "root" {
  certificate_authority_arn   = local.ca_root.arn
  certificate_signing_request = local.ca_root.certificate_signing_request
  signing_algorithm           = "SHA512WITHRSA"

  template_arn = "arn:aws:acm-pca:::template/RootCACertificate/V1"

  validity {
    type  = "YEARS"
    value = 10
  }
}

resource "aws_acmpca_certificate_authority" "subordinate" {
  certificate_authority_configuration {
    key_algorithm     = "RSA_4096"
    signing_algorithm = "SHA512WITHRSA"

    subject {
      common_name = "sub.${var.common_name}"
    }
  }

  type = "SUBORDINATE"
}

resource "aws_acmpca_certificate_authority_certificate" "subordinate" {
  certificate_authority_arn = local.ca_sub.arn

  certificate       = aws_acmpca_certificate.subordinate.certificate
  certificate_chain = aws_acmpca_certificate.subordinate.certificate_chain
}

resource "aws_acmpca_certificate" "subordinate" {
  certificate_authority_arn   = local.ca_root.arn
  certificate_signing_request = local.ca_sub.certificate_signing_request
  signing_algorithm           = "SHA512WITHRSA"

  template_arn = "arn:aws:acm-pca:::template/SubordinateCACertificate_PathLen0/V1"

  validity {
    type  = "YEARS"
    value = 5
  }
}

data "aws_caller_identity" "c" {}

resource "aws_s3_bucket" "ca_bucket" {
  bucket = "${data.aws_caller_identity.c.account_id}-ca-bucket"
  policy = <<POLICY
```

```
{
  "Version":"2012-10-17",
  "Statement":[
      {
        "Effect":"Allow",
        "Principal":{
          "Service":"acm-pca.amazonaws.com"
        },
        "Action":[
          "s3:PutObject",
          "s3:PutObjectAcl",
          "s3:GetBucketAcl",
          "s3:GetBucketLocation"
        ],
        "Resource":[
          "arn:aws:s3:::${data.aws_caller_identity.c.account_id}-ca-bucket/*",
          "arn:aws:s3:::${data.aws_caller_identity.c.account_id}-ca-bucket"
        ]
      }
  ]
}
POLICY
}

resource "aws_acm_certificate" "nginx" {
  domain_name             = ""
  certificate_authority_arn = aws_acmpca_certificate_authority.subordinate.arn
}
```

In Recipe 5.5, you used VPC endpoints to allow private network access to AWS serv-ices as well. This allows for private resources to still function within AWS and drasti-cally minimizes the amount of resources that need to be able to route to the public internet.

As endpoints come with an enduring cost, by combining this approach with Recipe 5.8, you can centralize the configuration. All VPCs within the hub-and-spoke Transit Gateway topology can utilize endpoints within the transit VPC itself, thereby signifi-cantly reducing cost. Additionally, other interconnectivity approaches on AWS, such as peering, require that the VPC CIDR ranges cannot overlap; with VPC endpoints that restriction does not apply.

 If access to an application needs to be restricted, such as an exter-nally hosted Kafka cluster, then deploy endpoints in the VPCs that require access, as opposed to centrally, to simplify access control.

Summary

Let's summarize what was learned and deployed in this recipe:

- VPC endpoints allow you to deploy private applications that can be accessed over private AWS networking.
- By utilizing AWS private networking, you can enable private resources to utilize services without giving them wider routing.
- In this recipe, an NGINX container was made accessible across accounts.
  — When creating a service endpoint, you define the IAM principals, such as AWS accounts, that are allowed to access it.
- Endpoints should also be used to access AWS services privately.
  — In Recipe 5.5, they are used to allow access to Systems Manager.
- If using a centralized Transit Gateway, endpoints should be configured centrally to reduce cost.

5.15 Private Application Access on Azure

Problem

You have an internal application you wish to make available directly to Azure subscriptions in your tenant without them having to traverse the public internet.

Solution

This recipe deploys the architecture shown in Figure 5-16. An NGINX container is exposed to the internet over HTTPS.

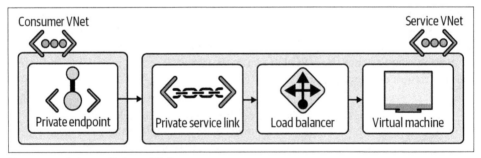

Figure 5-16. Azure Private Link

First, complete Recipe 5.3, and open the working directory.

Add the following variable definition to your *variables.tf* file:

```
...
variable "service_cidr" {
  type        = string
  description = "The CIDR for the Service Network"
}
```

And to your *terraform.tfvars* file:

```
...
service_cidr = ""
```

Create the following *service.tf* file and run `terraform plan`:

```
resource "azurerm_resource_group" "s" {
  name     = "service"
  location = var.location
}

resource "azurerm_virtual_network" "s" {
  name                = "service"
  resource_group_name = azurerm_resource_group.s.name
  location            = azurerm_resource_group.s.location
  address_space       = [var.service_cidr]
}

resource "azurerm_subnet" "service" {
  name                                           = "service"
  resource_group_name                            = azurerm_resource_group.s.name
  virtual_network_name                           = azurerm_virtual_network.s.name
  address_prefixes                               = [var.service_cidr]
  enforce_private_link_service_network_policies  = true
  enforce_private_link_endpoint_network_policies = true
}

resource "azurerm_lb" "service" {
  name                = "service"
  sku                 = "Standard"
  location            = azurerm_resource_group.s.location
  resource_group_name = azurerm_resource_group.s.name

  frontend_ip_configuration {
    name      = "frontend"
    subnet_id = azurerm_subnet.service.id
  }
}

resource "azurerm_private_link_service" "service" {
  name                = "service"
  resource_group_name = azurerm_resource_group.s.name
  location            = azurerm_resource_group.s.location

  load_balancer_frontend_ip_configuration_ids = [
```

```
      azurerm_lb.service.frontend_ip_configuration.0.id
    ]

    nat_ip_configuration {
      name      = "primary"
      subnet_id = azurerm_subnet.service.id
      primary   = true
    }
  }
```

Review the resources that are going to be created, and then run `terraform apply` to make the changes.

Discussion

To enable access to the service from other networks, you will need to add the following resources. It expects resources to be named as per Recipe 5.3.

```
locals {
  service = azurerm_private_endpoint.service
  psc     = local.service.private_service_connection[0]
}

resource "azurerm_private_endpoint" "service" {
  name                = "service"
  location            = azurerm_resource_group.network.location
  resource_group_name = azurerm_resource_group.network.name
  subnet_id           = azurerm_subnet.private.id

  private_service_connection {
    name                           = "service"
    private_connection_resource_id = azurerm_private_link_service.service.id
    is_manual_connection           = false
  }
}

resource "azurerm_network_security_rule" "endpoint_egress" {
  name                    = "endpoint-egress"
  priority                = 101
  direction               = "Outbound"
  access                  = "Allow"
  protocol                = "Tcp"
  source_port_range       = "*"
  destination_port_range  = "80"
  source_application_security_group_ids = [
    azurerm_application_security_group.application.id
  ]
  destination_address_prefixes = [
    local.psc.private_ip_address
  ]
  resource_group_name         = azurerm_resource_group.network.name
  network_security_group_name = azurerm_network_security_group.private.name
```

```
}

resource "azurerm_network_security_rule" "endpoint_ingress" {
  name                     = "endpoint-ingress"
  priority                 = 101
  direction                = "Inbound"
  access                   = "Allow"
  protocol                 = "Tcp"
  source_port_range        = "*"
  destination_port_range   = "80"
  source_application_security_group_ids = [
    azurerm_application_security_group.application.id
  ]
  destination_address_prefixes = [
    local.psc.private_ip_address
  ]
  resource_group_name      = azurerm_resource_group.network.name
  network_security_group_name = azurerm_network_security_group.private.name
}
```

Once these resources are created, you will be able to reach the service over the private endpoint.

By combining this recipe with Recipe 5.9, you can use private endpoints to make services available to all VNets and over ExpressRoute or VPNs. This allows you to deploy isolated applications that can only be accessed over specific paths, making the network security significantly easier to reason about. Additionally, it is possible to link endpoints to services in other regions, allowing for simple cross-region routing to specific services.

In this recipe, the Private Link service was configured to automatically accept connections from subscriptions within the tenancy. It is also possible to operate with a whitelist of subscriptions that are allowed to see that the Private Link service exists, and a separate whitelist for subscriptions that can automatically connect without manual approval.

Private Link is also the basis by which you can expose Azure APIs privately to virtual networks without configuring NAT or allowing public access. However, this is done by using the `service_endpoints` parameter in the subnet resource definition itself. Additionally, you can use endpoints with other Azure services, such as Azure Web Apps, to allow private access to applications hosted in higher-level managed services.

Summary

Let's summarize what was learned and deployed in this recipe:

- Azure private endpoints and service link allow you to deploy services that can only be accessed over private networking.
- As you can deploy the services into sandboxed network environments, you can protect against data leakage risks.
- By deploying a service link in one VNet, and an endpoint in another, you can expose services across subscriptions.
- Service endpoints are traversable from ExpressRoute and other connections, allowing you to centrally provision access.
- As Azure services are onboarded onto Private Link, it is possible to access applications hosted in managed services purely over private networking.
  - For example, applications hosted in Azure Web App can be made available privately.
- You can add `service_endpoints` to your subnet definitions to allow private access to Azure APIs.

CHAPTER 6

Infrastructure as Code

Infrastructure as code, or IAC, is a fundamental tool for cloud native environments. It should be the primary way resources are created, updated, and deleted across your estate. This book focuses on bringing a Terraform-first approach to fulfilling your security requirements, as that is how you drive impact at scale.

A common method for the initial management of cloud estates is to do everything through the console. This is inherently unrepeatable and difficult to audit, and it makes ensuring that changes don't result in insecure infrastructure effectively impossible. In Recipes 7.7 through 7.9, the book explores the options you have to prevent people from misconfiguring resources.

With the rapid pace of change in cloud environments, the previous methods of reviewing architecture diagrams on a regular cadence do not work. As the platform underneath the team matures, they need to be enabled to change their architecture on demand. Especially as teams encroach on serverless or Kubernetes-based architectures, the dynamic and elastic nature of cloud native services necessitates a different approach.

IAC enables you to create patterns that are secure by default. First, by producing infrastructure modules that are secure by default, you simplify the secure adoption of cloud for delivery teams. Second, by deploying your own serverless code, you can automate common tasks and dynamically react to changes in the environment. Third, by using CI/CD pipelines, you can embed DevSecOps tool chains that review every proposed change, ensuring that your security controls are not being bypassed or circumvented. Last, you can use IAC to rapidly deploy your security resources out across the entire estate, ensuring that all your systems and controls are in place and that as your estate scales, new accounts, projects, and subscriptions are automatically enrolled into your security posture.

6.1 Building Secure Infrastructure Defaults on GCP

Problem

You need to give delivery teams security-approved infrastructure patterns.

Solution

This recipe creates a Terraform module that deploys a Compute Engine instance with all disks encrypted by default.

If you haven't already done so, familiarize yourself with Terraform and the different authentication mechanisms in Chapter 11.

Create and enter an *instance* folder, and create a *variables.tf* file with the following contents:

```
variable "instance_name" {
  type        = string
  description = "The name of the instance"
}
```

Create a *main.tf* file with the following contents:

```
locals {
  required_apis = [
    "cloudkms.googleapis.com",
    "compute.googleapis.com",
  ]
}

resource "google_project_service" "api" {
  for_each        = toset(local.required_api)
  service         = each.value
  disable_on_destroy = false
}

resource "google_kms_key_ring" "keyring" {
  name       = "${var.instance_name}-keyring"
  location   = "global"
  depends_on = [google_project_service.api]
}

resource "google_kms_crypto_key" "key" {
  name     = "${var.instance_name}-key"
  key_ring = google_kms_key_ring.keyring.id
}

resource "google_compute_instance" "this" {
  name                = var.instance_name
  machine_type        = "f1-micro"
```

```
    allow_stopping_for_update = true

    boot_disk {
      initialize_params {
        image = "cos-cloud/cos-stable-89-16108-470-25"
      }
    }

    network_interface {
      network = "default"
      access_config {
      }
    }

    attached_disk {
      source             = google_compute_disk.encrypted.id
      kms_key_self_link = google_kms_crypto_key.key.id
    }
    depends_on = [google_project_service.api]
}

resource "google_service_account" "sensitive" {
  account_id   = "${var.instance_name}-sa"
  display_name = "Sensitive Data Handler"
}

resource "google_kms_crypto_key_iam_member" "service_account_use" {
  crypto_key_id = google_kms_crypto_key.key.id
  role          = "roles/cloudkms.cryptoKeyEncrypterDecrypter"
  member        = "serviceAccount:${google_service_account.sensitive.email}"
}

resource "google_compute_disk" "encrypted" {
  name = "${var.instance_name}-1"
  size = "10"
  type = "pd-standard"
  disk_encryption_key {
    kms_key_self_link     = google_kms_crypto_key.key.id
    kms_key_service_account = google_service_account.sensitive.email
  }

  depends_on = [
    google_project_service.api,
    google_kms_crypto_key_iam_member.service_account_use
  ]
}
```

Move up to the parent folder and create the following *variables.tf* file:

```
variable "project" {
  type        = string
  description = "The project to deploy the resources into"
}
```

```
variable "region" {
  type        = string
  description = "The region to deploy the resources into"
}

variable "zone" {
  type        = string
  description = "The zone to deploy the resources into"
}

variable "instance_name" {
  type        = string
  description = "The name of the instance"
}
```

Then fill out the corresponding *terraform.tfvars* file:

```
project       = ""
region        = ""
zone          = ""
instance_name = ""
```

Create the following *provider.tf* file and run `terraform init`:

```
provider "google" {
  project = var.project
  region  = var.region
  zone    = "${var.region}-${var.zone}"
}

terraform {
  required_providers {
    google = {
      source  = "hashicorp/google"
      version = "~> 4"
    }
  }
}
```

Create the following *main.tf* file and run `terraform plan`:

```
module "encrypted_instance" {
  source        = "./instance"
  instance_name = var.instance_name
}
```

Review the resources that are going to be created, and then run `terraform apply` to make the changes.

Discussion

In this recipe you created an `instance` module that created an encrypted Compute Engine instance. You then used the module to create an instance in your project. With Terraform modules, you can encapsulate the complexity and the mechanics of how the resources are secured, taking the cognitive load off the delivery teams. You write the module once, and it is deployed many times, saving significant time and effort. This is key to ensure secure infrastructure at scale by making the secure option the simplest and easiest.

 Be wary of opening up too many options on modules. When a module is adopted within the business, it becomes very hard to make breaking changes. Breaking changes include updates which force resource recreation, and the removal or modification of variables. It is significantly easier to add new variables than to change how an existing variable operates. Therefore, only add variables for today's requirements; don't try to predict what people will want tomorrow, as you will create more work in the future.

This module for a Compute Engine instance lacks variables that would be needed to use it across a business, for example, adding variables that allow for changing the instance size, boot disk image, or number of disks. As you understand the requirements of the business, you can iterate on modules selectively, opening up required options, while still preserving the secure defaults such as ensuring all disks are encrypted with distinct keys or that only certain boot disk images are allowed.

Next, let's look at how you can distribute modules. In the recipe, you locally sourced the module, which works for developing the module itself, but you need to be able to allow others to leverage the module in a secure way. Terraform provides a variety of module source options, the most common of which in GCP environments are using Cloud Storage buckets and Git repositories. For creating Git repositories on Google Cloud, see Recipe 6.7.

For a module hosted in a bucket, you can reference it as follows, filling in the variables as appropriate:

```
module "encrypted_instance" {
  source = join("", [
    "gcs::https://www.googleapis.com/storage/v1/",
    var.bucket_name,
    "/",
    var.module_name,
    ".zip"
  ])
}
```

For a module hosted in a Git repository, you can reference it as follows, filling in the variables as appropriate:

```
module "encrypted_instance" {
  source = "git::https://{var.git_url}/${var.repository_name}.git//{module_path}"
}
```

Modules work amazingly well for modern DevOps teams that are familiar with and are leveraging infrastructure as code-based workflows.

For teams within the business that are looking for a lower barrier to entry and pre-packaged solutions, you can set up Private Catalog. It enables you to load Terraform modules into catalogs that can be deployed with the Google Cloud console into user projects. However, the trade-off is that extending and building on top of these modules becomes significantly more challenging as they operate outside of the normal Terraform workflows, as elaborated on in Recipe 6.7.

Understanding the differences between these options—modules shared via buckets and Git versus modules deployed from Private Catalog—allows you to make an informed decision when faced with a business requirement. If a user needs a simplified experience where they need a fully prepackaged solution, then Private Catalog is more than likely the correct solution. If they are looking for a secure-by-default collection of resources to build on top of, then modules sourced from a central registry would be appropriate.

Summary

Let's summarize what was learned and deployed in this recipe:

- Terraform modules enable the encapsulation of complexity.
- You can build modules that enforce standard security practices.
- By building easy-to-use modules that reduce the cognitive load on teams, you will have a better security posture.
- To share modules on GCP, you can use buckets and Git repositories.
- If users are looking for a fully prepackaged solution, then Private Catalog gives a console-driven option.

6.2 Building Secure Infrastructure Defaults on AWS

Problem

You need to give delivery teams security-approved infrastructure patterns.

Solution

This recipe creates a Terraform module that deploys a Compute Engine instance with all disks encrypted by default.

If you haven't already done so, familiarize yourself with Terraform and the different authentication mechanisms in Chapter 11.

Create and enter an *instance* folder, and create a *variables.tf* file with the following contents:

```
variable "instance_name" {
  type        = string
  description = "The name for the instance"
}

variable "subnet_id" {
  type        = string
  description = "The subnet to place the instance into"
}
```

Create a *main.tf* file with the following contents:

```
data "aws_ami" "ubuntu" {
  most_recent = true

  filter {
    name   = "name"
    values = ["ubuntu/images/hvm-ssd/ubuntu-focal-20.04-amd64-server-*"]
  }

  filter {
    name   = "virtualization-type"
    values = ["hvm"]
  }

  owners = ["099720109477"] # Canonical
}

data "aws_caller_identity" "current" {}

resource "aws_instance" "this" {
  ami                  = data.aws_ami.ubuntu.id
  instance_type        = "t2.micro"
  iam_instance_profile = aws_iam_instance_profile.ssm_profile.name
  security_groups      = [aws_security_group.instance.id]
  subnet_id            = var.subnet_id

  root_block_device {
    delete_on_termination = true
    encrypted             = true
    kms_key_id            = aws_kms_key.this.arn
  }
```

```
}

data "aws_subnet" "target" {
  id = var.subnet_id
}

resource "aws_security_group" "instance" {
  vpc_id = data.aws_subnet.target.vpc_id
}

resource "aws_iam_instance_profile" "ssm_profile" {
  name = var.instance_name
  role = aws_iam_role.role.name
}

resource "aws_iam_role" "role" {
  name = var.instance_name

  managed_policy_arns = [
    "arn:aws:iam::aws:policy/AmazonSSMManagedInstanceCore"
  ]

  assume_role_policy = data.aws_iam_policy_document.assume.json
}

data "aws_iam_policy_document" "assume" {
  statement {
    actions = [
      "sts:AssumeRole",
    ]

    principals {
      type = "Service"
      identifiers = [
        "ec2.amazonaws.com"
      ]
    }
  }
}
```

Create a *key.tf* file with the following contents:

```
resource "aws_kms_key" "this" {
  policy = data.aws_iam_policy_document.key_policy.json
}

data "aws_iam_role" "current_principal" {
  name = split("/", data.aws_caller_identity.current.arn)[1]
}

data "aws_iam_policy_document" "key_policy" {
  statement {
    sid = "Allow access for Key Administrators"
```

```
    actions = [
      "kms:Create*",
      "kms:Describe*",
      "kms:Enable*",
      "kms:List*",
      "kms:Put*",
      "kms:Update*",
      "kms:Revoke*",
      "kms:Disable*",
      "kms:Get*",
      "kms:Delete*",
      "kms:TagResource",
      "kms:UntagResource",
      "kms:ScheduleKeyDeletion",
      "kms:CancelKeyDeletion"
    ]
    effect = "Allow"
    principals {
      type        = "AWS"
      identifiers = [data.aws_iam_role.current_principal.arn]
    }
    resources = ["*"]
}

statement {
  sid = "Allow use of the key"
  actions = [
    "kms:Encrypt",
    "kms:Decrypt",
    "kms:ReEncrypt*",
    "kms:GenerateDataKey*",
    "kms:DescribeKey"
  ]
  effect = "Allow"
  principals {
    type        = "AWS"
    identifiers = ["*"]
  }
  resources = ["*"]
}

statement {
  sid     = "Allow attachment of persistent resources"
  effect = "Allow"
  principals {
    type        = "AWS"
    identifiers = ["*"]
  }
  actions = [
    "kms:CreateGrant",
    "kms:ListGrants",
    "kms:RevokeGrant"
```

```
    ]
    resources = ["*"]
    condition {
      test     = "Bool"
      variable = "kms:GrantIsForAWSResource"
      values   = [true]
    }
  }
}
```

Move up to the parent folder and create the following *variables.tf* file:

```
variable "instance_name" {
  type        = string
  description = "The name for the instance"
}

variable "subnet_id" {
  type        = string
  description = "The subnet to place the instance into"
}
```

Then fill out the corresponding *terraform.tfvars* file:

```
instance_name = ""
subnet_id     = ""
```

Create the following *provider.tf* file and run `terraform init`:

```
provider "aws" {}

terraform {
  required_providers {
    aws = {
      source  = "hashicorp/aws"
      version = "~> 3"
    }
  }
}
```

Create the following *main.tf* file and run `terraform plan`:

```
module "encrypted_instance" {
  source        = "./instance"
  instance_name = var.instance_name
  subnet_id     = var.subnet_id
}
```

Review the resources that are going to be created, and then run `terraform apply` to make the changes.

Discussion

This recipe created a module that enforces several best practices into the EC2 instances created with it. For example, the volumes were encrypted with KMS keys, and the instance profile contained the base SSM permission set. Having modules such as these as the building blocks enables you to bake these core practices into the infrastructure without passing the burden on to development teams.

Looking at this module, you will see missing variables that would be needed to make use of it across a number of teams. Rather than locking to the most recent Ubuntu 20-04 server image, users will most likely need a choice of operating system, and a t2.micro instance size is too small for the majority of use cases.

 Although making modules with many possible configurations may sound appealing as users will be able to do more with them, the trade-off you make is one of value, stability, and maintainability. With more options come more possible configurations, some of which may be broken. If you produce modules that break consistently, you erode the trust that is key to getting teams to leverage them in the first place. A module is an abstraction; you're hiding complexity from the consumer. The wider the array of options, the weaker that abstraction becomes, negating the value you're trying to provide.

Authoring the module is only step one of the process; step two is making the module readily available to other teams and users across the business. To distribute modules across teams in AWS, there are two predominant options: hosting them in S3 buckets and hosting them in Git repositories. To see how to create Git repositories in AWS, see Recipe 6.8.

For a module hosted in a bucket, you can reference it as follows, filling in the variables as appropriate:

```
module "encrypted_instance" {
  source = join("", [
    "s3::https://s3-",
    var.region,
    ".amazonaws.com/",
    var.bucket_name,
    "/",
    var.module_name,
    ".zip"
  ])
}
```

For a module hosted in a Git repository, you can reference it as follows, filling in the variables as appropriate:

```
module "encrypted_instance" {
  source = "git::https://{var.git_url}/${var.repository_name}.git//{module_path}"
}
```

While modules are the right vehicle for delivery teams actively leveraging infrastructure as code, businesses often want a point-and-click option for deploying prepackaged solutions. Currently, Service Catalog on AWS is CloudFormation only, although the functionality exists within HashiCorp's Terraform Cloud for Business or Terraform Enterprise offerings.

Summary

Let's summarize what was learned and deployed in this recipe:

- Modules allow you to abstract away complexity from consuming teams.
- You can author modules to enforce security best practices, such as encryption configurations and instance profiles.
- As modules are adopted, the security posture of your estate increases.
- Producing well-written modules is key to their success.
- You can share modules using S3 buckets or Git repositories.
- The first-party Service Catalog offering on AWS does not support Terraform at this time.
- HashiCorp provides the functionality within its third-party offerings.

6.3 Building Secure Infrastructure Defaults on Azure

Problem

You need to give delivery teams security-approved infrastructure patterns.

Solution

This recipe creates a Terraform module that deploys a Compute Engine instance with all disks encrypted by default.

If you haven't already done so, familiarize yourself with Terraform and the different authentication mechanisms in Chapter 11.

Create and enter an *instance* folder and create a *variables.tf* file with the following contents:

```
variable "resource_group_name" {
  type        = string
  description = "The name of the resource group to use"
}
```

```
variable "instance_name" {
  type        = string
  description = "The name for the instance"
}

variable "subnet_id" {
  type        = string
  description = "The subnet to place the instance into"
}

variable "ssh_key_path" {
  type        = string
  description = "The path to the SSH key to upload"
}
```

Create a *provider.tf* file with the following contents:

```
terraform {
  required_providers {
    random = {
      source  = "hashicorp/random"
      version = "~> 3"
    }
  }
}
```

Create a *main.tf* file with the following contents:

```
data "azurerm_client_config" "current" {}

data "azurerm_resource_group" "this" {
  name = var.resource_group_name
}

resource "azurerm_network_interface" "primary" {
  name                = "${var.instance_name}-primary"
  location            = data.azurerm_resource_group.this.location
  resource_group_name = data.azurerm_resource_group.this.name

  ip_configuration {
    name                          = "internal"
    subnet_id                     = var.subnet_id
    private_ip_address_allocation = "Dynamic"
  }
}

resource "azurerm_linux_virtual_machine" "this" {
  name                = var.instance_name
  resource_group_name = data.azurerm_resource_group.this.name
  location            = data.azurerm_resource_group.this.location
  size                = "Standard_F2"
  admin_username      = "adminuser"
  network_interface_ids = [
```

```
      azurerm_network_interface.primary.id,
    ]


    os_disk {
      caching             = "ReadWrite"
      storage_account_type = "Standard_LRS"
      disk_encryption_set_id = azurerm_disk_encryption_set.des.id
    }

    admin_ssh_key {
      username   = "adminuser"
      public_key = file(var.ssh_key_path)
    }

    source_image_reference {
      publisher = "Canonical"
      offer     = "UbuntuServer"
      sku       = "16.04-LTS"
      version   = "latest"
    }

    depends_on = [
      azurerm_role_assignment.crypto_access
    ]
  }

  resource "random_string" "key_vault" {
    length  = 16
    number = false
    special = false
  }

  resource "azurerm_key_vault" "keys" {
    name                        = random_string.key_vault.result
    location                    = data.azurerm_resource_group.this.location
    resource_group_name         = data.azurerm_resource_group.this.name
    tenant_id                   = data.azurerm_client_config.current.tenant_id
    enable_rbac_authorization   = true
    enabled_for_disk_encryption = true
    soft_delete_retention_days  = 7
    purge_protection_enabled    = true
    sku_name                    = "standard"
  }

  resource "azurerm_disk_encryption_set" "des" {
    name                = "des"
    resource_group_name = data.azurerm_resource_group.this.name
    location            = data.azurerm_resource_group.this.location
    key_vault_key_id    = azurerm_key_vault_key.disk.id

    identity {
```

```
    type = "SystemAssigned"
  }
}

resource "azurerm_role_assignment" "crypto_officer" {
  scope                = azurerm_key_vault.keys.id
  role_definition_name = "Key Vault Crypto Officer"
  principal_id         = data.azurerm_client_config.current.object_id
}

resource "azurerm_role_assignment" "user_reader" {
  scope                = azurerm_key_vault.keys.id
  role_definition_name = "Reader"
  principal_id         = data.azurerm_client_config.current.object_id
}

resource "azurerm_role_assignment" "des_reader" {
  scope                = azurerm_key_vault.keys.id
  role_definition_name = "Reader"
  principal_id         = azurerm_disk_encryption_set.des.identity.0.principal_id
}

resource "azurerm_role_assignment" "crypto_access" {
  scope                = azurerm_key_vault.keys.id
  role_definition_name = "Key Vault Crypto User"
  principal_id         = azurerm_disk_encryption_set.des.identity.0.principal_id
}

resource "azurerm_key_vault_key" "disk" {
  name         = "disk"
  key_vault_id = azurerm_key_vault.keys.id
  key_type     = "RSA"
  key_size     = 2048
  key_opts     = ["decrypt", "encrypt", "sign", "unwrapKey", "verify", "wrapKey"]
}

resource "azurerm_managed_disk" "encrypted" {
  name                   = "${var.instance_name}-1"
  location               = data.azurerm_resource_group.this.location
  resource_group_name    = data.azurerm_resource_group.this.name
  storage_account_type   = "Standard_LRS"
  create_option          = "Empty"
  disk_size_gb           = "1"
  disk_encryption_set_id = azurerm_disk_encryption_set.des.id
}

resource "azurerm_virtual_machine_data_disk_attachment" "attachment" {
  managed_disk_id    = azurerm_managed_disk.encrypted.id
  virtual_machine_id = azurerm_linux_virtual_machine.this.id
  lun                = "10"
  caching            = "ReadWrite"
}
```

Move up to the parent folder and create the following *variables.tf* file:

```
variable "location" {
  type        = string
  description = "The Azure location for resources"
}

variable "instance_name" {
  type        = string
  description = "The name for the instance"
}

variable "ssh_key_path" {
  type        = string
  description = "The path to the SSH key to upload"
}
```

Then fill out the corresponding *terraform.tfvars* file:

```
location      = ""
instance_name = ""
ssh_key_path  = ""
```

Create the following *provider.tf* file and run `terraform init`:

```
terraform {
  required_providers {
    azurerm = {
      source  = "hashicorp/azurerm"
      version = "~> 2"
    }
  }
}

provider "azurerm" {
  features {}
}
```

Create the following *main.tf* file and run `terraform plan`:

```
resource "azurerm_resource_group" "workload" {
  name     = "workload"
  location = var.location
}

resource "azurerm_virtual_network" "this" {
  name                = "example"
  address_space       = ["10.0.0.0/16"]
  location            = azurerm_resource_group.workload.location
  resource_group_name = azurerm_resource_group.workload.name
}

resource "azurerm_subnet" "this" {
  name                = "internal"
```

```
  resource_group_name  = azurerm_resource_group.workload.name
  virtual_network_name = azurerm_virtual_network.this.name
  address_prefixes     = ["10.0.2.0/24"]
}

module "encrypted_instance" {
  source               = "./instance"
  instance_name        = var.instance_name
  resource_group_name  = azurerm_resource_group.workload.name
  ssh_key_path         = var.ssh_key_path
  subnet_id            = azurerm_subnet.this.id

  depends_on = [
    azurerm_resource_group.workload
  ]
}
```

 Due to the time delay in Key Vault RBAC permissions being properly propagated, if the first apply fails due to permission issues on the key, wait a couple of minutes and run `terraform apply` again. Currently there is no way in Terraform to explicitly wait on the propagation to occur.

Review the resources that are going to be created, and then run `terraform apply` to make the changes.

Discussion

In this recipe, you created a module that deployed a virtual machine with all disks encrypted by default. You also created an example VNet, workload subnet, and resource group to house the instance. Modules like this allow you to ensure that your security controls are not only being observed but are the default state for resources in the cloud. Chapter 7 covers how prevention of security issues is fundamental to having highly secure infrastructure.

A well-written module abstracts away complexity from the consumers. In this recipe, by invoking the module, you get the instance that you need. The other resources such as the Key Vault are created invisible to you as the consumer, thereby reducing the cognitive load. Modules are powerful because they encapsulate learning and practices, which are then applied en masse across your estate.

 Authoring well-written abstractions has proved to be one of the perennial challenges in IT. With modules, focus on having small interfaces, the smallest number of possible options. By only adding the variables that teams need today, you push design decisions into the future, where you will better understand how the module has been used and what the emerging requirements are.

Once you have a module, the next step is to share it across teams. Unlike with AWS and GCP buckets, Terraform doesn't provide support for hosting modules directly in Azure storage accounts. This leaves us with one preferred option of module hosting: Git repositories. For setting up repositories, see Recipe 6.9.

For a module hosted in a Git repository, you can reference it as follows, filling in the variables as appropriate:

```
module "encrypted_instance" {
  source = "git::https://{var.git_url}/${var.repository_name}.git//{module_path}"
}
```

For delivery teams that are actively using infrastructure as code, consuming modules in this way provides the lowest friction and highest velocity. For parts of the business that are looking for prepackaged, turnkey solutions, there is Azure Managed Applications. Unfortunately, as of the time of writing, it only supports ARM templates and not Terraform. For equivalent functionality, HashiCorp's Terraform Cloud for Business or Terraform Enterprise offerings both provide a similar service.

Summary

Let's summarize what was learned and deployed in this recipe:

- Modules are a key part of security at scale.
- A well-authored module enables you to embed best practices at the foundation.
- The recipe created a module that ensured disks were encrypted with keys from Key Vault.
- To share modules on Azure, use git repositories.
- For console-driven deployment of solutions, look at HashiCorp's offerings, as Azure Managed Applications does not support Terraform-based applications.

6.4 Functions as a Service on GCP

Problem

You need to deploy some code that needs to run every day, and be alerted via email when failures occur.

Solution

If you haven't already done so, familiarize yourself with Terraform and the different authentication mechanisms in Chapter 11.

Create the following *variables.tf* file:

```
variable "project" {
  type        = string
  description = "The project to deploy the resources into"
}

variable "region" {
  type        = string
  description = "The region to deploy the resources into"
}

variable "function_name" {
  type        = string
  description = "The name of the function"
}

variable "email_address" {
  type        = string
  description = "The email address to send alerts to"
}
```

Then fill out the corresponding *terraform.tfvars* file:

```
project       = ""
region        = ""
function_name = ""
email_address = ""
```

Create the following *provider.tf* file and run `terraform init`:

```
provider "google" {
  project     = var.project
  region      = var.region
}

terraform {
  required_providers {
    google = {
      source  = "hashicorp/google"
      version = "~> 4"
    }
    archive = {
      source  = "hashicorp/archive"
      version = "~> 2"
    }
  }
}
```

Create a *src* folder and the following *main.py* file:

```
import base64
from logging import getLogger, INFO

from google.cloud import error_reporting, logging
```

```
logging.Client().setup_logging()
logger = getLogger()
logger.setLevel(INFO)

error_client = error_reporting.Client()

def handle(event, _):
  try:
    logger.info(event)
    data = base64.b64decode(event["data"]).decode("utf-8")
    logger.info(data)
  except Exception as e:
    logger.error(e)
    error_client.report_exception()
```

And the following *requirements.txt* file:

```
google-cloud-logging
google-cloud-error-reporting
```

Last, in the parent folder, create the following *main.tf* file and run `terraform plan`:

```
locals {
  required_apis = [
    "cloudbuild.googleapis.com",
    "clouderrorreporting.googleapis.com",
    "cloudfunctions.googleapis.com",
    "logging.googleapis.com",
    "storage.googleapis.com",
  ]
}

resource "google_project_service" "api" {
  for_each           = toset(local.required_apis)
  service            = each.value
  disable_on_destroy = false
}

resource "google_storage_bucket" "bucket" {
  name     = "${var.function_name}-artifacts"
  location = var.region
}

data "archive_file" "code" {
  type        = "zip"
  source_dir  = "${path.module}/src"
  output_path = "${path.module}/main.zip"
}

resource "google_storage_bucket_object" "code" {
  name   = "${data.archive_file.code.output_md5}.zip"
  bucket = google_storage_bucket.bucket.name
  source = data.archive_file.code.output_path
```

```
}

resource "google_cloudfunctions_function" "function" {
  name    = var.function_name
  runtime = "python39"

  available_memory_mb   = 128
  source_archive_bucket = google_storage_bucket.bucket.name
  source_archive_object = google_storage_bucket_object.code.name
  entry_point           = "handle"

  event_trigger {
    event_type = "google.pubsub.topic.publish"
    resource   = google_pubsub_topic.trigger.name
  }

  depends_on = [
    google_project_service.api
  ]
}

resource "google_project_iam_member" "log_writer" {
  project = var.project
  role    = "roles/logging.logWriter"
  member  = join(":", [
    "serviceAccount",
    google_cloudfunctions_function.function.service_account_email
  ])
}

resource "google_cloud_scheduler_job" "daily" {
  name     = var.function_name
  schedule = "* 9 * * *"

  pubsub_target {
    topic_name = google_pubsub_topic.trigger.id
  }
}

resource "google_pubsub_topic" "trigger" {
  name = var.function_name
}

resource "google_monitoring_alert_policy" "errors" {
  display_name = "${var.function_name} Errors"
  combiner     = "OR"
  conditions {
    display_name = "Errors"
    condition_threshold {
      filter = join("", [
        "resource.type = \"cloud_function\" AND ",
        "resource.labels.function_name = \"",
```

```
      var.function_name,
      "\" AND ",
      "metric.type = \"logging.googleapis.com/log_entry_count\" AND ",
      "metric.labels.severity = \"ERROR\""
      ]
    )
    duration   = "0s"
    comparison = "COMPARISON_GT"
    aggregations {
      alignment_period   = "60s"
      per_series_aligner = "ALIGN_COUNT"
    }
    trigger {
      count = 1
    }
  }
}

notification_channels = [
  google_monitoring_notification_channel.email.id
]
}

resource "google_monitoring_notification_channel" "email" {
  display_name = "${var.function_name} Error Emails"
  type         = "email"
  labels = {
    email_address = var.email
  }
}
```

Review the resources that are going to be created, and then run `terraform apply` to make the changes.

Discussion

Cloud Functions are a low total-cost-of-ownership method of running code on GCP. Given a particular trigger, they allow you to perform any action you wish. For example, they are used in Recipe 7.10 to fix public buckets automatically, and in Recipe 3.1 to allow for automated actions on SCC findings. While this recipe uses Python, there are many more languages with first-class support.

This recipe shows how to deploy a timed dummy function triggered via Cloud Scheduler and also how to monitor and debug functions. The function is given explicit permissions to be able to write logs to Cloud Operations Suite and also to dispatch errors when they occur. This is then observed via a monitoring alert policy that sends emails when errors are detected. As you scale the amount of systems and services under the management of the security team, it is key that robust monitoring and alerting is wrapped around everything you support.

For serverless event-driven architectures on GCP, one option is Cloud Functions and the other is Cloud Run, which is container based. By adopting Cloud Functions, you have a shallower learning curve than with containers, and you will be able to more rapidly build out code to fulfill your needs on day one.

Eventarc is a managed service which looks to provide a unified event-driven approach to GCP and beyond. It automatically produces events from many GCP services by trailing audit logs and can handle events from third-party SaaS vendors, and even your own custom events. This gives you a wide range of triggers to execute your code, from every time a query is run on BigQuery to whenever a new network is created. Unfortunately, Cloud Run is the only service that can consume Eventarc messages at the current time, which comes with the aforementioned container learning curve.

Summary

Let's summarize what was learned and deployed in this recipe:

- Cloud Functions allow for the simple running of code from a variety of triggers.
- You should ensure that your functions are operable, with logging, monitoring, and alerting enabled by default.
- Cloud Functions support many languages, such as TypeScript, Python, and Java.
- There is also the Cloud Run service, which is container based but can also be triggered off of events.
- On day one, Cloud Functions provide a more managed service compared to container-based options.
- Eventarc, which is GCP's unified event platform, currently only interoperates with Cloud Run.

6.5 Functions as a Service on AWS

Problem

You need to deploy some code that needs to run every day, and be alerted via email when failures occur.

Solution

If you haven't already done so, familiarize yourself with Terraform and the different authentication mechanisms in Chapter 11.

Create the following *variables.tf* file:

```hcl
variable "function_name" {
  type        = string
  description = "The name for the function"
}

variable "email" {
  type        = string
  description = "The email address to send alarm notifications"
}
```

Then fill out the corresponding *terraform.tfvars* file:

```hcl
function_name = ""
email_address = ""
```

Create the following *provider.tf* file and run `terraform init`:

```hcl
provider "aws" {}

terraform {
  required_providers {
    aws = {
      source  = "hashicorp/aws"
      version = "~> 3"
    }
    archive = {
      source  = "hashicorp/archive"
      version = "~> 2"
    }
  }
}
```

Next, create a *src* folder and the following *main.py* file:

```python
from logging import getLogger, INFO

logger = getLogger()
logger.setLevel(INFO)

def handle(event, _):
    try:
        logger.info(event)
    except Exception as e:
        logger.error(e)
        raise e
```

Create the following *main.tf* file and run `terraform plan`:

```hcl
resource "aws_lambda_function" "this" {
  filename      = data.archive_file.code.output_path
  function_name = var.function_name
  role          = aws_iam_role.lambda.arn
  handler       = "main.handle"

  source_code_hash = filebase64sha256(data.archive_file.code.output_path)
```

```
  runtime = "python3.9"

  depends_on = [
    data.archive_file.code
  ]
}

data "archive_file" "code" {
  type        = "zip"
  source_dir  = "${path.module}/src"
  output_path = "${path.module}/main.zip"
}

resource "aws_cloudwatch_event_rule" "daily" {
  name                = "run-daily"
  schedule_expression = "cron(* 9 ? * * *)"
}

resource "aws_cloudwatch_event_target" "daily" {
  rule = aws_cloudwatch_event_rule.daily.name
  arn  = aws_lambda_function.this.arn
}

resource "aws_lambda_permission" "allow_cloudwatch" {
  statement_id  = "AllowExecutionFromEventBridge"
  action        = "lambda:InvokeFunction"
  function_name = aws_lambda_function.this.function_name
  principal     = "events.amazonaws.com"
  source_arn    = aws_cloudwatch_event_rule.daily.arn
}

resource "aws_iam_role" "lambda" {
  name               = var.function_name
  assume_role_policy = data.aws_iam_policy_document.assume.json
  managed_policy_arns = [
    "arn:aws:iam::aws:policy/service-role/AWSLambdaBasicExecutionRole",
  ]
}

data "aws_iam_policy_document" "assume" {
  statement {
    effect  = "Allow"
    actions = ["sts:AssumeRole"]

    principals {
      type = "Service"
      identifiers = [
        "lambda.amazonaws.com"
      ]
    }
  }
```

```
}

resource "aws_cloudwatch_metric_alarm" "foobar" {
  alarm_actions = [
    aws_sns_topic.alarm.arn
  ]
  alarm_name                = "${var.function_name}-failures"
  comparison_operator       = "GreaterThanOrEqualToThreshold"
  evaluation_periods        = "1"
  insufficient_data_actions = []
  metric_name               = "Errors"
  namespace                 = "AWS/Lambda"
  period                    = "60"
  statistic                 = "Sum"
  threshold                 = "1"
  treat_missing_data        = "notBreaching"
}

resource "aws_sns_topic" "alarm" {
  name = "${var.function_name}-failures"
}

resource "aws_sns_topic_subscription" "email" {
  topic_arn = aws_sns_topic.alarm.arn
  protocol  = "email"
  endpoint  = var.email
}
```

Review the resources that are going to be created, and then run `terraform apply` to make the changes.

Discussion

AWS Lambda functions are a fully serverless way of deploying code. They can be triggered from a wide array of events and allow you to easily extend AWS services with custom functionality. In this recipe, you deployed a function which is triggered at a particular time every day, often used for turning on and off resources to save money or for running daily reports.

Recipe 7.11 uses AWS-provided remediation actions, but where the action does not already exist, the easiest way to extend is with a Lambda function. You can trigger functions off almost everything in AWS using AWS EventBridge, as discussed in Recipes 4.11 and 7.5. Most AWS services natively publish events to EventBridge, and it is also possible to build rules to trail CloudTrail logs, or publish your own custom events.

The key to having success with functions is ensuring they are operable. In this recipe, you ensured that the function had enough permissions to write logs to CloudWatch and that an alert was configured to fire off an email whenever the function failed.

When looking to build more complex architectures with Lambda functions, AWS X-Ray provides a fully managed tracing solution which allows you to follow a particular request through all the services that make up your application.

AWS Lambda also possesses the capability to run containers. This can be a simple way to run certain tools within your AWS environment, as long as the 15-minute execution time is sufficient. Lambda functions, as used in this recipe, provide a lower total-cost-of-ownership approach to executing code, as the environment management is provided by AWS. In building custom containers, you bring much of that burden back on yourself, and you must have a container strategy and the supporting infrastructure.

Summary

Let's summarize what was learned and deployed in this recipe:

- AWS Lambda functions are a fully serverless way of running code.
- You need to ensure they are operable to derive value.
- By using CloudWatch, you can capture logs and errors, and alert as required.
- EventBridge allows for triggering functions off almost any event.
- These triggers allow you to easily extend AWS services with custom functionality.
- You can run containers directly on Lambda, but that introduces a container learning curve.

6.6 Functions as a Service on Azure

Problem

You need to deploy some code that needs to run every day, and be alerted via email when failures occur.

Solution

To complete this recipe, you will need the Azure Functions Core Tools installed, which you can find instructions for at Azure Functions Core Tools GitHub (*https://github.com/Azure/azure-functions-core-tools*).

If you haven't already done so, familiarize yourself with Terraform and the different authentication mechanisms in Chapter 11.

Create the following *variables.tf* file:

```
variable "location" {
    type        = string
```

```
  description = "The Azure location for resources"
}

variable "function_name" {
  type        = string
  description = "The name for the Azure function"
}

variable "email" {
  type        = string
  description = "The email address to notify on errors"
}
```

Then fill out the corresponding *terraform.tfvars* file:

```
location      = ""
function_name = ""
email_address = ""
```

Create the following *provider.tf* file and run `terraform init`:

```
terraform {
  required_providers {
    azurerm = {
      source  = "hashicorp/azurerm"
      version = "~> 2"
    }
    null = {
      source  = "hashicorp/null"
      version = "~> 3"
    }
    random = {
      source  = "hashicorp/random"
      version = "~> 3"
    }
    archive = {
      source  = "hashicorp/archive"
      version = "~> 2"
    }
  }
}

provider "azurerm" {
  features {}
}
```

Create the following *host.json* file:

```
{
  "version": "2.0",
  "logging": {
    "applicationInsights": {
      "samplingSettings": {
        "isEnabled": true,
```

```
        "excludedTypes": "Request"
      }
    }
  },
  "extensionBundle": {
    "id": "Microsoft.Azure.Functions.ExtensionBundle",
    "version": "[2.*, 3.0.0)"
  }
}
```

And the following *local.setting.json* file:

```
{
  "IsEncrypted": false,
  "Values": {
    "FUNCTIONS_WORKER_RUNTIME": "python",
    "AzureWebJobsStorage": ""
  }
}
```

And the following *requirements.txt* file:

```
azure-functions==1.7.2
```

Create and enter a folder called function_name from *terraform.tfvars*, and create the following *main.py* file:

```python
import logging

import azure.functions as func

logger = logging.getLogger(__name__)
logger.setLevel(logging.INFO)

def main(daily: func.TimerRequest):
    logger.info(daily)
```

And the following *function.json*:

```json
{
  "scriptFile": "main.py",
  "bindings": [
    {
      "type": "timerTrigger",
      "name": "daily",
      "direction": "in",
      "schedule": "* * 9 * * *"
    }
  ]
}
```

Move back up to the parent folder and create the following *main.tf* file, and run terraform plan:

```
```

```
locals {
  function = azurerm_application_insights.function
}

data "azurerm_subscription" "current" {}

data "azurerm_client_config" "current" {}

resource "azurerm_resource_group" "function" {
  name     = var.function_name
  location = var.location
}

resource "random_string" "sa_name" {
  length  = 16
  number = false
}

resource "azurerm_storage_account" "f" {
  name                     = random_string.sa_name.result
  resource_group_name      = azurerm_resource_group.function.name
  location                 = azurerm_resource_group.function.location
  account_tier             = "Standard"
  account_replication_type = "LRS"
}

resource "azurerm_app_service_plan" "function" {
  name                = var.function_name
  location            = azurerm_resource_group.function.location
  resource_group_name = azurerm_resource_group.function.name
  kind                = "functionapp"
  reserved            = true

  sku {
    tier = "Dynamic"
    size = "Y1"
  }
}

resource "azurerm_function_app" "function" {
  name                       = var.function_name
  location                   = azurerm_resource_group.function.location
  resource_group_name        = azurerm_resource_group.function.name
  app_service_plan_id        = azurerm_app_service_plan.function.id
  storage_account_name       = azurerm_storage_account.f.name
  storage_account_access_key = azurerm_storage_account.f.primary_access_key
  os_type                    = "linux"
  version                    = "~3"

  app_settings = {
    APPINSIGHTS_INSTRUMENTATIONKEY = local.function.instrumentation_key
    APPLICATIONINSIGHTS_CONNECTION_STRING = local.function.connection_string
```

```
    FUNCTIONS_WORKER_RUNTIME      = "python"
  }

  site_config {
    linux_fx_version = "PYTHON|3.9"
  }

  identity {
    type = "SystemAssigned"
  }
}

data "archive_file" "code" {
  type        = "zip"
  source_dir  = "${path.module}/${var.function_name}"
  output_path = "${path.module}/main.zip"
}

resource "null_resource" "deploy" {
  triggers = {
    checksum = filebase64sha256(
      data.archive_file.code.output_path
    )
  }
  provisioner "local-exec" {
    command = "func azure functionapp publish ${var.function_name}"
  }

  depends_on = [
    azurerm_function_app.function
  ]
}

resource "azurerm_application_insights" "function" {
  name                = var.function_name
  location            = azurerm_resource_group.function.location
  resource_group_name = azurerm_resource_group.function.name
  workspace_id        = azurerm_log_analytics_workspace.insights.id
  application_type    = "other"
}

resource "azurerm_log_analytics_workspace" "insights" {
  name                = var.function_name
  location            = azurerm_resource_group.function.location
  resource_group_name = azurerm_resource_group.function.name
  sku                 = "PerGB2018"
  retention_in_days   = 30
}

resource "azurerm_monitor_metric_alert" "exceptions" {
  name                = "exceptions"
  resource_group_name = azurerm_resource_group.function.name
```

```
  scopes = [
    azurerm_application_insights.function.id
  ]

  criteria {
    metric_namespace = "Microsoft.Insights/components"
    metric_name      = "exceptions/count"
    aggregation      = "Count"
    operator         = "GreaterThan"
    threshold        = 0
  }

  action {
    action_group_id = azurerm_monitor_action_group.email.id
  }
}

resource "azurerm_monitor_action_group" "email" {
  name                = var.function_name
  resource_group_name = azurerm_resource_group.function.name
  short_name          = var.function_name

  email_receiver {
    name          = "ops"
    email_address = var.email
  }
}
```

Review the resources that are going to be created, and then run `terraform apply` to make the changes.

Discussion

Azure Functions are a cheap and simple way of running code on Azure. In this recipe, you configured the timer trigger to run the function daily, a pattern which is often used for scheduling resources and running regular reporting. They're used in both Recipes 7.6 and 7.12 to notify and take action when compliance issues are discovered.

You need to ensure that the functions you deploy are operable, so you can understand when and what failures occur. To this end, the recipe configures Application Insights, which provides a holistic set of monitoring around the function, including a wide variety of metrics. One of those metrics, the amount of thrown exceptions, was used to configure an automatic failure alert. This automatically dispatches emails whenever there is a failure via an action group.

A key part of building out a suite of security solutions with Azure Functions is Event Grid, as seen in Recipes 7.6 and 7.12. As Event Grid natively produces a wide variety of Azure events, you can trigger a wide variety of automation tags, such as automatically putting virtual machine data into a configuration management database on creation or logging when a privileged role is leveraged in a production or sensitive subscription.

Summary

Let's summarize what was learned and deployed in this recipe:

- Azure Functions are a simple way of running code in the cloud.
- They are triggered by events.
- The recipe configured a timer trigger to run the function every day at a set time.
- By integrating the Event Grid, you can trigger functions off almost any event in Azure.
- By ensuring that the functions are configured with App Insights, you can simply manage functions.

6.7 Robust Deployment on GCP

Problem

You want to use version control and CI/CD pipelines to deploy your code.

Solution

If you haven't already done so, familiarize yourself with Terraform and the different authentication mechanisms in Chapter 11.

Create a *variables.tf* file and copy the following contents:

```
variable "project" {
  type        = string
  description = "The project to deploy the resources into"
}

variable "region" {
  type        = string
  description = "The region to deploy the resources into"
}

variable "repository_name" {
  type        = string
  description = "The name of the repository"
}
```

Then fill out the corresponding *terraform.tfvars* file:

```
project         = ""
region          = ""
repository_name = ""
```

Create the following *provider.tf* file and run `terraform init`:

```
provider "google" {
  project     = var.project
  region      = var.region
}

terraform {
  required_providers {
    google = {
      source  = "hashicorp/google"
      version = "~> 4"
    }
  }
}
```

Define the following *cloudbuild.yaml* file:

```
steps:
  - id: 'tf plan'
    name: 'hashicorp/terraform:1.0.0'
    entrypoint: 'sh'
    args:
    - '-c'
    - |
        echo $BRANCH_NAME
        terraform init
        terraform plan -no-color
  - id: 'tf apply'
    name: 'hashicorp/terraform:1.0.0'
    entrypoint: 'sh'
    args:
    - '-c'
    - |
        echo $BRANCH_NAME
        if [ $BRANCH_NAME == "main" ]; then
          terraform init
          terraform apply -no-color -auto-approve
        fi
options:
  logging: CLOUD_LOGGING_ONLY
```

Create the following *main.tf* file and run `terraform plan`:

```
data "google_project" "project" {}

locals {
  required_apis = [
    "cloudbuild.googleapis.com",
    "sourcerepo.googleapis.com",
```

```
    "storage.googleapis.com",
  ]
}

resource "google_project_service" "api" {
  for_each          = toset(local.required_apis)
  service           = each.value
  disable_on_destroy = false
}

resource "google_storage_bucket" "state" {
  name = "${var.repository_name}-state"
  location = var.region

  versioning {
    enabled = true
  }
}

resource "google_sourcerepo_repository" "this" {
  name = var.repository_name

  depends_on = [
    google_project_service.api
  ]
}

resource "google_cloudbuild_trigger" "main" {
  trigger_template {
    branch_name = "main"
    repo_name   = google_sourcerepo_repository.this.name
  }

  service_account = google_service_account.cloudbuild.id

  filename = "cloudbuild.yaml"

  depends_on = [
    google_project_service.api
  ]
}

resource "google_cloudbuild_trigger" "branches" {
  trigger_template {
    branch_name  = "main"
    invert_regex = true
    repo_name    = google_sourcerepo_repository.this.name
  }

  service_account = google_service_account.cloudbuild.id

  filename = "cloudbuild.yaml"
```

```
    depends_on = [
      google_project_service.api
    ]
}

resource "google_service_account" "cloudbuild" {
  account_id = "${var.repository_name}-cloudbuild"
}

resource "google_project_iam_member" "act_as" {
  project = data.google_project.project.project_id
  role    = "roles/iam.serviceAccountUser"
  member  = join(":", [
    "serviceAccount",
    google_service_account.cloudbuild.email
  ])
}

resource "google_project_iam_member" "editor" {
  project = data.google_project.project.project_id
  role    = "roles/editor"
  member  = join(":", [
    "serviceAccount",
    google_service_account.cloudbuild.email
  ])
}

output "git_credential_command" {
  value = join(" ", [
    "git config --global",
    "credential.https://source.developers.google.com.helper gcloud.sh"
  ])
}

output "add_remote_command" {
  value = join(" ", [
    "git remote add origin",
    google_sourcerepo_repository.this.url
  ])
}

output "backend" {
  value = <<BACKEND
  backend "gcs" {
    bucket = "${google_storage_bucket.state.name}"
  }
BACKEND
}
```

Review the resources that are going to be created, and then run `terraform apply` to make the changes.

Discussion

By completing the recipe, you now have a git repository and the CloudBuild jobs required to perform CI and CD operations. In order to work with Terraform in CI/CD, you need to upload state to the bucket that was created. Update your *provider.tf* file with the backend output in the `terraform apply` execution so it looks like the following:

```
provider "google" {
  project   = var.project
  region    = var.region
}

terraform {
  required_providers {
    google = {
      source  = "hashicorp/google"
      version = "~> 4"
    }
  }

  backend "gcs" {
    bucket = "..."
  }
}
```

 Keeping secure access to Terraform state is crucial. It can contain sensitive information, and also if corrupted or lost, it can be incredibly time consuming to recover. All buckets containing state should, at the very least, have versioning enabled, allowing you to recover from incidents.

Next, run `terraform init` to copy the state up into the bucket. After that, initialize Git by running `git init`, and add the remote origin by running the command from the `add_remote_command` output. Now run `git config --global credential .https://source.developers.google.com.helper gcloud.sh` to allow you to use your Cloud SDK credentials to authenticate against Git. Last, to get your code into the repository, run `git push -u origin main`. This will trigger the CloudBuild job, which will apply any changes pushed to that branch.

Unfortunately, at the current time, source repositories do not support pull requests, although the recipe includes an example CloudBuild trigger for a continuous integration job that runs a Terraform plan with the changes on the branch. In reality, to get the most out of version control and CloudBuild, you will want to explore software as a service options such as GitHub.

As seen in Recipe 7.7, there are tools which you should look to build into your CI/CD pipelines. For example, you can add a Checkov task by extending `cloudbuild.yaml` with a new task like the following:

```
steps:
  - id: 'checkov'
    name: 'bridgecrew/checkov'
```

With your CI jobs, you want to build as much confidence as you can that your change is of the highest quality and presents minimal risk. The following are common items to check as part of CI:

- Terraform files are formatted correctly.
- Python code passes all its tests.
- Static application security testing (SAST) tools such as semgrep find no new issues.

Using CI/CD as the primary mechanism of driving change in environments is key to achieving a true least-privilege identity posture. By pushing all change via auditable pipelines, you can remove the ability of end users to make changes in projects through the console or other mechanisms. Then as you bring tools into place, you can enforce standards across the entire organization.

Summary

Let's summarize what was learned and deployed in this recipe:

- CloudBuild is a fully managed platform for running CI and CD tasks.
- It allows you to pull in containers to perform a variety of tasks on the code in a repository.
- Cloud Source Repositories is a managed version control system on GCP.
- It is recommended to explore other version control options such as GitHub.
- To work with Terraform in a team, or via automation, state needs uploading to a Cloud Storage bucket.
- CI is about building confidence that the proposed change is of sufficient quality.

6.8 Robust Deployment on AWS

Problem

You want to use version control and CI/CD pipelines to deploy your code.

Solution

If you haven't already done so, familiarize yourself with Terraform and the different authentication mechanisms in Chapter 11.

Create a *variables.tf* file and copy the following contents:

```
variable "repository_name" {
  type        = string
  description = "The name for the repository"
}

variable "profile_name" {
  type        = string
  description = "The name of the AWS profile to use for codecommit auth"
  default     = "default"
}
```

Then fill out the corresponding *terraform.tfvars* file:

```
repository_name = ""
profile_name    = ""
```

Create the following *provider.tf* file and run `terraform init`:

```
provider "aws" {}

terraform {
  required_providers {
    aws = {
      source  = "hashicorp/aws"
      version = "~> 3"
    }
  }
}
```

Define the following *buildspec.yaml* file:

```
version: 0.2

phases:
  build:
    commands:
      - |
        if [ $CODEBUILD_SOURCE_VERSION != "main" ]; then
          terraform init
          terraform plan -no-color
        fi
      - |
        if [ $CODEBUILD_SOURCE_VERSION == "main" ]; then
          terraform init
          terraform apply -no-color -auto-approve
        fi
```

Create the following *main.tf* file and run `terraform plan`:

```
resource "aws_s3_bucket" "state" {
  bucket        = "${var.repository_name}-state"
  force_destroy = true

  versioning {
    enabled = true
  }
}

resource "aws_codecommit_repository" "this" {
  repository_name = var.repository_name
  default_branch  = "main"
}

resource "aws_iam_role" "codebuild" {
  name = "${var.repository_name}-codebuild"

  assume_role_policy = data.aws_iam_policy_document.cb_assume.json

  managed_policy_arns = [
    "arn:aws:iam::aws:policy/AdministratorAccess"
  ]
}

data "aws_iam_policy_document" "cb_assume" {
  statement {
    actions = [
      "sts:AssumeRole"
    ]

    principals {
      type = "Service"
      identifiers = [
        "codebuild.amazonaws.com"
      ]
    }
  }
}

resource "aws_codebuild_project" "main" {
  name = "${var.repository_name}-main"

  service_role = aws_iam_role.codebuild.arn

  artifacts {
    type = "NO_ARTIFACTS"
  }

  environment {
    compute_type = "BUILD_GENERAL1_SMALL"
```

```
    image         = "hashicorp/terraform:1.0.0"
    type          = "LINUX_CONTAINER"
  }

  source {
    type     = "CODECOMMIT"
    location = aws_codecommit_repository.this.clone_url_http
  }
}

resource "aws_codebuild_project" "pull_requests" {
  name = "${var.repository_name}-pull-requests"

  service_role = aws_iam_role.codebuild.arn

  artifacts {
    type = "NO_ARTIFACTS"
  }

  environment {
    compute_type = "BUILD_GENERAL1_SMALL"
    image        = "hashicorp/terraform:1.0.0"
    type         = "LINUX_CONTAINER"
  }

  source {
    type     = "CODECOMMIT"
    location = aws_codecommit_repository.this.clone_url_http
  }
}

resource "aws_cloudwatch_event_rule" "pull_requests" {
  name          = "${var.repository_name}-pull-requests"
  event_pattern = <<PATTERN
{
  "detail": {
    "event": [
      "pullRequestCreated",
      "pullRequestSourceBranchUpdated"
    ]
  },
  "detail-type": ["CodeCommit Pull Request State Change"],
  "resources": ["${aws_codecommit_repository.this.arn}"],
  "source": ["aws.codecommit"]
}
PATTERN
}

resource "aws_cloudwatch_event_rule" "main" {
  name          = "${var.repository_name}-main"
  event_pattern = <<PATTERN
{
```

```
    "detail": {
      "event": [
        "referenceUpdated"
      ],
      "referenceName": [
        "${aws_codecommit_repository.this.default_branch}"
      ]
    },
    "detail-type": ["CodeCommit Repository State Change"],
    "resources": ["${aws_codecommit_repository.this.arn}"],
    "source": ["aws.codecommit"]
}
PATTERN
}

resource "aws_cloudwatch_event_target" "main" {
  arn      = aws_codebuild_project.main.arn
  input    = <<TEMPLATE
{
  "sourceVersion": "${aws_codecommit_repository.this.default_branch}"
}
TEMPLATE
  role_arn = aws_iam_role.events.arn
  rule     = aws_cloudwatch_event_rule.main.name
  target_id = "Main"
}

resource "aws_cloudwatch_event_target" "pull_requests" {
  arn      = aws_codebuild_project.pull_requests.arn
  role_arn = aws_iam_role.events.arn
  rule     = aws_cloudwatch_event_rule.pull_requests.name
  target_id = "PullRequests"

  input_transformer {
    input_paths = {
      sourceVersion : "$.detail.sourceCommit"
    }

    input_template = <<TEMPLATE
{
  "sourceVersion": <sourceVersion>
}
TEMPLATE
  }
}

resource "aws_iam_role" "events" {
  name = "${var.repository_name}-events"

  assume_role_policy = data.aws_iam_policy_document.events_assume.json

  inline_policy {
```

```
    name = "execution"

    policy = data.aws_iam_policy_document.events_execution.json
  }
}

data "aws_iam_policy_document" "events_assume" {
  statement {
    actions = [
      "sts:AssumeRole"
    ]

    principals {
      type = "Service"
      identifiers = [
        "events.amazonaws.com"
      ]
    }
  }
}

data "aws_iam_policy_document" "events_execution" {
  statement {
    actions = [
      "codebuild:StartBuild"
    ]

    resources = [
      aws_codebuild_project.main.arn,
      aws_codebuild_project.pull_requests.arn,
    ]
  }
}

output "add_remote_command" {
  value = join("", [
    "git remote add origin ",
    "codecommit://",
    var.profile_name,
    "@",
    aws_codecommit_repository.this.repository_name
  ])
}

output "backend" {
  value = <<BACKEND
  backend "s3" {
    bucket = "${aws_s3_bucket.state.bucket}"
    key    = "terraform.tfstate"
  }
BACKEND
}
```

Review the resources that are going to be created, and then run `terraform apply` to make the changes.

Discussion

By completing the recipe, you now have a Git repository and the CodeBuild jobs required to perform CI and CD operations. In order to work with Terraform in CI/CD, you need to upload state for the bucket that was created. Update your *provider.tf* file with the backend output in the `terraform apply` execution so it looks like the following:

```
provider "aws" {}

terraform {
  required_providers {
    aws = {
      source  = "hashicorp/aws"
      version = "~> 3"
    }
  }
  backend "s3" {
    bucket = "..."
    key    = "terraform.tfstate"
  }
}
```

 It is imperative you keep the Terraform state files secure. First, they often contain sensitive information such as passwords and API keys. Second, if the state is lost or corrupted, it often takes a significant amount of time to recover. In this recipe, the S3 bucket was configured with versioning to allow previous state files to be recovered when a failure potentially occurs.

Next, run `terraform init` to copy the state up into the bucket. After that, initialize git by running `git init`, and add the remote origin by running the command from the `add_remote_command` output. Now follow the instructions found in the AWS CodeCommit documentation (*https://oreil.ly/8Lvaa*) to enable you to authenticate against the repository in CodeCommit. Lastly, to get your code into the repository, run `git push -u origin main`. This will trigger the CodeBuild job, which will apply any changes pushed to that branch.

If you were to push another branch and raise a pull request, then the corresponding CodeBuild job will execute and log out the planned changes. This allows you to understand before merging the pull request what the expected changes are so you can make an informed decision on whether to merge the change. There are examples online of people extending this pattern to automatically decorate the pull request with the details of the plan using Lambda functions.

By leveraging automation to verify and action your changes, you unlock the ability to bring tooling to bear to prevent changes that are of insufficient quality. In Recipe 7.8, Checkov is explored as a tool for preventing noncompliant infrastructure from being deployed. To add Checkov scanning to your CI/CD infrastructure, add and apply the following Terraform:

```
resource "aws_cloudwatch_event_target" "checkov" {
  arn       = aws_codebuild_project.checkov.arn
  role_arn  = aws_iam_role.events.arn
  rule      = aws_cloudwatch_event_rule.pull_requests.name
  target_id = "Checkov"

  input_transformer {
    input_paths = {
      sourceVersion : "$.detail.sourceCommit"
    }

    input_template = <<TEMPLATE
{
  "sourceVersion": <sourceVersion>
}
TEMPLATE
  }
}

resource "aws_codebuild_project" "checkov" {
  name = "${var.repository_name}-checkov"

  service_role = aws_iam_role.codebuild.arn

  artifacts {
    type = "NO_ARTIFACTS"
  }

  environment {
    compute_type = "BUILD_GENERAL1_SMALL"
    image        = "bridgecrew/checkov"
    type         = "LINUX_CONTAINER"
  }

  source {
    type     = "CODECOMMIT"
    location = aws_codecommit_repository.this.clone_url_http
  }
}
```

CI jobs are fundamentally about building confidence in the quality of the change, that it will provide value that far outstrips the potential risk. Based on what code is in the repository, there are a variety of checks that should be done, such as linting, formatting, and security scanning.

With auditable pipelines as the primary mechanism for delivering change, you can significantly reduce the permissions available to users. Rather than users being able to assume highly privileged roles, you can reduce their permissions to read only and have only the pipelines with the permission to create, update, and delete resources. With the path of change both automated and known, you can embed a toolchain into the workflows of every team to bring consistency to your estate.

Summary

Let's summarize what was learned and deployed in this recipe:

- CodeBuild is a fully managed build platform on AWS.
- CodeCommit is a managed version control system.
- You can use CodeBuild to automatically run builds on pull requests, or when a branch is pushed to.
- Terraform state should be uploaded to secure S3 buckets to allow multiple people to work on the same infrastructure.
- State files should be kept securely with versioning as they often contain sensitive information and are time consuming to reconstruct.
- By making CI/CD the way change happens, you can enforce security standards before changes occur.
- By embedding a toolchain into every pipeline, you bring standardization and consistency.

6.9 Robust Deployment on Azure

Problem

You want to use version control and CI/CD pipelines to deploy your code.

Solution

This recipe requires a preexisting Azure DevOps organization, with an owner-level personal access token locally available.

If you haven't already done so, familiarize yourself with Terraform and the different authentication mechanisms in Chapter 11.

Create a *variables.tf* file and copy the following contents:

```
variable "org_service_url" {
  type        = string
  description = "The Azure DevOps Organization URL"
}

variable "token" {
  type        = string
  description = "A personal access token with owner privileges"
}

variable "project_name" {
  type        = string
  description = "The name of the project to create"
}

variable "subscription_id" {
  type        = string
  description = "The ID of the subscription to deploy into"
}

variable "subscription_name" {
  type        = string
  description = "The name of the subscription to deploy into"
}

variable "location" {
  type        = string
  description = "The location to deploy resources into"
}
```

Then fill out the corresponding *terraform.tfvars* file:

```
org_service_url   = ""
token             = ""
project_name      = ""
location          = ""
subscription_id   = ""
subscription_name = ""
```

Create the following *provider.tf* file and run `terraform init`:

```
terraform {
  required_providers {
    azuredevops = {
      source  = "microsoft/azuredevops"
      version = "0.1.7"
    }
    azurerm = {
      source  = "hashicorp/azurerm"
      version = "~> 2"
    }
  }
}
```

```
provider "azuredevops" {
  org_service_url     = var.org_service_url
  personal_access_token = var.token
}

provider "azurerm" {
  features {}
}
```

Define the following *azure-pipelines.yaml* file:

```yaml
trigger:
- main

pool: Hosted Ubuntu 1604

steps:
- script: |
    OPTIONS="deb [arch=$(dpkg --print-architecture)]"
    URL="https://apt.releases.hashicorp.com"
    SUFFIX="$(lsb_release -cs) main"
    curl -fsSL https://apt.releases.hashicorp.com/gpg | sudo apt-key add -
    sudo apt-add-repository "$OPTIONS $URL $SUFFIX"
    sudo apt install terraform=1.0.0
  displayName: Install Terraform
- script: |
    if [ ${Build.SourceBranchName} != "main" ]; then
      terraform init
      terraform plan -no-color
    fi
  displayName: Plan
- script: |
    pip3 install checkov
    checkov --directory .
  displayName: Checkov
- script: |
    if [ ${Build.SourceBranchName} == "main" ]; then
      terraform init
      terraform apply -auto-approve
    fi
  displayName: Apply
```

Create the following *main.tf* file and run `terraform plan`:

```
data "azuredevops_git_repository" "repo" {
  project_id = azuredevops_project.project.id
  name       = var.project_name
}

resource "azuredevops_project" "project" {
  name = var.project_name
}
```

```
resource "azuredevops_git_repository" "infra" {
  project_id = azuredevops_project.project.id
  name       = "infra"
  initialization {
    init_type = "Uninitialized"
  }
}

resource "azuredevops_build_definition" "main" {
  project_id = azuredevops_project.project.id
  name       = "main"

  ci_trigger {
    use_yaml = true
  }

  repository {
    repo_type = "TfsGit"
    repo_id   = data.azuredevops_git_repository.repo.id
    yml_path  = "azure-pipelines.yml"
  }
}

data "azurerm_client_config" "current" {}

resource "azuredevops_serviceendpoint_azurerm" "endpointazure" {
  project_id               = azuredevops_project.project.id
  service_endpoint_name    = "Azure"
  azurerm_spn_tenantid     = data.azurerm_client_config.current.tenant_id
  azurerm_subscription_id  = var.subscription_id
  azurerm_subscription_name = var.subscription_name
}

resource "azurerm_resource_group" "terraform" {
  name     = var.project_name
  location = var.location
}

resource "azurerm_storage_account" "state" {
  name                     = "${var.project_name}state"
  resource_group_name      = azurerm_resource_group.terraform.name
  location                 = azurerm_resource_group.terraform.location
  account_tier             = "Standard"
  account_replication_type = "LRS"

  blob_properties {
    versioning_enabled = true
  }
}

resource "azurerm_storage_container" "state" {
```

```
    name                  = "state"
    storage_account_name  = azurerm_storage_account.state.name
    container_access_type = "private"
}

output "add_remote_command" {
  value = join("", [
    "git remote add origin ",
    azuredevops_git_repository.infra.remote_url
  ])
}

output "backend" {
  value = <<BACKEND
  backend "azurerm" {
    resource_group_name  = "${azurerm_resource_group.terraform.name}"
    storage_account_name = "${azurerm_storage_account.state.name}"
    container_name       = "state"
    key                  = "terraform.tfstate"
  }
BACKEND
}
```

Review the resources that are going to be created, and then run `terraform apply` to make the changes.

Discussion

By completing the recipe, you now have a Git repository and the Azure DevOps build definitions required to perform CI and CD operations. In order to work with Terraform in CI/CD, you need to upload state to the storage account that was created. Update your *provider.tf* file with the backend output in the `terraform apply` execution so it looks like the following:

```
terraform {
  required_providers {
    azuredevops = {
      source  = "microsoft/azuredevops"
      version = "0.1.7"
    }
    azurerm = {
      source  = "hashicorp/azurerm"
      version = "~> 2"
    }
  }
  backend "azurerm" {
    resource_group_name  = "..."
    storage_account_name = "..."
    container_name       = "state"
    key                  = "terraform.tfstate"
  }
```

```
}

provider "azuredevops" {
  org_service_url      = var.org_service_url
  personal_access_token = var.token
}

provider "azurerm" {
  features {}
}
```

 The storage accounts you store state in should have versioning enabled so that errors can be easily and quickly recoverable. Additionally, as state files often contain sensitive information, such as passwords and API keys, it is critical that access to the accounts is tightly controlled.

Next, run `terraform init` to copy the state up into the bucket. After that, initialize Git by running `git init`, and add the remote origin by running the command from the `add_remote_command` output. To get your code into the repository, run `git push -u origin main`. This will trigger the pipeline, which will apply any changes pushed to that branch.

When working with Git, a fundamental concept is a pull request, or PR. A PR is where you request to make changes to a shared branch. When someone raises a PR, you should run a Continuous Integration job to execute tests, or in this case, a Terraform plan. To set up automated PR building, and also prevent people from pushing directly to the main branch, add and apply the following resources:

```
resource "azuredevops_build_definition" "prs" {
  project_id = azuredevops_project.project.id
  name       = "prs"

  repository {
    repo_type = "TfsGit"
    repo_id   = data.azuredevops_git_repository.repo.id
    yml_path  = "azure-pipelines.yml"
  }
}

resource "azuredevops_branch_policy_build_validation" "prs" {
  project_id = azuredevops_project.project.id

  settings {
    build_definition_id = azuredevops_build_definition.prs.id
    display_name        = "Require clean build"
    valid_duration      = 720

    scope {
```

```
        repository_id  = azuredevops_git_repository.infra.id
        repository_ref = azuredevops_git_repository.infra.default_branch
        match_type     = "Exact"
      }
    }
  }
```

As shown in Recipe 7.9, there are tools which you should look to build into your CI/CD pipelines. For example, you can add a Checkov task by extending `azure-pipelines.yaml` with a new step like the following:

```
- script: |
    pip3 install checkov
    checkov --directory .
  displayName: Checkov
```

Embedding tools like Checkov into every change that happens in your estate is one of the fundamental ways to scale the impact of the security team. Delivery teams should also be following a CI/CD-driven approach and will naturally want to run a variety of tests, checks, and tools as part of their own workflows. By being able to make it as simple as possible to embed the security tools, you can enable teams to identify and potentially fix their own issues independently.

Having the organization be CI/CD first is critical to removing highly privileged access from users. If they can make all the changes they need to via code, then their console access can be reduced to read-only. The principle of least privilege is reliant on high levels of automation to be truly embraced.

Summary

Let's summarize what was learned and deployed in this recipe:

- Azure DevOps provides CI/CD capabilities on Azure.
- You can set up Git repositories and build definitions to store your code.
- By delivering change via automation, you can embed tooling into the workflow.
- In order to work with state across users and systems, you need to upload it to a storage account.
- These storage accounts should be closely guarded, as state contains sensitive information and is very time consuming to reconstruct if it's lost or corrupted.
- Becoming familiar with CI/CD is critical for being able to reduce the permissions of end users, as it allows them to make change in an audited, automated fashion.

6.10 Deployment at Scale on GCP

Problem

You wish to be able to deploy a set of baseline resources across a number of projects.

Solution

This recipe enables a base set of APIs across all projects in the organization and a specific set of APIs for serverless development under a particular folder.

If you haven't already done so, familiarize yourself with Terraform and the different authentication mechanisms in Chapter 11.

Create the following *variables.tf* file:

```
variable "folder_id" {
  type        = string
  description = "The folder ID containing serverless projects"
}
```

Then fill out the corresponding *terraform.tfvars* file:

```
folder_id = ""
```

Create the following *provider.tf* file and run `terraform init`:

```
provider "google" {}

terraform {
  required_providers {
    google = {
      source  = "hashicorp/google"
      version = "~> 4"
    }
  }
}
```

Create the following *main.tf* file and run `terraform plan`:

```
data "google_projects" "all_active" {
  filter = "lifecycleState:ACTIVE"
}

data "google_projects" "under_folder" {
  filter = "parent.id:${var.folder_id}"
}

locals {
  required_apis = [
    "logging.googleapis.com",
    "storage.googleapis.com",
  ]
```

```
    serverless_apis = [
      "cloudbuild.googleapis.com",
      "cloudfunctions.googleapis.com",
    ]
    all_project_ids = [
      for project in data.google_projects.all_active.projects :
      project.project_id
    ]
    required = setproduct(
      local.required_apis,
      local.all_project_ids
    )
    folder_project_ids = [
      for project in data.google_projects.under_folder.projects :
      project.project_id
    ]
    serverless = setproduct(
      local.serverless_apis,
      local.folder_project_ids
    )
  }

  resource "google_project_service" "all" {
    for_each        = {
      for req in local.required : index(local.required, req) => req
    }
    service         = each.value[0]
    project         = each.value[1]
    disable_on_destroy = false
  }

  resource "google_project_service" "serverless" {
    for_each        = {
      for req in local.serverless : index(local.serverless, req) => req
    }
    service         = each.value[0]
    project         = each.value[1]
    disable_on_destroy = false
  }
```

Review the resources that are going to be created, and then run `terraform apply` to make the changes.

Discussion

As every resource in the Google Terraform provider accepts an explicit project parameter, deploying across multiple projects can be done with a single provider definition. In Azure and AWS, it is complicated by the fact that iterating over accounts or subscriptions must be done outside of Terraform.

In this recipe, you used the `setproduct` function to build out a list of project and API tuples. By combining this with a `for_each` definition, you can easily create a distinct resource for each project and API pairing.

Due to the generally permissible boundaries between projects, commonly services in GCP are deployed centrally and reach out into the clients' projects. However, there are cases when having this as a pattern is useful. One is the recipe itself, where you wish to enable a set of default APIs automatically within a project. Another is granting a service account granular IAM access within a set of projects.

The filter option used in the recipe accepts a variety of different fields. In addition to filtering by state and parent, you can also filter by labels and names, allowing you to list only the projects you require. This avoids having to complicate the code by doing dynamic filtering within the Terraform itself.

Summary

Let's summarize what was learned and deployed in this recipe:

- All GCP resources in Terraform support a `project` parameter.
- This parameter allows you to dynamically deploy the same resource into multiple projects.
- By using the `google_projects` data provider, you can get a list of projects based on a filter.
- The `setproduct` function in Terraform allows you to build out a list of pairs to iterate over.

6.11 Deployment at Scale on AWS

Problem

You wish to able to deploy a set of baseline resources across a number of accounts.

Solution

This recipe requires `boto3` be available on the current Python path, which can be done by running `pip install boto3` and needs to be run from the organization root account.

If you haven't already done so, familiarize yourself with Terraform and the different authentication mechanisms in Chapter 11.

Create the following *variables.tf* file:

```
variable "target_account_id" {
  type = string
  description = "The account to deploy into"
}

variable "cross_account_role" {
  type = string
  description = "The account to deploy into"
}

variable "region" {
  type = string
  description = "The region to deploy into"
}
```

Then fill out the corresponding *terraform.tfvars* file, without defining a target_
account_id:

```
cross_account_role = ""
region             = ""
```

Create the following *provider.tf* file and run `terraform init`:

```
provider "aws" {
  region  = var.region
}

provider "aws" {
  alias = "target"
  region  = var.region
  assume_role {
    role_arn = join("", [
      "arn:aws:iam::",
      var.target_account_id,
      ":role/",
      var.cross_account_role
    ])
  }
}

terraform {
  required_providers {
    aws = {
      source  = "hashicorp/aws"
      version = "~> 3"
    }
  }
}
```

Then create an *account_iterator.py* file:

```
import subprocess

import boto3
```

```python
def init():
  subprocess.run(f"terraform init", check=True, shell=True)

def get_accounts():
  organizations = boto3.client('organizations')
  paginator = organizations.get_paginator("list_accounts")

  return [
      account["Id"]
      for page in paginator.paginate()
      for account in page["Accounts"]
      if account["Status"] != "SUSPENDED"
  ]

def workspace_exists(account):
  returncode = subprocess.run(
    f"terraform workspace list | grep {account}",
    shell=True
  ).returncode
  return returncode == 0

def create_workspace(account):
  subprocess.run(
    f"terraform workspace new {account}",
    check=True,
    shell=True
  )

def switch_to_workspace(account):
  subprocess.run(
    f"terraform workspace select {account}",
    check=True,
    shell=True
  )

def plan(account):
  subprocess.run(
    f"terraform plan -var target_account_id={account}",
    check=True,
    shell=True
  )

def apply(account):
  subprocess.run(
    f"terraform apply -var target_account_id={account} -auto-approve",
    check=True,
    shell=True
  )

def run(is_apply=False):
  init()
```

```
  for account in get_accounts():
    if not workspace_exists(account):
      create_workspace(account)
    switch_to_workspace(account)
    plan(account)
    if is_apply:
      apply(account)

if __name__ == "__main__":
  if len(sys.argv) == 2 and sys.argv[1] == "apply":
    run(True)
  else:
    run()
```

Discussion

Now, if you define any Terraform resources within the folder and run python account_iterator.py, it will output a plan against every active account in the organization. By running python account_iterator.py apply, you will apply the changes to every account in the organization. The code uses Terraform workspaces to create state files for each account, ensuring that each account is sandboxed from the others.

Due to the hard boundaries between accounts, this pattern is used for many tasks with an AWS estate. In Recipe 7.5, you need an AWS Config recorder configured in every account, in order to be able to deploy organization rules successfully. To do this, create the following *main.tf* file and run python account_iterator.py apply:

```
data "aws_caller_identity" "current" {
  provider = aws.target
}

resource "aws_config_delivery_channel" "this" {
  provider       = aws.target
  name           = "delivery_channel"
  s3_bucket_name = aws_s3_bucket.bucket.bucket
  depends_on     = [
    aws_config_configuration_recorder.this,
    aws_s3_bucket_policy.config
  ]
}

resource "aws_s3_bucket" "bucket" {
  provider = aws.target
  bucket   = join("-", [
    "config",
    data.aws_caller_identity.current.account_id
  ])
}

resource "aws_config_configuration_recorder" "this" {
  provider = aws.target
```

```
  name     = "recorder"
  role_arn = aws_iam_role.config.arn
}

resource "aws_iam_role" "config" {
  provider = aws.target
  name     = "config-delivery"

  assume_role_policy = data.aws_iam_policy_document.assume_role.json
}

data "aws_iam_policy_document" "assume_role" {
  statement {
    actions = [
      "sts:AssumeRole"
    ]

    effect = "Allow"

    principals {
      type        = "Service"
      identifiers = ["config.amazonaws.com"]
    }
  }
}

resource "aws_iam_role_policy_attachment" "a" {
  provider   = aws.target
  role       = aws_iam_role.config.name
  policy_arn = "arn:aws:iam::aws:policy/service-role/AWSConfigRole"
}

resource "aws_iam_role_policy" "config" {
  provider = aws.target
  name     = "config-delivery"
  role     = aws_iam_role.config.id
  policy   = data.aws_iam_policy_document.config_role.json
}

data "aws_iam_policy_document" "config_role" {
  statement {
    actions = [
      "s3:*"
    ]

    effect = "Allow"

    resources = [
      aws_s3_bucket.bucket.arn,
      "${aws_s3_bucket.bucket.arn}/*"
    ]
```

```
    }
  }
```

Other common use cases include bootstrapping a set of base roles into every account, deploying transit gateways attachments, and deploying log forwarding architectures.

Summary

Let's summarize what was learned and deployed in this recipe:

- To deploy into multiple accounts, you need multiple provider definitions.
- The Python code in the recipe collects a list of all active accounts in the organization.
- By using Terraform workspaces, you keep state sandboxed and distinct from other accounts.
- A common use case for this is configuring the AWS Config recorder in every account.

6.12 Deployment at Scale on Azure

Problem

You wish to able to deploy a set of baseline resources across a number of subscriptions.

Solution

This recipe requires `azure-mgmt-resource` and `azure-identity` to be available on the current Python path, which can be done by running `pip install azure-mgmt-resource azure-identity`.

If you haven't already done so, familiarize yourself with Terraform and the different authentication mechanisms in Chapter 11.

Create the following *variables.tf* file:

```
variable "location" {
  type        = string
  description = "The Azure location for resources"
}

variable "subscription_id" {
  type = string
  description = "The subscription to deploy into"
}
```

Then fill out the corresponding *terraform.tfvars* file without defining a `subscrip
tion_id` value:

```
location = ""
```

Define the following *provider.tf* file and run `terraform init`:

```
terraform {
  required_providers {
    azurerm = {
      source  = "hashicorp/azurerm"
      version = "~> 2"
    }
  }
}

provider "azurerm" {
  features {}
  subscription_id = var.subscription_id
}
```

Then create a *subscription_iterator.py* file:

```python
import subprocess
import sys

from azure.identity import AzureCliCredential
from azure.mgmt.resource import SubscriptionClient


def init():
  subprocess.run(
    f"terraform init",
    check=True,
    shell=True
  )


def get_subscriptions():
    credential = AzureCliCredential()
    client = SubscriptionClient(credential)

    return [
      return [
        subscription.subscription_id for
        subscription in client.subscriptions.list()
      ]
    ]


def workspace_exists(subscription):
    completed_process = subprocess.run(
      f"terraform workspace list | grep {subscription}",
      shell=True
    )
    return completed_process.returncode == 0
```

```python
def create_workspace(subscription):
    subprocess.run(
        f"terraform workspace new {subscription}",
        check=True,
        shell=True
    )


def switch_to_workspace(subscription):
    subprocess.run(
        f"terraform workspace select {subscription}",
        check=True,
        shell=True
    )


def plan(subscription):
    subprocess.run(
        f"terraform plan -var subscription_id={subscription}",
        check=True,
        shell=True,
    )


def apply(subscription):
    subprocess.run(
        f"terraform apply -var subscription_id={subscription} -auto-approve",
        check=True,
        shell=True,
    )


def run(run_plan=True):
    init()
    for subscription in get_subscriptions():
        if not workspace_exists(subscription):
            create_workspace(subscription)
        switch_to_workspace(subscription)
        if run_plan:
            plan(subscription)
        else:
            apply(subscription)


if __name__ == "__main__":
    if len(sys.argv) == 2:
        run(sys.argv[1] != "apply")
    else:
        run()
```

Discussion

Now, if you define any Terraform resources within the folder and run `python sub scription_iterator.py`, it will output a plan against every subscription in the tenant. By running `python subscription_iterator.py apply`, you will apply the changes to every subscription in the tenant. The code uses Terraform workspaces to create state files for each subscription, ensuring that each account is sandboxed from the others.

There are a variety of use cases in Azure, where you need to enable, deploy, or configure resources across an array of subscriptions. For example, to configure Security Center across all subscriptions within the organization, add the following *main.tf* file and run `python subscription_iterator.py apply`:

```
resource "azurerm_security_center_auto_provisioning" "this" {
  auto_provision = "On"
}

locals {
  resource_types = toset([
    "AppServices",
    "ContainerRegistry",
    "KeyVaults",
    "KubernetesService",
    "SqlServers",
    "SqlServerVirtualMachines",
    "StorageAccounts",
    "VirtualMachines",
    "Arm",
    "Dns"
  ])
}

resource "azurerm_security_center_subscription_pricing" "this" {
  for_each      = local.resource_types
  tier          = "Free"
  resource_type = each.value
}
```

Summary

Let's summarize what was learned and deployed in this recipe:

- To deploy into multiple subscriptions, you need multiple provider definitions.
- The Python code in the recipe iterates over every subscription in the tenant.
- By using Terraform workspaces, you keep state sandboxed and distinct from other subscriptions.
- A common use case for this is configuring the Azure Security Center across the entire organization.

CHAPTER 7

Compliance as Code

Compliance is a key concern for security functions across the world, as businesses need to operate within certain regulatory frameworks or are looking to enforce industry best practices as a standard.

With the speed of modern technical delivery, and the possibilities the cloud unlocks, compliance has become both harder and easier at the same time. This is the paradox at the heart of cloud native security. The velocity of change presents new challenges, which drive a transformation that leads to a new *continuous* reality. Rather than auditing applications and systems on a rolling schedule, instead you build a continuous understanding of compliance that moves at the speed of cloud. This new speed also allows compliance gaps to be resolved within unprecedented time frames.

With compliance, to make significant, enduring progress, you need to be equipped for the following three key activities:

- You need to be able to detect noncompliant infrastructure. If you cannot see the scope and scale of the problem, you cannot hope to make progress in the right direction.

- You need to be able to prevent noncompliant infrastructure. The ability to *stop the rot* is critical, otherwise all the effort invested merely gets eroded over time.

- You need to be able to remediate noncompliant infrastructure. This last step is the most complex of the three, as you will often need to transparently communicate and plan changes with business users, as all change comes with a potential risk to negatively impact systems.

A useful mental model for understanding the categories of compliance changes is shown in Figure 7-1. It is something I built through handling cloud compliance at some of the world's biggest regulated enterprises.

By moving from green changes to red changes, you build trust with the workload teams, and establish a shared responsibility model. This shared responsibility model will outline who is responsible for which compliance issues and ensures that a process for remediation is established and actioned.

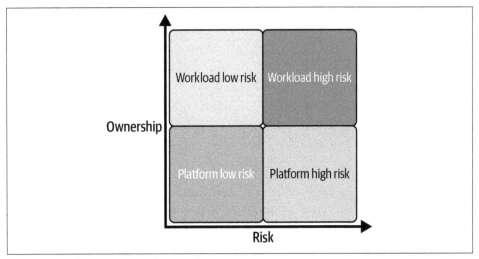

Figure 7-1. Classifying compliance changes

In this chapter, you will see how to assign metadata to resources to allow users and systems to make informed choices. Next, you will learn how to build detection mechanisms that allow you to be alerted the moment a resource becomes noncompliant and to build an aggregated view that allows you to see how your entire estate is fairing. Third, you will look at what options are available for preventing users from creating noncompliant infrastructure. Last, you will explore the options for automatic remediation that are available on each of the CSPs.

7.1 Labeling Resources on GCP

Problem

You need to add metadata to a resource so that cost allocation is accurate and the expected data classification of the objects is known.

Solution

This recipe creates a Cloud Storage bucket that has a `cost_center` and a `data_classification` label.

If you haven't already done so, familiarize yourself with Terraform and the different authentication mechanisms in Chapter 11.

Create a *variables.tf* file and copy the following contents:

```
variable "project_id" {
  type        = string
  description = "The project to deploy the resources into"
}

variable "region" {
  type        = string
  description = "The region to deploy the resources into"
}

variable "bucket_name" {
  type        = string
  description = "The name of the bucket"
}

variable "cost_center" {
  type        = string
  description = "The cost center to charge for the bucket"
}

variable "data_classification" {
  type        = string
  description = "The data classification of the bucket"
}
```

Then fill out the corresponding *terraform.tfvars* file:

```
project             = ""
region              = ""
bucket_name         = ""
cost_center         = ""
data_classification = ""
```

Create the following *provider.tf* file and run `terraform init`:

```
provider "google" {
  project = var.project
  region  = var.region
}

terraform {
  required_providers {
    google = {
      source  = "hashicorp/google"
      version = "~> 3"
    }
  }
}
```

Last, create the following *main.tf* file and run `terraform apply`:

```
locals {
  labels = {
    "cost_center"         = var.cost_center
    "data_classification" = var.data_classification
  }
}

resource "google_storage_bucket" "pii_bucket" {
  name          = var.bucket_name
  location      = var.region
  force_destroy = true

  labels = local.labels
}
```

 In this recipe, I have extracted the labels into a local variable. This allows you to set the labels in one location and readily apply them to all the resources defined in your code. You can override them on specific resources with the Terraform merge function, such as labels = merge(local.labels,{ data_classification = "Standard" }).

Discussion

Common security-related labels applied to resources in GCP include the following:

- Environment—for example, production
- Owner
- Data classification

In GCP, there are multiple mechanisms for annotating resources. Labels are for enriching resources with metadata, allowing you to group them across projects and folders. They are leveraged for ownership identification and environment classification and can be used to group and filter in Google Cloud's operations suite.

From a compliance perspective, Security Command Center (SCC), from Recipe 3.1, has the concept of *security marks*. These marks are only viewable from SCC and enable a security-centric view of resources. They are editable and viewable on resources even when the user does not have direct access to the resource itself. Marks exist purely within the sphere of control of the security team and as such are a much more stable basis around which to build monitoring and automation. To view the current marks assigned to assets, view the asset panel of the SCC web console. To mark assets, you can use the same asset panel, the gcloud scc assets update-marks command, or set them programmatically with languages such as Python.

As marks are defined independently of the resources, they work more effectively on static resources, such as production databases, rather than on highly dynamic and elastic resources, such as Cloud Functions.

There are two types of tags in GCP. First are *network tags*, which are assigned to Compute Engine virtual machines and are used to control network flows and firewalls, as seen in Recipe 5.1. Second are *resource tags*, which are only assigned to organizations, folders, and projects and are automatically inherited down the organization structure, i.e., a project will automatically be tagged the same as its parent folder unless explicitly tagged. They are used to implement conditional policies to manage access. Imagine a serverless-first organization that will want to by default lock users out of consuming the compute API. Following is the Terraform required to use tags to instantiate that policy.

The organization policy API requires that you use service account credentials to access it. If you are using end user credentials, you will need to create an appropriately privileged service account to be able to create all the necessary resources.

First, you need to define two variables in *variables.tf*:

```
variable "organization_domain" {
  type = string
  description = "The domain of the organization"
}

variable "target_projects" {
  type = list(string)
  description = "The projects to have compute access"
}
```

And input their corresponding values in *terraform.tfvars*:

```
organization_domain = ""
target_projects      = []
```

Then you will need to define the following resources in a *main.tf* file:

```
data "google_organization" "current" {
  domain = var.organization_domain
}

resource "google_org_policy_policy" "compute" {
  name = join("/", [
    data.google_organization.current.name,
    "policies/serviceuser.services"
  ])
```

```
      parent = data.google_organization.current.name

  spec {
    rules {
      condition {
        expression = join("", [
          "resource.matchTags('",
          data.google_organization.current.org_id,
          "/compute'",
          ", ",
          "'enabled')"
        ])
      }
    }

    rules {
      condition {
        expression = join("", [
          "resource.matchTags('",
          data.google_organization.current.org_id,
          "/compute'",
          ", ",
          "'disabled')"
        ])
      }

      values {
        denied_values = ["compute.googleapis.com"]
      }
    }
  }
}

resource "google_tags_tag_key" "compute" {
  parent     = data.google_organization.current.id
  short_name = "compute"
}

resource "google_tags_tag_value" "disabled" {
  parent     = "tagKeys/${google_tags_tag_key.compute.name}"
  short_name = "disabled"
}

resource "google_tags_tag_value" "enabled" {
  parent     = "tagKeys/${google_tags_tag_key.compute.name}"
  short_name = "enabled"
}

resource "google_tags_tag_binding" "org_compute_disabled" {
  parent = join("/", [
    "//cloudresourcemanager.googleapis.com/",
    data.google_organization.current.name
```

```
  ])
  tag_value = "tagValues/${google_tags_tag_value.disabled.name}"
}

resource "google_tags_tag_binding" "project_compute_enabled" {
  for_each = toset(var.target_projects)
  parent = "//cloudresourcemanager.googleapis.com/projects/${each.value}"
  tag_value = "tagValues/${google_tags_tag_value.enabled.name}"
}
```

After you run `terraform apply` on those resources, only those projects that you identified in the variables will be able to make any successful calls against the compute API.

Summary

Let's summarize what was learned and deployed in this recipe:

- Labels allow you to enrich resources with metadata.
- From a security point of view, you can mark resources through SCC.
- When looking to build security automation around resources, you should choose marks over labels.
  — They are within the security team sphere of control.
  — They are a more stable base to build around.
- Network tags can only be applied to Compute Engine instances and are purely for allowing and preventing traffic through firewalls.
- Resource tags are only applied at the organization, folder, and project levels.
  — You can use resource tags to create conditional policies at a per-project or higher level.

7.2 Tagging Resources on AWS

Problem

You need to add metadata to resources so that cost allocation is accurate and the expected data classification of the objects is known.

Solution

This recipe creates an S3 bucket that has a `cost_center` and a `data_classification` tag.

If you haven't already done so, familiarize yourself with Terraform and the different authentication mechanisms in Chapter 11.

Create a *variables.tf* file and copy the following contents:

```
variable "region" {
  type        = string
  description = "The region to deploy resources into"
}

variable "bucket_name" {
  type        = string
  description = "The name of the bucket"
}

variable "cost_center" {
  type        = string
  description = "The cost center to charge for the bucket"
}

variable "data_classification" {
  type        = string
  description = "The data classification of the bucket"
}
```

Then fill out the corresponding *terraform.tfvars* file:

```
region              = ""
bucket_name         = ""
cost_center         = ""
data_classification = ""
```

Create the following *provider.tf* file and run `terraform init`:

```
provider "aws" {
  region = var.region

  default_tags {
    tags = {
      cost_center         = var.cost_center
      data_classification = var.data_classification
    }
  }
}

terraform {
  required_providers {
    aws = {
      source  = "hashicorp/aws"
      version = "~> 3"
    }
  }
}
```

Last, create the following *main.tf* file and run `terraform apply`:

```
resource "aws_s3_bucket" "pii_bucket" {
  bucket        = var.bucket_name
  force_destroy = true
}
```

 In this recipe, you used the `default_tags` block in the provider definition to automatically apply tags to all taggable resources. This removes the burden of individually applying tags to every resource. You can override particular tags at the resource level by explicitly setting them in the resource definition. Terraform automatically merges the default tags with the explicit tags, with the latter taking precedence.

Discussion

Common security-related tags applied to resources in AWS include the following:

- Environment—for example, production
- Owner
- Data classification

Tagging unlocks the concept of Attribute Based Access Control (ABAC), which is explored in depth in Recipe 9.2. One of the perennial challenges in an AWS estate is ensuring resources are tagged according to your internal standards.

To support you in high levels of tagging compliance, AWS provides tag policies and resource groups. *Tag policies* are about setting, reporting on, and enforcing tag standardization across your organization. For example, let's look at a policy that outlines the cost center tag and its allowed values. First, you need to enable tag policies for your organization. You can do this by updating your `aws_organizations_organiza tion` resource to include the following line and applying the change:

```
resource "aws_organizations_organization" "this" {
  ...
  enabled_policy_types = [
    ...
    "TAG_POLICY",
  ]
  ...
}
```

With that done, you can create the policy and attach it to the entire organization with the following Terraform:

```
resource "aws_organizations_policy" "cost_center_tags" {
  name = "cost_center_tags"
  type = "TAG_POLICY"
```

```
      content = <<CONTENT
{
  "tags": {
    "Cost_Center": {
      "tag_key": {
        "@@assign": "Cost_Center",
        "@@operators_allowed_for_child_policies": ["@@none"]
      },
      "tag_value": {
        "@@assign": [
          "BU1",
          "BU2",
          "BU3",
          "BU4",
          "BU5"
        ]
      }
    }
  }
}
CONTENT
}

data "aws_organizations_organization" "current" {}

resource "aws_organizations_policy_attachment" "root" {
  policy_id = aws_organizations_policy.cost_center_tags.id
  target_id = data.aws_organizations_organization.current.roots[0].id
}
```

With that in place, you can review each account in turn, seeing the compliance level. When satisfied with a particular account's compliance, or when starting with a fresh account, you can modify the policy to have it enforce tagging for particular resource types. To enforce for EC2 instances, update the policy content to the following:

```
{
  "tags": {
    "Cost_Center": {
      "tag_key": {
        "@@assign": "Cost_Center",
        "@@operators_allowed_for_child_policies": ["@@none"]
      },
      "tag_value": {
        "@@assign": [
          "BU1",
          "BU2",
          "BU3",
          "BU4",
          "BU5"
        ]
      },
      "enforced_for": {
```

```
    "@@assign": [
        "ec2:instance"
    ]
      }
     }
    }
   }
  }
```

 Tag policies currently do not show untagged resources within their compliance results. So an account can appear to be significantly more compliant than is the case.

Resource groups allow you to create arbitrary collections within a region in an account. You build them by specifying a tag-based query, such as the following Terraform which collects all resources with a particular cost center tag:

```
resource "aws_resourcegroups_group" "BU1" {
  name = "cost-center-BU1"

  resource_query {
    query = <<JSON
{
  "ResourceTypeFilters": [
    "AWS::AllSupported"
  ],
  "TagFilters": [
    {
      "Key": "CostCenter",
      "Values": ["BU1"]
    }
  ]
}
JSON
  }
}
```

You can then use the tag editor service in the console to update tags on the resources contained within the group. This, combined with tag policies, gives us a general flow for bringing compliance up in an account. First, you create and assign the tag policy to an account. Then, you use resource groups and the tag editor to bring compliance up. Last, you update the tag policy to enforcement mode to ensure that tagging compliance does not drop.

Summary

Let's summarize what was learned and deployed in this recipe:

- Tags are a way of attaching metadata to resources within AWS.
- Terraform provides a `default_tags` configuration to simplify tagging resources.
- Tag policies allow you to implement reporting and enforcement against your tagging standards.
- Resource groups can be created by writing tag-based queries.
- Once a resource group is created, you can rapidly modify tags on all included resources.

7.3 Tagging Resources on Azure

Problem

You need to add metadata to a resource so that cost allocation is accurate and the expected data classification of the objects is known.

Solution

This recipe creates a storage account that has a `cost_center` and a `data_classifica tion` tag.

If you haven't already done so, familiarize yourself with Terraform and the different authentication mechanisms in Chapter 11.

Create a *variables.tf* file and copy the following contents:

```
variable "location" {
  type        = string
  description = "The location to deploy the resources into"
}

variable "storage_account_name" {
  type        = string
  description = "The name of the storage account"
}

variable "cost_center" {
  type        = string
  description = "The cost center to charge for the bucket"
}

variable "data_classification" {
  type        = string
```

```
    description = "The data classification of the bucket"
  }
```

Then fill out the corresponding *terraform.tfvars* file:

```
location              = ""
storage_account_name  = ""
cost_center           = ""
data_classification   = ""
```

Create the following *provider.tf* file and run `terraform init`:

```
terraform {
  required_providers {
    azurerm = {
      source  = "hashicorp/azurerm"
      version = "~> 2"
    }
  }
}

provider "azurerm" {
  features {}
}
```

Last, create the following *main.tf* file and run `terraform apply`:

```
locals {
  tags = {
    cost_center         = var.cost_center
    data_classification = var.data_classification
  }
}

resource "azurerm_resource_group" "this" {
  name     = "tagging-rg"
  location = var.location
  tags     = local.tags
}

resource "azurerm_storage_account" "this" {
  name                     = var.storage_account_name
  resource_group_name      = azurerm_resource_group.this.name
  location                 = azurerm_resource_group.this.location
  account_tier             = "Standard"
  account_replication_type = "GRS"
  tags                     = local.tags
}
```

In this recipe, I have extracted the tags into a local variable. This allows you to set the tags in one location and readily apply them to all the resources defined in your code. You can override them on specific resources with the Terraform merge function, such as labels = merge(local.tags,{ data_classification = "Stan dard" }).

Discussion

Common security-related tags applied to resources in Azure include the following:

- Environment—for example, production
- Owner
- Data classification

Azure is currently experimenting with Attribute Based Access Control (ABAC), which is discussed in Recipe 9.3. However, Azure Policy has a variety of built-in policies that allow you to build an understanding of tagging compliance, enforce the setting of tags, and remediate incorrectly tagged resources.

An effective built-in policy to assign is inheriting tags from resource groups. Let's look at the code required to assign the policy and automatically create remediation actions against every active subscription within the tenant.

In Azure, it is important to remember that resource groups are very malleable. It is possible to migrate resources between groups. When looking to inherit tags, it is worth ensuring that resources are correctly aligned to resource groups and that moving resources is done first so that they only inherit the correct tags.

First, you'll need to define the following variables in a *variables.tf* file:

```
variable "location" {
  type        = string
  description = "The location to deploy the resources into"
}

variable "root_management_group_uuid" {
  type = string
  description = "The UUID of the root management group"
}

variable "tags_to_inherit" {
  type = list(string)
  description = "The tags to inherit from the resource group"
}
```

And input their values in a corresponding *terraform.tfvars* file:

```
location                  = ""
root_management_group_uuid = ""
tags_to_inherit           = []
```

Next, define the following resources in a *main.tf* file:

```
data "azurerm_management_group" "root" {
  name = var.root_management_group_uuid
}

data "azurerm_policy_definition" "tag_inherit" {
  display_name = "Inherit a tag from the resource group if missing"
}

data "azurerm_subscriptions" "available" {}

resource "azurerm_policy_assignment" "tag_inherit" {
  for_each           = toset(var.tags_to_inherit)
  name               = "tag-${each.value}"
  scope              = data.azurerm_management_group.root.id
  policy_definition_id = data.azurerm_policy_definition.tag_inherit.id
  location           = var.location

  identity {
    type = "SystemAssigned"
  }

  parameters = <<PARAMETERS
{
  "tagName": {
    "value": "${each.value}"
  }
}
PARAMETERS

}

locals {
  remediation_data = toset(flatten([
    for tag in var.tags_to_inherit : [
      for subscription in data.azurerm_subscriptions.available.subscriptions : {
        tag = tag,
        scope_id = subscription.id
        subscription_id = subscription.subscription_id
      }
    ]
  ]))
}

resource "azurerm_policy_remediation" "inheritance" {
  for_each = {
```

```
    for datum in local.remediation_data :
      "${datum.tag}.${datum.subscription_id}" => datum
  }
  name                  = "${each.value.tag}_${each.value.subscription_id}"
  scope                 = each.value.scope_id
  policy_assignment_id = azurerm_policy_assignment.tag_inherit[each.value.tag].id
  location_filters      = [var.location]
}
```

When you apply these resource definitions, all the resources will inherit the specified tags from their resource groups if not explicitly set. Running this is made safer due to the fact that it will not override preexisting tags.

Azure Policy, as mentioned, can be used for enforcement as well. Let's quickly look at code that will configure the enforcement of particular tags on resource groups:

```
data "azurerm_policy_definition" "tag_enforcement" {
  display_name = "Require a tag on resource groups"
}

resource "azurerm_policy_assignment" "tag_enforcement" {
  for_each              = toset(var.tags_to_inherit)
  name                  = "enf-${each.value}"
  scope                 = data.azurerm_management_group.root.id
  policy_definition_id = data.azurerm_policy_definition.tag_enforcement.id
  location              = var.location

  identity {
    type = "SystemAssigned"
  }

  parameters = <<PARAMETERS
{
  "tagName": {
    "value": "${each.value}"
  }
}
PARAMETERS

}
```

Now whenever a user attempts to create a resource group without either of the tags specified in the variables, they will be denied.

Summary

Let's summarize what was learned and deployed in this recipe:

- Tags on Azure are resource-attached metadata.
- Their most common use case is cost attribution.

- Azure is currently exploring ABAC, but it is very limited in support.
- Azure Policy has a variety of built-in policies to support tagging standards.
- You can configure the inheritance of tags from resource groups to rapidly implement best-effort tagging.
- Azure Policy also allows you to configure tag enforcement.

7.4 Detecting Noncompliant Infrastructure on GCP

Problem

You wish to be notified when a noncompliant piece of infrastructure is deployed anywhere in your organization.

Solution

This recipe involves building a Cloud Asset Organization Feed that triggers a Cloud Function which posts to a Slack channel.

If you haven't already done so, familiarize yourself with Terraform and the different authentication mechanisms in Chapter 11.

As this recipe has a dependency-on-service account authentication, first create and enter an *auth* folder.

Create the following *variables.tf* file:

```
variable "project" {
  type        = string
  description = "The project to deploy the resources into"
}

variable "organization_domain" {
  type        = string
  description = "The organization domain of your Google Cloud estate"
}
```

And input your values into the following *terraform.tfvars* file:

```
project             = ""
organization_domain = ""
```

Define the following *provider.tf* file and run `terraform init`:

```
provider "google" {
  project = var.project
}

terraform {
  required_providers {
```

```
    google = {
      source  = "hashicorp/google"
      version = "~> 3"
    }
  }
}
```

Create the following *main.tf* file and run `terraform plan`:

```
data "google_organization" "current" {
  domain = var.organization_domain
}

resource "google_service_account" "cloud_assets" {
  account_id   = "cloud-assets"
  display_name = "Cloud Assets"
}

resource "google_service_account_key" "cloud_assets" {
  service_account_id = google_service_account.cloud_assets.name
  public_key_type    = "TYPE_X509_PEM_FILE"
}

resource "local_file" "cloud_assets" {
  content  = base64decode(google_service_account_key.cloud_assets.private_key)
  filename = "cloud_assets.json"
}

resource "google_organization_iam_member" "cloud_assets" {
  org_id = data.google_organization.current.org_id
  role   = "roles/cloudasset.owner"

  member = "serviceAccount:${google_service_account.cloud_assets.email}"
}

resource "google_project_iam_member" "cloud_assets" {
  role   = "roles/serviceusage.serviceUsageConsumer"

  member = "serviceAccount:${google_service_account.cloud_assets.email}"
}
```

Review the resources that are going to be created, and then run `terraform apply` to make the changes.

Move up one directory into the parent folder and create the following *variables.tf* file:

```
variable "project_id" {
  type        = string
  description = "The project to create the resources in"
}

variable "region" {
  type        = string
```

```
      description = "The region to create the resources in"
    }

    variable "organization_domain" {
      type        = string
      description = "The organization domain of your Google Cloud estate"
    }

    variable "channel" {
      type        = string
      description = "The Slack channel to post alerts into"
    }
```

Then fill out the corresponding *terraform.tfvars* file:

```
project_id          = ""
region              = ""
organization_domain = ""
channel             = ""
```

Then create the following *provider.tf* file and run `terraform init`:

```
provider "google" {
  project = var.project_id
  region  = var.region
}

provider "google" {
  alias       = "cloud_assets"
  project     = var.project_id
  region      = var.region
  credentials = "./auth/cloud_assets.json"
}

terraform {
  required_providers {
    google = {
      source  = "hashicorp/google"
      version = "~> 3"
    }
  }
}
```

And create the following *main.tf* file:

```
data "google_organization" "this" {
  domain = var.organization_domain
}

data "google_project" "current" {}

locals {
  required_apis = [
    "cloudasset.googleapis.com",
```

```
      "cloudbuild.googleapis.com",
      "cloudfunctions.googleapis.com",
      "secretmanager.googleapis.com"
    ]
}

resource "null_resource" "create_assets_service_account" {
  provisioner "local-exec" {
    command = join(" ", [
      "gcloud beta services identity create",
      "--service=cloudasset.googleapis.com"
    ])
  }
}

resource "google_project_service" "api" {
  for_each = toset(local.required_apis)
  service  = each.value
}

resource "google_cloud_asset_organization_feed" "networking_changes" {
  provider        = google.cloud_assets
  billing_project = data.google_project.current.name
  org_id          = data.google_organization.this.org_id
  feed_id         = "network-changes"
  content_type    = "RESOURCE"

  asset_types = [
    "compute.googleapis.com/Network",
  ]

  feed_output_config {
    pubsub_destination {
      topic = google_pubsub_topic.network_changes.id
    }
  }

  condition {
    expression  = <<EXP
    !temporal_asset.deleted
    EXP
    title       = "created_or_updated"
    description = "Notify on create or update"
  }

  depends_on = [
    google_pubsub_topic_iam_member.cloud_asset_writer,
    google_project_service.api
  ]
}

resource "google_pubsub_topic" "network_changes" {
```

```
  name = "network-changes"
}

resource "google_pubsub_topic_iam_member" "cloud_asset_writer" {
  topic  = google_pubsub_topic.network_changes.id
  role   = "roles/pubsub.publisher"
  member = join("", [
    "serviceAccount:service-",
    data.google_project.current.number,
    "@gcp-sa-cloudasset.iam.gserviceaccount.com"
  ])

  depends_on = [
    null_resource.create_assets_service_account
  ]
}

resource "google_storage_bucket" "bucket" {
  name = "${split(".", var.organization_domain)[0]}-asset-notifications"
}

data "archive_file" "code" {
  type        = "zip"
  source_dir  = "${path.module}/src"
  output_path = "${path.module}/main.zip"
}

resource "google_storage_bucket_object" "code" {
  name   = "${data.archive_file.code.output_md5}.zip"
  bucket = google_storage_bucket.bucket.name
  source = data.archive_file.code.output_path
}

resource "google_cloudfunctions_function" "function" {
  name    = name    = "asset-change-notifier"
  runtime = "python39"

  available_memory_mb   = 128
  source_archive_bucket = google_storage_bucket.bucket.name
  source_archive_object = google_storage_bucket_object.code.name
  entry_point           = "handle"

  environment_variables = {
    "CHANNEL"   = var.channel
    "SECRET_ID" = google_secret_manager_secret.slack_token.secret_id
  }

  event_trigger {
    event_type = "google.pubsub.topic.publish"
    resource   = google_pubsub_topic.network_changes.id

    failure_policy {
```

```
      retry = false
    }
  }

  depends_on = [
    google_project_service.api
  ]
}

resource "google_secret_manager_secret" "slack_token" {
  secret_id = "slack-token"

  replication {
    automatic = true
  }

  depends_on = [
    google_project_service.api
  ]
}

resource "google_secret_manager_secret_iam_member" "function" {
  secret_id = google_secret_manager_secret.slack_token.secret_id
  role      = "roles/secretmanager.secretAccessor"
  member = join("", [
    "serviceAccount:",
    google_cloudfunctions_function.function.service_account_email
  ])
}

output "update_secret_command" {
  value = join(" ", [
    "echo -n TOKEN |",
    "gcloud secrets versions add",
    google_secret_manager_secret.slack_token.secret_id,
    "--data-file=-"
  ])
}
```

Create a *src* folder, and add the following *main.py* file:

```python
import base64
import json
import os

import requests
from google.cloud import secretmanager

client = secretmanager.SecretManagerServiceClient()


def run(asset):
  response = client.access_secret_version(
```

```
      request={"name": f"{os.environ['SECRET_ID']}/versions/latest"}
    )
    token = response.payload.data.decode("utf-8")
    if asset["resource"]["data"]["autoCreateSubnetworks"]:
      requests.post(
        "https://slack.com/api/chat.postMessage",
        data={
          "token": token,
          "channel": f"#{os.environ['CHANNEL']}",
          "text": "".join(
            [
              "The following resource ",
              asset["name"],
              " is noncompliant, expected no automatic subnetworks",
            ]
          ),
        },
      )


def handle(event, _):
  if "data" in event:
    run(json.loads(base64.b64decode(event["data"]).decode("utf-8"))["asset"])
```

And add the following *requirements.txt* file:

```
requests==2.26.0
google-cloud-secret-manager==2.7.2
```

Run `terraform plan` to review the resources that are going to be created, and then run `terraform apply` to make the changes.

Run the command in the `update_secret_command` output, replacing *TOKEN* with your Slack API key.

Discussion

In GCP, SCC Premium runs compliance detection for many industry-standard benchmarks, such as CIS, PCI/DSS, NIST, and ISO 27001. In Recipe 3.1, the recipe builds a similar architecture which reacts based on SCC findings. This recipe enables building customized compliance rules and a fleet of functions that specifically handle particular resource types.

In this recipe, the only asset type that is configured is `compute.googleapis.com/Network`, and the function sends a notification if the network is configured with automatic subnets. As explored in Recipe 5.1, explicitly configuring subnets is required at scale; otherwise, CIDR range overlaps can derail any attempts to allow private network traffic in the future.

Where possible, you should rely on industry-standard compliance benchmarks. As you can see, building your own comes with a large maintenance burden, but this approach is also the underpinning of automatic remediation, which you can see in more detail in Recipe 7.10. Recipe 3.10 also similarly makes use of Cloud Assets to build a queryable asset registry on BigQuery. When developing these custom compliance policies, it is critical that you not only create the notification and remediation functions but also craft a BigQuery query that allows you to understand how many noncompliant resources currently exist within your organization. The nature of this architecture is that it captures compliance when change happens but cannot retroactively investigate preexisting noncompliant infrastructure.

Summary

Let's summarize what was learned and deployed in this recipe:

- To notify users when noncompliant infrastructure is provisioned, you have two options:
  - If the compliance control is from an SCC-supported benchmark, use the architecture in Recipe 3.1.
  - If it is a custom control, then use this recipe.
- This recipe notifies users when a network is created or updated, and is configured to use the automatic subnets.
- You can trigger Cloud Functions on infrastructure changes and use that to determine compliance.
- In Recipe 3.10, the recipe builds a BigQuery table of all assets, allowing you to determine overall compliance against your custom controls.

7.5 Detecting Noncompliant Infrastructure on AWS

Problem

You wish to deploy a set of compliance controls across your entire organization and view the aggregated data.

Solution

This recipe builds on top of Recipe 6.11, assumes an AWS Config recorder is configured in every account, and needs to be run from the organization management account.

If you haven't already done so, familiarize yourself with Terraform and the different authentication mechanisms in Chapter 11.

Update your `aws_organizations_organization` resource to include the `config-multiaccountsetup.amazonaws.com` service access principal.

Create a *variables.tf* file and copy the following contents:

```
variable "cross_account_role" {
  type        = string
  description = "The cross account role to assume"
}

variable "delegated_admin_account_id" {
  type        = string
  description = "The account ID to configure as the delegated admin"
}

variable "managed_config_rules" {
  type        = list(string)
  description = "The config rules to apply in all accounts"
}
```

Then fill out the corresponding *terraform.tfvars* file:

```
cross_account_role         = ""
delegated_admin_account_id = ""
managed_config_rules       = []
```

Create the following *provider.tf* file and run `terraform init`:

```
provider "aws" {}

provider "aws" {
  alias = "delegated_admin"
  assume_role {
    role_arn = join("", [
      "arn:aws:iam::",
      var.delegated_admin_account_id,
      ":role/",
      var.cross_account_role
    ])
  }
}

terraform {
  required_providers {
    aws = {
      source  = "hashicorp/aws"
      version = "~> 3"
    }
  }
}
```

Create the following *main.tf* file and run `terraform plan`:

```
resource "aws_organizations_delegated_administrator" "config-multiaccount" {
  account_id        = var.delegated_admin_account_id
  service_principal = "config-multiaccountsetup.amazonaws.com"
}

resource "aws_config_organization_managed_rule" "rule" {
  provider = aws.delegated_admin
  for_each = toset(var.managed_config_rules)

  name            = each.value
  rule_identifier = each.value

  depends_on = [
    aws_organizations_delegated_administrator.config-multiaccount
  ]
}

resource "aws_config_configuration_aggregator" "organization" {
  provider = aws.delegated_admin
  name     = "organization-aggregator"

  organization_aggregation_source {
    all_regions = true
    role_arn    = aws_iam_role.config_aggregator.arn
  }
}

resource "aws_iam_role" "config_aggregator" {
  provider = aws.delegated_admin
  name     = "config_aggregator"

  assume_role_policy  = data.aws_iam_policy_document.assume.json
  managed_policy_arns = [
    "arn:aws:iam::aws:policy/service-role/AWSConfigRoleForOrganizations"
  ]
}

data "aws_iam_policy_document" "assume" {
  statement {
    actions = [
      "sts:AssumeRole"
    ]

    principals {
      type = "Service"
      identifiers = [
        "config.amazonaws.com"
      ]
    }
  }
}
```

Review the resources that are going to be created, and then run `terraform apply` to make the changes.

Discussion

Because of the hard boundaries between accounts in AWS, the configuration of AWS Config requires the deployment of rules into each disparate account. The combination of organization rules and aggregators abstracts some of that complexity away from the end user. It is also possible to create your own rules, which integrate seamlessly into AWS Config. For example, the following Python shows the general flow of how to create your own rule:

```
def handler(event, context):
  config = boto3.client("config")

  LOGGER.info(event)

  invoking_event = json.loads(event.get("invokingEvent"))

  evaluations = check_compliance()

  for e in evaluations:
    response = config.put_evaluations(
      Evaluations=[
        {
          "ComplianceResourceType": e["compliance_resource_type"],
          "ComplianceResourceId": e["compliance_resource_id"],
          "ComplianceType": e["compliance_type"],
          "Annotation": e["annotation"],
          "OrderingTimestamp": invoking_event["notificationCreationTime"],
        },
      ],
      ResultToken=event["resultToken"],
    )
    LOGGER.info(response)
```

To build a centralized notification function, you need to use AWS EventBridge to funnel events centrally. The following Terraform creates a rule that captures compliance change events and forwards them to the delegated administrator account defined in the recipe. You will need to combine this with Recipe 6.11 to deploy into each account.

```
resource "aws_cloudwatch_event_rule" "compliance" {
  name        = "capture-compliance-changes"
  description = "Capture compliance changes"

  event_pattern = <<EOF
{
  "source": ["aws.config"],
  "detail-type": ["Config Rules Compliance Change"]
```

```
  }
EOF
}

resource "aws_cloudwatch_event_target" "compliance" {
  rule = aws_cloudwatch_event_rule.compliance.name
  arn  = join(":", [
    "arn:aws:events",
    var.region,
    var.delegated_admin_account_id,
    "event-bus/default"
  ])
  role_arn = aws_iam_role.event_forwarder.arn
}

resource "aws_iam_role" "event_forwarder" {
  name               = "event_forwarder"
  assume_role_policy = data.aws_iam_policy_document.assume.json
  managed_policy_arns = [
    aws_iam_policy.execution.arn
  ]
}

data "aws_iam_policy_document" "assume" {
  statement {
    effect  = "Allow"
    actions = ["sts:AssumeRole"]

    principals {
      type = "Service"
      identifiers = [
        "events.amazonaws.com"
      ]
    }
  }
}

resource "aws_iam_policy" "execution" {
  name   = "event_forwarder"
  policy = data.aws_iam_policy_document.execution.json
}

data "aws_iam_policy_document" "execution" {
  statement {
    effect  = "Allow"
    actions = ["events:PutEvents"]
    resources = [
      join(":", [
        "arn:aws:events",
        var.region,
        var.delegated_admin_account_id,
        "event-bus/default"
```

```
            ])
        ]
      }
    }
```

You can then use the same rule deployed into the delegated administrator account, with a lambda function as the target to fire off notifications.

To see the compliance adherence across all accounts, the organization aggregator provides a centralized per-account, per-rule breakdown. This allows you to rapidly identify which rules and which accounts have the greatest number of compliance issues, allowing you to build a data-driven approach to tackling the problem.

Summary

Let's summarize what was learned and deployed in this recipe:

- AWS Config allows you to rapidly deploy rules to every account in the organization.
- The organization-managed rule resources rely on the recorders being already configured in each account.
- The aggregator resource allows you to combine data from all accounts centrally.
- To centralize notifications, you need to deploy EventBridge rules to all accounts that forward their compliance status events.
- It is possible to develop and deploy custom rules which seamlessly integrate with AWS Config.

7.6 Detecting Noncompliant Infrastructure on Azure

Problem

You wish to be notified when a noncompliant piece of infrastructure is deployed anywhere in your tenant.

Solution

This recipe involves configuring an Azure Event Grid system topic that triggers an Azure Function which posts to a Slack channel.

To complete this recipe, you will need the Azure Functions Core Tools installed, which you can find instructions for in the Azure Functions Core Tools GitHub repository (*https://github.com/Azure/azure-functions-core-tools*).

If you haven't already done so, familiarize yourself with Terraform and the different authentication mechanisms in Chapter 11.

Create a *variables.tf* file and copy the following contents:

```
variable "location" {
  type        = string
  description = "The Azure location for resources"
}

variable "channel" {
  type        = string
  description = "The Slack channel to post notifications to"
}
```

Then fill out the corresponding *terraform.tfvars* file:

```
location = ""
channel  = ""
```

Create the following *provider.tf* file and run `terraform init`:

```
terraform {
  required_providers {
    azurerm = {
      source  = "hashicorp/azurerm"
      version = "~> 2"
    }
    null = {
      source  = "hashicorp/null"
      version = "~> 3"
    }
    random = {
      source  = "hashicorp/random"
      version = "~> 3"
    }
  }
}

provider "azurerm" {
  features {}
}
```

Create the following *host.json* file:

```
{
  "version": "2.0",
  "logging": {
    "applicationInsights": {
      "samplingSettings": {
        "isEnabled": true,
        "excludedTypes": "Request"
      }
    }
  },
  "extensionBundle": {
    "id": "Microsoft.Azure.Functions.ExtensionBundle",
```

```
    "version": "[2.*, 3.0.0)"
  }
}
```

Create the following *local.setting.json* file:

```
{
  "IsEncrypted": false,
  "Values": {
    "FUNCTIONS_WORKER_RUNTIME": "python",
    "AzureWebJobsStorage": ""
  }
}
```

Create the following *requirements.txt* file:

```
azure-functions==1.7.2
requests==2.26.0
azure-keyvault-secrets==4.3.0
```

Create a *ComplianceAlerting* folder and in it create two files. First, create an
__init__.py file:

```python
import json
import logging
import os

import azure.functions as func
import requests
from azure.identity import DefaultAzureCredential
from azure.keyvault.secrets import SecretClient


def main(event: func.EventGridEvent):

    result = json.dumps(
        {
            "id": event.id,
            "data": event.get_json(),
            "topic": event.topic,
            "subject": event.subject,
            "event_type": event.event_type,
        }
    )

    logging.info(result)

    credential = DefaultAzureCredential()

    secret_client = SecretClient(
        vault_url=os.environ["KEY_VAULT_URI"], credential=credential
    )
    token = secret_client.get_secret("token")
    requests.post(
```

```
            "https://slack.com/api/chat.postMessage",
            data={
                "token": token,
                "channel": f"#{os.environ['CHANNEL']}",
                "text": f"{result['data']}",
            },
        )
```

And second, create a *function.json* file:

```
{
  "scriptFile": "__init__.py",
  "bindings": [
    {
      "type": "eventGridTrigger",
      "name": "event",
      "direction": "in"
    }
  ]
}
```

Move back to the parent directory, create the following *main.tf* file, and run `terraform plan`:

```
data "azurerm_subscription" "current" {}

data "azurerm_client_config" "current" {}

resource "azurerm_resource_group" "compliance_alerting" {
  name     = "compliance_alerting"
  location = var.location
}

resource "azurerm_eventgrid_system_topic" "policy_state_changes" {
  name                   = "PolicyStateChanges"
  resource_group_name    = azurerm_resource_group.compliance_alerting.name
  location               = "global"
  source_arm_resource_id = data.azurerm_subscription.current.id
  topic_type             = "Microsoft.PolicyInsights.PolicyStates"
}

resource "azurerm_eventgrid_system_topic_event_subscription" "alerting" {
  name                = "policy-state-changes-alerting"
  system_topic        = azurerm_eventgrid_system_topic.policy_state_changes.name
  resource_group_name = azurerm_resource_group.compliance_alerting.name

  azure_function_endpoint {
    function_id = join("/", [
      azurerm_function_app.compliance_alerting.id,
      "functions",
      "ComplianceAlerting"
    ])
    max_events_per_batch              = 1
```

```
    preferred_batch_size_in_kilobytes = 64
  }

  depends_on = [
    null_resource.deploy
  ]
}

resource "azurerm_storage_account" "alerting" {
  name                     = "compliance_alerting"
  resource_group_name      = azurerm_resource_group.compliance_alerting.name
  location                 = azurerm_resource_group.compliance_alerting.location
  account_tier             = "Standard"
  account_replication_type = "LRS"
}

resource "azurerm_app_service_plan" "compliance_alerting" {
  name                = "compliance_alerting"
  location            = azurerm_resource_group.compliance_alerting.location
  resource_group_name = azurerm_resource_group.compliance_alerting.name
  kind                = "functionapp"
  reserved            = true

  sku {
    tier = "Dynamic"
    size = "Y1"
  }
}

resource "azurerm_function_app" "alerting" {
  name                      = "compliance_alerting"
  location                  = azurerm_resource_group.compliance_alerting.location
  resource_group_name       = azurerm_resource_group.compliance_alerting.name
  app_service_plan_id       = azurerm_app_service_plan.compliance_alerting.id
  storage_account_name      = azurerm_storage_account.alerting.name
  storage_account_access_key = azurerm_storage_account.alerting.primary_access_key
  os_type                   = "linux"
  version                   = "~3"

  app_settings = {
    FUNCTIONS_WORKER_RUNTIME = "python"
    KEY_VAULT_URI            = azurerm_key_vault.slack.vault_uri
    CHANNEL                  = var.channel
  }

  site_config {
    linux_fx_version = "Python|3.9"
  }

  identity {
    type = "SystemAssigned"
  }
}
```

```
}

resource "null_resource" "deploy" {
  provisioner "local-exec" {
    command = "func azure functionapp publish compliance_alerting"
  }

  depends_on = [
    azurerm_function_app.alerting
  ]
}

resource "random_string" "key_vault" {
  length  = 16
  special = false
}

resource "azurerm_key_vault" "slack" {
  name                      = random_string.key_vault.result
  location                  = azurerm_resource_group.compliance_alerting.location
  resource_group_name       = azurerm_resource_group.compliance_alerting.name
  enable_rbac_authorization = true

  sku_name  = "standard"
  tenant_id = data.azurerm_client_config.current.tenant_id
}

resource "azurerm_role_assignment" "secret_officer" {
  scope                = azurerm_key_vault.slack.id
  role_definition_name = "Key Vault Secrets Officer"
  principal_id         = data.azurerm_client_config.current.object_id
}

resource "azurerm_function_app" "alerting" {
  scope                = azurerm_key_vault.slack.id
  role_definition_name = "Key Vault Secrets User"
  principal_id         = azurerm_function_app.alerting.identity.0.principal_id
}

output "update_secret_command" {
  value = join(" ", [
    "az keyvault secret set -n token --vault-name",
    azurerm_key_vault.slack.name,
    "--value"
  ])
}
```

Review the resources that are going to be created, and then run `terraform apply` to make the changes.

Copy the command from the `update_secret_command` output, append your Slack token to the end, and run the command.

Discussion

Azure Policy gives you an aggregated view of the state of compliance across your tenant. What this recipe adds is an ability to notify users in real time as compliance changes occur. The Python code can be extended to filter for events of particular interest or criticality.

The recipe uses the `Microsoft.PolicyInsights.PolicyStates` topic type, which means that three different types of policy events will be routed: `Microsoft.Policy Insights.PolicyStateCreated` when a compliance state is first created, `Microsoft .PolicyInsights.PolicyStateChanged` when a compliance state changes, and `Micro soft.PolicyInsights.PolicyStateDeleted` when a compliance state is deleted. By tracking *hot* resources, those with many frequent changes, that consistently swap between compliance and noncompliance, you can diagnose situations where two different automation systems are in conflict. This becomes critical when looking at automated remediation activities, as in Recipe 7.12.

It is possible to create your own Azure Policies to detect compliance against custom controls. In Recipe 7.9, you'll create a custom policy to enforce a compliance requirement. Custom policies are treated by Azure Policy as first-class citizens, meaning they are automatically integrated into this recipe.

Summary

Let's summarize what was learned and deployed in this recipe:

- Azure Policy state changes can be automatically published to Azure Event Grid.
- Event Grid can invoke Azure Functions, which allow us to send notifications to users when events of interest occur.
- By collecting and looking for patterns in the events, you can see infrastructure that is caught between automation systems.
- You can craft custom policies for your custom compliance controls.
- Custom policies are treated no differently than built-in policies.

7.7 Preventing Noncompliant Infrastructure on GCP

Problem

You want to prevent users from creating noncompliant infrastructure through the console or APIs.

Solution

This recipe configures organization policies to prevent certain types of infrastructure configuration.

If you haven't already done so, familiarize yourself with Terraform and the different authentication mechanisms in Chapter 11.

Create a *variables.tf* file and copy the following contents:

```
variable "organization_domain" {
  type        = string
  description = "The organization domain of your Google Cloud estate"
}

variable "target_folder_id" {
  type        = string
  description = "The folder that requires only VPC connected functions"
}

variable "target_project_id" {
  type        = string
  description = "The project that requires restricted function ingresses"
}
```

Then fill out the corresponding *terraform.tfvars* file:

```
organization_domain = ""
target_folder_id    = ""
target_project_id   = ""
```

Create the following *provider.tf* file and run `terraform init`:

```
provider "google" {
  project = var.project
  region  = var.region
}

terraform {
  required_providers {
    google = {
      source  = "hashicorp/google"
      version = "~> 3"
    }
  }
}
```

Create the following *main.tf* file and run `terraform plan`:

```
data "google_organization" "current" {
  domain = var.organization_domain
}

resource "google_organization_policy" "vm_external_ips" {
```

```
    org_id     = data.google_organization.current.org_id
    constraint = "constraints/compute.vmExternalIpAccess"

    list_policy {
      deny {
        all = true
      }
    }
}

resource "google_folder_organization_policy" "vpc_connected_functions" {
    folder     = var.target_folder_id
    constraint = "constraints/cloudfunctions.requireVPCConnector"

    boolean_policy {
      enforced = true
    }
}

resource "google_project_organization_policy" "restricted_function_ingress" {
    project    = var.target_project_id
    constraint = "constraints/cloudfunctions.allowedIngressSettings"

    list_policy {
      allow {
        values = [
          "ALLOW_INTERNAL_ONLY"
        ]
      }
    }
}
```

Review the resources that are going to be created, and then run `terraform apply` to make the changes.

Discussion

In this recipe, you applied organization policies at the organization, folder, and project level. Where the policy exists for your requirement, enforcement through this mechanism should be your first choice. It affects every user, cannot be circumnavigated via identity and access management (IAM), and works the same whether you're making changes through the console or via automation.

As was discussed in Chapter 6, infrastructure as code should be the primary driver of change in your environment. Among the host of benefits you get, you can adopt tools to enforce compliance. A common tool in the space is Checkov. Let's take a look at how it handles noncompliant Terraform resource definitions. First, install Checkov, following the instructions at the Checkov home page (*https://www.checkov.io*).

Define a simple Cloud Storage bucket in a file called *bucket.tf*:

```
resource "google_storage_bucket" "test" {
  name = "checkov-test"
}
```

Now run `checkov -f bucket.tf`. It will fail with output that looks like the following:

```
Passed checks: 0, Failed checks: 2, Skipped checks: 0

Check: CKV_GCP_62: "Bucket should log access"
        FAILED for resource: google_storage_bucket.test
        File: /bucket.tf:1-3
        Guide: https://docs.bridgecrew.io/docs/bc_gcp_logging_2

                1 | resource "google_storage_bucket" "test" {
                2 |   name = "checkov-test"
                3 | }


Check: CKV_GCP_29: "Ensure that Cloud Storage buckets have uniform bucket-level
access enabled"
        FAILED for resource: google_storage_bucket.test
        File: /bucket.tf:1-3
        Guide: https://docs.bridgecrew.io/docs/bc_gcp_gcs_2

                1 | resource "google_storage_bucket" "test" {
                2 |   name = "checkov-test"
                3 | }
```

By working through the guides Checkov provides, you should end up with a bucket definition that looks like the following:

```
resource "google_storage_bucket" "test" {
  name = "checkov-test"
  uniform_bucket_level_access = true
  logging {
    log_bucket = "access_logs"
  }
}
```

Now, when running `checkov -f bucket.tf` again, you will get a clean bill of health. A tool like this is a fundamental part of shifting security left when combined with Recipe 6.7.

Summary

Let's summarize what was learned and deployed in this recipe:

- Organization policies allow enforcement of certain compliance guardrails.
- When an organization policy exists that fulfils your requirement, you should use it over other options.

- The recipe had examples of applying the policies to the entire organization, specific folders, and particular projects.

- Organization policies cannot be easily circumvented and are not flexible.

- When using infrastructure as code, you unlock the ability to use other tools to prevent noncompliant infrastructure.

- Checkov is a common, open source option.

- Given noncompliant infrastructure, it will provide guides that show you how to resolve the issues.

7.8 Preventing Noncompliant Infrastructure on AWS

Problem

You want to prevent users from creating noncompliant infrastructure through the console or APIs.

Solution

This recipe configures Service Control Policies (SCPs) to restrict access. It needs to run from your organization management account.

If you haven't already done so, familiarize yourself with Terraform and the different authentication mechanisms in Chapter 11.

Create the following *provider.tf* file and run `terraform init`:

```
provider "aws" {}

terraform {
  required_providers {
    aws = {
      source  = "hashicorp/aws"
      version = "~> 3"
    }
  }
}
```

Create the following *main.tf* file and run `terraform plan`:

```
data "aws_caller_identity" "current" {}

data "aws_organizations_organization" "current" {}

resource "aws_organizations_policy" "compliance" {
  name = "compliance_guardrails"

  content = data.aws_iam_policy_document.compliance.json
```

```
  }

  data "aws_iam_policy_document" "compliance" {
    statement {
      effect = "Deny"
      actions = [
        "ec2:DeleteFlowLogs",
        "logs:DeleteLogStream",
        "logs:DeleteLogGroup"
      ]
      resources = [
        "*"
      ]
    }
  }

  resource "aws_organizations_policy_attachment" "root" {
    policy_id = aws_organizations_policy.compliance.id
    target_id = data.aws_organizations_organization.current.roots[0].id
  }
```

Review the resources that are going to be created, and then run `terraform apply` to make the changes.

Discussion

This recipe restricts any principal within the account from disabling VPC flow logs or deleting the historical logs in CloudWatch. As flow logs are a critical piece of evidence for forensic analysis, they are a good candidate for locking with an SCP. By putting IAM restrictions in the SCP, you establish guardrails that cannot be circumvented from within the account, as the SCP is applied outside of the account boundary. It is possible to build exceptions into SCPs to deny users access by default but allow certain privileged individuals access.

> The following are a few situations where SCPs do not apply:
>
> - Actions taken in the organization root account
> - Service-linked roles
> - AWS principals from outside the organization, such as cross-account bucket access

For example, the following policy prevents any user from modifying a protected IAM role within the account, except a single exempted role:

```
{
  "Version": "2012-10-17",
  "Statement": [
    {
```

```
        "Sid": "ProtectRoleWithException",
        "Effect": "Deny",
        "Action": [
          "iam:AttachRolePolicy",
          "iam:DeleteRole",
          "iam:DeleteRolePermissionsBoundary",
          "iam:DeleteRolePolicy",
          "iam:DetachRolePolicy",
          "iam:PutRolePermissionsBoundary",
          "iam:PutRolePolicy",
          "iam:UpdateAssumeRolePolicy",
          "iam:UpdateRole",
          "iam:UpdateRoleDescription"
        ],
        "Resource": [
          "arn:aws:iam::*:role/protected-role"
        ],
        "Condition": {
          "StringNotLike": {
            "aws:PrincipalARN":"arn:aws:iam::*:role/privileged-role"
          }
        }
      }
    }
  ]
}
```

As long as you can write IAM policy that expresses your compliance requirement, you can prevent users from being able to create resources, whether they're using the console or APIs. However, as was discussed in Chapter 6, infrastructure as code should be the default way of enacting change, with the console reserved for read-only activities and break-glass operations. Let's look at how the open source tool Checkov can support us in our compliance journey. Install Checkov by following the instructions at the Checkov home page (*https://www.checkov.io*).

Define a simple S3 bucket in a file called *bucket.tf*:

```
resource "aws_s3_bucket" "test" {
  bucket = "test"
}
```

Now, run checkov -f bucket.tf. It will fail with output that looks like the following:

```
Check: CKV_AWS_19: "Ensure all data stored in the S3 bucket is securely encrypted
at rest"
        FAILED for resource: aws_s3_bucket.test
        File: /bucket.tf:1-3
        Guide: https://docs.bridgecrew.io/docs/s3_14-data-encrypted-at-rest

                1 | resource "aws_s3_bucket" "test" {
                2 |   bucket = "test"
                3 | }
```

```
Check: CKV_AWS_18: "Ensure the S3 bucket has access logging enabled"
        FAILED for resource: aws_s3_bucket.test
        File: /bucket.tf:1-3
        Guide: https://docs.bridgecrew.io/docs/s3_13-enable-logging

                1 | resource "aws_s3_bucket" "test" {
                2 |   bucket = "test"
                3 | }
```

...

By working through the guides Checkov provides, you should end up with a bucket
definition that looks like the following. In this example, the check for cross-region
replication is skipped:

```
resource "aws_s3_bucket" "test" {
  // checkov:skip=CKV_AWS_144
  bucket = "test"
  server_side_encryption_configuration {
    rule {
      apply_server_side_encryption_by_default {
        sse_algorithm = "aws:kms"
      }
    }
  }

  versioning {
    enabled = true
  }

  logging {
    target_bucket = "access_logging"
    target_prefix = "log/test"
  }
}

resource "aws_s3_bucket_public_access_block" "test" {
  bucket = aws_s3_bucket.test.id

  block_public_acls       = true
  block_public_policy     = true
  restrict_public_buckets = true
  ignore_public_acls      = true
}
```

Now, when running checkov -f bucket.tf again, you will get a clean bill of health.
A tool like this is a fundamental part of shifting security left when combined with
Recipe 6.8.

Summary

Let's summarize what was learned and deployed in this recipe:

- SCPs allow for the enforcement of certain compliance guardrails.
- SCPs are limited by what is expressible through IAM policies.
- You saw an example of building escape hatches into policies.
- Crafting complicated SCPs is difficult and error prone; having two organizations, as recommended in Recipe 2.2, helps with the testing of SCPs.
- By adopting infrastructure as code, you enable other tools to be used in addition to SCPs.
- Checkov is a common, open source option.
- Given noncompliant infrastructure, you can iteratively work to make the infrastructure compliant.

7.9 Preventing Noncompliant Infrastructure on Azure

Problem

You want to prevent users from creating noncompliant infrastructure through the console or APIs.

Solution

This recipe configures a custom Azure Policy in enforce mode to prevent users from creating resources.

If you haven't already done so, familiarize yourself with Terraform and the different authentication mechanisms in Chapter 11.

Create the following *provider.tf* file and run `terraform init`:

```
terraform {
  required_providers {
    azurerm = {
      source  = "hashicorp/azurerm"
      version = "~> 2"
    }
  }
}

provider "azurerm" {
  features {}
}
```

Create the following *main.tf* file and run `terraform plan`:

```
data "azurerm_subscription" "current" {}

resource "azurerm_policy_definition" "g_series_prevent" {
  name         = "Prevent G Series Virtual Machines"
  policy_type  = "Custom"
  mode         = "All"
  display_name = "Prevent G Series Virtual Machines"


  policy_rule = <<POLICY_RULE
{
  "if": {
    "allOf": [{
        "field": "type",
        "equals": "Microsoft.Compute/virtualMachines"
      },
      {
        "field": "Microsoft.Compute/virtualMachines/sku.name",
        "like": "Standard_G*"
      }
    ]
  },
  "then": {
    "effect": "deny"
  }
}
POLICY_RULE
}

resource "azurerm_subscription_policy_assignment" "g_series_prevent" {
  name                 = "g_series_prevent"
  policy_definition_id = azurerm_policy_definition.g_series_prevent.id
  subscription_id      = data.azurerm_subscription.current.id
}
```

Review the resources that are going to be created, and then run `terraform apply` to make the changes.

Discussion

After assigning this policy with the preceding Terraform, all users will be prevented from creating G-series virtual machines in the subscription. This will hold whether they use the portal or APIs to try to create the resources. When using Azure Policy, it is important to understand the variety of effects that it can enact:

Append
:   Adds additional fields to a resource

Audit
:   Creates a warning when a noncompliant resource is found but does not stop the request

---

AuditIfNotExists
    Creates a warning when a related resource does not exist

Deny
    Stops the request if noncompliant

DeployIfNotExists
    Deploys resources if missing

Disabled
    Stops the policy from doing anything

Modify
    Adds, updates, or removes properties or tags on a resource

When looking to prevent noncompliant infrastructure, audit, deny, and modify are the most interesting. When first creating a new policy, it is often best to initially deploy with an audit effect where you can review the accuracy and potential impact of the policy. Depending on whether you wish to stop users, or modify their requests in flight, you can then redeploy with the more invasive effects. The modify effect comes with some of the same downsides as automated remediation activities, as explored in Recipe 7.12. With deny policies, it can sometimes be hard to enable your users to fix their requests in a fully self-service manner. It can also present challenges to automated deployments, where the planned changes are successful, but they break when being applied.

Infrastructure as code, covered in depth in Chapter 6, is not only fundamental to truly leveraging the cloud but is also a requirement for a highly compliant environment. By using it, you have the option to embrace tools to support you on your compliance journey. Checkov can tell you, prior to deployment, that your infrastructure will be noncompliant; and for the built-in checks, it provides fully documented self-service guides for users.

Let's explore how it can ensure you deploy compliant storage accounts. First, install Checkov by following the instructions at the Checkov home page (*https:// www.checkov.io*).

Define a simple storage account in an *sa.tf* file:

```
resource "azurerm_resource_group" "test" {
  name     = "test"
  location = "us"
}

resource "azurerm_storage_account" "test" {
  resource_group_name      = azurerm_resource_group.test.name
  location                 = azurerm_resource_group.test.location
  name                     = "test"
  account_tier             = "Standard"
```

```
    account_replication_type = "GRS"
}
```

Now, run checkov -f sa.tf. It will fail with output that looks like the following:

```
Check: CKV2_AZURE_18: "Ensure that Storage Accounts use customer-managed key for
encryption"
        FAILED for resource: azurerm_storage_account.test
        File: /sa.tf:6-12
        Guide: https://docs.bridgecrew.io/docs/ensure-that-storage-accounts-use-
customer-managed-key-for-encryption

                6 | resource "azurerm_storage_account" "test" {
                7 |   resource_group_name      = azurerm_resource_group.test.name
                8 |   location                 = azurerm_resource_group.test.location
                9 |   name                     = "test"
               10 |   account_tier             = "Standard"
               11 |   account_replication_type = "GRS"
               12 | }


Check: CKV2_AZURE_8: "Ensure the storage container storing the activity logs is
not publicly accessible"
        FAILED for resource: azurerm_storage_account.test
        File: /sa.tf:6-12
        Guide: https://docs.bridgecrew.io/docs/ensure-the-storage-
container-storing-the-activity-logs-is-not-publicly-accessible

                6 | resource "azurerm_storage_account" "test" {
                7 |   resource_group_name      = azurerm_resource_group.test.name
                8 |   location                 = azurerm_resource_group.test.location
                9 |   name                     = "test"
               10 |   account_tier             = "Standard"
               11 |   account_replication_type = "GRS"
               12 | }

...
```

By working through the guides Checkov provides, you should end up with a storage account definition that looks like the following. In this example, two rules were skipped: CKV2_AZURE_8 and CKV_AZURE_112.

```
resource "azurerm_resource_group" "test" {
  name     = "test"
  location = "us"
}

resource "azurerm_storage_account" "test" {
  // checkov:skip=CKV2_AZURE_8
  resource_group_name      = azurerm_resource_group.test.name
  location                 = azurerm_resource_group.test.location
  name                     = "test"
  account_tier             = "Standard"
```

```
    account_replication_type = "GRS"
    min_tls_version          = "TLS1_2"
    enable_https_traffic_only = true

    queue_properties {
      logging {
        delete                = true
        read                  = true
        write                 = true
        version               = "1.0"
        retention_policy_days = 10
      }
    }


    network_rules {
      default_action = "Deny"
    }
}

resource "azurerm_key_vault" "example" {
  name                = "examplekv"
  location            = "location"
  resource_group_name = "group"
  tenant_id           = data.azurerm_client_config.current.tenant_id
  sku_name            = "standard"

  purge_protection_enabled = true

  network_acls {
    default_action = "Deny"
    bypass         = "AzureServices"
  }
}

resource "azurerm_key_vault_key" "example" {
  // checkov:skip=CKV_AZURE_112
  name         = "tfex-key"
  key_vault_id = azurerm_key_vault.example.id
  key_type     = "RSA"
  key_size     = 2048
  key_opts     = [
    "decrypt",
    "encrypt",
    "sign",
    "unwrapKey",
    "verify",
    "wrapKey"
  ]
  expiration_date = "2022-12-30T20:00:00Z"
}
```

```
resource "azurerm_storage_account_customer_managed_key" "key" {
  storage_account_id = azurerm_storage_account.test.id
  key_vault_id       = azurerm_key_vault.example.id
  key_name           = azurerm_key_vault_key.example.name
  key_version        = "1"
}
```

Now, if you run checkov -f bucket.tf again, you will get a clean bill of health. Combining this with Recipe 6.9 is one of the first steps in building out a cloud native DevSecOps pipeline.

Summary

Let's summarize what was learned and deployed in this recipe:

- Azure Policy has a variety of effects it can enact when finding a noncompliant resource.

- You can define custom policies to enforce particular compliance controls.

- By assigning a policy with a deny effect, you prevent users from being able to breach that control.

- Azure Policy, while effective, is not the best at supporting self-service fixing.

- Checkov is an open source tool that can identify noncompliant infrastructure from the Terraform resource definitions.

- It automatically provides self-service documentation for each finding.

7.10 Remediating Noncompliant Infrastructure on GCP

Problem

You wish to automatically fix high-risk infrastructure as soon as it is discovered.

Solution

This recipe involves building a Cloud Asset Organization Feed that triggers a Cloud Function which prevents public Cloud Storage buckets.

If you haven't already done so, familiarize yourself with Terraform and the different authentication mechanisms in Chapter 11.

As this recipe has a dependency-on-service account authentication, first create and enter an *auth* folder.

Create the following *variables.tf* file:

```
variable "project" {
  type        = string
```

```
  description = "The project to deploy the resources into"
}

variable "organization_domain" {
  type        = string
  description = "The organization domain of your Google Cloud estate"
}

variable "target_projects" {
  type        = list(string)
  description = "The project to enable the remediator for"
}
```

Then fill out the corresponding *terraform.tfvars* file:

```
project             = ""
organization_domain = ""
target_projects     = [""]
```

Create the following *provider.tf* file and run `terraform init`:

```
provider "google" {
  project = var.project
}

terraform {
  required_providers {
    google = {
      source  = "hashicorp/google"
      version = "~> 3"
    }
  }
}
```

Create the following *main.tf* file and run `terraform plan`:

```
data "google_organization" "current" {
  domain = var.organization_domain
}

resource "google_service_account" "cloud_assets" {
  account_id   = "cloud-assets"
  display_name = "Cloud Assets"
}

resource "google_service_account_key" "cloud_assets" {
  service_account_id = google_service_account.cloud_assets.name
  public_key_type    = "TYPE_X509_PEM_FILE"
}

resource "local_file" "cloud_assets" {
  content  = base64decode(google_service_account_key.cloud_assets.private_key)
  filename = "cloud_assets.json"
}
```

```
resource "google_organization_iam_member" "cloud_assets" {
  org_id = data.google_organization.current.org_id
  role   = "roles/cloudasset.owner"

  member = "serviceAccount:${google_service_account.cloud_assets.email}"
}

resource "google_project_iam_member" "cloud_assets" {
  for_each = toset(var.target_projects)
  project  = each.value
  role     = "roles/serviceusage.serviceUsageConsumer"

  member = "serviceAccount:${google_service_account.cloud_assets.email}"
}
```

Review the resources that are going to be created, and then run `terraform apply` to make the changes.

Move up to the parent folder and create the following *variables.tf* file:

```
variable "project_id" {
  type        = string
  description = "The project to create the resources in"
}

variable "region" {
  type        = string
  description = "The region to create the resources in"
}

variable "organization_domain" {
  type        = string
  description = "The organization domain of your Google Cloud estate"
}

variable "target_projects" {
  type        = list(string)
  description = "The project to enable the remediator for"
}
```

Then fill out the corresponding *terraform.tfvars* file:

```
project             = ""
region              = ""
organization_domain = ""
target_projects     = [""]
```

Create the following *provider.tf* file and run `terraform init`:

```
provider "google" {
  project = var.project_id
  region  = var.region
}
```

```
provider "google" {
  alias       = "cloud_assets"
  project     = var.project_id
  region      = var.region
  credentials = "./auth/cloud_assets.json"
}

terraform {
  required_providers {
    google = {
      source  = "hashicorp/google"
      version = "~> 3"
    }
  }
}
```

Create the following *main.tf* file:

```
data "google_project" "current" {}

locals {
  required_apis = [
    "cloudasset.googleapis.com",
    "cloudbuild.googleapis.com",
    "cloudfunctions.googleapis.com",
    "storage.googleapis.com",
  ]
}

resource "null_resource" "create_assets_service_account" {
  for_each = toset(var.target_projects)
  provisioner "local-exec" {
    command = join(" ", [
      "gcloud beta services identity create",
      "--service=cloudasset.googleapis.com",
      "--project=${each.value}"
    ])
  }
}

resource "google_project_service" "api" {
  for_each           = toset(local.required_apis)
  service            = each.value
  disable_on_destroy = false
}

resource "google_project_service" "assets" {
  for_each           = toset(var.target_projects)
  project            = each.value
  service            = "cloudasset.googleapis.com"
  disable_on_destroy = false
}
```

```
resource "google_cloud_asset_project_feed" "bucket_changes" {
  provider = google.cloud_assets
  for_each      = toset(var.target_projects)
  project       = each.value
  feed_id       = "bucket-changes"
  content_type = "RESOURCE"

  asset_types = [
    "storage.googleapis.com/Bucket",
  ]

  feed_output_config {
    pubsub_destination {
      topic = google_pubsub_topic.bucket_changes.id
    }
  }

  condition {
    expression  = <<EXP
    !temporal_asset.deleted
    EXP
    title         = "created_or_updated"
    description = "Notify on create or update"
  }

  depends_on = [
    google_pubsub_topic_iam_member.cloud_asset_writer,
    google_project_service.api,
    google_project_service.assets,
  ]
}

resource "google_pubsub_topic" "bucket_changes" {
  name = "bucket-changes"
}

data "google_project" "targets" {
  for_each = toset(var.target_projects)
  project_id = each.value
}

resource "google_pubsub_topic_iam_member" "cloud_asset_writer" {
  for_each = toset(var.target_projects)
  topic  = google_pubsub_topic.bucket_changes.id
  role   = "roles/pubsub.publisher"
  member = join("", [
    "serviceAccount:service-",
    data.google_project.targets[each.value].number,
    "@gcp-sa-cloudasset.iam.gserviceaccount.com"
  ])
```

```
  depends_on = [
    null_resource.create_assets_service_account
  ]
}

resource "google_storage_bucket" "bucket" {
  name = "${split(".", var.organization_domain)[0]}-bucket-remediator"
}

data "archive_file" "code" {
  type        = "zip"
  source_dir  = "${path.module}/src"
  output_path = "${path.module}/main.zip"
}

resource "google_storage_bucket_object" "code" {
  name   = "${data.archive_file.code.output_md5}.zip"
  bucket = google_storage_bucket.bucket.name
  source = data.archive_file.code.output_path
}

resource "google_cloudfunctions_function" "function" {
  name    = "public-bucket-remediation"
  runtime = "python39"

  available_memory_mb   = 128
  source_archive_bucket = google_storage_bucket.bucket.name
  source_archive_object = google_storage_bucket_object.code.name
  entry_point           = "handle"

  event_trigger {
    event_type = "google.pubsub.topic.publish"
    resource   = google_pubsub_topic.bucket_changes.id

    failure_policy {
      retry = false
    }
  }

  depends_on = [
    google_project_service.api
  ]
}

resource "google_project_iam_member" "function" {
  for_each = toset(var.target_projects)
  project  = each.value
  role     = google_project_iam_custom_role.bucket-remediator[each.key].id
  member   = join("", [
    "serviceAccount:",
    google_cloudfunctions_function.function.service_account_email
  ])
```

```
}
resource "google_project_iam_custom_role" "bucket-remediator" {
  for_each = toset(var.target_projects)
  project  = each.value
  role_id  = "bucketRemediator"
  title    = "Role used to remediate noncompliant bucket configurations"
  permissions = [
    "storage.buckets.get",
    "storage.buckets.setIamPolicy",
    "storage.buckets.update"
  ]
}
```

Last, create a *src* folder, and create two files in it. First, create a *main.py* file:

```python
import base64
import json

from google.cloud.storage import Client
from google.cloud.storage.constants import PUBLIC_ACCESS_PREVENTION_ENFORCED

client = Client()


def public_access_allowed(iam_configuration):
    return (
        "publicAccessPrevention" in iam_configuration
        and iam_configuration["publicAccessPrevention"] != "enforced"
    ) or ("publicAccessPrevention" not in iam_configuration)


def run(asset):
    if public_access_allowed(asset["resource"]["data"]["iamConfiguration"]):
        bucket_name = asset["resource"]["data"]["name"]
        bucket = client.get_bucket(bucket_name)

        bucket.iam_configuration.public_access_prevention = (
            PUBLIC_ACCESS_PREVENTION_ENFORCED
        )
        bucket.patch()


def handle(event, _):
    if "data" in event:
        run(json.loads(base64.b64decode(event["data"]).decode("utf-8"))["asset"])
```

And second, create a *requirements.txt* file:

```
google-cloud-storage==1.42.3
```

Run `terraform plan`, review the resources that are going to be created, and then run `terraform apply` to make the changes.

Discussion

Unintentional public data storage has been in the newspapers with frightening regularity since cloud usage has accelerated. It is one of those critical compliance controls that needs rectifying as it happens. This recipe is architecturally similar to Recipe 7.4, although in this instance the Cloud Function is privileged in specific projects to actively fix noncompliant buckets.

Although great in theory, automated remediation of this sort has potential issues.

First, it undermines the approach in Chapter 6, by making the infrastructure drift from what the code has defined. In these instances, adopting an approach more like Checkov in Recipe 7.7 is more appropriate, as it forces the change to happen through infrastructure as code.

Second, you run the risk of system impacts. In Figure 7-1, I showed how you can segment changes based on ownership and risk. Automated remediation is fantastic for low-risk changes, especially those that are workload owned. Not all workload teams may be using infrastructure as code, which means that other options aren't available.

Third, often the end user doesn't learn how to do it correctly next time. Depending on the specific compliance finding, this may or may not be important. For public buckets, it is critical that people understand how to configure them properly; for not deleting a user who hasn't logged in for 90 days, letting automation clear that up is probably OK.

As you saw in this recipe, building automated remediation is not trivial; it requires a level of coding ability and is its own maintenance burden. By investing in prevention, you reduce the need for mass remediation. Focus on the highest-value remediation targets, but if it's a case of something that once fixed will stay fixed, a more manual fix is the correct way to go.

For critical compliance issues, automated remediation is the last line of defense, as the impact of the issue far outweighs any other impacts. For small, dynamic resources, you'll end up in a loop of always fixing the symptom and never the cause.

Summary

Let's summarize what was learned and deployed in this recipe:

- By triggering Cloud Functions of Cloud Assets, you can automatically remediate identified compliance issues.
- To build out an automated remediation framework, you accept an ongoing maintenance burden.
- Beware the conflict between automated remediation and infrastructure as code.

- If teams are using infrastructure as code, determine how best to prevent non-compliant infrastructure in the first place.

- Automated remediation works best for low-operational-risk, high-security-risk changes.

- Remediating resources automatically stops end users from learning; for high-risk items, it is better they learn how to configure the resource properly in the future.

7.11 Remediating Noncompliant Infrastructure on AWS

Problem

You wish to automatically fix high-risk infrastructure as soon as it is discovered.

Solution

This recipe involves configuring an AWS Config remediation action to automatically close off public S3 buckets. It also requires a Python environment with boto3 available.

If you haven't already done so, familiarize yourself with Terraform and the different authentication mechanisms in Chapter 11.

Create the following *provider.tf* file and run terraform init:

```
provider "aws" {}

terraform {
  required_providers {
    aws = {
      source  = "hashicorp/aws"
      version = "~> 3"
    }
    null = {
      source  = "hashicorp/null"
      version = "~> 3"
    }
  }
}
```

Create the following *main.py* file:

```
from sys import argv

from boto3 import client

def update_configuration(configuration):
    config = configuration.copy()
    config["Automatic"] = True
    config["MaximumAutomaticAttempts"] = 1
```

```
            config["RetryAttemptSeconds"] = 60
            return config

    def run(rule_name):
        config = client("config")

        configurations = config.describe_remediation_configurations(
            ConfigRuleNames=[
                rule_name,
            ]
        )["RemediationConfigurations"]
        auto_configurations = [
            update_configuration(configuration) for configuration in configurations
        ]
        config.put_remediation_configurations(
          RemediationConfigurations=auto_configurations
        )

    if __name__ == "__main__":
        run(argv[1])
```

Create the following *main.tf* file and run `terraform plan`:

```
resource "aws_config_config_rule" "s3_public" {
  name = "S3_BUCKET_LEVEL_PUBLIC_ACCESS_PROHIBITED"

  source {
    owner            = "AWS"
    source_identifier = "S3_BUCKET_LEVEL_PUBLIC_ACCESS_PROHIBITED"
  }
}

resource "aws_config_remediation_configuration" "s3_public" {
  config_rule_name = aws_config_config_rule.s3_public.name
  target_type      = "SSM_DOCUMENT"
  target_id        = "AWSConfigRemediation-ConfigureS3BucketPublicAccessBlock"

  parameter {
    name         = "AutomationAssumeRole"
    static_value = aws_iam_role.remediator.arn
  }

  parameter {
    name           = "BucketName"
    resource_value = "RESOURCE_ID"
  }
}

resource "null_resource" "turn_on_auto_remediate" {
  provisioner "local-exec" {
    command = "python main.py ${aws_config_config_rule.s3_public.name}"
  }
```

```
  depends_on = [
    aws_config_remediation_configuration.s3_public
  ]
}

resource "aws_iam_role" "remediator" {
  name = "s3_public_bucket_remediator"

  assume_role_policy = data.aws_iam_policy_document.assume.json
  managed_policy_arns = [
    aws_iam_policy.s3_public_bucket_remediator.arn
  ]
}

data "aws_iam_policy_document" "assume" {
  statement {
    actions = [
      "sts:AssumeRole"
    ]

    principals {
      type = "Service"
      identifiers = [
        "ssm.amazonaws.com"
      ]
    }
  }
}

resource "aws_iam_policy" "s3_public_bucket_remediator" {
  name   = "s3_public_bucket_remediator"
  policy = data.aws_iam_policy_document.remediation.json
}

data "aws_iam_policy_document" "remediation" {
  statement {
    effect = "Allow"
    actions = [
      "s3:GetBucketPublicAccessBlock",
      "s3:PutBucketPublicAccessBlock"
    ]
    resources = ["*"]
  }
}
```

Review the resources that are going to be created, and then run `terraform apply` to
make the changes.

Discussion

Public S3 buckets are the source of most data breaches in company AWS environments. Being able to shut them off automatically is a key capability to have as part of

your compliance suite. In this recipe, you configured an AWS-provided remediation action to automatically fire if the S3_BUCKET_LEVEL_PUBLIC_ACCESS_PROHIBITED rule found any noncompliant S3 buckets. Unfortunately, there is no remediation equivalent of the aws_config_organization_managed_rule resources from Recipe 7.5. To get around this, you can either use AWS Config conformance packs, which break away from Terraform by using CloudFormation to deploy resources across accounts, or combine this recipe with Recipe 6.11 to use Terraform.

Automatic remediation comes into conflict with the concept of infrastructure as code, as explored fully in Chapter 6. The remediation action causes drift between reality and what is defined in the code, which can cause resources to continually flip between compliant and noncompliant states. In Recipe 7.8, you saw Checkov act as a strong compliance prevention tool when using infrastructure as code. This should be the primary method of compliance enforcement of teams.

Another potential issue in a highly automated compliance world is that end users stop learning how to configure infrastructure properly and instead learn to lean more heavily on security to clean up after them. Back in Chapter 1, I wrote about how security in a modern organization is an enablement function—you are looking to scale through upskilling and enabling teams. Automated remediation should be focused on where the risk is too great to allow the learning feedback loop to occur. Public S3 buckets are a classic example of exactly that.

It is possible to roll your own remediation actions. The same AWS EventBridge rule from Recipe 7.5 can be used to trigger AWS SSM runbooks, the same mechanism used for the recipe's AWS Config remediation, or AWS Lambda functions to perform any necessary actions. With the Lambda function approach, you can either combine with Recipe 6.11 to deploy the function to all accounts and trigger locally, or centralize the events and have the function assume a role in the other accounts. The advantage to a centralized function is that the role it assumes can be more readily shaped to fit the end user's requirements, as they can deploy it themselves.

Summary

Let's summarize what was learned and deployed in this recipe:

- AWS Config provides a variety of pre-canned remediation tasks.
- They are deployed in an account targeting a particular rule.
- To deploy across an organization, use Recipe 6.11.
- You can configure them to automatically remediate noncompliant infrastructure.
- Automated remediation and infrastructure as code come into conflict.
  — The remediation action induces drift from the code.

- For teams adopting infrastructure as code, you should look to ideally leverage tools like Checkov from Recipe 7.8.

- For custom remediation actions, you can use EventBridge rules with SSM runbooks or Lambda functions.

7.12 Remediating Noncompliant Infrastructure on Azure

You wish to automatically fix high-risk infrastructure as soon as it is discovered.

Solution

This recipe involves configuring an Azure Event Grid system topic that triggers an Azure Function which automatically remediates the noncompliant resource.

If you haven't already done so, familiarize yourself with Terraform and the different authentication mechanisms in Chapter 11.

Create a *variables.tf* file and copy the following contents:

```
variable "location" {
  type        = string
  description = "The Azure location for resources"
}
```

Then fill out the corresponding *terraform.tfvars* file:

```
location = ""
```

Create the following *provider.tf* file and run `terraform init`:

```
terraform {
  required_providers {
    azurerm = {
      source  = "hashicorp/azurerm"
      version = "~> 2"
    }
    null = {
      source  = "hashicorp/null"
      version = "~> 3"
    }
    random = {
      source  = "hashicorp/random"
      version = "~> 3"
    }
  }
}

provider "azurerm" {
  features {}
}
```

Next, create the following *host.json* file:

```json
{
  "version": "2.0",
  "logging": {
    "applicationInsights": {
      "samplingSettings": {
        "isEnabled": true,
        "excludedTypes": "Request"
      }
    }
  },
  "extensionBundle": {
    "id": "Microsoft.Azure.Functions.ExtensionBundle",
    "version": "[2.*, 3.0.0)"
  }
}
```

Create the following *local.setting.json* file:

```json
{
  "IsEncrypted": false,
  "Values": {
    "FUNCTIONS_WORKER_RUNTIME": "python",
    "AzureWebJobsStorage": ""
  }
}
```

And create the following *requirements.txt* file:

```
azure-functions==1.7.2
azure-mgmt-policyinsights==1.0.0
azure-identity==1.7.0
azure-mgmt-resource==20.0.0
```

Create a *Remediation* folder, and in it create two files. First, create an *__init__.py* file:

```python
import logging

import azure.functions as func
from azure.identity import DefaultAzureCredential
from azure.mgmt.policyinsights import PolicyInsightsClient
from azure.mgmt.policyinsights.models import Remediation
from azure.mgmt.resource.policy import PolicyClient


credential = DefaultAzureCredential()

def main(event: func.EventGridEvent):
  logging.info(event)

  compliance_state = event.get_json()["complianceState"]

  if compliance_state == "NonCompliant":
```

```python
    policyAssignmentId = event.get_json()["policyAssignmentId"]
    policyDefinitionId = event.get_json()["policyDefinitionId"]

    policy_insights = PolicyInsightsClient(credential=credential)
    policy = PolicyClient(credential=credential)

    definition = policy.policy_definitions.get(
      policy_definition_name=policyDefinitionId
    )
    if definition.policy_rule:
      effect = definition.policy_rule["then"]["effect"]
      if (
        "append" == effect or
        "modify" == effect
      ):

        parameters = Remediation(policy_assignment_id=policyAssignmentId)
        result = policy_insights.remediations.create_or_update_at_subscription(
          remediation_name="AutomatedRemediation", parameters=parameters
        )

        logging.info(result)
    else:
      logging.info("Policy definition had no remediation action available")
  else:
    logging.info("Resource is compliant, taking no action")
```

And second, create a *function.json* file:

```json
{
  "scriptFile": "__init__.py",
  "bindings": [
    {
      "type": "eventGridTrigger",
      "name": "event",
      "direction": "in"
    }
  ]
}
```

Now, move back to the parent directory, create the following *main.tf* file, and run
`terraform plan`:

```
data "azurerm_subscription" "current" {}

resource "azurerm_resource_group" "remediation" {
  name     = "remediation"
  location = var.location
}

resource "azurerm_eventgrid_system_topic" "policy_state_changes" {
  name                = "PolicyStateChanges"
  resource_group_name = azurerm_resource_group.remediation.name
```

```
  location                = "global"
  source_arm_resource_id = data.azurerm_subscription.current.id
  topic_type              = "Microsoft.PolicyInsights.PolicyStates"
}

resource "azurerm_eventgrid_system_topic_event_subscription" "remediation" {
  name                  = "policy-state-changes-alerting"
  system_topic          = azurerm_eventgrid_system_topic.policy_state_changes.name
  resource_group_name = azurerm_resource_group.remediation.name

  azure_function_endpoint {
    function_id = join("/", [
      azurerm_function_app.remediation.id,
      "functions",
      "Remediation"
    ])
    max_events_per_batch            = 1
    preferred_batch_size_in_kilobytes = 64
  }

  depends_on = [
    null_resource.deploy
  ]
}

resource "random_string" "storage_account" {
  length  = 16
  special = false
  upper   = false
}

resource "azurerm_storage_account" "r" {
  name                    = random_string.storage_account.result
  resource_group_name   = azurerm_resource_group.remediation.name
  location                = azurerm_resource_group.remediation.location
  account_tier            = "Standard"
  account_replication_type = "LRS"
}

resource "azurerm_app_service_plan" "remediation" {
  name                  = "remediation"
  location                = azurerm_resource_group.remediation.location
  resource_group_name = azurerm_resource_group.remediation.name
  kind                    = "functionapp"
  reserved                = true

  sku {
    tier = "Dynamic"
    size = "Y1"
  }
}
```

```
resource "random_string" "functionapp" {
  length  = 16
  special = false
  upper   = false
}

resource "azurerm_storage_account" "r" {
  name                      = random_string.functionapp.result
  location                  = azurerm_resource_group.remediation.location
  resource_group_name       = azurerm_resource_group.remediation.name
  app_service_plan_id       = azurerm_app_service_plan.remediation.id
  storage_account_name      = azurerm_storage.r.name
  storage_account_access_key = azurerm_storage.r.primary_access_key
  os_type                   = "linux"
  version                   = "~3"

  app_settings = {
    FUNCTIONS_WORKER_RUNTIME = "python"
  }

  site_config {
    linux_fx_version = "Python|3.9"
  }

  identity {
    type = "SystemAssigned"
  }
}

resource "null_resource" "deploy" {
  provisioner "local-exec" {
    command = join(" ", [
      "func azure functionapp publish",
      azurerm_function_app.remediation.name
    ])
  }

  depends_on = [
    azurerm_function_app.remediation
  ]
}

resource "azurerm_role_assignment" "remediation" {
  scope                = data.azurerm_subscription.current.id
  role_definition_name = azurerm_role_definition.remediation.name
  principal_id         = azurerm_function_app.remediation.identity.0.principal_id
}

resource "azurerm_role_definition" "remediation" {
  name  = "automated-remediation"
  scope = data.azurerm_subscription.current.id
```

```
permissions {
  actions     = ["Microsoft.PolicyInsights/remediations/write"]
  not_actions = []
}

assignable_scopes = [
  data.azurerm_subscription.current.id
]
}
```

Review the resources that are going to be created, and then run `terraform apply` to make the changes.

Discussion

Unlike the AWS and GCP equivalent recipes, this Azure recipe uses the library of remediation actions in Azure Policy to handle a large amount of noncompliant resources.

Azure Policy gives a robust remediation mechanism for policies that have either an append or modify effect. Unfortunately, there is no built-in mechanism for automatically remediating resources within Azure Policy. Hence the recipe here, which is architecturally similar to Recipe 7.6. Rather than sending Slack notifications, the function app is given the privilege to execute remediations against Azure Policy.

It is possible to extend the function to perform any action against Azure in response to the compliance status event. Rather than create a remediation task against Azure Policy, you could directly modify the resource. However, by going through Azure Policy, you retain the history of the remediation tasks that have been attempted during the life of your subscription.

Remediating in this way works amazingly well for resources that are not managed via infrastructure as code and carry low operational risk. With modern ways of working, as explored in Chapter 6, the focus should be more on building the toolchain around the infrastructure as code, rather than applying fixes around it. It actively undermines the power of the code as it drifts further from reality. This is why evaluating tools such as Checkov, from Recipe 7.9, is fundamental to DevSecOps. If possible, prevent the noncompliant infrastructure in the first place; idiomatically, "an ounce of prevention is worth a pound of cure."

Summary

Let's summarize what was learned and deployed in this recipe:

- Azure Policy provides remediation tasks for many policies.
- They can be created ad hoc, but no built-in functionality allows them to be automated.

- This recipe used Event Grid to trigger an Azure Function to create the remediations on demand.
- Be careful when applying remediations to an environment with high levels of infrastructure as code.
  — The remediations cause drift, which undermines the value.
- An ounce of prevention is worth a pound of remediation.

CHAPTER 8

Providing Internal Security Services

As part of managing a growing cloud estate, a security function needs to be able to provide scalable services. These services provide a secure baseline that ensures that known vulnerable resources are automatically rectified and that recovery is possible during a potential incident.

First, you must be able to control your identity perimeter. Delivery teams will require the ability to self-manage identity in order to be able to move at speed. As their architectures evolve, to maintain the principle of least privilege, they need to create roles without the delay of going through a centralized team. As the ability to create roles is decentralized, it is key that they are not able to accidentally or intentionally escalate their privilege and start to compromise the guardrails in the cloud estate.

Second, being able to manage the virtual machine fleet becomes critical. The highly volatile nature of resources in a cloud environment needs modern tooling built for that reality. Each cloud service provider has services dedicated to giving overviews of the active machines while also enabling drilling down to specifics such as inventory. As new machines emerge continuously, your tooling needs to build a real-time lens onto the vulnerabilities that exist.

Third, running scheduled patches and updates is mandatory for proactively handling vulnerabilities and operating a healthy fleet. All three providers again provide a managed service that allows for the deployment and management of scheduled updates across your estate.

Last, having robust backup processes is key to restoring service due to malicious or accidental incidents. As ransomware and similar attacks become more prevalent, business continuity is dependent on modern backup strategies that allow for recovery.

8.1 Protecting Security Assets and Controls on GCP

Problem

You need to prevent people from escalating their own permissions within a project.

Solution

This recipe gives a specific user the ability to only grant certain roles to other IAM principals.

If you haven't already done so, familiarize yourself with Terraform and the different authentication mechanisms in Chapter 11.

Create a *variables.tf* file and copy the following contents:

```
variable "project" {
  type        = string
  description = "The project to deploy the resources into"
}

variable "customer_id" {
  type        = string
  description = <<DESCRIPTION
Customer ID for your Google Workspace account
Can be found at https://admin.google.com/ac/accountsettings
DESCRIPTION
}

variable "organization_domain" {
  type        = string
  description = "The domain of your organization"
}

variable "user_email" {
  type        = string
  description = "The email of the user to give IAM admin"
}
```

Then fill out the corresponding *terraform.tfvars* file:

```
project             = ""
customer_id         = ""
organization_domain = ""
user_email          = ""
```

Create the following *provider.tf* file and run `terraform init`:

```
provider "google" {
  project               = var.project
  billing_project       = var.project
  user_project_override = true
```

```
  }

terraform {
  required_providers {
    google = {
      source  = "hashicorp/google"
      version = "~> 3"
    }
  }
}
```

Create the following *main.tf* file and run `terraform plan`:

```
resource "google_project_service" "resource_manager" {
  service            = "cloudresourcemanager.googleapis.com"
  disable_on_destroy = false
}

resource "google_project_iam_member" "compute_admin" {
  role = "roles/resourcemanager.projectIamAdmin"

  member = "user:${var.user_email}"

  condition {
    title       = "only_compute_engine"
    description = "Only allows granting compute engine roles"
    expression = join("", [
      "api.getAttribute('iam.googleapis.com/modifiedGrantsByRole', [])",
      ".hasOnly([",
      "'roles/computeAdmin'",
      "])"
    ])
  }

  depends_on = [
    google_project_service.resource_manager
  ]
}
```

Review the resources that are going to be created, and then run `terraform apply` to make the changes.

Discussion

To protect security assets in GCP, the critical aspect is controlling how IAM privileges are assigned. For teams to operate autonomously, they need to be able to assign their own permissions. However, it is best practice to prevent a user assigning more privileges than they currently possess. This recipe allows the specified user to grant and revoke only the `computeAdmin` role on any user within the project. By matching the list of roles in the condition expression with the roles assigned to the user, you block this variant of privilege escalation.

Now imagine that the user needs to be able to give other users the power to grant and revoke the set of roles. In theory, you could give the user the `roles/resourceman ager.projectIamAdmin` role, but this would allow them to modify their own condition and escalate their privileges. Instead, to achieve this, you need to create a group, assign the permissions to the group, and make the original user the manager of the group. Then, by toggling group membership, they can give other users the privilege to grant those roles. The following Terraform implements this pattern:

```
resource "google_cloud_identity_group" "iam_admins" {
  display_name = "${var.project} IAM Admins"

  parent = "customers/${var.customer_id}"

  group_key {
    id = "${var.project}-iam-admins@${var.organization_domain}"
  }

  labels = {
    "cloudidentity.googleapis.com/groups.discussion_forum" = ""
  }
}

resource "google_cloud_identity_group_membership" "manager" {
  group = google_cloud_identity_group.iam_admins.id

  preferred_member_key {
    id = var.user_email
  }

  roles {
    name = "MEMBER"
  }

  roles {
    name = "MANAGER"
  }
}

resource "google_project_iam_member" "compute_admin_group" {
  role = "roles/resourcemanager.projectIamAdmin"

  member = "group:${google_cloud_identity_group.iam_admins.group_key[0].id}"

  condition {
    title       = "only_compute_engine"
    description = "Only allows granting compute engine roles"
    expression = join("", [
      "api.getAttribute('iam.googleapis.com/modifiedGrantsByRole', [])",
      ".hasOnly([",
      "'roles/computeAdmin'",
      "])"
  }
```

```
    ])
  }

  depends_on = [
    google_project_service.resource_manager
  ]
}
```

When creating and managing service accounts in your estate, care should be taken to not allow users to assume more highly privileged service accounts unless explicitly required. When a user assumes a service account, they gain equivalent privilege, and it is therefore a vector for privilege escalation. The following is a nonexhaustive list of permissions that enable service account assumption:

- `iam.serviceAccounts.getAccessToken`
- `iam.serviceAccounts.getOpenIdToken`
- `iam.serviceAccounts.actAs`
- `iam.serviceAccounts.implicitDelegation`
- `iam.serviceAccountKeys.create`
- `iam.serviceAccountKeys.get`
- `deploymentmanager.deployments.create`
- `cloudbuild.builds.create`

A service account's IAM policy dictates who can assume it. Therefore, any user with the `iam.serviceAccounts.setIamPolicy` permission on the service account can modify who can assume that role. This permission should be granted sparingly and only when explicitly required to stop lateral movement between principals.

To prevent rogue access to service accounts, the `Disable service account key cre ation` and `Disable service account key upload` organization policy constraints should be applied in all projects where service account keys are not explicitly required. Service account keys that are compromised or leaked become persistent, direct attack vectors into your estate. As such, their creation should be when required, not a default enabled option.

Google Cloud Recommender provides three kinds of insights into how your identity and access management are configured. First are lateral movement insights, where Recommender determines opportunities for service accounts to assume a different service account in another project. These are a primary vector for a security incident to break out of a project and spread across the state. Second are policy insights, where Recommender identifies excess permissions assigned to users. Third are service account insights, which finds potentially redundant service accounts to delete.

Summary

Let's summarize what was learned and deployed in this recipe:

- By using conditions on the `roles/resourcemanager.projectIamAdmin` role, you can prevent users from assigning privileges outside of an approved list.
- If that list is equivalent to the permissions assigned to the user, then they cannot create a principal that is more privileged than themselves.
- Use groups to share the limited IAM administration between users in a project.
- Service accounts are another vector for privilege escalation.
- The service account IAM policies, and who can edit them, need to be tightly controlled.
- Two organization policy constraints to curtail the usage of service account keys should be enforced by default on all projects.
- Use Google Cloud Recommender to provide feedback on your identity perimeter, and identify areas where users are too privileged, service accounts present a vector for lateral movement, and service accounts are redundant.

8.2 Protecting Security Assets and Controls on AWS

Problem

You need to prevent people from escalating their own permissions within an account.

Solution

This recipe restricts a principal escalating privilege by creating another principal with higher permissions.

If you haven't already done so, familiarize yourself with Terraform and the different authentication mechanisms in Chapter 11.

Create the following *provider.tf* file and run `terraform init`:

```
provider "aws" {}

terraform {
  required_providers {
    aws = {
      source  = "hashicorp/aws"
      version = "~> 3"
    }
  }
}
```

Create the following *main.tf* file and run `terraform plan`:

```
data "aws_caller_identity" "current" {}

locals {
  all_roles = join("", [
    "arn:aws:iam::",
    data.aws_caller_identity.current.account_id,
    ":role/*"
  ])
  all_users = join("", [
    "arn:aws:iam::",
    data.aws_caller_identity.current.account_id,
    ":user/*"
  ])
  policy_arn = join("", [
    "arn:aws:iam::",
    data.aws_caller_identity.current.account_id,
    ":policy/",
    local.policy_name
  ])
  policy_name = "general_permissions_boundary"
}

resource "aws_iam_policy" "permissions_boundary" {
  name        = local.policy_name
  path        = "/"
  description = "General Permission Boundary for Principals"

  policy = data.aws_iam_policy_document.permissions_boundary.json
}

data "aws_iam_policy_document" "permissions_boundary" {
  statement {
    sid       = "AllowFullAccess"
    actions   = ["*"]
    effect    = "Allow"
    resources = ["*"]
  }

  statement {
    sid = "DenyCostAndBillingAccess"
    actions = [
      "account:*",
      "aws-portal:*",
      "savingsplans:*",
      "cur:*",
      "ce:*"
    ]
    effect    = "Deny"
    resources = ["*"]
  }
```

```
statement {
  sid = "DenyEditAccessThisPolicy"
  actions = [
    "iam:DeletePolicy",
    "iam:DeletePolicyVersion",
    "iam:CreatePolicyVersion",
    "iam:SetDefaultPolicyVersion"
  ]
  effect = "Deny"
  resources = [
    local.policy_arn
  ]
}

statement {
  sid = "DenyRemovalOfPermissionBoundary"
  actions = [
    "iam:DeleteUserPermissionsBoundary",
    "iam:DeleteRolePermissionsBoundary"
  ]
  effect = "Deny"
  resources = [
    local.all_users,
    local.all_roles
  ]

  condition {
    test     = "StringEquals"
    variable = "iam:PermissionsBoundary"
    values = [
      local.policy_arn
    ]
  }
}

statement {
  sid = "DenyPrincipalCRUDWithoutPermissionBoundary"
  actions = [
    "iam:PutUserPermissionsBoundary",
    "iam:PutRolePermissionsBoundary",
    "iam:CreateUser",
    "iam:CreateRole"
  ]
  effect = "Deny"
  resources = [
    local.all_users,
    local.all_roles
  ]

  condition {
    test     = "StringNotEquals"
```

```
      variable = "iam:PermissionsBoundary"
      values = [
        local.policy_arn
      ]
    }
  }
}
```

Review the resources that are going to be created, and then run `terraform apply` to make the changes.

Discussion

Consuming teams in AWS need the ability to create their own IAM roles and policies. But once their initial permission sets have been applied, you need the ability to ensure they cannot create roles and policies that exceed those permissions. This is where permission boundaries are required. To understand how permission boundaries interact with policies and Service Control Policies (SCPs), see Figure 8-1.

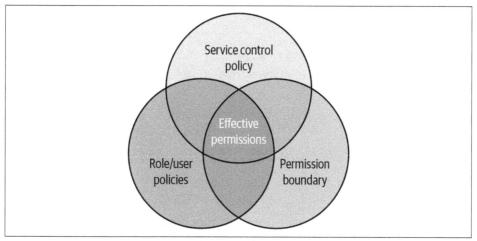

Figure 8-1. Effective IAM permissions

IAM principals acting from outside your organization, for example, an IAM user that has cross-account S3 bucket access, are not affected by SCPs.

Instead, if they must assume a role in the account, then they are beholden to the SCPs in place.

The permissions a principal has are the cross-section among the SCP, the permissions boundary, and the policies attached to the role or user. The permissions boundary policy defined in the recipe blocks a principal from accessing the services related to costs and billing, enforces that any roles or users they create must have the same permissions boundary applied, and prevents them from editing the permissions boundary itself. So given the following role defined in Terraform, although it has the AdministratorAccess managed policy attached, users who assume that role still cannot access any APIs related to cost and billing:

```
resource "aws_iam_role" "example" {
  name = "permissions_boundary_example"

  assume_role_policy = data.aws_iam_policy_document.assume.json
  managed_policy_arns = [
    "arn:aws:iam::aws:policy/AdministratorAccess"
  ]
  permissions_boundary = aws_iam_policy.permissions_boundary.arn
}

data "aws_iam_policy_document" "assume" {
  statement {
    effect = "Allow"

    principals {
      type = "AWS"
      identifiers = [
        join("", [
          "arn:aws:iam::",
          data.aws_caller_identity.current.account_id,
          ":root"
        ])
      ]
    }

    actions = ["sts:AssumeRole"]
  }
}
```

As shown in Figure 8-1, SCPs can also be used to restrict access. A common use case for SCPs is locking all principals from accessing certain resources, apart from a known administration role. For example, if you were looking to prevent users within an account from modifying AWS Config rules, you can apply the following SCP once you have filled out the target_id and role_name variables:

```
resource "aws_organizations_policy" "prevent_config_access" {
  name    = "prevent_config_access"
  content = data.aws_iam_policy_document.prevent_config_access.json
}

data "aws_iam_policy_document" "prevent_config_access" {
  statement {
    sid = "PreventConfigAccess"
    action = [
      "config:*"
    ]
```

```
      effect = "Deny"
      resources = [
        "*"
      ]

      condition {
        test     = "StringNotLike"
        variable = "aws:PrincipalARN"
        values = [
          "arn:aws:iam::*:role/${var.role_name}"
        ]
      }
    }
  }
}

resource "aws_organizations_policy_attachment" "account" {
  policy_id = aws_organizations_policy.prevent_config_access.id
  target_id = var.target_id
}
```

Summary

Let's summarize what was learned and deployed in this recipe:

- On AWS, a principal's effective permissions are determined by the cross-section of the SCPs, the attached policies, and the permission boundary.

- You can write permission boundaries that require their attachment to new roles and users.

- By doing so, you can prevent a principal from escalating their privilege while still allowing them to create principals as required.

- You can also use SCPs to lock all principals in an account from accessing certain APIs, apart from explicitly exempted principals.

8.3 Protecting Security Assets and Controls on Azure

Problem

You need to prevent people from escalating their own permissions within an account.

Solution

This recipe prevents a principal from elevating their privilege on a given resource.

If you haven't already done so, familiarize yourself with Terraform and the different authentication mechanisms in Chapter 11.

Create a *variables.tf* file and copy the following contents:

```
variable "location" {
  type        = string
  description = "The location to deploy the resources into"
}

variable "group_name" {
  type        = string
  description = "The AAD group that can edit role assignments"
}
```

Then fill out the corresponding *terraform.tfvars* file:

```
location   = ""
group_name = ""
```

Create the following *provider.tf* file and run `terraform init`:

```
terraform {
  required_providers {
    azurerm = {
      source  = "hashicorp/azurerm"
      version = "~> 2"
    }
    azuread = {
      source = "hashicorp/azuread"
      version = "~> 2"
    }
  }
}

provider "azurerm" {
  features {}
}
```

Create the following *main.tf* file and run `terraform plan`:

```
resource "azurerm_resource_group" "workload" {
  name     = "workload"
  location = var.location
}

data "azuread_user" "access_admin" {
  user_principal_name = var.upn
}

resource "azurerm_role_assignment" "access_admin" {
  scope                = azurerm_resource_group.workload.id
  role_definition_name = "User Access Administrator"
  principal_id         = data.azuread_user.access_admin.object_id
}

resource "azurerm_policy_definition" "psep" {
  name        = "prevent-self-edit-permissions"
  policy_type = "Custom"
```

```
  mode          = "All"
  display_name = "Prevent self editing of permissions"

  metadata = <<METADATA
{
  "category": "IAM"
}
METADATA

  policy_rule = <<RULE
{
  "if": {
    "anyOf": [
      {
        "allOf": [
          {
            "field": "type",
            "equals": "Microsoft.Authorization/roleAssignments"
          },
          {
            "field": "Microsoft.Authorization/roleAssignments/principalId",
            "equals": "[parameters('principalId')]"
          }
        ]
      }
    ]
  },
  "then": {
    "effect": "Deny"
  }
}
RULE

  parameters = <<PARAMETERS
{
  "principalId": {
    "type": "string",
    "defaultValue": "",
    "metadata": {
      "description": "The principal ID",
      "displayName": "The principal ID"
    }
  }
}
PARAMETERS
}

resource "azurerm_resource_group_policy_assignment" "prevent_self_edit" {
  name                 = "prevent-self-edit"
  resource_group_id    = azurerm_resource_group.workload.id
  policy_definition_id = azurerm_policy_definition.psep.id
  parameters = <<PARAMETERS
```

```
{
  "principalId": {
    "value": "${data.azuread_user.access_admin.object_id}"
  }
}
PARAMETERS

  depends_on = [
    azurerm_role_assignment.access_admin
  ]
}
```

Review the resources that are going to be created, and then run `terraform apply` to make the changes.

Discussion

In Azure, permissions are attached directly to resources as extensions and are inherited down from management groups, to subscriptions, to resource groups, and finally to individual resources. Although subscriptions are often highly multitenanted, team boundaries should be enforced with resource groups at a minimum.

The built-in role for managing permissions is the User Access Administrator role, as used in the recipe. However, this role by default allows a user to give themselves owner permissions on the resource. In the recipe, through the creation of a custom Azure Policy, you can prevent a user from modifying their own permissions for a given scope. By matching that scope to the resource they are administrating permissions on, be that a subscription, resource group, or resource, you prevent them from escalating privilege.

However, through the usage of managed identities, a user can still look to elevate their privilege. A *managed identity* is a principal that can only be assumed by a given Azure resource but cannot be assumed by a human user. For example, if a user has the ability to edit the code within an Azure function, and manage the permissions of the managed identity used by the function, they can operate with elevated permissions. Any user that has the User Access Administrator role on a resource in reality has the full permissions of an Owner on that resource unless specifically blocked by Azure Policy.

To prevent this, you can configure Azure Policy to block the setting of Owner permissions on an existing resource with the following Azure Policy definition, feeding in the role definition ID as a parameter:

```
resource "azurerm_policy_definition" "prevent_specific_role_assignment" {
  name         = "prevent-specific-role-assignment"
  policy_type  = "Custom"
  mode         = "All"
  display_name = "Prevent specific role assignment"
```

```
  metadata = <<METADATA
{
  "category": "IAM"
}
METADATA

  policy_rule = <<RULE
{
  "if": {
    "anyOf": [
      {
        "allOf": [
          {
            "field": "type",
            "equals": "Microsoft.Authorization/roleAssignments"
          },
          {
            "field": "Microsoft.Authorization/roleAssignments/roleDefinitionId",
            "equals": "[parameters('definitionId')]"
          }
        ]
      }
    ]
  },
  "then": {
    "effect": "Deny"
  }
}
RULE

  parameters = <<PARAMETERS
{
  "definitionId": {
    "type": "string",
    "defaultValue": "",
    "metadata": {
      "description": "The role definition ID to prevent",
      "displayName": "The role definition ID to prevent"
    }
  }
}
PARAMETERS
}
```

Rather than assigning users long-term privileged access, the Privileged Identity Management (PIM) service on Azure provides an auditable approach to providing just-in-time, time-bound elevated access. Currently, managing PIM is not possible through Terraform. However, the general workflow for allowing access to a particular privileged role is as follows:

1. An access review is configured, outlining the required approval steps for the role.

2. The role is assigned to principals within the tenant.

3. When the user requests to assume the role, the approval steps are triggered, which, if successful, give the user the permissions for a specific time.

It is also possible to use PIM to give certain principals eternal elevated access, such as the managed identities that are used as part of the CI/CD pipelines, as in Recipe 6.9, where waiting for a human approval every time you deploy would be a significant drag on productivity.

Summary

Let's summarize what was learned and deployed in this recipe:

- In Azure, permissions are applied directly to resources.
- To protect resources, it is often easiest to segment into different resource groups.
- By default, a principal with the User Access Administrator role can escalate their privilege up to Owner level.
- You can use Azure Policy to prevent certain privilege escalation paths.
- Azure PIM allows for audited break-glass access to privileged roles.

8.4 Understanding Machine Status at Scale on GCP

Problem

You need inventory management for the virtual machines in your estate.

Solution

If you haven't already done so, familiarize yourself with Terraform and the different authentication mechanisms in Chapter 11.

Create a *variables.tf* file and copy the following contents:

```
variable "project" {
  type        = string
  description = "The project to deploy the resources into"
}

variable "zone" {
  type        = string
  description = "The zone to deploy resources into"
}
```

Then fill out the corresponding *terraform.tfvars* file:

```
project    = ""
zone       = ""
```

Create the following *provider.tf* file and run `terraform init`:

```
provider "google" {
  project = var.project
}

terraform {
  required_providers {
    google = {
      source  = "hashicorp/google"
      version = "~> 4"
    }
  }
}
```

Create the following *main.tf* file and run `terraform plan`:

```
resource "google_project_service" "containerscanning" {
  service           = "containerscanning.googleapis.com"
  disable_on_destroy = false
}

resource "google_project_service" "osconfig" {
  service           = "osconfig.googleapis.com"
  disable_on_destroy = false
}

resource "google_compute_project_metadata_item" "osconfig" {
  key   = "enable-osconfig"
  value = "TRUE"
}

resource "google_compute_project_metadata_item" "guest_attrs" {
  key   = "enable-guest-attributes"
  value = "TRUE"
}

resource "google_project_service_identity" "containerscanning" {
  provider = google-beta
  service = "containerscanning.googleapis.com"
}

resource "google_project_service_identity" "osconfig" {
  provider = google-beta
  service = "osconfig.googleapis.com"
}

resource "google_project_iam_member" "containerscanning" {
  project = var.project
```

```
    role = "roles/containeranalysis.ServiceAgent"
    member = join("", [
      "serviceAccount:",
      google_project_service_identity.containerscanning.email
    ])
}

resource "google_project_iam_member" "osconfig" {
  project = var.project
  role = "roles/osconfig.serviceAgent"
  member = join("", [
    "serviceAccount:",
    google_project_service_identity.osconfig.email
  ])
}
```

Review the resources that are going to be created, and then run `terraform apply` to make the changes.

Discussion

VM Manager on GCP provides three primary functions for supporting fleets of virtual machines: inventory management, configuration management, and patch management (covered in Recipe 8.7). Let's quickly deploy a simple VM by adding and applying the following Terraform:

```
resource "google_compute_instance" "example" {
  name                     = "example"
  machine_type             = "f1-micro"
  zone                     = var.zone
  allow_stopping_for_update = true

  boot_disk {
    initialize_params {
      image = "debian-cloud/debian-10-buster-v20211105"
    }
  }

  network_interface {
    network = "default"

    access_config {}
  }

  service_account {
    email  = google_service_account.example.email
    scopes = ["cloud-platform"]
  }
}

resource "google_service_account" "example" {
```

```
    account_id  = "example"
    display_name = "example"
}
```

As the Google disk images come with the OS Config agent preinstalled, the recently launched virtual machine will automatically appear in inventory listings. Run `gcloud alpha compute os-config inventories list` to get a list of all the managed machines in the project. Make a note of the ID of the bastion machine you created.

To get a breakdown of the packages installed on a particular instance, run the command `gcloud alpha compute os-config inventories describe <your-instance-id> --view=full`. This will print out to the console a list of all the installed packages and pending updates. If Cloud Assets is configured, as in Recipe 3.10, then the enriched data will automatically flow to your asset registry.

To install new packages, create and assign OS policies to the instances. An OS policy is a YAML definition that is then assigned to machines on a zone-by-zone basis. This allows you to ensure that a baseline set of packages is installed on the machines and to manage package updates via code. For example, a policy that ensures the stackdriver agent, for integration with Cloud Operations Suite, is installed is the following *policy.yaml*:

```yaml
osPolicies:
  - id: install-stackdriver-agent
    mode: ENFORCEMENT
    resourceGroups:
      - inventoryFilters:
          - osShortName: debian
        resources:
          - id: setup-repo
            repository:
              apt:
                archiveType: DEB
                uri: https://packages.cloud.google.com/apt
                distribution: google-cloud-monitoring-buster-all
                components:
                  - main
                gpgKey: https://packages.cloud.google.com/apt/doc/apt-key.gpg
          - id: install-pkg
            pkg:
              desiredState: INSTALLED
              apt:
                name: stackdriver-agent
instanceFilter:
  inventories:
    - osShortName: debian
rollout:
  disruptionBudget:
    fixed: 10
  minWaitDuration: 300s
```

To create the policy, run the command gcloud alpha compute os-config os-policy-assignments create stackdriver-debian --file=./policy.yaml. With that policy in place, all Debian virtual machines in the project, in the zone specified in your gcloud compute/zone property, will have the Stackdriver agent installed automatically if it is missing.

Summary

Let's summarize what was learned and deployed in this recipe:

- VM Manager allows you manage large fleets of virtual machines.
- Once configured with machines that have the OS Config agent installed, you can get detailed information on each instance, including installed packages.
- With OS Config properly configured, you can use OS policies to enforce the existence of packages on your machines.

8.5 Understanding Machine Status at Scale on AWS

Problem

You need inventory management for the virtual machines in your estate.

Solution

If you haven't already done so, familiarize yourself with Terraform and the different authentication mechanisms in Chapter 11.

Create the following *provider.tf* file and run `terraform init`:

```
provider "aws" {}

terraform {
  required_providers {
    aws = {
      source  = "hashicorp/aws"
      version = "~> 3"
    }
  }
}
```

Create the following *main.tf* file and run `terraform plan`:

```
resource "aws_iam_instance_profile" "ssm_profile" {
  name = "fleet"
  role = aws_iam_role.role.name
}

resource "aws_iam_role" "role" {
```

```
    name = "fleet"

    managed_policy_arns = [
      "arn:aws:iam::aws:policy/AmazonSSMManagedInstanceCore"
    ]

    assume_role_policy = data.aws_iam_policy_document.assume.json
}

data "aws_iam_policy_document" "assume" {
  statement {
    actions = [
      "sts:AssumeRole",
    ]

    principals {
      type = "Service"
      identifiers = [
        "ec2.amazonaws.com"
      ]
    }
  }
}

resource "aws_ssm_association" "inventory" {
  name                = "AWS-GatherSoftwareInventory"
  schedule_expression = "rate(1 day)"
  targets {
    key    = "InstanceIds"
    values = ["*"]
  }

  parameters = {
    "applications"                = "Enabled"
    "awsComponents"               = "Enabled"
    "billingInfo"                 = "Enabled"
    "customInventory"             = "Enabled"
    "instanceDetailedInformation" = "Enabled"
    "networkConfig"               = "Enabled"
    "services"                    = "Enabled"
    "windowsRoles"                = "Enabled"
    "windowsUpdates"              = "Enabled"
  }
}
```

Review the resources that are going to be created, and then run `terraform apply` to make the changes.

Discussion

For AWS Systems Manager, SSM, and the variety of services that run under the banner, including Fleet Manager, Inventory, and Session Manager, all rely on the SSM agent being installed and configured. Recipe 5.5 configures private endpoints so that the required APIs are accessible. For a simplified example, the following Terraform deploys an EC2 machine, using the instance profile from the recipe, into the default VPC with a public IP address so it can access the APIs:

```
data "aws_ami" "ubuntu" {
  most_recent = true

  filter {
    name   = "name"
    values = ["ubuntu/images/hvm-ssd/ubuntu-focal-20.04-amd64-server-*"]
  }

  filter {
    name   = "virtualization-type"
    values = ["hvm"]
  }

  owners = ["099720109477"] # Canonical
}

resource "aws_instance" "this" {
  ami                         = data.aws_ami.ubuntu.id
  associate_public_ip_address = true
  instance_type               = "t2.micro"
  iam_instance_profile        = aws_iam_instance_profile.ssm_profile.name
}

output "instance_id" {
  value = aws_instance.this.id
}
```

With that instance deployed, run `aws ssm describe-instance-information` to get a high-level listing of all the SSM-managed EC2 machines in the account and region. As part of the `AWS-GatherSoftwareInventory` SSM document association, the SSM agent is also automatically reporting back inventory data on each instance. There are currently 10 predefined inventory types available in SSM:

- `AWS:AWSComponent`
- `AWS:Application`
- `AWS:File`
- `AWS:InstanceDetailedInformation`
- `AWS:InstanceInformation`
- `AWS:Network`
- `AWS:Service`
- `AWS:WindowsRegistry`

- AWS:WindowsRole

- AWS:WindowsUpdate

You can directly query the inventory information of a particular instance by running the command `aws ssm list-inventory-entries --instance-id <instance_id> --type <inventory_type>`.

Additionally, SSM provides the ability to install packages at scale across instances. The following Terraform shows an example of deploying the Amazon CloudWatch agent to all instances with a `Type` tag with the value `Workload`:

```
resource "aws_ssm_association" "cloudwatch_install" {
  name                = "AWS-ConfigureAWSPackage"
  schedule_expression = "rate(1 day)"

  targets {
    key    = "tag:Type"
    values = ["Workload"]
  }

  parameters = {
    "action"           = "Install"
    "installationType" = "In-place update"
    "name"             = "AmazonCloudWatchAgent"
  }
}
```

The compliance of each instance within the account is automatically tracked based on the associations that have been configured. To view compliance in the aggregate across all instances, run the command `aws ssm list-resource-compliance-summaries`. To drill down on compliance for a particular resource, run the command `aws ssm list-compliance-items --resource-ids <instance_id>`.

Summary

Let's summarize what was learned and deployed in this recipe:

- AWS SSM allows for the management of EC2 instances at scale.
- For instances to appear in SSM, they need three things:
  — The SSM agent is installed.

  — An instance profile with the required permissions is attached.

  — Access to the SSM APIs is available.

- By configuring an SSM document association for `AWS-GatherSoftwareInventory`, you enable automated inventory reporting.

- By configuring an SSM document association for `AWS-ConfigureAWSPackage`, you can automatically install packages on targeted machines.

8.6 Understanding Machine Status at Scale on Azure

Problem

You need inventory management for the virtual machines in your estate.

Solution

Create the following *provider.tf* file and run `terraform init`:

```
terraform {
  required_providers {
    azurerm = {
      source  = "hashicorp/azurerm"
      version = "~> 2"
    }
  }
}

provider "azurerm" {
  features {}
}
```

Create the following *main.tf* file and run `terraform plan`:

```
resource "azurerm_resource_group" "management" {
  name     = "instance-management"
  location = var.location
}

resource "azurerm_automation_account" "this" {
  name                = "instance-management"
  location            = azurerm_resource_group.management.location
  resource_group_name = azurerm_resource_group.management.name

  sku_name = "Basic"
}

resource "azurerm_log_analytics_workspace" "inventory" {
  name                = "inventory"
  location            = azurerm_resource_group.management.location
  resource_group_name = azurerm_resource_group.management.name
  sku                 = "PerGB2018"
  retention_in_days   = 30
}

resource "azurerm_log_analytics_linked_service" "automation_account" {
  resource_group_name = azurerm_resource_group.management.name
```

```
    workspace_id        = azurerm_log_analytics_workspace.inventory.id
    read_access_id      = azurerm_automation_account.this.id
}

resource "azurerm_log_analytics_solution" "updates" {
  resource_group_name = azurerm_resource_group.management.name
  location            = azurerm_resource_group.management.location

  solution_name           = "Updates"
  workspace_resource_id = azurerm_log_analytics_workspace.inventory.id
  workspace_name          = azurerm_log_analytics_workspace.inventory.name

  plan {
    publisher = "Microsoft"
    product   = "OMSGallery/Updates"
  }
}

resource "azurerm_log_analytics_solution" "change_tracking" {
  resource_group_name = azurerm_resource_group.management.name
  location            = azurerm_resource_group.management.location

  solution_name           = "ChangeTracking"
  workspace_resource_id = azurerm_log_analytics_workspace.inventory.id
  workspace_name          = azurerm_log_analytics_workspace.inventory.name

  plan {
    publisher = "Microsoft"
    product   = "OMSGallery/ChangeTracking"
  }
}
```

Review the resources that are going to be created, and then run `terraform apply` to make the changes.

Discussion

Azure Automation allows for the management of fleets of virtual machines. It provides three broad areas of capability: configuration management; update management, covered in Recipe 8.9; and process automation. Additionally, it supports both Windows and Linux instances and can be configured to manage virtual machines either on premises or in other clouds.

For a virtual machine to correctly report data into your Automation account, you will need to configure a virtual machine extension. The extension configures the agents on the machine to push data to the correct Log Analytics workspace. The following Terraform sets up a Linux machine with the extension preconfigured:

```
locals {
  inventory_workspace = azurerm_log_analytics_workspace.inventory
}
```

```
resource "azurerm_linux_virtual_machine" "inventory" {
  name                 = "inventory-example"
  resource_group_name  = azurerm_resource_group.management.name
  location             = azurerm_resource_group.management.location
  size                 = "Standard_B1s"
  admin_username       = "adminuser"
  network_interface_ids = [
    azurerm_network_interface.inventory.id,
  ]

  admin_ssh_key {
    username   = "adminuser"
    public_key = file("~/.ssh/id_rsa.pub")
  }

  os_disk {
    caching              = "ReadWrite"
    storage_account_type = "Standard_LRS"
  }

  source_image_reference {
    publisher = "Canonical"
    offer     = "UbuntuServer"
    sku       = "16.04-LTS"
    version   = "latest"
  }

  identity {
    type = "SystemAssigned"
  }
}

resource "azurerm_virtual_machine_extension" "example" {
  name                 = "OmsAgentForLinux"
  virtual_machine_id   = azurerm_linux_virtual_machine.inventory.id
  publisher            = "Microsoft.EnterpriseCloud.Monitoring"
  type                 = "OmsAgentForLinux"
  type_handler_version = "1.13"

  settings = <<SETTINGS
{
    "workspaceId": "${local.inventory_workspace.workspace_id}"
}
SETTINGS

  protected_settings = <<SETTINGS
{
    "workspaceKey": "${local.inventory_workspace.primary_shared_key}"
}
SETTINGS
}
```

Once deployed, the instance inventory will be available in the Azure Portal, allowing you to track the installed software across your fleet.

To install software to machines, and track their compliance against a baseline, you can use Desired State Configuration, or DSC. DSC uses PowerShell scripts to declaratively set the expected machine state, and takes actions to bring the machine into line. The following Terraform outlines a basic DSC configuration that manages the installation of the apache2 package on Linux virtual machines:

```
locals {
  custom_data = <<CONTENT
wget ${join("/", [
  "https://github.com/microsoft/omi/releases/download",
  "v1.6.8-1/omi-1.6.8-1.ssl_100.ulinux.x64.deb"
)}
dpkg -i ./omi-1.6.8-1.ssl_100.ulinux.x64.deb

wget ${join("/", [
  "https://github.com/microsoft/PowerShell-DSC-for-Linux",
  "releases/download/v1.2.1-0/dsc-1.2.1-0.ssl_100.x64.deb"
)}
dpkg -i ./dsc-1.2.1-0.ssl_100.x64.deb

${join(" ", [
  "/opt/microsoft/dsc/Scripts/Register.py",
  azurerm_automation_account.this.dsc_primary_access_key,
  azurerm_automation_account.this.dsc_server_endpoint,
  azurerm_automation_dsc_configuration.example.name
])}
CONTENT
}

resource "azurerm_automation_module" "nx" {
  name                  = "nx"
  resource_group_name   = azurerm_resource_group.management.name
  automation_account_name = azurerm_automation_account.this.name

  module_link {
    uri = "https://www.powershellgallery.com/api/v2/package/nx/1.0"
  }
}

resource "azurerm_automation_dsc_configuration" "example" {
  name                  = "LinuxConfig"
  resource_group_name   = azurerm_resource_group.management.name
  location              = azurerm_resource_group.management.location
  automation_account_name = azurerm_automation_account.this.name
  content_embedded      = <<CONTENT
Configuration LinuxConfig
{
    Import-DscResource -ModuleName 'nx'
```

```
        Node IsPresent
        {
                nxPackage apache2
                {
          Name              = 'apache2'
          Ensure            = 'Present'
          PackageManager    = 'Apt'
        }
        }

        Node IsNotPresent
        {
                nxPackage apache2
                {
          Name              = 'apache2'
          Ensure            = 'Absent'
        }
        }
    }
    CONTENT

    depends_on = [
      azurerm_automation_module.nx
    ]
}
```

With that defined, the virtual machine will need enrolling into DSC on boot up,
which can be achieved with custom data:

```
resource "azurerm_linux_virtual_machine" "inventory" {
  ...
  custom_data = base64(local.custom_data)
  ...
}
```

Summary

Let's summarize what was learned and deployed in this recipe:

- Azure Automation is a centralized fleet management service.

- By configuring virtual machines to report to the correct Log Analytics workspace, you can gather inventory data.

- Using desired state configuration allows you to install packages on machines and
  track compliance against expected packages.

- For Linux virtual machines, you need to install the Open Management Infrastructure (OMI) and DSC packages.

- For Windows machines, the required packages for DSC are preinstalled as part of
  the operating system.

8.7 Patching at Scale on GCP

Problem

You need to ensure that virtual machines are patched appropriately.

Solution

This recipe relies on VM Manager, as configured in Recipe 8.4. So if you haven't already completed that process for the project, do so first.

If you haven't already done so, familiarize yourself with Terraform and the different authentication mechanisms in Chapter 11.

Create a *variables.tf* file and copy the following contents:

```
variable "project" {
  type        = string
  description = "The project to deploy the resources into"
}

variable "time_zone" {
  type        = string
  description = "The IANA time zone to use for the schedule"
}

variable "time_of_day" {
  type = object({
    hours   = number
    minutes = number
    seconds = number
  })
  description = "The time of day to run patching"
}

variable "week_ordinal" {
  type        = number
  description = "The week of the month to run patching"
}

variable "day_of_week" {
  type        = string
  description = "The day of the week to run patching"
}

variable "disruption_budget" {
  type        = number
  description = "The max percentage of machines to disrupt with patching"
}
```

Then fill out the corresponding *terraform.tfvars* file:

```
day_of_week       = ""
disruption_budget = 0
project           = ""
time_of_day = {
  hours   = 9
  minutes = 0
  seconds = 0
}
time_zone      = ""
week_ordinal = 0
```

Create the following *provider.tf* file and run `terraform init`:

```
provider "google-beta" {
  project = var.project
}

terraform {
  required_providers {
    google-beta = {
      source  = "hashicorp/google-beta"
      version = "~> 4"
    }
  }
}
```

Create the following *main.tf* file and run `terraform plan`:

```
resource "google_os_config_patch_deployment" "patch" {
  project             = var.project
  patch_deployment_id = "debian-patching"

  instance_filter {
    group_labels {
      labels = {
        os = "debian"
      }
    }
  }

  patch_config {
    reboot_config = "ALWAYS"

    apt {
      type = "DIST"
    }
  }

  recurring_schedule {
    time_zone {
      id = var.time_zone
    }
```

```
      dynamic "time_of_day" {
        for_each = toset([var.time_of_day])
        content {
          hours   = time_of_day.value["hours"]
          minutes = time_of_day.value["minutes"]
          seconds = time_of_day.value["seconds"]
          nanos   = 0
        }
      }

      monthly {
        week_day_of_month {
          week_ordinal = var.week_ordinal
          day_of_week  = var.day_of_week
        }
      }
    }

    rollout {
      mode = "ZONE_BY_ZONE"
      disruption_budget {
        percentage = var.disruption_budget
      }
    }
  }
}
```

Review the resources that are going to be created, and then run `terraform apply` to make the changes.

Discussion

With VM Manager configured, you can use GCP's managed patching service to keep your virtual machines up to date. In the recipe, you created a patching plan targeting Debian machines by means of labels. At present, the service also supports RHEL/Centos, Rocky Linux, SUSE Enterprise, Ubuntu, and Windows Server. In each case, on Linux it leverages the local package management solution for each distribution and uses the Update Agent on Windows.

Within the GCP console, you have a dashboard that provides an overview of patch compliance for the project. It shows a breakdown of the virtual machines by operating system and provides a compliance breakdown by operating system type. Currently, although SUSE Enterprise and Rocky Linux are supported for patching, they do not report compliance data and appear as "No data" in the operating system breakdown.

When looking to patch systems, you will often need to patch machines on different schedules to reduce operational risk. Patch management provides multiple filtering mechanisms to identify machine groups. The recipe leverages label-based filtering.

Other options include filtering by zone, selecting specific instances, or targeting based on instance name prefix.

When patching live systems, they often need to be taken out of circulation while the patching is ongoing. Patch manager provides pre- and post-patch hooks to run scripts on machines. The scripts can either be hosted directly on the machine or dynamically pulled from a Cloud Storage bucket. For example, to run a script on a Linux host prior to patching, add the following block to the `patch_config` block in your Terraform resource definition:

```
pre_step {
  linux_exec_step_config {
    gcs_object {
      bucket = "bucket-name"
      object = "pre_patch.sh"
      generation_number = "1"
    }
  }
}
```

As part of VM Manager, periodic scans are done to understand the active, known vulnerabilities on the machines. To inspect a particular machine, first run `gcloud alpha compute os-config inventories list` and make a note of the `INSTANCE_ID` of your chosen machine. Next, run `gcloud alpha compute os-config vulnerability-reports describe <your_instance_id>` to list all the known CVEs currently affecting your machine.

Summary

Let's summarize what was learned and deployed in this recipe:

- VM Manager provides a fully managed patching solution, OS patch management.
- Patch management supports an array of Linux operating systems, Windows Server, and Windows SQL Server.
- It provides a dashboard that summarizes compliance for the current project.
- When defining a patch deployment, you can specify filters to target only the expected machines.
- You can also define pre- and post-patch hooks to run arbitrary scripts.
- As part of VM Manager, you also get vulnerability reports of all known CVEs active on a given machine.

8.8 Patching at Scale on AWS

Problem

You need to ensure that virtual machines are patched appropriately.

Solution

If you haven't already done so, familiarize yourself with Terraform and the different authentication mechanisms in Chapter 11.

Create a *variables.tf* file and copy the following contents:

```
variable "schedule" {
  type        = string
  description = "The schedule for patching, e.g. cron(0 16 ? * TUE *)"
}
```

Then fill out the corresponding *terraform.tfvars* file:

```
schedule = ""
```

Create the following *provider.tf* file and run `terraform init`:

```
provider "aws" {}

terraform {
  required_providers {
    aws = {
      source  = "hashicorp/aws"
      version = "~> 3"
    }
  }
}
```

Create the following *main.tf* file and run `terraform plan`:

```
resource "aws_ssm_maintenance_window" "patching" {
  name     = "maintenance-window-patching"
  schedule = var.schedule
  duration = 2
  cutoff   = 1
}

resource "aws_ssm_maintenance_window_task" "patching" {
  max_concurrency = 50
  max_errors      = 0
  priority        = 1
  task_arn        = "AWS-RunPatchBaseline"
  task_type       = "RUN_COMMAND"
  window_id       = aws_ssm_maintenance_window.patching.id

  targets {
```

```
    key    = "WindowTargetIds"
    values = [
      aws_ssm_maintenance_window_target.patch_group.id
    ]
  }

  task_invocation_parameters {
    run_command_parameters {
      timeout_seconds     = 600

      parameter {
        name   = "Operation"
        values = ["Install"]
      }

      parameter {
        name   = "SnapshotId"
        values = ["{{WINDOW_EXECUTION_ID}}"]
      }
    }
  }
}

resource "aws_ssm_maintenance_window_target" "patch_group" {
  window_id     = aws_ssm_maintenance_window.patching.id
  name          = "PatchingTarget"
  resource_type = "INSTANCE"

  targets {
    key    = "tag:Patch Group"
    values = ["production"]
  }
}
```

Review the resources that are going to be created, and then run `terraform apply` to make the changes.

Discussion

This recipe configures patching so that any instance with a Patch Group tag of "production" will get patched as per the maintenance window you set. The patches to be installed are defined by the default patch baselines AWS provides for common operating systems.

To create custom baselines, the Patch Group tag is used, where AWS will automatically check for an existing patch group of the same name and use the custom baselines as appropriate. The following Terraform configures a custom Ubuntu baseline and assigns it to the "production" patch group:

```
resource "aws_ssm_patch_baseline" "ubuntu" {
  name             = "CustomUbuntu20.10"
  description      = "All patches, including non-security"
  operating_system = "UBUNTU"

  approval_rule {
    approve_after_days  = 0
    compliance_level    = "CRITICAL"
    enable_non_security = true

    patch_filter {
      key = "PRODUCT"
      values = [
        "Ubuntu20.10",
      ]
    }
    patch_filter {
      key = "SECTION"
      values = [
        "*",
      ]
    }
    patch_filter {
      key = "PRIORITY"
      values = [
        "*",
      ]
    }
  }
}

resource "aws_ssm_patch_group" "production" {
  baseline_id = aws_ssm_patch_baseline.ubuntu.id
  patch_group = "production"
}
```

With those resources created, any Ubuntu 20.10 instances with a Patch Group tag with the value "production" will now be patched as per the custom baseline. All other Ubuntu instances will be patched with the AWS default baseline.

As well as scheduled patching, AWS Patch Manager also has the option for running on-demand patching when required. When running an on-demand patch execution, you can also use lifecycle hooks to trigger SSM documents before patching, after patching but before rebooting, after patching and rebooting if needed, and after a scheduled reboot. What hooks are available is defined by the reboot option you selected when triggering the patch job: "reboot if needed," "do not reboot," and "schedule a reboot time."

Summary

Let's summarize what was learned and deployed in this recipe:

- AWS Patch Manager handles the patching of instances on AWS.
- It can be configured to run on a schedule and also allow on-demand patching.
- Scheduled patching occurs as per the schedule defined in the maintenance window.
- On-demand patching allows for lifecycle hooks to run SSM documents as required to configure the system before and after patching.
- Patch Manager comes with default patch baselines for each supported operating system.
- You can define custom baselines and associate them with a patch group.
- Patch group membership is defined by the "Patch Group" tag on an instance.

8.9 Patching at Scale on Azure

Problem

You need to ensure that virtual machines are patched appropriately.

Solution

This recipe is built on top of Recipe 8.6, so complete that recipe before continuing.

If you haven't already done so, familiarize yourself with Terraform and the different authentication mechanisms in Chapter 11.

Create a *variables.tf* file and copy the following contents:

```
variable "tag_key" {
  type        = string
  description = "The tag key to use for machine selection"
}

variable "tag_values" {
  type        = list(string)
  description = "The tag values to use for machine selection"
}

variable "time_zone" {
  type        = string
  description = "The time zone to use for running updates"
}

variable "update_time" {
```

```
    type        = string
    description = "The time to run updates"
}
```

Then fill out the corresponding *terraform.tfvars* file:

```
tag_key     = ""
tag_values  = [""]
time_zone   = ""
update_time = ""
```

Create the following *provider.tf* file and run `terraform init`:

```
terraform {
  required_providers {
    azurerm = {
      source  = "hashicorp/azurerm"
      version = "~> 2"
    }
  }
}

provider "azurerm" {
  features {}
}
```

Create the following *main.tf* file and run `terraform plan`:

```
data "azurerm_subscription" "current" {}

resource "time_offset" "tomorrow" {
  offset_days = 1
}

locals {
  update_date = substr(time_offset.tomorrow.rfc3339, 0, 10)
  datetime = replace(
    "${local.update_date}T${var.update_time}",
    "/:/",
    "-"
  )
  classifications = [
    "Critical",
    "Other",
    "Security",
    "Unclassified"
  ]
}

resource "azurerm_resource_group_template_deployment" "linux" {
  name                = "linux-weekly-patching"
  resource_group_name = azurerm_resource_group.management.name

  template_content = <<DEPLOY
```

```
{
  "$schema": ${join("", [
    "https://schema.management.azure.com/,
    "schemas/2019-04-01/deploymentTemplate.json#"
  ])},
  "contentVersion": "1.0.0.0",
  "parameters": {},
  "resources": [
    {
      "type": ${join("/", [
        "Microsoft.Automation",
        "automationAccounts",
        "softwareUpdateConfigurations",
      ])},
      "apiVersion": "2019-06-01",
      "name": "${azurerm_automation_account.this.name}/linux-weekly",
      "properties": {
        "scheduleInfo": {
          "advancedSchedule": {
            "weekDays": [ "Friday" ]
          },
          "frequency": "Week",
          "interval": "1",
          "startTime": "${local.update_date}T${var.update_time}:00-00:00",
          "timeZone": "${var.time_zone}"
        },
        "updateConfiguration": {
          "duration": "PT2H",
          "linux": {
            "includedPackageClassifications": ${local.classifications},
            "rebootSetting": "IfRequired"
          },
          "operatingSystem": "Linux",
          "targets": {
            "azureQueries": [
              {
                "scope": [
                  "${data.azurerm_subscription.current.id}"
                ],
                "tagSettings": {
                  "filterOperator": "Any",
                  "tags": {
                    "${var.tag_key}": ${var.tag_values}
                  }
                }
              }
            ]
          }
        }
      }
    }
  ]
}
```

```
    }
      DEPLOY

    deployment_mode = "Complete"
}
```

Review the resources that are going to be created, and then run `terraform apply` to make the changes.

Discussion

This recipe configures a weekly update schedule for Linux machines. It automatically targets all Linux machines with the given tags within the subscription. It is also possible to configure the patching schedule to target specific machines for updates, which is useful to specifically exclude patches from particular machines. The following JSON snippet shows how to target specific machines:

```
{
  ...
  "properties": {
    ...
    "updateConfiguration": {
      "duration": "PT2H",
      "linux": {
        "includedPackageClassifications": ${local.classifications},
        "rebootSetting": "IfRequired"
      },
      "operatingSystem": "Linux",
      "azureVirtualMachines": [
        "${azurerm_linux_virtual_machine.example.id}"
      ]
    },
    ...
  }
  ...
}
```

When patching machines, pre- and post-patch tasks are often required for safe operation. The template also provides a tasks key for configuring those tasks. The tasks must exist as Azure Automation runbooks, which can be created with the following Terraform:

```
resource "azurerm_automation_runbook" "pre_patch" {
  name                    = "Pre-Patch"
  location                = azurerm_resource_group.management.location
  resource_group_name     = azurerm_resource_group.management.name
  automation_account_name = azurerm_automation_account.this.name
  log_verbose             = "true"
  log_progress            = "true"
  description             = "Runs required pre-patch activities"
  runbook_type            = "PowerShellWorkflow"
```

```
    content = <<CONTENT
...
CONTENT
}
```

The runbook can then be referenced by adding a `tasks` object under the `properties` key in the template, as shown in the following JSON snippet:

```
{
  ...
  "properties": {
    ...
    "tasks": {
      "preTask": {
        "parameters": {},
        "source": "${azurerm_automation_runbook.pre_patch.name}"
      }
    },
    ...
  }
  ...
}
```

By viewing the Azure Automation account in the portal and browsing to the update management blade, you can see a dashboard that summarizes update compliance across your fleet. It includes a per-instance breakdown of missing patches, allowing you to understand how many known, active vulnerabilities exist.

Summary

Let's summarize what was learned and deployed in this recipe:

- Azure Automation handles the patching and updating of machines.
- It can be configured to run on a schedule and also allows on-demand patching.
- You can either explicitly set which machines are covered under the schedule or use tagging to filter for machines.
- It is possible to define the schedule at both resource group and subscription scopes.
- To cover the entire estate, combine with Recipe 6.12.
- You can define runbooks to perform operations on machines before and after patches are applied to ensure that patching can happen successfully.

8.10 Data Backup on GCP

Problem

You need to securely back up data to protect from data loss.

Solution

If you haven't already done so, familiarize yourself with Terraform and the different authentication mechanisms in Chapter 11.

Create a *variables.tf* file and copy the following contents:

```
variable "project" {
  type        = string
  description = "The project to deploy the resources into"
}

variable "region" {
  type        = string
  description = "The region to deploy the resources into"
}

variable "secondary_zone" {
  type        = string
  description = "The second zone to deploy the resources into"
}

variable "start_time_utc" {
  type        = string
  description = "The snapshot start time in UTC"
}

variable "storage_locations" {
  type        = list(string)
  description = "The locations to store the snapshot"
}

variable "zone" {
  type        = string
  description = "The zone to deploy the resources into"
}
```

Then fill out the corresponding *terraform.tfvars* file:

```
project           = ""
region            = ""
secondary_zone    = ""
start_time_utc    = ""
storage_locations = [""]
zone              = ""
```

Create the following *provider.tf* file and run `terraform init`:

```
provider "google" {
  project = var.project
  region  = var.region
}

terraform {
  required_providers {
    google = {
      source  = "hashicorp/google"
      version = "~> 4"
    }
  }
}
```

Create the following *main.tf* file and run `terraform plan`:

```
resource "google_compute_resource_policy" "daily_snapshot" {
  name = "daily-snapshots"
  snapshot_schedule_policy {
    schedule {
      daily_schedule {
        days_in_cycle = 1
        start_time    = var.start_time_utc
      }
    }
    retention_policy {
      max_retention_days    = 10
      on_source_disk_delete = "APPLY_RETENTION_POLICY"
    }
    snapshot_properties {
      guest_flush       = true
      storage_locations = var.storage_locations
    }
  }
}

resource "google_compute_disk_resource_policy_attachment" "attachment" {
  name = google_compute_resource_policy.daily_snapshot.name
  disk = google_compute_disk.zonal.name
  zone = "${var.region}-${var.zone}"
}

resource "google_compute_disk" "zonal" {
  name = "daily-snapshot"
  size = 10
  type = "pd-ssd"
  zone = "${var.region}-${var.zone}"
}

resource "google_compute_region_disk" "regional" {
  name = "daily-snapshot"
```

```
    replica_zones = [
      "${var.region}-${var.zone}",
      "${var.region}-${var.secondary_zone}"
    ]
    size   = 10
    type   = "pd-ssd"
    region = var.region
}

resource "google_compute_region_disk_resource_policy_attachment" "snapshot" {
    name   = google_compute_resource_policy.daily_snapshot.name
    disk   = google_compute_region_disk.regional.name
    region = var.region
}
```

Review the resources that are going to be created, and then run `terraform apply` to make the changes.

Discussion

As large volumes of business-critical data are stored in running virtual machines, this recipe looks at how to take regular snapshots of disks on a schedule. As policies must be explicitly applied to disks, this recipe should be combined with Recipe 6.10 to push the resource policy out to all projects, and Recipe 6.1 to ensure that all disks have a policy attached.

When running backups against live systems, it is critical to ensure that the snapshots are application consistent. Imagine an application that stores data across multiple attached disks. You need to complete snapshots of all the disks before another transaction can be processed. To take application-consistent snapshots, you need to enable `guest_flush` in the resource policy. On Windows, this will cause the snapshot to be a Volume Shadow Copy Service (VSS) snapshot, which will preserve consistency. On Linux, this will call the /etc/google/snapshots/pre.sh script before taking the snapshot, and the /etc/google/snapshots/post.sh script afterwards. These two scripts can be used to run any application-specific backup requirements, such as flushing memory or stopping accepting requests.

Holistic and reliable data backup is central to an effective disaster recovery strategy. By appropriately configuring the `storage_locations` variable, you can ensure that your snapshots are available in the event of a regional failure. For example, putting "EU" as the storage location will redundantly store the snapshot in multiple regions in the EU.

When deploying backup schedules at scale, it is important to wrap them up in sufficient monitoring. Few things are worse than finding your backups have failed at the exact moment you need to restore them. You should configure a logging metric and metric policy to trigger an alert whenever backups fail. The following Terraform creates both required resources:

```
resource "google_logging_metric" "snapshot_failures" {
  name   = "snapshot_failures"
  filter = <<FILTER
resource.type="gce_disk"
logName="projects/${var.project}/logs/cloudaudit.googleapis.com%2Fsystem_event"
protoPayload.methodName="ScheduledSnapshots"
severity="INFO"
FILTER
  metric_descriptor {
    metric_kind = "DELTA"
    value_type  = "INT64"
    labels {
      key        = "status"
      value_type = "STRING"
    }
    display_name = "Snapshot Failures"
  }
  label_extractors = {
    "status" = "EXTRACT(protoPayload.response.status)"
  }
}

resource "google_monitoring_alert_policy" "snapshot_failures" {
  display_name = "Snapshot Failures"
  combiner     = "OR"
  conditions {
    display_name = "Failures"
    condition_threshold {
      aggregations {
        alignment_period  = "60s"
        per_series_aligner = "ALIGN_SUM"
      }
      filter = join("", [
        "resource.type=\"gce_disk\" ",
        "metric.type=\"logging.googleapis.com/user/",
        google_logging_metric.snapshot_failures.name,
        "\" metric.label.\"status\"=\"DONE\""
      ])
      duration   = "0s"
      comparison = "COMPARISON_GT"
      trigger {
        count = 1
      }
    }
  }
}
```

Managed database services on GCP have their own specific backup solutions. For BigQuery, a table is recoverable for seven days by using time decorators to perform queries against a particular point in time. Additionally, BigQuery transfers allow you to copy datasets on a schedule to back up data or move data between regions to enable regional failover. Cloud SQL automatically takes backups every four hours, retaining the most recent seven by default, which, combined with transaction logs, allows you to do point-in-time recovery. BigTable allows users to take manual back-ups, which you can automate and schedule with Cloud Scheduler and Cloud Functions. Spanner allows for the configuration of a retention period to enable point-in-time recovery and manual backups, which can be handled similarly to BigTable backups. Last, for Cloud Storage buckets, versioning enables the recovery of previous objects, and turbo replication asynchronously replicates objects between buckets with a 15-minute recovery point objective.

Summary

Let's summarize what was learned and deployed in this recipe:

- Backups on GCP are handled on a service-by-service basis.
- Part of any backup strategy is ensuring that the proper monitoring is in place to alert on failed backups.
- BigQuery, Cloud SQL, and Spanner all offer point-in-time recovery up to a certain time period.
- For services that do not have a managed backup schedule option, you can build your own with Cloud Scheduler and Cloud Functions.

8.11 Data Backup on AWS

Problem

You need to securely back up data to protect from data loss.

Solution

If you haven't already done so, familiarize yourself with Terraform and the different authentication mechanisms in Chapter 11.

Create the following *provider.tf* file and run `terraform init`:

```
provider "aws" {}

terraform {
  required_providers {
    aws = {
      source  = "hashicorp/aws"
      version = "~> 3"
    }
```

```
    }
  }
```

Create the following *main.tf* file and run `terraform plan`:

```
resource "aws_backup_vault" "this" {
  name = "backups"
}

resource "aws_backup_plan" "weekly" {
  name = "weekly"

  rule {
    rule_name         = "Weekly"
    target_vault_name = aws_backup_vault.this.name
    schedule          = "cron(0 12 ? * MON *)"
  }
}

resource "aws_backup_region_settings" "test" {
  resource_type_opt_in_preference = {
    "Aurora"          = true
    "DocumentDB"      = true
    "DynamoDB"        = true
    "EBS"             = true
    "EC2"             = true
    "EFS"             = true
    "FSx"             = true
    "Neptune"         = true
    "RDS"             = true
    "Storage Gateway" = true
  }
}

resource "aws_backup_selection" "weekly" {
  iam_role_arn = aws_iam_role.backups.arn
  name         = "weekly"
  plan_id      = aws_backup_plan.weekly.id

  selection_tag {
    type  = "STRINGEQUALS"
    key   = "backup"
    value = "weekly"
  }
}

resource "aws_iam_role" "backups" {
  name                = "backups"
  assume_role_policy  = data.aws_iam_policy_document.assume.json
  managed_policy_arns = [
    "arn:aws:iam::aws:policy/service-role/AWSBackupServiceRolePolicyForBackup"
  ]
}
```

```
data "aws_iam_policy_document" "assume" {
  statement {
    actions = ["sts:AssumeRole"]
    effect  = "Allow"
    principals {
      type        = "Service"
      identifiers = ["backup.amazonaws.com"]
    }
  }
}
```

Review the resources that are going to be created, and then run `terraform apply` to make the changes.

Discussion

This recipe creates the simplest possible weekly backup schedule that targets all supported resources that have a `backup` tag of `weekly`. It also creates a backup vault called "backups" where all the backups are stored indefinitely.

For cost and practicality reasons, data generally does not need retaining after a certain time period, as more recent backups cover the business needs. AWS Backup plans have a lifecycle configuration that can be applied to the rule. The following Terraform, for example, archives backups after a month to lower storage costs and deletes backups after a year:

```
rule {
  rule_name         = "Weekly"
  target_vault_name = aws_backup_vault.this.name
  schedule          = "cron(0 12 ? * MON *)"

  lifecycle {
    cold_storage_after = 30
    delete_after       = 365
  }
}
```

To enable point-in-time recovery for all supported resources, you need to enable continuous backups for your backup rule. This can be done by adding a second rule block in the following Terraform to your plan resource. Note that continuous backups cannot be automatically moved to cold storage, and they must be deleted after 35 days.

```
rule {
  rule_name                = "WeeklyContinuous"
  target_vault_name        = aws_backup_vault.this.name
  schedule                 = "cron(0 12 ? * MON *)"
  enable_continuous_backup = true

  lifecycle {
    delete_after           = 35
```

```
    }
  }
```

For Windows machines, to achieve application consistent recovery, you should enable VSS-based recovery by adding the following block to your backup plan definition:

```
advanced_backup_setting {
  backup_options = {
    WindowsVSS = "enabled"
  }
  resource_type = "EC2"
}
```

You can also configure copy actions to automatically copy backups to other regions or accounts. The following Terraform shows how to set up a centralized vault for an organization:

```
data "aws_organizations_organization" "current" {}

resource "aws_backup_vault" "central" {
  name = "central"
}

resource "aws_backup_vault_policy" "org" {
  backup_vault_name = aws_backup_vault.central.name

  policy = data.aws_iam_policy_document.vault.json
}

data "aws_iam_policy_document" "vault" {
  statement {
    actions = ["backup:CopyIntoBackupVault"]
    principals {
      type = "AWS"
      identifiers = ["*"]
    }
    resources = ["*"]

    condition {
      test = "StringEquals"
      values = [
        data.aws_organizations_organization.current.id
      ]
      variable = "aws:PrincipalOrgID"
    }
  }
}
```

With that configured, you can set up the backup rule to automatically copy backups to the vault with the following configuration in a rule block:

```
copy_action {
  destination_vault_arn = aws_backup_vault.central.arn
```

```
    lifecycle {
      cold_storage_after = "1"
    }
  }
}
```

Although you could combine this recipe with Recipe 6.11 to deploy plans to multiple accounts, it is possible to configure backup policies at the organization level. First, ensure your organization is configured to allow backup policies by updating your organization resource like the following:

```
resource "aws_organizations_organization" "this" {
  ...
  enabled_policy_types = [
    ...
    "BACKUP_POLICY",
  ]
}
```

Then, create a backup policy and attach it to the organization, organizational unit, or account you require. For example, the following Terraform creates a daily backup policy that is applied to the entire organization:

```
resource "aws_organizations_policy" "daily_backups" {
  name    = "daily_backups"
  type    = "BACKUP_POLICY"
  content = <<CONTENT
{
  "plans": {
    "daily": {
      "regions": {
        "@@assign": [
          "${data.aws_region.current.name}"
        ]
      },
      "rules": {
        "daily": {
          "schedule_expression": { "@@assign": "cron(0 9 * * ? *)" },
          "target_backup_vault_name": { "@@assign": "backups" }
        }
      },
      "selections": {
        "tags": {
          "datatype": {
            "iam_role_arn": { "@@assign": "arn:aws:iam::$account:role/backups" },
            "tag_key": { "@@assign": "backup" },
            "tag_value": { "@@assign": [ "daily" ] }
          }
        }
      }
    }
  }
}
```

```
  CONTENT
}

resource "aws_organizations_policy_attachment" "root" {
  policy_id = aws_organizations_policy.daily_backups.id
  target_id = data.aws_organizations_organization.current.roots[0].id
}
```

Summary

Let's summarize what was learned and deployed in this recipe:

- AWS Backup provides a managed backup service for many resource types.
- You can automatically configure lifecycle events to archive and delete redundant backups.
- Protect against account compromise and regional failures by automatically copying backups to other regions and accounts.
- By configuring a backup policy at the organization level, you create centrally managed backup plans.

8.12 Data Backup on Azure

Problem

You need to securely back up data to protect from data loss.

Solution

If you haven't already done so, familiarize yourself with Terraform and the different authentication mechanisms in Chapter 11.

Create the following *variables.tf* file:

```
variable "location" {
  type        = string
  description = "The location to deploy resources into"
}
```

Then fill out the corresponding *terraform.tfvars* file:

```
location = ""
```

Create the following *provider.tf* file and run `terraform init`:

```
terraform {
  required_providers {
    azurerm = {
      source  = "hashicorp/azurerm"
      version = "~> 2"
```

```
        }
      }
    }

    provider "azurerm" {
      features {}
    }
```

Create the following *main.tf* file and run `terraform plan`:

```
resource "azurerm_resource_group" "backups" {
  name     = "backups"
  location = var.location
}

resource "azurerm_recovery_services_vault" "this" {
  name                = "vault"
  location            = azurerm_resource_group.backups.location
  resource_group_name = azurerm_resource_group.backups.name
  sku                 = "Standard"
}

resource "azurerm_backup_policy_vm" "daily" {
  name                = "daily-vm-backups"
  resource_group_name = azurerm_resource_group.backups.name
  recovery_vault_name = azurerm_recovery_services_vault.this.name

  backup {
    frequency = "Daily"
    time      = "23:00"
  }

  retention_daily {
    count = 14
  }
}
```

Review the resources that are going to be created, and then run `terraform apply` to make the changes.

Discussion

This recipe created a backup policy for virtual machines that runs daily and retains backups for 14 days. In order to associate this policy with a virtual machine, you will need to apply the following Terraform, replacing `azurerm_linux_vir tual_machine.example.id` with a reference to your machine ID:

```
resource "azurerm_backup_protected_vm" "vm1" {
  resource_group_name = azurerm_resource_group.backups.name
  recovery_vault_name = azurerm_recovery_services_vault.this.name
  source_vm_id        = azurerm_linux_virtual_machine.example.id
```

```
  backup_policy_id    = azurerm_backup_policy_vm.daily.id
}
```

In addition to specifying daily retention, it is also possible to define weekly, monthly, and yearly retention periods to fulfill audit requirements.

To ensure that virtual machines are backed up correctly, Azure Policy provides a few built-in policies that allow for reporting when machines are not actively covered by backups, and that machines be assigned to a backup policy by default. To configure these policies, apply the following Terraform:

```
data "azurerm_subscription" "current" {}

resource "azurerm_subscription_policy_assignment" "vm_backups" {
  name                 = "vm_backups"
  location             = azurerm_resource_group.backups.location
  subscription_id      = data.azurerm_subscription.current.id
  policy_definition_id = join("", [
    "/providers/Microsoft.Authorization/policyDefinitions/",
    "013e242c-8828-4970-87b3-ab247555486d"
  ])
  identity {
    type = "SystemAssigned"
  }
}

resource "azurerm_resource_group_policy_assignment" "default_vm_backups" {
  name                 = "default_vm_backups"
  location             = azurerm_resource_group.backups.location
  resource_group_id    = azurerm_resource_group.backups.id
  policy_definition_id = join("", [
    "/providers/Microsoft.Authorization/policyDefinitions/",
    "09ce66bc-1220-4153-8104-e3f51c936913"
  ])

  parameters = <<PARAMETERS
{
  "vaultLocation": {
    "value": "${azurerm_resource_group.backups.location}"
  },
  "backupPolicyId": {
    "value": "${azurerm_backup_policy_vm.daily.id}"
  }
}
PARAMETERS

  identity {
    type = "SystemAssigned"
  }
}
```

Both virtual machines and file shares are backed up using recovery services, whereas other resources, such as managed PostgreSQL databases, are managed via data protection. Both are managed via the portal in the backup center; however, they use different APIs and therefore Terraform resources. The following is the Terraform required to set up a backup policy for a specified database instance. It requires that a connection string be configured and accessible in the Key Vault secret defined in the secret_id variable.

```
locals {
  vault = local.vault
}

resource "azurerm_data_protection_backup_vault" "this" {
  name                = "this"
  resource_group_name = azurerm_resource_group.backups.name
  location            = azurerm_resource_group.backups.location
  datastore_type      = "VaultStore"
  redundancy          = "LocallyRedundant"

  identity {
    type = "SystemAssigned"
  }
}

resource "azurerm_data_protection_backup_policy_postgresql" "weekly" {
  name                            = "weekly"
  resource_group_name             = azurerm_resource_group.backups.name
  vault_name                      = local.vault.name
  backup_repeating_time_intervals = ["R/2021-11-24T11:30:00+00:00/P1W"]
  default_retention_duration      = "P1Y"
}

resource "azurerm_role_assignment" "reader" {
  scope                = var.database_id
  role_definition_name = "Reader"
  principal_id         = local.vault.identity.0.principal_id
}

resource "azurerm_data_protection_backup_instance_postgresql" "target" {
  name             = "target"
  location         = azurerm_resource_group.backups.location
  vault_id         = azurerm_data_protection_backup_vault.example.id
  database_id      = var.database_id
  backup_policy_id = azurerm_data_protection_backup_policy_postgresql.weekly.id

  database_credential_key_vault_secret_id = var.secret_id
}
```

Summary

Let's summarize what was learned and deployed in this recipe:

- Azure Backup provides secure resource backups.

- It uses recovery services for virtual machines and file shares.

- It uses data protection services for other resources.

- You can use Azure Policy to report on whether resources are actively being backed up, and apply default backup policies to resources.

CHAPTER 9
Enabling Teams

Back in Chapter 1, I talked about how the modern security function is one of enablement, instead of the historical gatekeeping which is prevalent. In this chapter, you will see patterns that allow you to overcome the challenge of shared resources: how you can enable two teams to safely work on resources within the same account, project, or subscription. The final three recipes look at how you can implement OWASP top 10–focused security scanning on applications, allowing you to use those findings to open up conversations with delivery teams about their DevSecOps practices and approach.

A common challenge a security team has when working with a mature cloud organization is how to scale your impact without an ever-increasing headcount. In Chapter 6, the recipes show how engineering is a force multiplier for both yourself and your team. The reason this book contains full Terraform implementations is to equip you for what is now the minimum bar for modern security engineers.

When looking at how two teams interact at an organization, there are three modes of interactivity (*Team Topologies*):

- Collaboration—highest throughput but highest cost
- Facilitation—short-term focus on enablement and upskilling of a team
- "As-a-service"—removes dependencies by allowing teams to self-service

The more teams are able to interact with security in an "as-a-service" modality, the wider and greater impact the security function can have.

Be mindful about how you interact with teams. Collaborating between teams gives you high-throughput communication to work through a challenge or problem; facilitate to teach teams new tools, approaches, and mindsets; and look for opportunities to enable self-service because they unlock the time to focus on higher-level activities.

9.1 Enabling Project Sharing on GCP

Problem

A team has now split into two teams. Both need to work in the same project but need to keep data secure from each other.

Solution

This recipe creates IAM policies that use conditions to selectively allow access to resources.

If you haven't already done so, familiarize yourself with Terraform and the different authentication mechanisms in Chapter 11.

Create a *variables.tf* file and copy the following contents:

```
variable "project" {
  type        = string
  description = "The project to deploy the resources into"
}
```

Then fill out the corresponding *terraform.tfvars* file:

```
project = ""
```

Create the following *provider.tf* file and run `terraform init`:

```
provider "google" {
  project = var.project
}

terraform {
  required_providers {
    google = {
      source  = "hashicorp/google"
      version = "~> 3"
    }
  }
}
```

Create the following *main.tf* file and run `terraform plan`:

```
resource "google_service_account" "red_team" {
  account_id   = "red-team"
  display_name = "Red Team"
}

resource "google_service_account_key" "red_team" {
  service_account_id = google_service_account.red_team.name
  public_key_type    = "TYPE_X509_PEM_FILE"
}

resource "local_file" "red_team" {
  content  = base64decode(google_service_account_key.red_team.private_key)
  filename = "red_team.json"
}

resource "google_project_iam_member" "red_secrets" {
  role = "roles/secretmanager.admin"

  member = "serviceAccount:${google_service_account.red_team.email}"

  condition {
    title      = "requires_red_team_name"
    expression = "resource.name.endsWith('_red')"
  }
}
```

Review the resources that are going to be created, and then run `terraform apply` to make the changes.

Discussion

The condition defined in the recipe uses the resource name to ensure that the red team can only interact with their own resources within the project. Conditions in GCP IAM are defined using the Common Expression Language (CEL). For writing conditions about resource properties, there are four pieces of data you can leverage: the resource type, the resource name, the service being used, and the resource tags. As tags are applied directly to the project, and not to resources within the project, there is no way of leveraging those to allow for the sharing of projects.

As a test, the following Terraform installs a provider using the service account you created earlier:

```
provider "google" {
  project = var.project
}

provider "google" {
  alias       = "red_team"
  project     = var.project
  credentials = local_file.red_team.filename
}
```

```
terraform {
  required_providers {
    google = {
      source  = "hashicorp/google"
      version = "~> 3"
    }
  }
}
```

This Terraform creates a secret with the correct naming convention and uses the red team service account to access it:

```
resource "google_project_service" "secrets_manager" {
  service           = "secretmanager.googleapis.com"
  disable_on_destroy = false
}

resource "google_secret_manager_secret" "secret-basic" {
  secret_id = "secret_red"

  replication {
    automatic = true
  }

  depends_on = [
    google_project_service.secrets_manager
  ]
}

data "google_secret_manager_secret" "secret" {
  provider  = google.red_team
  secret_id = google_secret_manager_secret.secret-basic.secret_id
}
```

When looking to apply conditions based on the resource name, you need to consult the list of resources that support conditions based on that attribute, including Compute Engine, Secret Manager, and a handful of others. In addition to the endsWith function used in the recipe, CEL also includes a startsWith function and an extract function that allows for the extraction of particular values from properties. For example, resource.name.extract("projects/{project}/") extracts the project ID.

In addition to resource attributes in conditions, GCP provides a selection of request attributes. These include the date and time of the request, the URL path specified, and the destination IP and port. Common patterns using these include providing time-limited privileges or rejecting if the user has not explicitly accessed via IAP.

Depending on the complexity of the architecture and the security requirements, part of the application may need to be moved to another project to implement stronger controls. Currently, there is no automated way of migrating resources between projects; instead you will need to take and restore backups or stream the data into a new project.

In realistic terms, sharing projects between teams is not an enduring model, as IAM on GCP does not really support a form of ABAC that would be sufficient.

Summary

Let's summarize what was learned and deployed in this recipe:

- GCP IAM allows you set conditions based on resource properties.
- When splitting a project between teams, the resource name attribute is the most versatile.
- Conditions are not supported on all resource types.
- Although you can have tag-based conditions, they are applied at the organization, folder, or project only.
- You can also have conditions based on the request attributes, such as date and time.
- You should evaluate migrating parts of the application to new projects if you need strong controls and boundaries.

9.2 Enabling Account Sharing on AWS

Problem

A team has now split into two teams. Both need to work in the same account but need to keep data secure from each other.

Solution

This recipe creates IAM policies that use conditions to selectively allow access to resources.

First, create the following *provider.tf* file and run `terraform init`:

```
provider "aws" {}

terraform {
  required_providers {
    aws = {
      source  = "hashicorp/aws"
      version = "~> 3"
    }
  }
}
```

Then, create the following *main.tf* file and run `terraform apply`:

```
data "aws_caller_identity" "current" {}

resource "aws_iam_role" "red_team" {
  name = "red_team"
  assume_role_policy = data.aws_iam_policy_document.assume_policy.json

  tags = {
    "team-name": "red"
  }
}

data "aws_iam_policy_document" "assume_policy" {
  statement {
    effect = "Allow"
    actions = ["sts:AssumeRole"]
    principals {
      type = "AWS"
      identifiers = [data.aws_caller_identity.current.account_id]
    }
  }
}

resource "aws_iam_policy" "secrets_management" {
  name = "secrets_management"
  path = "/"
  policy = data.aws_iam_policy_document.secrets_management.json
}

resource "aws_iam_role_policy_attachment" "red_secrets_management" {
  role = aws_iam_role.red_team.name
  policy_arn = aws_iam_policy.secrets_management.arn
}

data "aws_iam_policy_document" "secrets_management" {
  statement {
    effect = "Allow"
    actions = ["secretsmanager:*"]
    resources = ["*"]

    condition {
      test    = "StringEquals"
      variable = "aws:ResourceTag/team-name"
      values = [
        "$${aws:PrincipalTag/team-name}"
      ]
    }

    condition {
      test    = "ForAllValues:StringEquals"
      variable = "aws:TagKeys"
```

```
      values = [
        "team-name"
      ]
    }

    condition {
      test     = "StringEqualsIfExists"
      variable = "aws:ResourceTag/team-name"
      values = [
        "$${aws:PrincipalTag/team-name}"
      ]
    }
  }
}
```

Discussion

IAM in AWS allows you to implement sophisticated Attribute Based Access Control (ABAC), which dynamically leverages the properties on the principal when determining access. In this recipe, the team-name tag is used to determine access, meaning that you can apply the same policy to multiple principals and get the desired outcomes. For example, the following provider definition and Terraform resource will work:

```
provider "aws" {
  alias = "red"
  assume_role {
    role_arn = join("", [
      "arn:aws:iam::",
      data.aws_caller_identity.current.account_id,
      ":role/red_team"
    ])
  }
}

resource "aws_secretsmanager_secret" "red" {
  provider = aws.red
  name     = "red"

  tags = {
    "team-name": "red"
  }
}
```

If you then created the same role but with a team-name tag value of blue, that role would be unable to interact with the secret.

Not only does the ABAC approach enable account segregation where required, it also allows for the creation of policies that are much closer to least privilege. It is important to note that not all resources support ABAC equally. In such cases it becomes difficult or impossible to safely enable multiple team access to those resources. If those edge cases are too critical to allow, then you will need to investigate options for migrating part of the application into another account. This will leverage the hard permission boundaries that exist between accounts to ensure safe operation.

ABAC is rightly seen as an advanced IAM topic, as it requires a solid understanding of IAM policies to manage effectively. When first starting out in AWS, adopting role-based access control (RBAC) will allow you to move much faster. Look for low-risk, high-reward areas to experiment with ABAC as your understanding of AWS matures.

 Other types of conditions are available on AWS; for example, you can provide time-limited access to a particular role in a break-glass situation or enforce particular KMS keys be used when interacting with S3.

Summary

Let's summarize what was learned and deployed in this recipe:

- AWS provides a sophisticated ABAC model.
  — It allows for dynamic policies based on the attributes of the principal.
- You deployed a role that had full access to Secrets Manager as long as the secret was tagged appropriately.
- ABAC is powerful but comes with a learning curve and should be adopted with caution.
- Some resources do not support ABAC, and those that do often only support ABAC on a subset of API calls.
- IAM conditions can be used for limited time access to permissions.

9.3 Enabling Resource Group Sharing on Azure

Problem

A team has now split into two teams. They need to migrate resources to separate resource groups to establish new security boundaries.

Solution

This recipe shows how to migrate resources between resource groups.

If you haven't already done so, familiarize yourself with Terraform and the different authentication mechanisms in Chapter 11.

Create a *variables.tf* file and copy the following contents:

```
variable "location" {
  type        = string
  description = "The Azure location for resources"
}
```

Then fill out the corresponding *terraform.tfvars* file:

```
location = ""
```

Create the following *provider.tf* file and run `terraform init`:

```
provider "azurerm" {
  features {}
}

terraform {
  required_providers {
    azurerm = {
      source  = "hashicorp/azurerm"
      version = "~> 2"
    }
  }
}
```

Create the following *main.tf* file and run `terraform plan`:

```
resource "azurerm_resource_group" "before" {
  name     = "before"
  location = var.location
}

resource "azurerm_resource_group" "after" {
  name     = "after"
  location = var.location
}

resource "azurerm_app_service_plan" "this" {
  name                = "this"
  location            = azurerm_resource_group.before.location
  resource_group_name = azurerm_resource_group.before.name

  sku {
    tier = "Standard"
    size = "S1"
  }
}

output "move_command" {
  value = join(" ", [
    "az resource move --destination-group",
    azurerm_resource_group.after.name,
    "--ids",
    azurerm_app_service_plan.this.id
  ])
```

```
  }

output "import_command" {
  value = join(" ", [
    "terraform import azurerm_app_service_plan.this",
    replace(
      azurerm_app_service_plan.this.id,
      azurerm_resource_group.before.name,
      azurerm_resource_group.after.name
    )
  ])
}
```

Review the resources that are going to be created, and then run `terraform apply` to make the changes.

Copy and run the `move_command` output, then the `import_command` output.

Update the `azurerm_app_service_plan` resource to look like the following:

```
resource "azurerm_app_service_plan" "this" {
  name                = "this"
  location            = azurerm_resource_group.after.location
  resource_group_name = azurerm_resource_group.after.name

  sku {
    tier = "Standard"
    size = "S1"
  }
}
```

Discussion

When looking to move resources between resource groups and subscriptions, it is worth sorting them into *stateless* resources, such as Azure Functions, and *stateful* resources, such as databases. For *stateless* resources, it is often easier to re-create the resources using IAC than migrate. For *stateful* resources, you can move the resource or stand up a new resource and migrate the state.

In this recipe, you saw how to migrate a resource between two resource groups. The general process is as follows:

1. Migrate the resource outside of Terraform.

2. Re-import the resource.

3. Update the Terraform to match.

4. Run `terraform plan` to verify there are no planned changes.

In preparation for the move, you can use the `az resource invoke-action --action validateMoveResources` CLI command to validate that the resources will move successfully.

To move resources between subscriptions, instead of the `--destination-group` flag, use the `destination-subscription-id` flag.

Currently, ABAC on Azure is in preview and is restricted purely to storage blobs. It is possible to restrict access to blobs with particular tags with conditions that look like the following:

```
(
  (
    !(ActionMatches{'Microsoft.Storage/storageAccounts/blobServices/
      containers/blobs/read'}
    AND
    @Request[subOperation] ForAnyOfAnyValues:StringEqualsIgnoreCase
      {'Blob.Read.WithTagConditions'})
  )
  OR
  (
    @Resource[Microsoft.Storage/storageAccounts/blobServices/containers/
      blobs/tags:Project<$key_case_sensitive$>] StringEquals 'Cookbook'
  )
)
```

Until ABAC is expanded to include a much wider resource pool, you should look to stand up new versions of resources with IAC for *stateless* components and determine on a case-by-case basis how to handle *stateful* components.

Summary

Let's summarize what was learned and deployed in this recipe:

- Azure provides commands to move resources between resource groups and subscriptions.
- After moving resources around, you will need to re-import them into Terraform.
- By using the `invoke-action` command, you can test whether resources are movable in a risk-free way.
- ABAC is in its very early stages on Azure.
  — Currently the only supported resource is storage blobs.

9.4 Application Security Scanning on GCP

Problem

As delivery teams are standing up applications in GCP, you want to run standard security testing for common threats.

Solution

This recipe stands up an application in App Engine and runs a Web Security Scanner scan.

If you haven't already done so, familiarize yourself with Terraform and the different authentication mechanisms in Chapter 11.

Create a *variables.tf* file and copy the following contents:

```
variable "project" {
  type        = string
  description = "The project to deploy the resources into"
}

variable "location" {
  type        = string
  description = "The location to deploy into"
}
```

Then fill out the corresponding *terraform.tfvars* file:

```
project  = ""
location = ""
```

Create the following *provider.tf* file and run `terraform init`:

```
provider "google" {
  project = var.project
}

provider "google-beta" {
  project = var.project
}

terraform {
  required_providers {
    google = {
      source  = "hashicorp/google"
      version = "~> 3"
    }
  }
}
```

Create the following *main.tf* file and run `terraform plan`:

```
data "google_project" "current" {}

locals {
  required_apis = [
    "websecurityscanner.googleapis.com",
    "appengine.googleapis.com"
  ]
}

resource "google_project_service" "api" {
  for_each           = toset(local.required_apis)
  service            = each.value
  disable_on_destroy = false
}

resource "google_app_engine_application" "app" {
  project     = data.google_project.current.project_id
  location_id = var.location

  depends_on = [
    google_project_service.api
  ]
}

resource "local_file" "app_yaml" {
  filename = "app.yaml"
  content  = <<FILE
runtime: python39

instance_class: F2

handlers:
  - url: '/(.*)'
    secure: always
    static_files: index.html
    upload: index.html
FILE
}

resource "local_file" "index_html" {
  filename = "index.html"
  content  = <<FILE
<html>
  <body>
    <h1>Welcome to your App Engine application.</h1>
  </body>
</html>
FILE
}

resource "null_resource" "deploy_app" {
  provisioner "local-exec" {
```

```
    command = "gcloud app deploy --project ${var.project}"
  }

  depends_on = [
    google_app_engine_application.app,
    local_file.app_yaml,
    local_file.index_html
  ]
}

resource "google_security_scanner_scan_config" "app" {
  provider        = google-beta
  display_name    = "app-engine-scan"
  starting_urls   = [
    "https://${google_app_engine_application.app.default_hostname}"
  ]
  target_platforms = ["APP_ENGINE"]
}

resource "null_resource" "run_scan" {
  provisioner "local-exec" {
    command = join(" ", [
      "gcloud alpha web-security-scanner scan-runs start",
      google_security_scanner_scan_config.app.id
    ])
  }
}
```

Review the resources that are going to be created, and then run `terraform apply` to make the changes.

Discussion

The Web Security Scanner on GCP can perform two kinds of scans: *managed* and *custom*. Managed scans are only available as part of the premium tier of the Security Command Center. They run automatically on a weekly schedule, only performing GET requests so as to not flood production applications with garbage data. They centralize website vulnerability detection and don't involve interacting with project teams until problems are found.

Custom scans are configured at the project level and should be run initially against nonproduction applications, as they attempt to enter data. When you have confidence in using Web Security Scanner, it should also be run against production sites. Custom scans can also be configured to run on an explicit schedule: daily, weekly, every two weeks, and every four weeks. To limit the scope of the scan, you should both leverage the excluded URLs feature and apply the `inq-no-click` CSS class to particular DOM objects.

Both scan types report their findings into the Security Command Center. By combining this recipe with Recipe 3.1, you can ensure that you get notified when high-severity findings are uncovered.

When configuring custom scans, it is possible to allow the scan to impersonate a Google account, or provide it with credentials to authenticate as a non-Google account. Also, when using IAP to protect your applications, give the Web Security Scanner service account, `service-project-number@gcp-sa-websecurityscanner.iam.gservi ceaccount.com`, the IAP Secured Web App User role on your application.

For applications hosted on Compute Engine or Google Kubernetes Engine, you can configure the scan to come from known, predictable IP ranges, allowing you to understand which traffic is induced by the source IP range. If you select this option for the scan, all traffic will come from IPs in the `34.66.18.0/26` and `34.66.114.64/26` ranges.

Summary

Let's summarize what was learned and deployed in this recipe:

- GCP provides Web Security Scanner to perform application testing.
- Managed scans are part of the Security Command Center Premium Tier.
  — They centralize website vulnerability management for the organization.
  — Managed scans run weekly and only perform GET requests.
- Custom scans are available to all GCP customers.
  — They perform a more invasive test which attempts to enter data.
  — Because of this, they should ideally be run against nonproduction systems.
- Scans can be run against any public application hosted in App Engine, Google Kubernetes Engine, or Compute Engine.
- You can give custom scans credentials to authenticate with the application.

9.5 Application Security Scanning on AWS

Problem

As delivery teams are standing up applications in AWS, you want to run standard security testing to protect against common threats.

Solution

This recipe creates a CodeBuild project that runs the OWASP Zed Attack Proxy (ZAP) container.

If you haven't already done so, familiarize yourself with Terraform and the different authentication mechanisms in Chapter 11.

Create a *variables.tf* file and copy the following contents:

```
variable "target_url" {
  type        = string
  description = "The URL to scan"
}
```

Then fill out the corresponding *terraform.tfvars* file:

```
target_url = ""
```

Create the following *provider.tf* file and run `terraform init`:

```
provider "aws" {}

terraform {
  required_providers {
    aws = {
      source  = "hashicorp/aws"
      version = "~> 3"
    }
  }
}
```

Create the following *main.tf* file and run `terraform plan`:

```
resource "aws_iam_role" "codebuild_service_role" {
  name = "codebuild_service_role"

  assume_role_policy = data.aws_iam_policy_document.assume.json
  managed_policy_arns = [
    "arn:aws:iam::aws:policy/service-role/AWSLambdaBasicExecutionRole"
  ]
}

data "aws_iam_policy_document" "assume" {
  statement {
    effect = "Allow"
    actions = [
      "sts:AssumeRole"
    ]

    principals {
      type = "Service"
      identifiers = [
        "codebuild.amazonaws.com"
      ]
    }
  }
}
```

```
resource "aws_codebuild_project" "zap" {
  name         = "owasp-zap"
  service_role = aws_iam_role.codebuild_service_role.arn

  artifacts {
    type = "NO_ARTIFACTS"
  }

  environment {
    compute_type                = "BUILD_GENERAL1_SMALL"
    image                       = "owasp/zap2docker-stable"
    type                        = "LINUX_CONTAINER"
    image_pull_credentials_type = "CODEBUILD"
  }

  source {
    buildspec = <<BUILDSPEC
version: 0.2

phases:
  build:
    commands:
      - zap-baseline.py -t ${var.target_url} -I
BUILDSPEC
    type      = "NO_SOURCE"
  }
}
```

Review the resources that are going to be created, and then run `terraform apply` to make the changes.

Discussion

AWS does not provide a managed web application security scanning tool. Instead, this recipe set up a CodeBuild project that can be easily bolted onto CI/CD pipelines, like those in Recipe 6.8, or invoked on demand. The results of the test are available in the build logs but currently are not preserved anywhere.

Let's look at how you can preserve the reports in S3. First, you'll need to add the following resources to the recipe to create the bucket and a policy for access:

```
data "aws_caller_identity" "current" {}

data "aws_iam_policy_document" "s3" {
  statement {
    effect = "Allow"
    actions = [
      "s3:PutObject"
    ]
    resources = [
      aws_s3_bucket.reports.arn
```

```
      ]
    }
  }

  resource "aws_s3_bucket" "reports" {
    bucket = "${data.aws_caller_identity.current.account_id}-reports"
  }
```

Then you'll need to attach that policy to the CodeBuild service role. Update the following resource:

```
  resource "aws_iam_role" "codebuild_service_role" {
    name = "codebuild_service_role"

    assume_role_policy = data.aws_iam_policy_document.assume.json
    managed_policy_arns = [
      "arn:aws:iam::aws:policy/service-role/AWSLambdaBasicExecutionRole"
    ]
    inline_policy {
      name = "s3access"
      policy = data.aws_iam_policy_document.s3.json
    }
  }
```

Last, update the CodeBuild project to look like the following:

```
  resource "aws_codebuild_project" "zap2" {
    name         = "owasp-zap2"
    service_role = aws_iam_role.codebuild_service_role.arn

    artifacts {
      type = "NO_ARTIFACTS"
    }

    environment {
      compute_type                = "BUILD_GENERAL1_SMALL"
      image                       = "aws/codebuild/standard:1.0"
      type                        = "LINUX_CONTAINER"
      image_pull_credentials_type = "CODEBUILD"
      privileged_mode             = true
    }

    source {
      buildspec = <<BUILDSPEC
version: 0.2

phases:
  build:
    commands:
      - ${join(" ", [
        "docker run -v $${PWD}:/zap/wrk owasp/zap2docker-stable",
        "zap-baseline.py -t",
        var.target_url,
```

```
        "-I -x report_xml"
      ])}
      - ${join(" ", [
        "aws s3api put-object --bucket",
        aws_s3_bucket.reports.bucket,
        "--key report.xml --body report_xml"
      ])}
  BUILDSPEC
    type        = "NO_SOURCE"
  }
}
```

As the OWASP container expects a volume to be mounted to produce a report, the project now runs a standard AWS image and runs the OWASP container explicitly. This then allows us to mount the volume and use the AWS CLI to upload the report to S3.

Summary

Let's summarize what was learned and deployed in this recipe:

- AWS doesn't provide a managed web application scanning tool.
- By using CodeBuild, you can easily run the OWASP containerized scanning tool.
  — By hosting it in CodeBuild, it is easy to add it to a CI/CD pipeline.

  — You can see the scan output in the project logs.

    — To persist the reports, upload them to S3.

9.6 Application Security Scanning on Azure

Problem

As delivery teams are standing up applications in Azure, you want to run standard security testing for common threats.

Solution

This recipe creates an Azure Container Instance that runs the OWASP Zed Attack Proxy (ZAP) container.

If you haven't already done so, familiarize yourself with Terraform and the different authentication mechanisms in Chapter 11.

Create a *variables.tf* file and copy the following contents:

```
variable "location" {
  type        = string
  description = "The Azure location for resources"
}
```

```
variable "target_url" {
  type        = string
  description = "The URL to scan"
}
```

Then fill out the corresponding *terraform.tfvars* file:

```
location   = ""
target_url = ""
```

Create the following *provider.tf* file and run `terraform init`:

```
provider "azurerm" {
  features {}
}

terraform {
  required_providers {
    azurerm = {
      source  = "hashicorp/azurerm"
      version = "~> 2"
    }
  }
}
```

Create the following *main.tf* file and run `terraform plan`:

```
resource "azurerm_resource_group" "zap" {
  name     = "zap"
  location = var.location
}

resource "azurerm_container_group" "zap" {
  name                = "zap"
  location            = azurerm_resource_group.zap.location
  resource_group_name = azurerm_resource_group.zap.name
  ip_address_type     = "public"
  os_type             = "Linux"
  restart_policy      = "Never"
  exposed_port        = []

  container {
    name   = "zap"
    image  = "owasp/zap2docker-stable"
    cpu    = "0.5"
    memory = "1.5"
    commands = [
      "zap-baseline.py",
      "-t",
      var.target_url,
      "-I"
    ]
```

```
    ports {
      port    = 443
      protocol = "TCP"
    }
  }
 }
}
```

Review the resources that are going to be created, and then run `terraform apply` to make the changes.

Discussion

Azure does not provide a managed web application scanning tool, so in this recipe, you are using Azure container images to host an open source tool. To see the results of the scan, run `az container logs --resource-group zap --name zap`. To preserve the reports from the scan, mount an Azure storage container into the container.

First, create the storage account and the share with the following resources, filling in the storage account name:

```
resource "azurerm_storage_account" "reports" {
  name                     = ""
  resource_group_name      = azurerm_resource_group.zap.name
  location                 = azurerm_resource_group.zap.location
  account_tier             = "Standard"
  account_replication_type = "GRS"
}

resource "azurerm_storage_share" "reports" {
  name                 = "reports"
  storage_account_name = azurerm_storage_account.reports.name
  quota                = 50
}
```

Next, update the `azurerm_container_group` resource to look like the following:

```
resource "azurerm_container_group" "zap" {
  name                = "zap"
  location            = azurerm_resource_group.zap.location
  resource_group_name = azurerm_resource_group.zap.name
  ip_address_type     = "public"
  os_type             = "Linux"
  restart_policy      = "Never"
  exposed_port        = []

  container {
    name    = "zap"
    image   = "owasp/zap2docker-stable"
    cpu     = "0.5"
    memory  = "1.5"
    commands = [
      "zap-baseline.py",
```

```
        "-t",
        var.target_url,
        "-I",
        "-x",
        "report"
      ]

      ports {
        port     = 443
        protocol = "TCP"
      }

      volume {
        name                  = "reports"
        mount_path            = "/zap/wrk"
        storage_account_name  = azurerm_storage_account.reports.name
        storage_account_key   = azurerm_storage_account.reports.primary_access_key
        share_name            = azurerm_storage_share.reports.name
      }
    }
  }
}
```

Now, once the scan has completed, a *report.xml* file will be in the storage account.

By combining this recipe with Recipe 6.9, and integrating scanning into the CI/CD pipelines that delivery teams use, you can make sure that every change to an application goes through a scan before it's allowed into production. When looking to run the scans in an ad hoc fashion, you will need to delete and re-create the container instance. You can delete just the container instance by running `terraform destroy -t azurerm_con tainer_group.zap`. This will leave the storage account with the historical reports untouched, and the container instance will be re-created next time `apply` is run.

Summary

Let's summarize what was learned and deployed in this recipe:

- Azure Container Instances allow you to run arbitrary containers.
- As Azure doesn't provide a managed web scanning service, you ran the OWASP ZAP container.
- To save reports, you can mount a storage account share into the container.
- By building scanning into CI/CD pipelines, you can ensure that applications with known vulnerabilities don't make it to production.
- To run scans on demand, you need to delete specifically the container instance with `terraform destroy -t azurerm_container_group.zap`.

CHAPTER 10
Security in the Future

The pace of innovation in the IT sector is continually increasing. With the shift from IT as a cost center to IT as a source of competitive advantage, although the principles of IT security have not fundamentally changed, the expectations from the business demand a revolution in approach. By adopting cloud native tooling as part of your security estate, you benefit from the rapid innovation of the cloud service providers, which keeps pace with how cloud adoption is changing over time.

As cloud service provider solutions are most often offered as managed services, their adoption also lowers the total cost of ownership (TCO) of your security tool chain. Through a low-TCO approach, you unlock the ability to invest time and money in higher-order initiatives, which enables a superior security posture. For example, running a self-hosted patching service requires maintenance, ongoing server costs, and recovery. By using the cloud vendor's solution, you reduce the human effort required and are provided with a contractually backed service-level agreement.

This book has shown, throughout the recipes, that you can solve the same set of security problems across each cloud. Sometimes the components of the solution look similar, such as with patching, and sometimes they look radically different, such as with preventing privilege escalation. In real terms, being fluent across two clouds is not twice as hard as being fluent in one, but it's not far removed.

To prepare for the unknown, unpredictable, and emergent requirements, the best defense is protecting the team's capacity. A team that is operating at full capacity cannot absorb new work without compromise. Little's law (*https://en.wikipedia.org/wiki/Little%27s_law*) tells us that as you add more work to a system or team, the response time gets exponentially worse as the arrival rate of work outstrips the throughput. By adopting low-TCO approaches, you reduce the draw on the team from their existing responsibilities, allowing them to broaden their domain of control and scale their impact.

10.1 The Infinite Game

The recipes in this book focused on core security problems, but security is an infinite game (*https://en.wikipedia.org/wiki/Finite_and_Infinite_Games*). There is no way to *win* or achieve *complete* security. Your efforts are an attempt to continue the game by preventing fatal breaches, enabling the business to produce value securely, and ensuring that the teams remains healthy, happy, and capable.

The recipes in this book target the fundamental and common problems that exist across businesses of all sizes and domains. Moving past the scope of the book, there are two key areas of security that are being explored currently.

Zero Trust

First coined by the BeyondCorp whitepaper (*https://research.google/pubs/pub43231*) from Google, zero trust models are about placing identity at the center of determining access.

Historically, network addresses determined your level of access. Once on the trusted corporate intranet, you were often presented with highly privileged access, making it easy for threat actors to spread throughout your estate.

To explore how Google made the transition to a zero trust model, with recommendations about how your organization can do the same, read the "Migrating to Beyond-Corp: Maintaining Productivity While Improving Security Whitepaper" (*https://research.google/pubs/pub46134*).

Supply Chain Security

Brought into the spotlight through compromises such as the SolarWinds breach, there has been a renewed focus on how to build software from known safe components and being able to identify and remediate components that are discovered to have vulnerabilities. In mid-2021, Google announced the Supply Chain Levels for Software Artifacts (SLSA) framework (*https://oreil.ly/m4Wdx*), which aims to ensure the integrity of software artifacts.

Going back to Chapter 1, I discussed how your security is only as strong as your weakest link. Zero trust and supply chain security both solve real problems, but there is a high likelihood that they are not the biggest problems you're facing today.

As you mature your cloud native security approach, focusing on maintaining the lowest possible TCO, you can preserve the capacity to explore new domains as they emerge, as opposed to being forever on the back foot.

10.2 Building Capability

As part of ensuring the enduring effectiveness of the security function, you require an effective plan for continually building new capability. A helpful model in this space is the three tiers of knowledge, skills, and operational capability (*https://oreil.ly/Go2eM*).

Knowledge is the total of what you understand, for example, understanding the KMS service in your cloud of choice, how IAM works, or what the OSI model is. You obtain knowledge by reading, taking online courses, and taking certification exams. The discussion sections of the recipes in this book provide the knowledge required to understand how security in the cloud works.

Skills are what you are able to do, for example, being able to write queries to parse audit logs, write least-privilege IAM policies, or configure cloud resources in Terraform. To build skills, you need to get hands-on experience in labs and sandboxes. The recipes in this book are focused on giving you the skills required to complete required tasks as a modern security engineer.

Operational capabilities are the problems you can solve, for example, being able to respond to active threats in your environment, performing forensic analysis, or remediating compliance issues across your estate. Building these capabilities comes from a variety of sources, such as mentoring, pairing, and game days. In Chapter 1 and the overview of other chapters, I have talked about the necessary capabilities for a modern security team.

With the ability to rapidly build replica or sandbox environments, game days are becoming an increasingly popular training method. The worst time to learn how to respond to an active threat in your environment is when one is happening. By investing in simulating threats and reacting authentically to them, you build capability in a safe and timely manner. Additionally, these investments become cornerstones of the culture within the business; they show a real, visceral intent to make security job zero. For an in-depth story of when I first ran an internal game day with lessons learned targeting our cloud environments, see "Red Teaming AWS." (*https://oreil.ly/dPohf*) Additionally, the book *Security Chaos Engineering* by Aaron Rinehart and Kelly Shortridge (O'Reilly) explores this topic in depth.

When evaluating training, you should start at the operational capability you're trying to gain or expand. The capability is what is of value, as you're then able to solve a problem. To have a capability, you need the requisite knowledge and skills within the team. So this leads us to a high-level framework for planning. First, outline a capability that needs cultivating or refining. Next, plan how to provide the team with the required experience, whether that's created internally or outsourced, and supplement with other training to fill known knowledge and skills gaps. This allows you to ensure your finite training resources are invested effectively and will drive business impact.

10.3 Building Situational Awareness

As the team's capability matures, it can be difficult to see where the next logical step is. What is the correct next problem to solve? To support the team in understanding the current landscape and context, Wardley Mapping is a powerful tool. Initially created by Simon Wardley in 2005, you collaboratively produce a map that aligns technologies and capabilities to the evolutionary axis shown in Figure 10-1.

Figure 10-1. Evolutionary axis

The cloud can be seen as a movement of compute resources from the product to commodity, as shown in Figure 10-2. Rather than having to purchase capacity with large data center contracts, or self-hosting the infrastructure, it becomes akin to any other commodity such as water or electricity: it's available on demand.

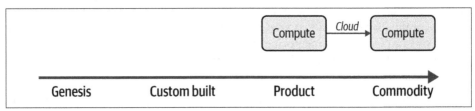

Figure 10-2. The evolution of compute

By mapping out domains under the purview of your team, you can identify cases where capabilities are misaligned. Imagine a scenario where the creation and hardening of machine images is done with custom scripting that the team maintains and extends over time. Adopting a tool such as HashiCorp Packer can drastically simplify and reduce the total cost of ownership of the solution. By creating and revisiting maps over time, you can identify opportunities and dependencies within your domain. Taking the example of providing secure machines to your end users, you can map that to include all the constituent components, as in Figure 10-3.

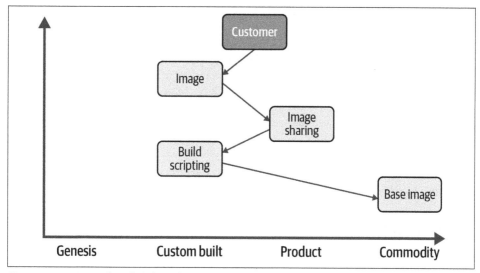

Figure 10-3. Providing hardened images

When looking at the map, you may disagree with the position of certain points or think things are missing. That is by design. The power of mapping comes from the conversations through the mapping process, more than the artifacts themselves. By reaching a common understanding of the current landscape, you can plan the next move while being mindful of the current context. Potentially, on reviewing this you may decide that the hardening done on images has become standardized to the point where the marketplace provides an image of sufficient quality. In that case, you can redraw the map, as in Figure 10-4, showing a significant reduction in complexity and maintenance.

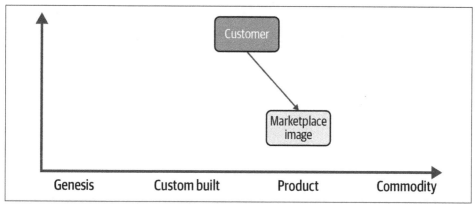

Figure 10-4. Marketplace images

Both the proposed training model and Wardley Maps are customer-centric in their orientation. Everything is done working back from the customer and their needs. By taking this empathetic approach to managing security, you align your plans with the needs of the business and are able to have more productive relationships. As explained in Recipe 1.3, security teams operate as enabling teams, focusing on uplifting and enabling value-stream-aligned teams: this customer centricity is fundamental to your success as an enabling team.

To explore Wardley Mapping further, a great starting point is the Learn Wardley Mapping (LWM) website (*https://learnwardleymapping.com*).

10.4 Conclusion

Cloud native security is both the same and different as security in other domains. Armed with the recipes, you will be able to quickly create and configure resources to provide a secure platform and guardrails for your engineering function. You will also get the visibility to understand your security posture and compliance at scale and leverage automation and the cloud native tooling to maintain and iteratively improve your posture over time.

The twin pressures of cost and time will always be pushing you to achieve more with less. The secret to achieving this is by evaluating tools and processes by their enduring total cost of ownership, both human and financial. Investing in modern, predominantly managed options frees up you and your team to constantly attack higher-level concerns and deliver greater value to the business.

As time passes from the publication of this book, newer services, approaches, and options will become available. This chapter on exploring mindful training and Wardley Mapping will hopefully prepare you for the future, enabling you to pick the correct choice for your context and success.

CHAPTER 11

Terraform Primer

Terraform, made by HashiCorp, is an open source infrastructure-as-code (IaC) tool. It allows you to work in a multicloud environment, keeping the tooling, processes, and patterns the same. By having a library of providers, you can use Terraform to interact with an ever-growing array of systems and platforms.

HashiCorp Configuration Language (HCL) is the common language that underlies the HashiCorp tool suite. It is a declarative language, where you describe *what* you want, rather than an imperative language, where you describe *how* you want something done. For infrastructure, this means you describe your architecture, and Terraform handles the mechanics of making that happen.

In the recipes, there is a general flow for writing and executing the Terraform configurations:

1. Define and enter the recipe's variables.
2. Define and install the providers by running `terraform init`.
3. Define the infrastructure and generate a *plan* by running `terraform plan`, which outlines the changes Terraform will make.
4. Execute the changes by running `terraform apply`.

Common additional commands that form part of a Terraform workflow include

- `terraform fmt`, which formats the file in the working directory
- `terraform validate`, which checks whether your HCL is syntactically correct
- `terraform destroy`, which tears down provisioned infrastructure

11.1 Authenticating with GCP

The quickest approach to authenticate with the Google provider is by running `gcloud auth application-default login`.

For production scenarios, changes should be made via service accounts, not user accounts. The usage of automation and service accounts to run Terraform can be seen in Recipe 6.7.

For full authentication instructions, refer to the Google provider documentation (*https://oreil.ly/vM5jR*).

11.2 Authenticating with AWS

The quickest approach to authenticate with the AWS provider is by configuring the AWS CLI tool. Terraform will use the default role defined in the CLI configuration, unless overridden by environment variables. To assume other defined roles, tools like AWSume (*https://awsu.me*) simplify the process.

For production scenarios, changes should be made via roles assumed by automation tooling, not user accounts. The usage of automation to run Terraform can be seen in Recipe 6.8.

For full authentication instructions, refer to the AWS provider documentation (*https://oreil.ly/9QvPw*).

11.3 Authenticating with Azure

The quickest approach to authenticate with the AzureRM provider is by running `az login`.

For production scenarios, changes should be made via Managed Service Identities, not user accounts. The usage of automation and Managed Service Identities to run Terraform can be seen in Recipe 6.9.

For full authentication instructions, refer to the AzureRM provider documentation (*https://oreil.ly/1W6XZ*).

Index

About the Author

Josh Armitage is a self-described "professional loudmouth," a distinguished technologist at Contino (a digital transformation consultancy), and an international conference speaker. Across his career, he has worked with many technologies, including everything from mainframes to machine learning, as well as architecting world-first event-sourced serverless architectures and running the first Australian production Elastic Kubernetes Service application.

Experienced and certified across the three primary clouds, he works with regulated enterprises, helping them digitally transform and taking them on a journey from the command and control models of the past to IT as the key to business differentiation. He has been recognized as both an AWS partner and a HashiCorp ambassador for his speaking and writing to audiences around the world.

Outside of work, he spends evenings and weekends getting overly competitive at board games with friends, going on adventures with his family, and cooking British food to have a very literal slice of home.

Colophon

The animal on the cover of *Cloud Native Security Cookbook* is a hooked-bill kite (*Chondrohierax uncinatus*). It is named for the distinct shape of its beak, which it uses to break open the shells of tree snails. These snails form the bulk of its diet, though it is also known to eat other small animals, including frogs, salamanders, small mammals, and insects. The hooked-bill kite's range stretches from the Rio Grande Valley of Texas to northern Argentina, and it is usually found in wooded areas where tree snails are plentiful. It usually hunts by climbing and walking around tree branches, looking for snails. When a kite finds a snail, it holds it with one foot while cracking the shell open with its hooked bill.

Hooked-bill kites are slender, midsized raptors, ranging about 15 to 20 inches long with a wingspan of about 30 to 40 inches. They have striped bellies and banded tails, though they show a great deal of variation in their plumage from one region to another. Males generally have gray or blackish undersides, while females are usually brown or reddish. Their bill size also varies greatly according to the size of the snails found in their range.

Hook-billed kites are considered a species of least concern, though deforestation and climate change both pose threats to their habitat, and the closely related Cuban kite is critically endangered. Many of the animals on O'Reilly covers are endangered; all of them are important to the world.

The cover illustration is by Karen Montgomery, based on a black and white engraving from *Wood's Illustrated Natural History*. The cover fonts are Gilroy Semibold and Guardian Sans. The text font is Adobe Minion Pro, the heading font is Adobe Myriad Condensed, and the code font is Dalton Maag's Ubuntu Mono.

O'REILLY®

Learn from experts.
Become one yourself.

Books | Live online courses
Instant Answers | Virtual events
Videos | Interactive learning

Get started at oreilly.com.

Lightning Source UK Ltd.
Milton Keynes UK
UKHW030618301122
413005UK00006B/16

9 781098 106300